BODIES OF DISORDER
GENDER AND DEGENERATION IN BAROJA AND BLASCO IBÁÑEZ

LEGENDA

LEGENDA is the Modern Humanities Research Association's book imprint for new research in the Humanities. Founded in 1995 by Malcolm Bowie and others within the University of Oxford, Legenda has always been a collaborative publishing enterprise, directly governed by scholars. The Modern Humanities Research Association (MHRA) joined this collaboration in 1998, became half-owner in 2004, in partnership with Maney Publishing and then Routledge, and has since 2016 been sole owner. Titles range from medieval texts to contemporary cinema and form a widely comparative view of the modern humanities, including works on Arabic, Catalan, English, French, German, Greek, Italian, Portuguese, Russian, Spanish, and Yiddish literature. Editorial boards and committees of more than 60 leading academic specialists work in collaboration with bodies such as the Society for French Studies, the British Comparative Literature Association and the Association of Hispanists of Great Britain & Ireland.

The MHRA encourages and promotes advanced study and research in the field of the modern humanities, especially modern European languages and literature, including English, and also cinema. It aims to break down the barriers between scholars working in different disciplines and to maintain the unity of humanistic scholarship. The Association fulfils this purpose through the publication of journals, bibliographies, monographs, critical editions, and the MHRA Style Guide, and by making grants in support of research. Membership is open to all who work in the Humanities, whether independent or in a University post, and the participation of younger colleagues entering the field is especially welcomed.

ALSO PUBLISHED BY THE ASSOCIATION

Critical Texts
Tudor and Stuart Translations • New Translations • European Translations
MHRA Library of Medieval Welsh Literature

MHRA Bibliographies
Publications of the Modern Humanities Research Association

The Annual Bibliography of English Language & Literature
Austrian Studies
Modern Language Review
Portuguese Studies
The Slavonic and East European Review
Working Papers in the Humanities
The Yearbook of English Studies

www.mhra.org.uk
www.legendabooks.com

STUDIES IN HISPANIC AND LUSOPHONE CULTURES

Studies in Hispanic and Lusophone Cultures are selected and edited by the Association of Hispanists of Great Britain & Ireland. The series seeks to publish the best new research in all areas of the literature, thought, history, culture, film, and languages of Spain, Spanish America, and the Portuguese-speaking world.

The Association of Hispanists of Great Britain & Ireland is a professional association which represents a very diverse discipline, in terms of both geographical coverage and objects of study. Its website showcases new work by members, and publicises jobs, conferences and grants in the field.

Editorial Committee
Chair: Professor Trevor Dadson (Queen Mary, University of London)
Professor Catherine Davies (University of Nottingham)
Professor Andrew Ginger (University of Bristol)
Professor Hilary Owen (University of Manchester)
Professor Christopher Perriam (University of Manchester)
Professor Alison Sinclair (Clare College, Cambridge)
Professor Philip Swanson (University of Sheffield)

Managing Editor
Dr Graham Nelson
41 Wellington Square, Oxford OX1 2JF, UK

www.legendabooks.com/series/shlc

STUDIES IN HISPANIC AND LUSOPHONE CULTURES

1. *Unamuno's Theory of the Novel*, by C. A. Longhurst
2. *Pessoa's Geometry of the Abyss: Modernity and the* Book of Disquiet, by Paulo de Medeiros
3. *Artifice and Invention in the Spanish Golden Age*, edited by Stephen Boyd and Terence O'Reilly
4. *The Latin American Short Story at its Limits: Fragmentation, Hybridity and Intermediality*, by Lucy Bell
5. *Spanish New York Narratives 1898–1936: Modernisation, Otherness and Nation*, by David Miranda-Barreiro
6. *The Art of Ana Clavel: Ghosts, Urinals, Dolls, Shadows and Outlaw Desires*, by Jane Elizabeth Lavery
7. *Alejo Carpentier and the Musical Text*, by Katia Chornik
8. *Britain, Spain and the Treaty of Utrecht 1713-2013*, edited by Trevor J. Dadson and J. H. Elliott
9. *Books and Periodicals in Brazil 1768-1930: A Transatlantic Perspective*, edited by Ana Cláudia Suriani da Silva and Sandra Guardini Vasconcelos
10. *Lisbon Revisited: Urban Masculinities in Twentieth-Century Portuguese Fiction*, by Rhian Atkin
11. *Urban Space, Identity and Postmodernity in 1980s Spain: Rethinking the Movida*, by Maite Usoz de la Fuente
12. *Santería, Vodou and Resistance in Caribbean Literature: Daughters of the Spirits*, by Paul Humphrey
13. *Reprojecting the City: Urban Space and Dissident Sexualities in Recent Latin American Cinema*, by Benedict Hoff
14. *Rethinking Juan Rulfo's Creative World: Prose, Photography, Film*, edited by Dylan Brennan and Nuala Finnegan
15. *The Last Days of Humanism: A Reappraisal of Quevedo's Thought*, by Alfonso Rey
16. *Catalan Narrative 1875-2015*, edited by Jordi Larios and Montserrat Lunati
17. *Islamic Culture in Spain to 1614: Essays and Studies*, by L. P. Harvey
18. *Film Festivals: Cinema and Cultural Exchange*, by Mar Diestro-Dópido
19. *St Teresa of Avila: Her Writings and Life*, edited by Terence O'Reilly, Colin Thompson and Lesley Twomey
20. *(Un)veiling Bodies: A Trajectory of Chilean Post-Dictatorship Documentary*, by Elizabeth Ramírez Soto

Bodies of Disorder

Gender and Degeneration in Baroja and Blasco Ibáñez

KATHARINE MURPHY

LEGENDA

Studies in Hispanic and Lusophone Cultures 26
Modern Humanities Research Association
2017

Published by Legenda
an imprint of the Modern Humanities Research Association
Salisbury House, Station Road, Cambridge CB1 2LA

ISBN 978-1-910887-30-1 (HB)
ISBN 978-1-78188-405-8 (PB)

First published 2017

All rights reserved. No part of this publication may be reproduced or disseminated or transmitted in any form or by any means, electronic, mechanical, photocopying, recording or otherwise, or stored in any retrieval system, or otherwise used in any manner whatsoever without written permission of the copyright owner, except in accordance with the provisions of the Copyright, Designs and Patents Act 1988, or under the terms of a licence permitting restricted copying issued in the UK by the Copyright Licensing Agency Ltd, Saffron House, 6–10 Kirby Street, London EC1N 8TS, *England, or in the USA by the Copyright Clearance Center, 222 Rosewood Drive, Danvers MA 01923. Application for the written permission of the copyright owner to reproduce any part of this publication must be made by email to legenda@mhra.org.uk.*

Disclaimer: Statements of fact and opinion contained in this book are those of the author and not of the editors or the Modern Humanities Research Association. The publisher makes no representation, express or implied, in respect of the accuracy of the material in this book and cannot accept any legal responsibility or liability for any errors or omissions that may be made.

Trademark notice: Product or corporate names may be trademarks or registered trademarks, and are used only for identification and explanation without intent to infringe.

© Modern Humanities Research Association 2017

Copy-Editor: Richard Correll

CONTENTS

	Acknowledgements	ix
	Introduction	1
	PART I: DETERMINISM AND HEREDITY	
1	The Nordau Effect: Degeneracy and the Artist in Baroja's *Camino de perfección* (1902) and Blasco's *La maja desnuda* (1906)	28
2	Trauma and the Origins of Neurosis: From Degeneration to the Unconscious in Two Novels of 1900	52
	PART II: URBAN DEGENERATION IN THE NATURALIST NOVEL	
3	Prostitution and Criminality in Turn-of-the-Century Madrid: Baroja's *La busca* (1904)	76
4	Crowd Psychology and the Urban Masses: Blasco Ibáñez's *La horda* (1905)	97
	PART III: PATHOLOGIES OF BODY AND MIND, GENDER AND NATION	
5	Adultery, Infanticide and Sensation Fiction: The Morality of Reproduction in Blasco Ibáñez's *Cañas y barro* (1902)	118
6	Eugenics and National Decline: The Failure of Maternity in Baroja's *El árbol de la ciencia* (1911)	137
	Conclusion	155
	Bibliography	176
	Index	187

For my boys,
Louis and Joseph Harding

ACKNOWLEDGEMENTS

The College of Humanities, University of Exeter, has supported the writing of this book through periods of Research Leave in 2011 and 2014, and research funds for visits to Valencia, the Biblioteca Nacional in Madrid, and the British Library in London. I presented earlier versions of chapters at the Association of Hispanists of Great Britain and Ireland Annual Conference hosted by the University of Nottingham (2011), University of Oxford (2013) and Sixtieth Anniversary Conference at the University of Exeter (2015); and as a Visiting Speaker at the University of Edinburgh (2011). Other conferences were invaluable in the development of this research, particularly Women in Spanish and Portuguese Studies, University of London (2011), and Wrongdoing in Spain, 1800–1936: Realities and Representations, University of Cambridge (2013).

I am indebted to Pío Caro Baroja Jr for enabling me to visit Baroja's library and house 'Itzea' in Vera de Bidasoa. Belén Villanueva provided me with access to the archives at the Casa-Museo Blasco Ibáñez in Valencia in 2014. Isabel Guardiola Selles at the Hemeroteca de Valencia kindly sent archival material on *El Pueblo* and other elusive research sources. I am grateful also to the Biblioteca de Valencia for allowing me to consult original editions of Blasco's novels.

This book has evolved over a number of years. Carlos-Alex Longhurst inspired my original interest in Baroja, the subject of my first book (published in 2004), and has continued to provide generous advice. The following colleagues in Modern Languages at the University of Exeter have been particularly helpful in responding to my work: Sally Faulkner, Danielle Hipkins, Katharine Hodgson, Ricarda Schmidt, Michael Stannard, Maria Thomas and Adam Watt. Thanks to my final-year students for engaging productively with new research for this book, and Alex Cattell, a former PhD student, for sourcing archival materials at the Biblioteca Nacional in Madrid. At other institutions, Rhian Davies, Andrew Ginger, Geraldine Lawless, Samuel Llano, Nicholas Round, and Alison Sinclair have all offered ideas and contributions to the ways in which I have framed this project. Rocío Rødtjer and Oscar Vázquez have shared useful discussions about gender and degenerationism respectively. Thanks also to Caragh Wells for exchanges about research and working motherhood, and to Isabel Moros and Sara Smart for moral support.

Some sections of Chapters 1, 2 and 6 of this book develop and extend my earlier work published in the following journals: 'Monstrosity and the Modernist Consciousness: Pío Baroja Versus Rosa Chacel', in 'Spanish Modernism', ed. by Christopher Soufas, *Anales de la literatura española contemporánea*, 35.1 (2010), 141–75;

'Images of Pleasure: Goya, Ekphrasis and the Female Nude in Blasco Ibáñez's *La maja desnuda*', *Bulletin of Spanish Studies*, 87.7 (2010), 939–57; 'En la encrucijada de 1900: los límites del naturalismo en *Entre naranjos* de Blasco Ibáñez y *La casa de Aizgorri* de Pío Baroja', ed. by Paul Smith and Christopher Anderson, *Revista de Estudios sobre Blasco Ibáñez*, 1, Ajuntament de Valencia (2012), 55–67; and 'The Female Subject in Pío Baroja: Sexual Ideology and the New Woman in *El árbol de la ciencia* and *El mundo es ansí*', *Modern Language Review*, 107.4 (2012), 1121–42. All the material on degeneration is entirely new to this book.

I acknowledge the contribution of the Museu de Montserrat, the Museu Nacional d'Art de Catalunya, Barcelona, the Museum of Modern Art / Scala, Florence and DACS, London for kindly facilitating permission to reproduce images for the cover and illustrations of this book. I would like to thank the editors at Legenda, Richard Correll, Trevor Dadson and Graham Nelson, for their considerate assistance in preparing the manuscript for publication.

Personal acknowledgements are due to family and friends who have taken a particular interest. My parents, John and Margaret Murphy, deserve special mention for their continuous support and willingness to help. Thanks as ever to my husband, Peter Harding, for his commitment and understanding, and for taking care of our children so generously while I was writing this volume. The book is dedicated to my sons, Louis and Joseph Harding, for the energy and intelligence with which they have distracted me from research. Bringing up boys has allowed me to consider questions of gender in an entirely new light.

K.M., Exeter, July 2017

INTRODUCTION

Degenerationism in Spain and Europe

Discourses of degeneration (social, moral, political, medical) peaked in the 1890s and posited the collective decline, even the eventual sterility, of European nations. *Bodies of Disorder* assesses the striking engagements with these ideas by two authors of early twentieth-century Spain. It does so through a unique analysis of the novels' assimilation and subversion of the work of influential European theorists, most notably Bénédict Morel, Cesare Lombroso and Max Nordau. As a physician, Pío Baroja took a particular interest in biological theories of heredity and environment in the late nineteenth century, as evidenced by the treatment of the themes of poverty and alcoholism in a number of his early novels. Vicente Blasco Ibáñez's early twentieth-century novels likewise engage with powerful contemporary degenerationist debates about poverty and criminality that circulated both in the political sphere and the popular press. My study assesses the compelling interactions between medicine, science and cultural production during this period. These myriad engagements are abundantly evident not just in the canonical works of the so-called 'Generation of 1898' authors but also contemporaneous popular fiction, often labelled pejoratively as 'ficción de masas'.

The representation of physical, psychological and social pathologies in the early twentieth-century novels of Baroja and Blasco Ibáñez provides ample testimony of the dominant influence of late nineteenth-century theories of degeneration. Yet these cultural narratives are not embraced and assimilated wholeheartedly. Beneath the evident interest in degeneration theory lies a notable scepticism towards positivist discourses that is apparent — I contend — in the works of both authors under scrutiny. My study seeks to demonstrate that the early novels of Baroja and Blasco Ibáñez drew profoundly on the cultural myths of degeneration, both echoing and simultaneously subverting widespread, alarmist fears about progressive national decadence. The nexus of interactions between disciplines and discourses — medical, social, and literary — has provided the foundations for recent academic interest in the medical writers of *fin-de-siglo* Spain, among whom Baroja is a prominent figure.

Bodies of Disorder seeks to explore and extend the critical analysis of the resonant impact of the biological sciences on the public imagination during this period. This influence is succinctly demonstrated by the widespread infusion of literature by pathological, anthropological and psychological discourses. My book is founded on an interdisciplinary approach to the multiple interactions between popular versions of scientific theories, the cultural narratives they sustained and prose fiction in early twentieth-century Spain. It thereby addresses a critical gap maintained by traditional hierarchies and divisions between academic disciplines.

The unconventional pairing of Baroja and Blasco Ibáñez is undertaken for the purposes of illuminating similarities between the early twentieth-century fictional production of each author, through a case study of the treatment by each author of biological, social and moral pathologies that align with cultural narratives of degenerationism. The comparison of two early twentieth-century authors placed traditionally in such different literary groups seeks to revitalize standard literary histories of the period by challenging artificial divisions between canonical and popular culture. In the particular context of early twentieth-century Spain, *Bodies of Disorder* reformulates the conventional distinction between the elitism and intellectualism of canonical modernist authors (or the 'Generation of 1898') and popular, bestselling fiction (often dismissed as 'ficción de masas'). Baroja was embraced by the academy; Blasco by popular culture and later Hollywood. The latter won the famous public polemic between the two authors, at least in terms of the financial profit generated by his fiction, if not the security of his place in literary history.

Through the sustained comparison of Baroja and Blasco, my book seeks to subvert the existing barriers between distinct groups of writers of this period. These divisions, reinforced through dominant categories such as highbrow, modernist or elitist literature on one hand, and mass cultural production on the other — I argue — have emphasized the divergences rather than commonalities between separate groups. My book seeks to counter assumptions still dominant in existing scholarship and standard literary histories of the period that reinforce the segregation of elite versus popular fiction and culture. It is entirely logical to draw examples across the literary spectrum of this period in order to break down these barriers via an analysis of the representation of gendered and degenerate bodies in Baroja and Blasco Ibáñez.

The case study offered by this book offers three key routes for revising critical histories of this period. Firstly, it aims to emphasize the connections between canonical and popular fiction in relation to the 'Generation of 1898' and their contemporaries. Secondly, it underscores the significance of popular versions of medicine and science in Spanish narrative fiction of the early twentieth century, and interprets early twentieth-century cultural production in Spain in the context of national and European influences. In relation to both imported and autochthonous models, Spain was a key European player (alongside France, Britain and Italy) for widespread cultural debate and exchange regarding degeneration theory. Finally, the book aims to recuperate the striking active agency of women, beyond their conventional role as literary consumers, in the formation of a critical readership during this period. Whilst men were assumed to constitute active, judicious readers, by contrast women were seen as susceptible through their weak nervous systems to the intellectual demands and emotive content of literary fiction of this period. Medical, social and judicial authorities sought to contain and control the biological function of reproduction and the moral role of education in order to safeguard the health of the nation's children and future. I propose that women readers were not passive consumers of regulatory discourses that sought to contain the degenerate female body and mind, but instead exercised active agency in response to prevalent paradigms of social medicine and bourgeois morality.

The genealogy of gender and degeneration traced by my book seeks to illuminate both literary representation of the period and its consumption by a contemporary market. My analysis of Blasco's commercially successful fiction recuperates and emphasizes the influence of the posited female reader in the creation of the author's sensationalist plots and transgressive anti-heroines such as Leonora (*Entre naranjos*) and Neleta (*Cañas y barro*). The representation of women in the works of both authors draws to a large extent on prevalent iconography — such as the figure of the Amazon, the *mujer fatal* and the *mujer serpiente* — and cultural assumptions that maintained the social status quo, bourgeois morality and gender roles. This statement does not preclude, however, the cultural function of women readers of the period in shaping literary fiction, a role that my study examines in the book's Conclusion.

In sum, *Bodies of Disorder* offers an original, interdisciplinary approach to the compelling assimilation of discourses of degeneration in two early twentieth-century Spanish male authors, one canonical, one bestselling. The book assesses the extent to which these discourses were informed — or indeed subverted — by the novels' representations of women, their biological, moral and intellectual functions. Prevalent anxieties in early twentieth-century Spain about the decline of the nation and its future in the wake of the Disaster of 1898 centred upon the regulation of human reproduction through the containment of the female body. These attempts to control the biological and moral health of women through the spheres of medicine, law, society and politics were thus viewed as key to halting the progressive decline of the Spanish nation, and instead providing a route for its regeneration.

Within the medico-scientific discourse of the period, women were construed as primitive or uncivilized 'Other', a source of fear and the dangerous object of moral containment. These formulations of the cultural myths and meta-narratives of degeneration drew momentum from bourgeois fears of the proletariat, the working-class crowd, and in particular the feminine masses. In their occupation of a public sphere, working-class women and the figure of the prostitute represented a notable threat to accepted feminine norms that centred on the bourgeois female in a domestic and maternal setting. The city thus became a site of moral and biological corruption, both in relation to the poverty of the working classes and the prevalent figure of the urban prostitute. The latter was construed as a key source of contamination through her dangerous role in the spread of venereal diseases, notably syphilis. The hiring of wet-nurses, too, constituted a potential threat of infection to children of the upper and middle classes. *Nodrizas* were frequently sourced from agricultural areas in the search for wholesome values and healthy bodies, removed from the dangers of urban prostitution.

Alcoholism, promiscuity and disease were associated particularly with urban areas and the indigent masses as sources of contagion. The effects of drinking mothers on urban working-class children received widespread attention. The presence of distilleries and alcoholism in agricultural areas, however, was also of primary concern. In the mid-nineteenth-century British press, for example, it was claimed that the growth of animals fed on the spoils of distilleries was weakened, provoking comparisons with working-class children in towns and cities. In a Spanish context, the analysis of Baroja's *La casa de Aizgorri* in Chapter 2 and Blasco Ibáñez's *Cañas y barro* in Chapter 5 demonstrates the rural reach of cultural narratives of degeneration, its association with alcohol (the insidious influence of the distillery in Valverde; the tavern in El Palmar as a source of corruption) and sexual morality.

Both Baroja and Blasco Ibáñez ultimately reject a positivist approach to these questions, despite their compelling interest in biological, social and political narratives of degeneration of the period. Through their uneasy association with eugenicist theories, both degenerationist and regenerationist ideologies would eventually seep into the fascist discourses of the interwar period in Europe. The complex and profoundly problematic relationship between degenerationism in its post-Darwinian context, the political ideologies of 'Generation of 1898' authors such as Baroja, and the appropriation of these ideas by the rhetoric of Francoism in the 1930s and beyond is the subject of the final section of my book.

Degenerationism in Baroja and Blasco Ibáñez

Degeneration theory construed heredity as the accumulation of latent pathological tendencies within subsequent generations. The early novels of Baroja and Blasco Ibáñez were strongly informed by the medical and pseudo-scientific discourses that centred on human reproduction. A pan-European disorder, degeneration both posited biological decadence and drew momentum through its appeal to fears of 'otherness', including non-white 'races', femininity and the masses. Authority was secured instead from the white bourgeois male, the doctor and the scientist.[1] In the wake of nineteenth-century theories of degeneration, femininity was more than ever a category both to explain and to contain. Discourses of degeneration in Spain, as elsewhere in Europe, were informed by the scientific, pseudo-scientific, medical and moral study of criminality (including physiognomy and the physical stigmata of degeneration), infanticide, promiscuity and other forms of 'deviance'. These debates were inseparable from social anxieties around reproduction, gender categories and changing women's roles at the turn of the twentieth century.

The influence of late nineteenth-century theories of degeneration in Baroja's novels has been acknowledged by a small number of studies. Weston and Noma Flint analyse the impact of Nordau on the representation of Fernando's pseudo-mysticism, morbid eroticism and ego-mania in *Camino de perfección*.[2] Longhurst addresses poverty and alcoholism in the context of turn-of-the-century medical and scientific theories in *La casa de Aizgorri*, literary naturalism and urban indigence in Baroja and Blasco.[3] Otis offers an overview of pathology and organic memory in three key novels by Baroja, through contextual comparison with Émile Zola, Thomas Mann, Miguel de Unamuno, Pardo Bazán and Thomas Hardy.[4] The 2009 volume *La mala vida* edited by Richard Cleminson and Teresa Fuentes Peris tackles the concept of national decline in turn-of-the-century Spain.[5] Most recently, in his analysis of medical writers in Spain, Sosa-Velasco examines nineteenth-century theories of race and biology. This perceptive study, however, assumes a consistent adherence to the premises of degenerationism that I seek to problematize.[6] Richard Cardwell's scholarship of the 1990s provides a knowledgeable overview of the *finisecular* novel in Spain in the light of discourses of pathology and naturalism.[7] *Bodies of Disorder* builds on these foundations by offering an original genealogy of the largely neglected symbiosis between gender and degenerationism in early twentieth-century Spain. It explores the key roles ascribed to the female body by degeneration theory and challenges existing studies by providing a sustained analysis of the ways in which Baroja and Blasco Ibáñez distance themselves from a secure adherence both to degenerationism and the premises of the naturalist novel. My book seeks to extend these critical perspectives through my focused alignment of degenerationism and cultural representations of the female body in the context of reproductive, social and moral health.

The interaction between representations of gender and degeneration in the early works of Baroja and Blasco Ibáñez is of particular interest for its literary expression of powerful debates about national decadence, its relationship to human reproduction and collective decline at the turn of the twentieth century in Spain. Also of relevance to my analysis are existing studies that focus specifically on nineteenth-century realist authors in Spain. Fuentes has addressed filth and deviancy in Galdós. Tsuchiya explores gendered deviance in the works of Galdós, Pardo Bazán and Clarín.[8] The critical approaches cited above provide valuable context for further extended scrutiny of Baroja and his Spanish contemporaries in early twentieth-century Spain. In particular, the complex and varied responses of each author to specific strands of influential scientific discourses both national and international in origin, demand further critical attention. Degeneration theory and the cultural history of heredity are among the most salient examples.

Most significantly, my book counters the dominant assumptions of existing criticism that Baroja wholeheartedly espoused the premises of degenerationism. The sustained and original comparison between the early twentieth-century works of Baroja and Blasco allows me to challenge these critical norms, thereby proposing a new scholarly perspective both in relation to the elitist fiction of 'Generation of 1898' authors and popular fiction of the period. *Bodies of Disorder* applies the paradigms of gender and degenerationism for the first time to the works of Blasco Ibáñez, in order to illuminate the parallels between his own contradictory engagements with pervasive moral and socio-cultural myths of the period and those of Baroja. With his medical training, his interest in physiology and pathology, and his characteristic agnosticism towards received ideas, Baroja was ideally placed to inherit the role of successor to the naturalist novel in Spain. However, the author did not consider his artistic production as fundamentally naturalist, since he regarded naturalism by this time as outmoded. As he wrote in 1899, 'El artista moderno no es, respecto a la Naturaleza, un espejo que trate de reflejarla: es más bien un instrumento delicado que vibra con sus latidos y amplifica sus vibraciones'.[9] Baroja did not reject naturalism *per se*. By the 1890s, however, his comments imply that this literary mode had run its course and was no longer an adequate means to convey a rapidly changing vision of reality. The author maintained a profound interest in experimental science, but diverged from the naturalist school of Émile Zola in his scepticism towards the theoretical application of scientific methods to art and literature.

In the case of Blasco Ibáñez, as for Baroja, the undeniable influence of popular theories of degeneration is mitigated by a contradictory adherence to their premises. Both authors engaged with and simultaneously resisted the pervasive cultural narratives of degenerationism. This revision of dominant critical perspectives proposed by my study has powerful implications both with regard to our understanding of the political views and the cultural legacy of each author in twentieth-century Spain. Without Baroja's clinical background, Blasco's own representations of moral, sexual and biological deviance are obviously eclectic in origins and influences. Blasco was familiar with well-known international scientific, philosophical and literary works, as his editorial work with Sempere demonstrates. By 1910, their catalogue included the publication of works by Darwin, Nietzsche, Nordau, Spencer and Zola. One of their collections, 'La novela literaria' was dedicated to translating early twentieth-century French literature into Spanish.[10] At the turn of the twentieth century, Blasco's own novels espoused a particularly idiosyncratic version of naturalism. Contrary to his reputation as 'el Zola español', his Valencian novels do not convey a scientifically neutral or detached version of the world, or indeed the premises of hereditary determinism through any consistent thesis. Instead, like Baroja's fiction of the first decade, Blasco's turn-of-the-century novels interweave a number of powerful cultural myths of the period that found authority within scientific discourse. In this sense, we find a notable similarity between the literary responses of Baroja and Blasco Ibáñez to degenerationism. Discourses of pathology infuse their early fiction, but neither accepts positivist models uncritically.

Baroja read Nordau and Lombroso with interest, but distanced himself from these theorists in unambiguous terms. Degenerationism spanned the various disciplines of science, social and hygienic medicine, psychiatry, anthropology, criminology and morality both in Spain and other parts of Europe. Theories of degeneration drew profoundly on fears around reproduction and maternity in relation to the future of the 'race', a term that referred variously to 'la raza humana', the 'pueblo' or nation, and to sub-categories and typologies within this overarching definition. In Spain, Sanz del Río's *Ideal de la humanidad* (1860) referred to the 'pueblo' as synonymous with 'raza'. During the late nineteenth century, the decadence of the Spanish nation was subject to widespread debate, as explored by Enrique Diego Madrazo in his book ¿*El pueblo español ha muerto? Impresiones sobre el estado actual de la sociedad española*, published in 1903. Regenerationists such as Lucas Mallada critiqued the Spanish nation in order to propose energetic solutions for its future. In 1916, Diego Guigou y Costa defended 'el matrimonio eugénico' (the medical licensing of marriage) as a means of achieving the 'perfeccionamiento físico y moral de la raza humana'.[11] The anticipation of fascist discourses could not be clearer.

Informed by Schopenhauer and Nietzsche among other prominent figures, the question of Will or *voluntad* was widely debated in late nineteenth-century Spain. This concern was reinvigorated by the examination of *aboulia* or lack of Will in the works of Spanish intellectuals, such as Unamuno's *En torno al casticismo* (1895), Ganivet's *Idearium español* (1897), and Azorín's *La voluntad* (1902). The lack of Will had already become gendered in the second half of the nineteenth century, as evidence of effeminacy and lack of virility. These cultural discourses had implications for concerns about low population increases in France and Spain, by comparison with the growing populations of Germany and England. The 'depopulation paranoia' fuelled debate about the biological inferiority of Mediterranean nations by contrast with Anglo-Saxon nations, as Oscar Vázquez attests in a recent study of degeneration in Spanish visual culture.[12]

Baroja's racial theories are notably problematic. He drew strong identification with Northern Europeans and his Basque origins, and in his essays distinguished between Aryan reason, science and strength of Will versus Semitic intrigue, commerce and rhetoric. He was particularly interested in the racial classifications of Vacher de Lapouge, who divided Europeans into *brachycephalics* (round-heads, whom Lapouge identified as Catholic and vulgar) and *dolichocephalics* (long-heads, identified as Protestant, cultured and civilized). Baroja questioned the dubious validity of this anthropological typology, yet it continued to exert a long-standing fascination in numerous essays and novels. In 'La raza y la cultura' of 1938, he concluded retrospectively that 'estas etiquetas de arios, semitas, latinos, germanos y eslavos' are scientifically worthless (*OC*, VIII, 942).

Throughout the nineteenth century, 'race' was frequently synonymous with 'nation', 'people', 'blood' and 'tribes'; the idea of race was both speculative and empirically grounded, the latter exemplified by the Latin American *castas* system.[13] In other words, the concepts of race and species lent useful elasticity to the myths of degeneration through their changing and contradictory set of definitions, national, biological and cultural. Within a pan-European context, debates within biological sciences about the definition of 'species' drew powerfully on degenerationism, since it provided information about variation in humans, as well as what was erroneously regarded as cross-racial reproduction. As Nancy Stepan has argued, degeneration thus became a compelling racial metaphor since it supplied social and political meanings to these debates. The long-standing scientific assumption that all human 'races' belonged to the same species, which was subject to the forces of environmental degeneration that produced racial varieties, gave way by the mid-nineteenth century to the notion that races formed distinct types that could not transform into one another.[14] Degeneration theory thus provided a biological argument against sexual freedom and racial hybridity that underpinned Victorian values about class and gender. Degeneracy also responded powerfully to colonial ideology, in its positioning of racial types in designated geographical places. Transgression of any of these boundaries would result in degeneration that posed a threat to accepted social relations and the concept of progress that defined European identities. This construct of civilization and racial superiority was therefore under attack from an 'unnatural' merging of different races and classes.[15]

It is by now a commonplace that the cultural power of science lies in its claims to authority in explaining human nature, including health, heredity and the mind. In the course of the nineteenth century, reproduction was conceived of, not in relation to the individual, but as the means of transmission of biological characteristics. Heredity thereby assumed a 'powerful bio-political dimension'.[16] By the mid-nineteenth century, the concept of degeneration within race biology began to be appropriated by medicine, psychiatry and criminology. In other words, the healthy reproduction of body and mind was seen as vital for the very future of European nations.

In 1857 the French physician Dr Bénédict Augustin Morel published his *Traité des dégénérescences physiques, intellectuelles et morales de l'espèce humaine*, a work that would have a strong influence on subsequent research in psychiatry, criminology and anthropology in the second half of the nineteenth century. Morel was not the first to posit a theory of degeneration. The concept is rooted in Biblical paradigms, it found expression in Classical literature, and was revitalized in the eighteenth century, well before its use as the basis of medical and social ills in mid-nineteenth-century France, as Michael Stannard has argued.[17] However, the discourses of degeneration were of particular appeal in the wake of evolutionary theory. Greenslade comments in relation to a British context that degeneration was 'an important resource of myth for the post-Darwinian world'. In the light of anxieties of the propertied classes about poverty and crime, public health and imperial fitness, 'degeneration offered boundless scope for both attacking the irrational and sustaining it'.[18]

In the second half of the nineteenth century, degeneration theories were constructed upon the foundation of fears about collective decline within Europe. According to this view, growing rates of crime, suicide, alcoholism, prostitution, neurasthenia and hysteria, syphilis and so on constituted evidence of social disease, and a process of degeneration within the European 'races' or nations. In other words, degeneration was seen, not as the product, but as the cause of crime and disease. To take a salient example, the prostitute was defined during this period through her marginal status as an outsider beyond the normal, the healthy or the civilized. According to dominant discourses, the prostitute was not a symptom of social inequities, but instead a source of contagion. In this context, degeneracy denoted deviation from the norm, a transgression of social and moral regulations. Prostitutes, like the urban poor, were construed as a degenerate class or type.

There is a substantial body of scholarship on the influence of Darwinism and evolutionary theory.[19] By contrast the nineteenth-century concept of degeneration remains a more nebulous term, one that was assimilated and redefined through the interactions between science, literature and socio-political debate. Ambitious studies on degeneration in a European context have been complemented by a recent body of research by the Consejo Superior de Investigaciones Científicas into the assimilation, development and modification of degeneration theory in Spain, with attention to the varied fields of psychiatry, medical discourses, crime, childhood, and social medicine.[20] My book does not set out to provide a comprehensive overview of Spanish degenerationism. Instead it seeks to explore the literary manifestation of degeneration theories in early twentieth-century Spain. It does so through examining the ways in which the novels of Baroja and Blasco Ibáñez engage with the ideas and language of degeneration that held such powerful appeal during the period in Spain as across Western Europe.

Discourses of degeneration, originally founded on racial and biological theories, were assimilated by historians, sociologists, anthropologists, doctors, scientists, politicians and novelists. These debates crossed the disciplines of medicine, politics, socio-cultural debate and literature, among other fields. The early novels of Baroja and Blasco Ibáñez inflect these broader scientific and social debates, at times echoing their conjectures, at others challenging them. My study traces in particular the striking interdependency between gender ideologies and degeneration theories in early twentieth-century Spain, and their relevance to the works of Baroja and Blasco Ibáñez as prominent case studies of their literary and cultural generation.

In the late nineteenth century, degeneration provided a resonant foundation for the naturalist novel, which was profoundly concerned with physiology and the metaphor of disease. The scientific foundations of naturalism presented a disturbing vision of decay, entropy, and the disintegration of biological and social bodies. Novelists of the period were at the forefront of popularizing these debates. Émile Zola's brand of naturalism in late nineteenth-century France inflamed an already alarmist form of social and moral discourse. The dominance of the naturalist novel in Spain coincided with an increasing public concern with criminal behaviour, penal and social reform in the 1890s, as demonstrated by the publication of Azorín's *La sociología criminal* (1899), Constancio Bernaldo de Quirós's *Las nuevas teorías de la criminalidad* (1898) and, co-authored with José-María Llanas Aguilaniedo, *La mala vida en Madrid* (1901). The assassination of Cánovas de Castillo in 1897 and the growing threat of anarchism and socialism all served to fuel public interest in criminality and degenerative disease.[21]

The exposition of pathologies formed the foundation of naturalist fiction and the 'novela médico-social'. It underpinned both the writings of the 'Generation of 1898' — Azorín's *Diario de un enfermo* (1901) and *La voluntad*, Unamuno's *Amor y pedagogía* (1902), Baroja's *Camino de perfección* (1902) — as well as popular fiction by Eduardo Zamacois, Felipe Trigo, and many others. As Fernández Villegas claimed in *La España Moderna* in 1892, literature of the period depicted a society that resembled 'un hospital enorme, un manicomio colosal o un presidio suelto'.[22]

Baroja has long been feted as a canonical figure of the 'Generation of 1898' and, more latterly, the development of Spanish modernism. The term 'Generation of 1898' is notoriously problematic, not least because it has tended to emphasize national concerns at the expense of a broader transnational perspective. The use of this label has frequently assumed recourse to elitist categories, and privileged a canonical and intellectual male perspective, something that scholars have begun more recently to address.[23] By contrast with Baroja, Blasco occupies an altogether different literary camp, defined by his successful use of mass media through journalism, bestselling fiction and in particular film adaptation. Despite these divergent backgrounds, the construction of 'deviant' subjects in the context of discourses of gender and degeneration in both authors is markedly similar.

Blasco, certainly, cannot be reclaimed as a modernist in its elitist, highbrow or formally innovative sense. However, his commercial success and widespread appeal could certainly be regarded as an effective modern vehicle for the public transmission of ideas in a social and political context. The comparison undertaken by this book between Baroja and his popular contemporary Blasco Ibáñez casts new light on their common interest in the contemporary obsession at the turn of the century with national pathologies in Spain. These questions centred on widespread debates about social deviance, criminality, poverty and gender. Baroja's medical fiction frequently incorporates naturalist representations of pathology characteristic of the *fin de siglo*. Yet he was scathing about what he considered to be decadent naturalist fiction of the period. Although it is beyond the scope of this study, the medical fiction of fellow-doctor Felipe Trigo provides a fertile source of comparison with Baroja's early novels.

Pathology, Degeneration and Regenerationism

Baroja enrolled in the School of Medicine at the University of Madrid in 1887, and submitted his medical thesis entitled 'El dolor: estudio de psico-física' in 1893. This dissertation combined knowledge of physiology, psychology and philosophy in the analysis of pain. It is common knowledge that Baroja pursued a brief career as a doctor in Cestona in his early twenties, before devoting himself fully to writing. The death of his eldest brother, Darío, from tuberculosis in February 1894 had a profound emotional impact on Baroja, as he records in his memoirs. This experience added a significant personal dimension to the author's reading of Schopenhauer, which strongly influenced his doctoral thesis.[24] Alongside Schopenhauer, Baroja found particular inspiration in Claude Bernard's *Introduction à l'étude de la médecine expérimentale* (*OC*, VII, 986).

In the context of dominant European theories of degeneration, and their relevance to gender ideologies, the figures of particular interest in my study are the French physician Bénédict Morel (1809–1873), the Italian criminal anthropologist Cesare Lombroso (1835–1909) and the Austro-Hungarian journalist Max Nordau (1849–1923). In his *Traité des dégénérescences* Morel identified a complex interaction between heredity and environment as the root cause of the accumulated degeneration of humanity, a negative trajectory evidenced by the high levels of alcoholism, syphilis, hysteria, criminality and idiocy across European countries. Within this negative trajectory of evolution, he theorized that physical and moral development were co-dependent. According to this view, the latent predisposition towards disease and negative characteristics combined with a harmful environment (poverty, poor nutrition, alcoholism) to produce a progressive burden in relation to the physical, moral and mental health of generations of offspring. Eventual sterility was the most extreme point in the trajectory of degeneration. Morel's hypothesis drew profoundly on Biblical metaphors of the Fall from grace. For both Morel and Lombroso, degenerates embodied atavism, the reversion to a primitive form of evolution. In *Criminal Man* (1885), Lombroso's key contribution to the field of criminal anthropology put forward the notion of the 'born' criminal, and proposed that criminals formed a distinct 'race' that could be classified according to salient physical characteristics, including skull shape and jawline. He grouped women, children, deviants and savages together as examples of atavistic throwbacks to primitive evolution.

Nordau viewed hysteria as the product of the impending *fin de siècle*, and deplored the rejection of accepted morality. As he wrote in his alarmist work *Degeneration* (1892): 'We stand now in the midst of a severe mental epidemic; of a sort of black death of degeneration and hysteria'.[25] The rapid expansion of cities in industrialized nations (Britain, France, Germany, Italy) and the social changes associated with the urban environment were at the heart of these debates. Morel and Lombroso, along with the English psychiatrist Henry Maudsley (1835–1918), had already posited that urban life was leading to physical, moral and mental enervation, and that this was exacerbated with each generation. To some extent, Nordau drew on Morel's physical explanation for degenerate traits: alcohol, drugs, and an unwholesome social environment. Nordau, however, underscored the deleterious effects of industrial society: the fatigue and exhaustion of the human organism, and particularly the frenzied environment of the city.[26] Focusing primarily on the diagnosis of the art and cultural world of the *fin de siècle*, Nordau's conceptualization of neurasthenia and hysteria in *Degeneration* finds salient echoes in the representation of the degenerate artist in Baroja and Blasco Ibáñez.

Pseudo-scientific theories from France, Italy and other European countries informed and accompanied the development of autochthonous ideologies in late nineteenth- and early twentieth-century Spain through a paradigm of cultural assimilation and modification.[27] The theories of key figures of degeneration identified above are specific to their national contexts and particular historical period, but they also inform wider medical, psychiatric and social debates across national borders. These ideas were discussed, assimilated and modified in Spain by scientists, medics and intellectuals. Primary routes for their broader dissemination were through contemporary fiction and the popular press. The newspaper *El Pueblo*, which Blasco founded in Valencia in 1894, exemplifies the broad circulation of French naturalist novels through the serialized fiction of the *folletín*. French medical texts were particularly influential in late nineteenth-century Spain, as Comenge comments: 'la invasión de escritos médicos fue más considerable en lengua primaria y traducidos al castellano; diríase que nuestra península se convirtió en mercado espléndido de los franceses, y así nuestra ciencia siguió un feudo del extranjero'.[28] Morel's doctrine of degenerative disease strongly influenced a number of Spanish medical works, including Esquerdo's *Locos que no lo parecen* (1881), which asserts that 'el insigne Morel afirma [...] que los descendientes de padres entregados al alcoholismo crónico [...] ofrecen a menudo los caracteres de una degeneración progresiva'.[29]

It is commonly accepted that the translation of French medical texts and their assimilation by Spanish physicians such as Pedro Felipe Monlau and Pedro Mata, as well as the widespread transmission of the French naturalist novel, were dominant influences on the development of degeneration theory in Spain. However, it should also be noted that the 1846 study of pauperism by the Catalan hygienist Monlau anticipated Morel in its discussion of the hereditary and environmental factors in the physical and moral degeneration suffered by the poor. The reproduction of the impoverished represents 'la enervación de las generaciones. A la degeneración física acompaña la degradación moral [...] de embriaguez y de libertinaje que se observan en la población indigente'.[30] Degeneration was a contentious issue for debate in Spain as in other parts of Europe, and one that retained a powerful momentum within the regenerationist debates of the early twentieth century.

Late nineteenth-century Spain, in common with other European countries, witnessed the publication of research that underlined biological causes of mental illness. These studies provide evidence of profound anxieties within *fin-de-siglo* society about criminality, sexuality and morality that transgressed expected norms and bourgeois values, as Campos Marín, Martínez Pérez and Huertas García-Alejo have shown.[31] The publication of psychiatrist J. M. Escuder's *Locos y anómalos* in 1895 exemplifies this trend, through its essentialist connection between madness, biological conception and the development of the foetus *in utero*: 'La locura viene casi siempre desde la fecundación. [...] La simiente de la locura se recibe en el claustro materno, y desde allí germina, crece, se reproduce, invade todo el organismo, y al llegar su época conquista el cerebro'.[32] The female body and its responsibility for reproductive health was thus placed at the centre of the conceptualization of what was deemed normal or abnormal, and was subject to moral and medical vigilance. Within this type of discourse, illness, poverty, prostitution, madness and alcoholism were all defined as beyond the norm in terms of both nature and society. Individuals who displayed these characteristics were deemed outcasts. In Spain degeneration theory offered a scientific basis for the connection between biological degeneration and social or spiritual decadence. A sick society in the process of degeneration was therefore in need of cure and regeneration.[33] Theories about biological degeneration in Spain became a metaphor for history and its ideological interpretation. These discourses focused both on human reproduction (through regulation of the female body) and the nation as Motherland, which was frequently personified during this period in female form.[34]

The pathological metaphors of degenerationism provided a vital foundation for the degeneration–regeneration polarity common in the 1880s. These debates gained increasing momentum over the subsequent two decades.[35] Following the Cuban disaster in 1898 and the loss of Spain's colonies, regenerationism gained even greater currency as an urgent polemic, not least the growing lack of faith in the country's political system. This perspective centred upon what the historian Sebastian Balfour terms a 'pathology of the nation; Spain was suffering from a severe, if not terminal, illness and needed an immediate and radical cure'. At the turn of the century, the politician and economist Joaquín Costa employed the metaphor of an 'iron surgeon' to symbolize the leadership required to 'operate on the sick body of the nation'.[36] In other words, the diagnosis of a diseased turn-of-the-century Spanish society demonstrates the process of identification between biology and history, through the transposition of biological degeneration to a society that was perceived within this ideological framework as a living organism and, more specifically, a female body or Mother. Across Western Europe, the anxieties produced by social, cultural, technological and scientific change in the late nineteenth century were inextricably tied to the myth of degeneration as a social and cultural resource. In Spain, this process was magnified and perpetuated by the 1898 Disaster and calls on the part of intellectuals, politicians and economists for regeneration of the nation.[37] Regenerationism cannot be understood without reference to its corollary degenerationism.[38]

Degenerationism in Spain was not limited to theory or abstraction, but instead informed social action through the findings of hygienists, and the objective to protect the future of the nation through reproductive purity. In 1886, J. Viñeta-Bellaserra reinforced the view that syphilis was a primary cause of the degeneration of the human race, stating that 'la sociedad debe estar compuesta de individuos fuertes, vigorosos y mejorarse sin cesar'.[39] Theories of degenerationism in late nineteenth-century Spain rested fundamentally on questions of rhetoric. Although founded on biology, the social and moral drive of these discourses was paramount within the question of national identity and widespread lament of 'los males de España' in the early twentieth century. In 1890, the regenerationist Lucas Mallada published his well-known work on the causes of Spain's decline, *Los males de la patria*, arguing that '[la] juventud, noble y generosa, que no querrá una patria envilecida y despreciada, que no querrá una patria corroída por bajas pasiones y miserables rivalidades; esa juventud, que no querrá una patria empobrecida y sin aliento, se alzará con brío para regenerarla'.[40] A nation that has exhausted itself through over-exertion, by contrast, would produce weak and degenerate descendants. Fatigue and lack of Will were at the heart of biological and spiritual explanations of Spanish decadence. 1899 saw the publication of lawyer Ricardo Macías Picavea's *El Problema Nacional*: the National or Spanish Problem.

The cultural myths of degeneration that extended across much of Western Europe were susceptible to appropriation and reinvention in Spain in the wake of 'el desastre', and the ensuing political, economic and spiritual consequences for the nation. If anything, the historical events of 1898 only intensified the appeal of — and recourse to — warnings about biological catastrophe. Morel's thesis of degeneration was cautiously optimistic in the sense that improved social conditions would provide the means to halt the degeneration of the nation. Lombroso's 'born' criminal, by contrast, could not be eliminated due to hereditary predisposition; the only solution was a model of negative eugenics that would remove these toxic elements from society.

In the field of psychiatry, degenerationism proved a powerful tool for interpreting society and politics in the final decades of the nineteenth century. As Campos Marín has demonstrated, Spanish psychiatrists were initially more cautious than their French counterparts, analysing clinical questions such as heredity, physical and psychological stigmata in relation to the degenerate individual, without adherence to an apocalyptic vision of national degeneration or social decadence.[41] This stance was counter to the role of hygienic and social medicine which operated both within an interpretative framework and as a tool of social action. In 1876, in his study *Tratado Teórico-Práctico de Frenopatología*, J. Giné y Partagás accepted the positivist connection between mental illness and brain pathology, but failed to subscribe to Morel's theory of degeneration in relation to his clinical analysis of insanity.[42] By the 1880s, however, young Spanish psychiatrists would be drawn to the anthropological dimensions of degenerationism. José María Escuder's *Locos y anómalos* of 1895 demonstrates the influence of Lombroso's work in its classification of the criminal in anthropological terms.[43] The reinvigoration of degeneration theories provided by the Italian positivist school, including Lombroso and his disciples, would prove enormously influential in Spain of the 1880s and 1890s, leading to a more homogenous acceptance of degeneration as the explanation for mental illness by the turn of the century. Lombroso's work on degeneration and criminal anthropology was publicly debated in Spain at the trial of Garayo el Sacamantecas in 1881.[44]

Alienism was pioneered famously in France by Jean-Étienne Esquirol and others, and was predicated on the positivist perspective that mental disease could be explained through neurological abnormality. This view would later be challenged by the proponents of psychodynamic theory. In Spain, the Valencian José María Esquerdo was a leading *alienista*, and disciple of the medico-legal scholar Pedro Mata. Esquerdo argued tirelessly for legal recognition of criminal insanity under the banner *Locos que no lo parecen*. Among his students was the medical journalist and politician, Ángel Pulido. The latter strongly supported Esquerdo's campaign, and publicly praised the private asylums founded at Carabanchel in an article published in 1882 by *El siglo médico*. Twenty years later Pulido would criticize the backward medical practices of Spain that had failed to adopt the use of vaccination to halt the extensive spread of infectious diseases, notably the outbreak of smallpox in Madrid in 1900–01 that had resulted in 2000 deaths.[45] Other *alienistas* who were disciples of Esquerdo include the criminal anthropologist Rafael Salillas, Victoriano Garrido, author of *La cárcel o el manicomio: estudio médico-legal sobre la locura* (1888), and the degenerationist José María Escuder.[46]

Like physical pathologies, mental degeneration was like a bacterium that could infect healthy individuals in the social body; degeneration thus threatened the evolution and progress of the human race. In the light of this growing threat, science was employed to control society, morality and culture, including artistic values. In Spain, these ideas were widely debated in the intellectual sphere: by the Krausists, the Institución Libre de Enseñanza, and in reviews including the *Revista Europea*, the *Revista Contemporánea* and *La España Moderna*. Scientists such as Santiago Ramón y Cajal, critics such as Pompeyo Gener and Francisco Giner de los Ríos, and authors of the period incorporated these debates in resounding terms.[47] Pathology and scientific discourses of course underpinned the naturalist novel, in Spain as in France. Many prominent Spanish cultural figures, such as Leopoldo Alas and Pardo Bazán, were sceptical about the methods of Lombroso and Nordau. Yet the discursive influence of degenerationism triumphed through the assimilation of its social and cultural premises, if not its methodologies. In the late nineteenth century the biological sciences exerted an enormous influence both on officialdom and the broader public in shaping attitudes to sanitation and public health. The powerful interweaving of medical science and literature, in Spain as elsewhere in the final decades of the nineteenth century, is noteworthy in this context.

In sum, degenerationism profoundly informed and shaped social and scientific disciplines in late nineteenth-century Spain, from hygienic medicine and social sanitation to criminal anthropology and psychiatry. Its dominance was rooted in the compelling and widespread appeal to varied forms of cultural explanation and discourse, whether scientific, social, political or literary. It afforded fundamental privilege to the authority of the white, bourgeois male and his status of superiority to all forms of otherness, in relation to race, class and gender.

The novels by Baroja and Blasco Ibáñez analysed in the current study were all published between 1895 and 1911. In early works such as *La casa de Aizgorri* and *Camino de perfección*, Baroja drew on nineteenth-century theories of the unconscious, notably those of Eduard von Hartmann and Arthur Schopenhauer. Despite his overt denigration of Freudian psychoanalysis, I contend that Baroja intuited in incipient form certain ideas developed contemporaneously by Sigmund Freud in seminal works such as *The Interpretation of Dreams* (1900) and *Three Essays on the Theory of Sexuality* (1905). Baroja was particularly fascinated by the effects of early childhood. The complex convergences and contradictions between nineteenth-century discourses of degeneration (Lombroso, Nordau, and others) and the development of psychoanalysis are key to the nuanced understanding of Baroja's concept of biological paradigms, heredity and determinism, and their interactions with the psyche. His interest in a subconscious world beneath rational thought was evident from his earliest writings.

Nineteenth-century philosophers of the unconscious (Hartmann, Schopenhauer) presented an inextricable connection between mind and body. As Schopenhauer wrote: 'the Materialists endeavour to show that *all*, even *mental phenomena*, are *physical*, and rightly, only they do not see that, on the other hand, everything physical is *at the same time metaphysical*'.[48] Schopenhauer's definition of Will as a blind, unconscious force was fundamentally driven by biology, the clearest affirmation of Will being the instinct for reproduction. Hartmann admired both Schopenhauer and Darwin; Freud in turn was acquainted with Hartmann's *Philosophy of the Unconscious* (1868). Freud's intellectual formation was in biological science, and was profoundly influenced by Darwin.[49]

This biological foundation for interpreting the psyche is demonstrated by Baroja's (frequently tentative and suggestive) exploration of repressed instincts, often sexual in nature, as evident in both *La casa de Aizgorri* and *Camino de perfección*. A number of his early short stories published in *Vidas sombrías* demonstrate an incipient interest in literary explorations of the unconscious. This convergence between Baroja's own literary representation of the workings of the psyche in his early works and the development of psychoanalysis is unlikely to be a case of straightforward or direct influence. Rather, in my view, it is one of convergence or parallel paths towards similar thinking. Baroja openly rejected Freud's theories, viewing his work as evidence of an obsession with eroticism and sexuality. Given the bluntness of his dismissal of Freud, it is particularly intriguing to trace incipient similarities in his conceptualization of psychological processes. Baroja was also well acquainted with nineteenth-century theories of the unconscious in Hartmann and Schopenhauer.

Freud's work of the 1890s on the origins of neurosis is especially relevant in this regard. In 'Heredity and the Aetiology of the Neuroses', of 1896, Freud argued that all neuroses originated in the subject's sexual history, and gave primacy to the legacy of sexual abuse in childhood. By 1897, however, he modified his seduction theory in favour of the early formulation of the Oedipus complex and the view that neuroses originated within the psyche. The child's sexual life, later explored in his *Three Essays on the Theory of Sexuality* (1905), was produced by internal psychological development and its interactions with external experience. None the less, Freud drew on evolutionary theory with regard to the inheritance of mental characteristics, transmitted via the memory of the species. This appeal to primitivism is evident in his assertion that dream symbols are remnants of 'an ancient but extinct mode of expression'.[50] The Oedipus complex accounted for the survival of the primitive human race, a theory developed in *Totem and Taboo* (1913).

The frequently tentative and experimental rendering of the workings of the unconscious has received little critical attention in either Baroja or Blasco Ibáñez. Yet the influence of childhood, psychological trauma and the psychodynamics of the family underpin the representation of unconscious motivation in Blasco's *Entre naranjos*, as they do more obviously in Baroja's *La casa de Aizgorri* and *Camino de perfección*. Baroja clearly conceptualized art as a means to explore covert realities and the hidden workings of the mind. In a similar vein, Blasco wrote in a letter about the creation of art or literature stemming from the depths of the subconscious, beneath rational thought.[51]

Gender and Deviance

One of the salient characteristics of degeneration, according to pseudo-scientific discourses, was the breakdown of categories of gender and the boundaries of sexual difference. The aesthetes of Oscar Wilde's *The Picture of Dorian Gray* (1891) and in Spain, Carmen de Burgos's *El veneno del arte* (1910), exemplify the androgynous gender hybridity so typical of the period, as effeminacy became equated with decline. The feared feminization of culture represented the inversion of civilization founded on masculine intellect and reason. The cigarette-smoking, bicycling, independent 'New Woman' was a particular object of satire in the British magazine *Punch*, due to the social implications of these newfound freedoms. Carmen de Burgos was a *mujer moderna* in her own right, and was an outspoken supporter of divorce. Following the breakdown of her marriage, she had a relationship with Ramón Gómez de la Serna. She was also a female foreign correspondent for the Spanish–Moroccan

War in 1909.[52] The widespread success of Nordau's infamous *Degeneration* rested on its expression of European anxieties about the perceived deviation from gender norms. The masculine women and the effeminate man represented this threatening gender ambivalence or hybridity founded on its transgression of social and cultural boundaries.[53] Salient examples in Spanish literature are the feminization of Galdós's Ángel Guerra (1890–91) and the androgyny of Feíta in Pardo Bazán's *Memorias de un solterón* (1896).[54] As the assumed norm or ideal was increasingly blurred, containment through categories became even more essential.

For Lombroso, like other criminal anthropologists, sexual ambiguity was a characteristic of degeneration and the associated concept of atavism, or reversion to a primitive state. In her study of gender deviance in Spanish realist authors, Tsuchiya argues that 'the feminine' came to signal all subjects beyond established norms and who were designated as transgressive, disorderly or degenerate, including the hysteric, the feminist, the homosexual and the revolutionary.[55] Degeneration thus became intertwined, through a false syllogism, with the perceived feminization of masculine culture and the concurrent drive for normativity, in which women were inherently represented as Other. Lombroso's *Criminal Woman* (1893) famously claimed a scientific basis for pathologies of female sexuality as deviant.[56]

Many of the novels selected for analysis in my comparison of Baroja and Blasco draw on the pervasive misogynist iconography of the European *fin de siècle*. Bram Dijkstra's exceptional study of visual art of the period assesses these images, although with little reference to Spain.[57] There are numerous examples in Spanish painting and the illustrated press during this period of languid, exhausted women, who visually demonstrate their perceived inability to revitalize the health of the nation.[58] Baroja's and Blasco Ibáñez's early novels coincide with recurrent tropes in visual art of the period in relation to misogynist representations of women as sexual temptation and danger (*la mujer fatal*) or as passive spectators, in each case providing models that are objectified in relation to male trajectories. The many appearances of the prostitute and the adulteress in the works of Blasco in particular echo essentialist ideologies that commented on, and attempted to control, the economy of the female body and the social effects of reproduction. The two generic figures are represented through the iconography of Eve, or *la mujer serpiente*, of the Amazon and siren in Blasco's works. These visual and literary representations of feminine identities are inseparable from social anxieties about the changing social roles and identities of women in the late nineteenth and early twentieth centuries.

The fear of woman as sexual danger is demonstrated succinctly by the spread of syphilis at the turn of the century, exemplified in visual art by Picasso's *Les Demoiselles d'Avignon* (1907). The early controversy surrounding the painting can be explained, as is well known, not just by the fracturing of the plane of vision which foreshadowed Cubism, but also by the violent treatment of the female body and its depiction of prostitutes. The female body is presented, through the confrontational eroticism of the painting, not as fertile (ironically denoted by the fruit in the foreground of the composition) but as threatening, reflecting Picasso's fears about sexually transmitted disease. Just a few years earlier, Ramon Casas's

Fig. I.1. Pablo Picasso (Málaga, 1881–1973), *Les Demoiselles d'Avignon* (Paris, June-July 1907). New York, Museum of Modern Art (MoMA). Oil on canvas, 243.9 × 233.7 cm. Acquired through the Lillie P. Bliss Bequest. 333.1939
© 2017. Digital image, The Museum of Modern Art, New York / Scala, Florence and © Succession Picasso / DACS, London 2017

poster *Sífilis* (1900) advertises a clinic in Barcelona that promises a permanent cure. In this well-known image, the disfiguring physical symptoms of syphilis are not represented. Instead the poster presents a sanitized version of a prostitute of pale complexion and delicate constitution holding a lily, a sign of her former purity. On her back, a serpent signifies her sexual decadence and downfall. The prostitute's physical vulnerability (her pale, slender and frail physique) is referenced both as her charm and sexual danger: the peril she represents as the perceived source of disease and degeneration. These well-known images provide stark illustration of prevalent visual and literary tropes of the period that inform in compelling ways the representation of gender and degeneration in the works of Baroja, Blasco and their contemporaries.

By the turn of the century, the concept of women's innate sexual continence was being questioned. As Showalter has argued in an Anglophone context, 'moving away from a mid-Victorian notion of female "passionlessness", or sexual anaesthesia, advanced late nineteenth-century thinkers acknowledged women's capacity for sexual pleasure and discussed the psychological and biological harmfulness of celibacy. One of the significant factors in this change was the recognition of female sexual desire, both as a physical function and as a health requirement'.[59] In early twentieth-century Western Europe, liberal thinkers recognized the existence of female sexual desire predominantly in relation to its role in marriage and motherhood.[60] On the surface, it may appear a troubling contradiction that a number of female authors of British New Woman fiction urged women to suppress their instincts and passions. The suffragette leader Christabel Pankhurst promoted female celibacy as a response to oppressive relations with men and the risks of venereal disease.[61] Others, by contrast, pointed to the dangers to health of sexual abstinence in women; some advocated rational reproduction as the means to physical regeneration.

In Spain, Carmen de Burgos, Concha Espina and Margarita Nelken defended dominant moral values, both in relation to the rejection of female sexual passion and the definition of women in relation to maternity, as Celaya Carrillo has shown in her study of sexuality in early twentieth-century Spain.[62] This position (the call for women to repress sexual instinct) by some *fin-de-siècle* feminists shares surprising commonality with traditional arguments against female emancipation on the basis of biology: the idea that the female body and mind were not fit for suffrage or intellectual pursuits, and that female education would damage healthy reproduction. Biological science could thus be used both in support of, and opposition to, social change.[63]

Bodies of Disorder assesses the ways in which literary constructions of gender during this period engage with dominant scientific, psychological and medical theories that sought to diagnose and contain the female body. One of the most salient of such theories was degeneration. Although pertinent to novels such as *Camino de perfección*, *Cañas y barro* and *La barraca*, an extended examination of the relationship between masculinity and degeneration is beyond the scope of this study. Likewise, my approach is necessarily selective in the number of works by Baroja and Blasco Ibáñez included, and analyses those which most clearly represent

FIG. 1.2. Ramon Casas (Barcelona, 1866–1932), *Sífilis* (1900). Lithograph. 80 × 34.3 cm © Museu Nacional d'Art de Catalunya, Barcelona

the connections and interactions of interest to the study of gender and degeneration. For this reason, Baroja's *Aventuras, inventos y mixtificaciones de Silvestre Paradox* (1901) has not been included, despite its compelling satire of positivism.

The opening chapter examines late nineteenth-century cultural myths surrounding the artist. Max Nordau's alarmist work *Degeneration* (*Entartung*) strongly informs Baroja's portrait of the neurasthenic artist in *Camino de perfección*. Four years later, Blasco Ibáñez's own portrait of the artist in *La maja desnuda* (1906) would draw directly on nineteenth-century theories of hysteria as both a feminine condition that manifested itself through symptoms of uncontrolled emotions and incoherence and a physiological disorder of the female body. Both *Camino de perfección* and *La maja desnuda* echo salient popular aspects of Nordau's concept of the degenerate artist. However, both novels ultimately fail to subscribe to the more extreme premises of Nordau's theories of degeneration.

Chapter 2 develops the analysis of degeneration and neurosis through comparison of two works published in 1900, and explores the coexistence of naturalist and symbolist elements in each author's representation of heredity and the unconscious. In Baroja's *La casa de Aizgorri*, the female protagonist Águeda rejects marriage and maternity, believing that she inherits the alcoholic traits of her father, a position that draws on Morel's theories of *dégénérescence* and generational or pathological decline. In a national context, the novel echoes studies of hereditary alcoholism by Spanish doctors such as Muñoz Ruiz de Pasanis and Cervera Barat. The intuitive parallels with contemporary developments in psychoanalysis, sexology and theories of the crowd exemplified by *Entre naranjos* were, I suggest, key to the commercial success of Blasco's turn-of-the-century novels.

Part II presents a comparison of each author's Madrid novels, Baroja's *La busca* (1904) and Blasco's *La horda* (1905). Existing critical studies have identified the documentary veracity of Baroja's portrait of the slums of the capital. The salient influence of Lombroso, however, has been accepted uncritically on the whole in the analysis of Baroja's depiction of deviance and degeneration in anthropological terms. Our interpretation of gender paradigms in his early novels is significant in this regard. I argue that Lombroso's concept of the 'born' prostitute in his work *Criminal Woman* offers a revealing contextual foundation for our understanding of Baroja's representation of criminality and prostitution in his Madrid novel *La busca*. My analysis aims to challenge critical assumptions regarding Baroja's anachronistic adherence to naturalist, determinist and positivist paradigms. Although there are echoes of atavism and degeneration, the portrait of prostitution does not rest in any consistent way on the notion of innate immorality sustained by criminal anthropology. Instead Baroja's urban portrait shares a degree of cautious optimism with French theories of *dégénérescence* in the wake of Morel about the possibility of social recovery. Social regeneration, rather than the removal of deviant individuals or negative eugenics, provides the key for the nation's future.

Baroja claimed that *La horda* was directly inspired by his own portrait of the poverty of the urban masses in *La busca* (*OC*, VII, 870). By contrast to Baroja's clinical diagnosis of the existence, if not the causes of, social pathology, Blasco's interest in the representation of urban indigence and vice in *La horda* is primarily political and sociological. None the less, the representation of social injustice draws on influential French theories of crowd psychology which underpinned Zola's naturalism, most notably Gustave Le Bon's *Psychologies des foules* which posited the inevitable and atavistic regression of the degenerate urban masses. The novel echoes fears of the working classes, and particularly working-class women, which inspired political and medical approaches to the 'cuestión social' in Spain. The dominant metaphor of the body, which functioned simultaneously as an equivalent for the nation in Krausism and for the 'cuerpo social' in social medicine, produced a contradictory discourse of social control in the late nineteenth century, as Labanyi has argued.[64] Naturalist discourse is thus present in both Baroja's and Blasco's urban novels through the function of the female body as a cypher for social fears. The revolutionary statement of the closing pages of *La horda* presents the failure of idealism, alongside a tentative model of regenerationism, in political rather than biological terms. The progressive accumulation of degenerative or pathological traits posited by theories of heredity is not an inevitable outcome in either *La busca* or *La horda*.

The final part of the book analyses fictional representations of the female body as the locus of social fears about reproduction, maternity and generational decadence. *Cañas y barro* has long held a reputation for being Blasco's naturalist novel *par excellence*. Following the success of his early serialized fiction, Blasco's novel of 1902 presents a sensationalist exposition of social issues of interest to a large audience, notably adultery, infanticide and criminality. Historical accounts of infanticide in the late nineteenth century posit popular stereotypes of this crime as the result of puerperal insanity that afflicted childbearing women. This commonly assumed paradigm is contested by the gruesome neonaticide and suicide of the novel's ending, both of which are committed by the child's father. The correlation between degeneration and the female body sustained by contemporaneous social and medical discourses and underpinned by parts of the text is finally overturned by a reversal of gender roles at the end of the novel. Interpreted frequently as the source of moral destruction and an obvious incarnation of the *mujer fatal*, the representation of Neleta does not convincingly sustain either a model of hereditary generational pathologies or the notion of 'born' criminality that led (according to Lombroso and his followers) to infanticide.

Developing my analysis of maternal dysfunction in *Cañas y barro*, the final chapter provides a gendered account of the disruptive engagement in Baroja's *El árbol de la ciencia* (1911) with discourses relating to reproduction and national decline within the urban environment of Madrid. In the final part of his trilogy *La raza*, Baroja's preoccupation with biological decline and degenerationism culminates in a potent symbol of national decadence through the failure of maternity/paternity and the still-born baby at the end of the novel. By contrast to existing criticism, however, I argue that the *abulia* from which the protagonist Andrés Hurtado and his wife Lulú both suffer is fundamentally metaphysical rather than hereditary or biological. According to my reading, the deaths of Andrés, Lulú and their ill-fated child denote their position as spiritual precursors, and not primarily as biological failures. In other words, the weak-willed protagonists represent the entrenched spiritual ailment of early twentieth-century Spain, and not the inevitable, biological sterility of the nation's future. Despite his profound fascination with heredity, for Baroja national character was more than a question of biology.

The well-known polemic between Baroja and Blasco Ibáñez focused particularly on the latter's remarkable commercial success: following Hollywood film adaptations of his novels he became a millionaire. Baroja's resentment about the perceived disjunction between literary authenticity and economic reward is evident in a number of pejorative statements about his Valencian contemporary. Long-dismissed as an 'escritor de masas', Blasco has commonly been placed in an altogether different literary camp from the elitist intellectualism of Baroja and other members of his generation. My study assesses the extent to which each author's early twentieth-century novels are comparable in their treatment of deviance and pathology, each a key trope of late nineteenth-century naturalism. Ultimately Baroja's and Blasco's early novels engage with, but fail to endorse in any cohesive and unequivocal sense, the arguments of degeneration theorists, dominant models of hereditary determinism, or the norms of literary naturalism that accompanied them.

This book seeks to extend recent but sporadic critical interest in the influence of Baroja's scientific training on his early novels, by countering the author's frequently assumed adherence to positivist ideologies. It also applies popular cultural interest in degenerationism to an extended analysis of the works of Blasco Ibáñez. The chameleonic nature of Baroja's political views has frequently been downplayed. I seek to problematize existing critical readings by drawing attention to the contradictions inherent within Baroja's approach to positivism and degenerationism, politics and social reform. Blasco's famous Republicanism provides a useful point of reference for addressing these questions across the spectrum of canonical and popular fiction.

Secondly, *Bodies of Disorder* examines the representation of women and the female body in the works of both Baroja and Blasco in order to trace the genealogy of gender and degeneration during this period with regard to reproductive health and the nation's future. The emphasis on the agency of discerning women readers and the exigencies of the literary market is an original strand of the book that aims to redress the weighty emphasis within 'Generation of 1898' and modernist literary history on the intellectualism of the male subject, author and reader. Finally, the present study explores the ways in which Spanish intellectuals framed degeneration and regeneration, producing both parallels and differences with other parts of Europe. In the particular case of Spain, the Disaster of 1898 and ensuing debate about the 'Spanish problem' served to intensify existing, impassioned debates about Spanish decadence and degeneration. The analysis of the early twentieth-century novels of Baroja and Blasco Ibáñez are offered as a case study that casts new light on this phenomenon.

Notes to the Introduction

1. See Daniel Pick, *Faces of Degeneration: A European Disorder, c.1848–c.1918* (Cambridge: Cambridge University Press, 1989), p. 230.

2. Weston and Noma Flint, *Pío Baroja: Camino de perfección* (London: Grant and Cutler, 1983).
3. Carlos-Alex Longhurst, 'Entre el naturalismo y el simbolismo: la primera novela de Baroja', *Ínsula*, 719 (2006), 19–21; 'La mala vida en Madrid según Blasco y Baroja: *La horda* y *La busca*', *Revista de Estudios sobre Blasco Ibáñez*, Ajuntament de Valencia, 1(2012), 105–17; 'Representations of the "Fourth Estate" in Galdós, Blasco and Baroja', in *New Galdós Studies: Essays in Memory of John Varey*, ed. and intro. by Nicholas G. Round (Woodbridge: Tamesis, 2003), pp. 73–97.
4. Laura Otis, *Organic Memory: History and the Body in the Late Nineteenth and Early Twentieth Centuries* (Lincoln and London: University of Nebraska Press, 1994).
5. Richard Cleminson and Teresa Fuentes Peris, Introduction to '"*La mala vida*": Source and Focus of Degeneration, Degeneracy and Decline', ed. by Cleminson and Fuentes Peris, *Journal of Spanish Cultural Studies*, 10.4 (2009), 385–97. Of specific relevance to the current study are the articles by Rafael Huertas, 'Los niños de la "mala vida": la patología del "golfo" en la España de entresiglos', 423–40. and Teresa Fuentes Peris, 'Alcoholismo, anarquismo y degeneración en *La bodega* de Vicente Blasco Ibáñez', 485–503.
6. Alfredo J. Sosa-Velasco, *Médicos escritores en España, 1885–1955: Santiago Ramón y Cajal, Pío Baroja, Gregorio Marañón y Antonio Vallejo Nágera* (Woodbridge: Tamesis, 2010).
7. Richard A. Cardwell, 'The Mad Doctors: Medicine and Literature in *fin de siglo* Spain', *Journal of the Institute of Romance Studies*, 4 (1996), 167–86; 'Degeneration, Discourse and Differentiation: *Modernismo frente a noventa y ocho* Reconsidered', in *Critical Essays on the Literatures of Spain and Spanish America*, ed. by Luis T. González-del-Valle and Julio Baena (Boulder, CO: Society of Spanish and Spanish-American Studies, 1991), pp. 29–46; 'Oscar Wilde and Spain: Medicine, Morals, Religion and Aesthetics in the *Fin de Siglo*', in *Crossing Fields in Modern Spanish Culture*, ed. by Federico Bonaddio and Xon de Ros (Oxford: Legenda, 2003), pp. 35–53.
8. Teresa Fuentes Peris, *Visions of Filth: Deviancy and Social Control in the Novels of Galdós* (Liverpool: Liverpool University Press, 2003); Akiko Tsuchiya, *Marginal Subjects: Gender and Deviance in Fin-de-Siècle Spain* (Toronto: University of Toronto Press, 2011).
9. Pío Baroja, *Obras completas*, 8 vols (Madrid: Biblioteca Nueva, 1946–51), VIII, 851. All subsequent references are to this edition.
10. Joan Fuster, *Recuerdo y juicio de Blasco Ibáñez en su centenario*, ed. by Manuel Bas Carbonell (Valencia: Societat Bibliogràfica Valenciana Jerònima Galés, 1998), p. 61.
11. Diego Guigou y Costa, *Discurso leído en la sesión inaugural del año 1916 por el Académico numerario Dr D. Diego Guigou y Costa* (Santa Cruz de Tenerife: El Comercio, 1916), p. 17. On medical approaches in Spain to the social concern with infant mortality in the closing decades of the nineteenth century, see María José Betancor Gómez, 'Eugenesia y pediatría: higiene infantil y "degeneración de la raza" en España a principios del siglo XX', in *Darwinismo social y eugenesia en el mundo latino*, ed. by Marisa Miranda and Gustavo Vallejo (Buenos Aires: Siglo XXI de Argentina Editores, 2005), pp. 641–63.
12. Oscar E. Vázquez, 'Regenerating the "Man-Beast": Embodying Brutishness in *Fin de Siglo* Spanish Art', in *Picturing Evolution and Extinction: Regeneration and Degeneration in Modern Visual Culture*, ed. by Fae Brauer and Serena Kshavjee (Newcastle: Cambridge Scholars Publishing, 2015), pp. 107–25 (pp. 112–13).
13. Staffan Müller-Wille and Hans-Jörg Rheinberger, *A Cultural History of Heredity* (Chicago, IL, and London: University of Chicago Press, 2012), pp. 102–03.
14. Nancy Stepan, 'Biological Degeneration: Races and Proper Places', in *Degeneration: The Dark Side of Progress*, ed. by J. Edward Chamberlin and Sander L. Gilman (New York: Columbia University Press, 1985), pp. 97–120 (p. 97).
15. Stepan, 'Biological Degeneration', p. 109.
16. See Müller-Wille and Rheinberger, *A Cultural History of Heredity*, pp. x–xi.
17. Michael W. Stannard, *The Theme of Degeneration in the Work of Benito Pérez Galdós: A Study of Four Naturalist Novels* (Saarbrücken: Lambert Academic Publishing, 2012), p. 6.
18. William Greenslade, *Degeneration, Culture and the Novel, 1880–1940* (Cambridge: Cambridge University Press, 1994), pp. 1–2.
19. On Darwin in Spain, see *The Reception of Darwinism in the Iberian World: Spain, Spanish America and Brazil*, ed. by Thomas F. Glick, Miguel Angel Puig-Samper and Rousaura Ruíz (Boston, MA: Kluwer Academic Publishers, 2001).

20. Noteworthy volumes include among others: Greenslade, *Degeneration*; Chamberlin and Gilman, eds, *Degeneration: The Dark Side of Progress*; Ricardo Campos Marín, José Martínez Pérez, Rafael Huertas García-Alejo, *Los ilegales de la naturaleza: medicina y degeneracionismo en la España de la restauración (1876–1923)* (Madrid: Consejo Superior de Investigaciones Científicas, 2000).
21. Richard A. Cardwell, 'Deconstructing the Binaries of *enfrentismo*: José-María Llanas Aguilaniedo's *Navegar pintoresco* and the Finisecular novel', in *Spain's 1898 Crisis: Regenerationism, Modernism, Post-Colonialism*, ed. by Joseph Harrison and Alan Hoyle (Manchester: Manchester University Press, 2000), 156–69 (pp. 156–57).
22. F. Fernández Villegas ('Zeda'), 'Impresiones literarias', *La España Moderna*, 70 (1892), 202.
23. On the critical recuperation of Baroja and Spanish authors in relation to European modernism, the reader is referred to C. A. Longhurst, '*Camino de perfección* and the Modernist Aesthetic', *Bulletin of Hispanic Studies*, special issue in honour of Geoffrey Ribbans, ed. by Ann L. Mackenzie and Dorothy S. Severin (1992), 191–203; Roberta Johnson, *Gender and Nation in the Spanish Modernist Novel* (Nashville, TN: Vanderbilt University Press, 2003); Katharine Murphy, *Re-reading Pío Baroja and English Literature* (Oxford: Peter Lang, 2004); and C. Christopher Soufas, *The Subject in Question: Early Contemporary Spanish Literature and Modernism* (Washington, DC: Catholic University of America Press, 2007).
24. 'La tuberculosis era una de esas enfermedades que el pensar en ellas era para mí una obsesión de terror' (*OC*, VII, 609). The death of Darío provides semi-autobiographical material for the death of Luisito in *El árbol de la ciencia*, and contributes to Andrés's Schopenhauerian view of life.
25. Max Nordau, *Degeneration*, ed. by George L. Mosse (Lincoln and London: University of Nebraska Press, 1993), p. 537.
26. George L. Mosse, Introduction, in Nordau, *Degeneration*, pp. xiii–xxxvi (p. xxi).
27. On cultural exchange across European borders in relation to early twentieth-century Spain, the reader is referred to Alison Sinclair, *Trafficking Knowledge in Early Twentieth-Century Spain: Centres of Exchange and Cultural Imaginaries* (Woodbridge: Tamesis, 2009).
28. Luis Comenge y Ferrer, *La medicina en el siglo XIX* (Barcelona: José Espasa, 1914), p. 413.
29. José María Esquerdo, *Locos que no lo parecen: Garayo el Sacamantecas* (Madrid: Imprenta del Hospicio, 1881), p. 25.
30. Pedro Felipe Monlau, *Remedios del pauperismo: memoria para optar al premio ofrecido por la Sociedad Económica Matritense el 1 de mayo de 1845* (Madrid: Sociedad Económica, 1846), p. 25. Stannard's *The Theory of Degeneration* provides rich contextual background on medicine and degeneracionism in Spain.
31. Campos et al., *Los ilegales*, p. ix. This study analyses the ways in which degeneration theories in France and elsewhere in Europe were assimilated and modified by Spanish medicine, including psychiatry, hygienic medicine and social medicine.
32. J. M. Escuder, *Locos y anómalos* (Madrid: Sucesores de Rivadeneyra, 1895), p. 43.
33. Campos et al., *Los ilegales*, p. x.
34. On the influence of Nordau in Spain and its connections with regenerationism, see Lisa Davis, 'Max Nordau, "Degeneración" y la decadencia de España', *Cuadernos hispanoamericanos*, 326–27 (1977), 307–23.
35. Jo Labanyi, *Gender and Modernization in the Spanish Realist Novel* (Oxford: Oxford University Press, 2000), p. 28.
36. Sebastian Balfour, 'The Loss of Empire, Regenerationism, and the Forging of a Myth of National Identity', in *Spanish Cultural Studies: An Introduction*, ed. by Helen Graham and Jo Labanyi (Oxford: Oxford University Press, 1995), pp. 25–31 (pp. 25–28).
37. On medicine and regenerationism, see Rafael Huertas, 'Niños degenerados. Medicina mental y regeneracionismo en la España del cambio de siglo', *Dynamis*, 18 (1998), 157–79.
38. '1898 supuso, en este sentido, como 1870 para el caso francés, una toma de conciencia sobre la decadencia del país'. Ricardo Campos Marín, 'La teoría de la degeneración y la profesionalización de la psiquiatría en España (1876–1920), *Asclepio*, 51.1 (1999), 185–203.
39. José Viñeta-Bellaserra, *La sífilis como hecho social punible y como una de las causas de la degeneración de la raza humana* (Barcelona: La Academia, 1886), p. 59.
40. Lucas Mallada, *Los males de la patria* (Madrid: Alianza, 1969), p. 222.
41. Campos Marín, 'La teoría de la degeneración', p. 187.

42. Campos Marín, 'La teoría de la degeneración', pp. 188–89.
43. Campos Marín, 'La teoría de la degeneración', pp. 191–93.
44. Labanyi, *Gender and Modernization*, p. 79.
45. Ángel Pulido y Fernández, *Sanidad pública en España y ministerio social de las clases médicas* (Madrid: Enrique Teodoro y Alonso, 1902), pp. 22–24.
46. On the significance of these medical discourses in the works of Galdós, see Michael Stannard, *Galdós and Medicine* (Oxford: Peter Lang, 2015).
47. See Cardwell, 'Degeneration, Discourse and Differentiation', p. 36.
48. Cited by Eduard von Hartmann, *Philosophy of the Unconscious: Speculative Results According to the Inductive Method of Physical Science*, trans. by William Chatterton Coupland, 2nd edn, 3 vols (London: Trübner & Co., 1893), I, 57.
49. Frank Sulloway, *Freud, Biologist of the Mind: Beyond the Psychoanalytic Legend*, 1st paperback edn (Cambridge, MA: Harvard University Press, 1992).
50. 'Symbolism in Dreams', *The Standard Edition of the Complete Psychological Works of Sigmund Freud*, trans. from the German under the general editorship of James Strachey, in collaboration with Anna Freud, assisted by Alix Strachey, Alan Tyson, and Angela Richards, 24 vols (London: Hogarth Press and the Institute of Psycho-Analysis, 1953–74), XV [1915–1916] (1963), 166.
51. Emilio Gascó Contell, *Genio y figura de Blasco Ibáñez: agitador, aventurero y novelista* (Madrid: Afrodisio Aguado, 1957), p. 92.
52. See Roberta Johnson, 'Carmen de Burgos and Spanish Modernism', *South Central Review*, 18.1–2 (2001), 66–77 (p. 67).
53. As Sandra Siegel notes: 'For the Victorians, any confusion of gender was bound to have implications for "civilization"', 'Literature and Degeneration: The Representation of "Decadence"', in *Degeneration: The Dark Side of Progress*, ed. by J. Edward Chamberlin and Sander L. Gilman (New York: Columbia University Press, 1985), pp. 199–219 (p. 209).
54. Catherine Jagoe, 'Monstrous Inversions: Decadence and Degeneration in Galdós's *Ángel Guerra*', in *Culture and Gender in Nineteenth-Century Spain*, ed. by Lou Charnon-Deutsch and Jo Labanyi (Oxford: Oxford University Press, 1996), pp. 161–81.
55. Tsuchiya, *Marginal Subjects*, p. 17.
56. Nicole Hahn Rafter and Mary Gibson, Introduction, in Cesare Lombroso and Guglielmo Ferrero, *Criminal Woman, the Prostitute, and the Normal Woman* (Durham, NC: Duke University Press, 2004), pp. 3–33 (pp. 28–29).
57. Bram Dijkstra, *Idols of Perversity: Fantasies of Feminine Evil in Fin-de-siècle Culture* (New York and Oxford: Oxford University Press, 1986).
58. For Spanish examples see Lou Charnon-Deutsch, *Fictions of the Feminine in the Nineteenth-Century Press* (University Park: Pennsylvania State University Press, 2000).
59. Elaine Showalter, *Sexual Anarchy: Gender and Culture at the Fin de Siècle* (London: Virago, 2009), p. 21.
60. Angus McLaren, *Twentieth-Century Sexuality: A History* (Oxford: Blackwell, 1999), p. 7.
61. Showalter, *Sexual Anarchy*, p. 22.
62. Beatriz Celaya Carrillo, *La mujer deseante: sexualidad femenina en la cultura y novela españolas (1900–1936)* (Newark, DE: Juan de la Cuesta, 2006), p. 52.
63. Angelique Richardson, 'The Biological Sciences', in *A Companion to Modernist Literature and Culture*, ed. by David Bradshaw and Kevin J. H. Dettmar (Oxford: Blackwell, 2005), pp. 50–65 (p. 59).
64. Labanyi, *Gender and Modernization*, p. 67.

PART I

Determinism and Heredity

CHAPTER 1

The Nordau Effect: Degeneracy and the Artist in Baroja's *Camino de perfección* (1902) and Blasco's *La maja desnuda* (1906)

By the time Max Nordau's flamboyant *Degeneration* (*Entartung*, 1892) was translated into Spanish by Nicolás Salmerón in 1902, Baroja was already familiar with the French translation of 1894. Coinciding with the ongoing momentum of Nordau's work and its appearance in Spanish translation, in 1902 Baroja published his famous portrait of the artist *Camino de perfección*. From the outset of the novel, the protagonist Fernando Ossorio defines himself as degenerate, pinpointing as the roots of his condition a combination of hereditary elements, education (his Jesuit schooling and family upbringing) and the corrupt, disordered urban environment of Madrid. He suffers from neurotic symptoms that are closely allied to nineteenth-century theories of determinism, both hereditary and environmental. However the most compelling exposition of degenerationism in *Camino de perfección* is to be found in the figure of the neurotic or neurasthenic artist. Fernando suffers from hallucinatory visions, physiological symptoms such as convulsions, mystical tendencies, and arguably ego-mania. In Madrid the protagonist diagnoses himself with cerebral anaemia, a prominent symptom of neurasthenia alongside morbid fears, bad dreams and exhaustion. In Baroja's novel of 1902 there are undeniable echoes of Nordau's model of the degenerate artist that proved so influential in the 1890s across Europe and continued to resonate loudly at the turn of the century. Nordau famously transposed the diagnosis of organic degeneration to *fin-de-siècle* culture, and placed its immoral, decadent artists at the heart of his exposition.

Baroja's response to degenerationism in *Camino de perfección*, however, is not uncritical. The novel draws on prevalent ideas that defined the artist in relation to pathology, but fails to adhere to the more outlandish premises of Nordau's alarmist theories. In an essay of 1899, 'Nietzsche y la filosofía', Baroja wrote of *Degeneration*: '¡Qué libro más extraño el de Max Nordau! Yo le clasificaría entre los más insanos, entre los más perturbadores que se han escrito. Recuerdo la impresión que me produjo su lectura. Al dejar de leerlo, me parecía escapar de un manicomio, de un manicomio en el cual, como en un cuento de Poe, su director estuviera también loco' (*OC*, VIII, 854). Baroja thus concurs with contemporaneous criticism of Nordau's sensationalist book: that his theories were obsessed with diagnosing madness to the point of insanity.

Just as significantly, *Camino de perfección* explores the workings of the unconscious mind and subjective perception through the experimental narrative techniques employed to represent Fernando's artistic vision. This transitional novel, poised between naturalism and modernism, overtly incorporates elements of degenerationist theory in relation to neurosis and artistic production as demonstrated by the linguistic terminology used by Fernando to diagnose his own nervous state. However, the novel simultaneously echoes contemporaneous developments in the understanding of the mind at the time of its publication that move beyond biological explanation towards psychoanalytic theory and the significance of internal psychic processes. The cross-currents between science, biology, psychiatry and literature, both national and international in origin, provide a rich intertextual foundation for Baroja's novel of 1902.

Just four years after the publication of *Camino de perfección*, in 1906 Blasco's Ibáñez's own portrait of the artist in *La maja desnuda* appeared. In this opening chapter I draw parallels between the two novels in their exposition of degenerationism through a particular focus on neurosis, hysteria and neurasthenia as driving biological and psychological forces behind the impulse to create art. These pathological symptoms also constitute — at least to an uncritical eye — the powerful emotional consequences of degenerate visual art for the susceptible spectator, something that preoccupied Nordau in his treatise on the pernicious influence of immoral artistic production. My analysis seeks to illuminate the hidden points of convergence between the novels in question. These two works are not traditionally read in relation to one another, and are commonly placed in very different literary categories according to common assumptions regarding their intellectual focus, authorial preoccupations and narrative demands. I seek to counter these hierarchical divisions by pointing to commonalities in the novels' representation of the artist in the wake of Nordau and his warnings about the pernicious effects of artistic production for an impressionable society. Baroja and Blasco shared a predominantly middle-class readership for whom bourgeois debate of the leading social issues of the day was particularly pertinent.

Camino de perfección has long enjoyed secure status as a canonical text of the 'Generation of 1898' and more latterly as a key example of the development of Spanish modernism. In 1902 a banquet of honour was held to celebrate the work, the same 'golden year' that Azorín's *La voluntad* and Unamuno's *Amor y pedagogía* were published. In this context, *Camino de perfección* provides a fertile point of comparison with Blasco's apparently lowbrow production. *La maja desnuda* has frequently been dismissed as 'light' fiction, lending itself effectively to storytelling and entertainment rather than any more serious concerns. My analysis of degeneration and psychopathology in *Camino de perfección* and *La maja desnuda* makes an original contribution to the critical renegotiation of traditional divisions between high and low art during this period, between the 'Generation of 1898' and contemporaneous Spanish writers frequently invoked as inferior, popular or second-rate, including Blasco Ibáñez. By analysing their common focus on the degenerate artist as a dominant cultural figure of the day, this chapter compares similarities in the social and cultural preoccupations of two authors long segregated by the demands of literary history. The famous polemic between Baroja and Blasco has only obscured these convergences and their common appeal to middle-class audiences.

Both *Camino de perfección* and *La maja desnuda* take as their foundation the prevalent contemporary interest in the pathological figure of the artist. Nordau drew powerfully on this tradition through his diagnosis of *fin-de-siècle* artists, notably the decadents, as both diseased and a source of contagion within wider society. Nordau dismissed modern art forms as collectively degenerate, citing the examples of Nietzsche, Wagner, Zola and the French symbolists, including Baudelaire. As he wrote in *Degeneration*: 'All these new tendencies, realism and naturalism, decadentism, neo-mysticism, and their sub-varieties are manifestations of degeneration and hysteria'.[1] Naturalism, then, was one manifestation of a pervasive cultural disorder of the *fin de siècle*, as manifested by 'the filth of Zola's art and of his disciples in literary canal-dredging'.[2] For Nordau, artistic production was evidence of pathology; the authors of literature were ego-maniacs who suffered from mental disorders. This view drew on a long tradition of association between artistic genius and madness, an idea that gathered momentum in the 1880s and 1890s in the wake of Lombroso's *L'uomo di genio* (1888) and the work of Havelock Ellis.[3] As Legrain asserted, 'the degenerate may be a genius': a brilliant but morally deranged figure.[4] Nordau thus stigmatized the artist as the embodiment of insanity or mental pathology. Lombroso, however, distanced himself from Nordau's 'errors', in particular his disciple's failure to identify degenerative neurosis as the accompaniment to genius.[5]

In *L'uomo di genio* Lombroso identified the modern artist, specifically the symbolists and Parnassians, as exhibiting symptoms of madness and delirium, and dubbed his subjects as *mattoide* (crazoid). Moral and medical discourses were combined strikingly within this diagnosis in order to argue for the control and eventual elimination from society of criminal individuals that threatened evolutionary development. By the early 1890s, the Latin American writers Gómez Carrillo and Rubén Darío would respond to dominant pathologies of the modern artist in Lombroso and Nordau through their defence of the 'degenerate' Oscar Wilde. The arguments in favour of aestheticism in Spain, of course, held little currency in an environment of regenerationism.[6] In Spain as elsewhere, accusations of effeminacy and fatigue were levelled in particular at the artists of aestheticism, decadence and *modernismo*.

Nordau's ideas enjoyed significant popularity in Spain during the late nineteenth and early twentieth centuries, with a number of his works translated into Spanish between the 1880s and 1915.[7] His *Degeneration* was widely read and cited in Spain well before it appeared in translation in 1902. Nordau's theories provoked mixed reactions in Spain, with a number of prominent intellectuals of the time responding scornfully to his obsessive diagnosis of degeneration and insanity. Pardo Bazán described the Austro-Hungarian as the 'fatal' successor to Lombroso.[8] Leopoldo Alas was similarly sceptical. Unamuno responded to Nordau's work with ill-disguised contempt: 'Hay críticos verdaderamente horrendos, y el prototipo de ellos es acaso Max Nordau, el cual me hace el efecto de un ciego de nacimiento [que] juzgando por el tacto hace crítica de pintura'.[9] Others, by contrast, absorbed Nordau's theories much more favourably. Either way, his powerful model of the diseased artist continued to hold resonant currency.

Pompeyo Gener's *Literaturas malsanas* (1894) is one such example that was both derivative in ideas of *Degeneration* and provided a means of dissemination of Nordau's work in a Spanish context.[10] One year after *Entartung*, Gener set out to diagnose the abnormal qualities of contemporary literature as examples of pathology.[11] One of the leading proponents of evolutionary theory, and the ideas of Lombroso and Nordau in Spain, Gener interpreted Spanish literature of the period in relation to degenerative pathologies. Llanas Aguilaniedo would follow this diagnosis of contemporary ills in his *Alma contemporánea* (1899), but unlike Gener, he would offer a remedy in the form of *emotivismo*: the stimulation of emotions by literature.[12]

One of Nordau's fundamental arguments in his now infamous *Degeneration* is the view that decadent forms of art and literature are manifestations of degeneration and should therefore be objects of study via the application of the theories developed by his predecessors Bénédict Morel and Cesare Lombroso. In the dedication to Lombroso, he states that 'degenerates are not always criminals, prostitutes, anarchists, and pronounced lunatics; they are often authors and artists'.[13] For Nordau, works of art wield a powerful influence on the masses, and can corrupt an entire generation. 'Absurd' and 'anti-social' works enthuse their audiences with evidence of 'moral insanity, imbecility, and dementia'.[14]

This chapter seeks to ascertain the extent to which each of the two chosen novels reflects or indeed resists dominant discourses of degeneration in relation to art and the degenerate artist. As in the case of literature, Spanish visual art was strongly influenced by the contemporary national interest in fatigue and exhaustion, as key symptoms of degeneration. In his study of *fin-de-siglo* Spanish art, Oscar Vázquez documents the concept of *embrutecimiento* in the artwork of Carles Mani y Roig (1867–1911), the Catalan sculptor and assistant to Antoni Gaudí, as exemplified by his sculpture *Els Degenerats* (1891–1904). In visual art as in literary fiction of the period, degeneration had become part of prevalent cultural terminology in turn-of-the-century Spain.[15]

Blasco's novels have not been subject to any sustained analysis of their interactions with degeneration theory, including Nordau's famous work. Yet the artist's final descent into insanity at the end of *La maja desnuda* confirms the pervasive *fin-de-siècle* association between abstract art, emotional subject matter and degeneracy or mental pathology. Symptomatic of the protagonist Mariano Renovales's journey towards psychological disintegration, the final portrait of his wife and muse Josefina exemplifies the rejection of rationalism and the articulation of turmoil within expressionist art as well as the artist's unbalanced emotional state. I argue that this trajectory towards expressionism, in turn, approximates Nordau's concept of abstract art. In particular, Renovales's decline echoes the lack of willpower and discipline of Nordau's degenerates, who 'fail to make clear and coherent connections. They are unable to grasp cause and effect. They can only associate ideas, throwing rational connections to the wind. This [...] was exactly the way in which such new artistic forms as expressionism sought to give vent to the turmoil of men's souls'.[16]

In *Camino de perfección* Fernando Ossorio defines himself as a hysteric and a degenerate, although his symptoms are more accurately evidence of neurasthenia, commonly designated as a minor stage of hysteria. In his obsession with the artistic representation of the female nude in *La maja desnuda*, Blasco's fictional artist Mariano Renovales confirms the association defended by Nordau between art, unrestrained sensuality and eroticism.[17] Whilst the language of degeneration is more overt in Baroja's *Camino de perfección*, I propose that Blasco's novel of 1906 references in striking ways dominant concepts of decadent or degenerate art and hysteria in relation to the female body and mind that continued to grip the public imagination at the turn of the twentieth century.

My reading of both novels provides new insight into the dissemination through popular fiction of dominant cultural narratives of the period, notably contemporary ideas about the artist that were fuelled by Nordau's *Degeneration*. Early twentieth-century Spanish literature provides compelling examples of the myriad engagements with scientific disciplines, including biology, anthropology and medicine across the spectrum of the arts. In *La maja desnuda* Josefina's physical decline, the product of a progressive disorder of the female body, engages with degenerationism in its biological sense: literally as the decay of organs and physiological disintegration. Her condition, by contrast, is interpreted by her husband and other male characters as a nervous disorder, the product of hysterical jealousy. Blasco's linguistic designation of neurosis is not developed as clearly as Baroja's in *Camino de perfección*. None the less, *La maja desnuda* draws evidently on the medical metaphors of degeneration in the doctor's diagnosis of Josefina's neurasthenia, demonstrating a resonant literary transposition of the dominant cultural and pseudo-scientific narratives of the day. Furthermore, I contend that the association of Josefina's illness with degenerationism, nervous ailments and particularly hysteria are false cultural readings of a menstrual disorder that affects Josefina following childbearing. Josefina's death is not ultimately evidence of biological degenerationism, a nervous malady or hysteria, but a common physiological disorder of the female body.

The portrait of artistic degeneracy in *Camino de perfección* is inherently contradictory. Baroja's engagement with Nordau's degenerate artist is not fully aligned with the obviously Freudian echoes of neurosis in Fernando Ossorio. Freud met Nordau in Paris in 1886, but wrote disparagingly of the latter as 'vain and stupid'.[18] Psychoanalysis was crucial to moving beyond the discourses of nineteenth-century positivism. Conversely Nordau's *Degeneration* viewed artists as corrupting reality at a time when the very concept of external reality was in doubt. Of course the echoes and discrepancies between degeneration theories and psychoanalysis are not straightforward. James Strachey clearly emphasizes Freud's belief in 'the universal validity of the law of determinism' as the foundation for all his work.[19] Furthermore, Freud's understanding and appropriation of the term 'degeneration' changed over time, creating both continuity and divergence between the earlier conception of degeneration in anthropology and physiognomy and later psychoanalytic writing. As Pick argues: 'the question of degeneration and the degenerate were not one and the same. Freud, it could be said, rejected the latter, but returned to the former'.[20] Biology continued to provide a powerful foundation for the analysis of the mind in the early twentieth century. In this context, I explore the powerful interactions between degeneracy, psychopathology and the unconscious in the representation of Fernando's neurosis, and emphasize Baroja's deliberate rejection of a unifying scientific narrative.

In the context of these crossings and counter-crossings between late nineteenth-century and early twentieth-century discourses, I begin with an analysis of family and Fernando's childhood experiences in Baroja's *Camino de perfección*. My reading focuses particularly on the effects of maternal absence on the protagonist's development. I do so in order to investigate the competing explanations of Fernando's deterministic familial legacy, alongside a speculative exploration of the internal psychic experience of maternal loss. Fernando's neurosis is explained, according to his own views, through recourse to biology and heredity. However, my own reading points to resonant parallels with psychoanalytic paradigms in *Camino de perfección* that provide alternative reasons for the protagonist's undeniably precarious psychological predicament: his neurosis or diseased psyche. Baroja's conscious refusal to adhere to one defined set of theories is nowhere more apparent than in his experimental novel of 1902.

Camino de perfección

Nordau claimed that physical degeneration caused psychological disordering to permeate through society, and viewed the causes of degeneration and hysteria as both genetic and the product of urban life. His work *Degeneration* provides a physiological explanation of the fatigue and exhaustion of human civilization, which 'breathes an atmosphere charged with organic detritus; he eats stale, contaminated, adulterated food; he feels himself in a state of constant nervous excitement'. Nordau's vocabulary in fact anticipates our modern diagnosis of the sources of stress, experiential overload, and the pace of change of society and technology still current over a century later, and he does so in alarmist and censorious terms. For Nordau, rapid progress and urbanization have overtaken the ability of human beings to adjust to the new pace of life: 'In our times [...] steam and electricity have turned the customs of life of every member of the civilized nations upside down. [...] All these activities, however, even the simplest, involve an effort of the nervous system and a wearing of tissue'.[21] Nordau developed Morel's theories of the toxic influence of narcotics and stimulants through his underscoring of the deleterious effects of industrial society: the fatigue and exhaustion of the human organism, and particularly the frenzied environment of the city. In *Camino de perfección*,

Madrid embodies 'la impresión de la fatiga, del aniquilamiento de un pueblo',[22] a description obviously influenced by Nordau's view of the tumult and exhausting effect of the city as causes of degeneration and hysteria.

Baroja's protagonist Fernando Ossorio appears to embody a number of the symptoms of degeneracy identified by Nordau. Fernando's subjective interpretations of perceived degenerate traits through hereditary and environmental explanations provide an obvious foundation for the language of degeneration in *Camino de perfección*. Most pertinently, however, the protagonist's vocation as an artist is crucial to the exploration of his degeneracy and neurosis. Nordau's 'three cardinal marks of degeneration' have already been identified by Noma and Weston Flint as pertinent to the depiction of Baroja's fictional artist: 'an exaggerated importance given to art, pseudo-mysticism in association with morbid eroticism, and egomania'.[23] The last of these can be understood as an impaired knowledge of the outside world accompanied by pathological self-absorption, a characteristic that underpins Fernando's perception of reality as frequently hostile. Indeed there is little to contradict these three characteristics that echo Nordau's degenerate artist in Fernando's trajectory. However, my reading of Baroja's neurotic artist extends this earlier analysis of Nordau's influence on *Camino de perfección* by emphasizing both the novel's conformity and its divergence from prevalent degenerationist theories of the day.

In *Camino de perfección* Fernando places the blame for his perceived degeneracy on education and family. 'Soy un histérico, un degenerado', Fernando asserts in the opening chapter (9). He goes on to describe his childhood, and the factors within his family which account, in his view, for the degeneration of his innate talents: 'mis brillantes facultades desaparecieron, sobre todo mi portentosa memoria. [...] Total: que gracias a mi educación han hecho de mí un degenerado' (9–11). The death of his grandfather and the emotional legacy of family life are both identified as sources of psychological trauma. As in the case of the protagonist Águeda in *La casa de Aizgorri*, Fernando believes that hysteria is inherited, as demarcated by the examples of madness, alcoholism, suicide and degeneracy in his family. Fernando narrates the familial, religious, and educational aspects of his childhood, in particular his strict Jesuit schooling in Yécora, and views his condition as the inevitable outcome of this background and upbringing. Within the discourses of degeneration, hysteria was not a condition that affected only, or even predominantly, women, but was associated instead with excessive emotionalism and susceptibility to suggestion.

The dominant nineteenth-century view of hysteria as a disorder of the female body through its association with physiology and the uterus was questioned to some extent by its subsequent classification as a neurological disorder. However, as Beizer has argued, medical discourses of the late nineteenth century continued to posit hysteria as a feminine condition, which manifested itself through symptoms of uncontrolled emotions and incoherence.[24] At the Salpêtrière, the Paris hospital for nervous disorders, the French doctor Jean Martin Charcot asserted in 1882 that hysteria was not unique to women and did not originate in the sexual organs, stating that men also suffered from the disorder. Charcot instead situated the cause of hysteria in the brain and argued that it was provoked by a nervous system weakened by degeneration.[25] These ideas have strong resonance in the two novels under scrutiny.

Baroja's protagonist asserts his belief in the inheritance of the degenerative traits of hysteria. However the physical symptoms he displays over the course of the novel, including visual disturbances, fainting and dizziness, convulsions and neuralgia, conform more accurately to contemporaneous definitions of neurasthenia. This condition affected both men and women, and was caused according to contemporary medical theory by excessive pressure on the nervous system due to the frenzy of modern urban life. In Spain, the condition was termed 'neurosismo', and was described by the hygienist Monlau in 1868 as 'la endemia de la civilización contemporánea': a symptom of degeneration caused by loss of energy.[26]

In *Camino de perfección*, the protagonist defines himself through overt reference to sickness and degeneracy, and identifies the sexual decadence that affects his family. Fernando refers to himself as 'el animal que cumple una ley orgánica' (197), 'un perdido, un vicioso' (312), and perceives monstrosity or deviance in his genetic lineage: 'si la naturaleza había creado en su hijo un monstruo [...]' (335). From the outset Fernando is defined as suffering from *aboulia*, a powerlessness to Will characteristic for Nordau of degeneracy. The protagonist lacks identity and self-definition. Within discourses of degeneration, he also lacks the will-power and discipline required for human progress. The notion of *aboulia* in this novel intersects both with French theories of paralysis of the Will as evidence of hereditary mental disease (or *dégénérescence*) and the philosophical foundations of regenerationism in Spain, which in turn rested on the concept of spiritual malaise and lack of *voluntad*. In late nineteenth-century Spain, as Shaw explains, national decline was explained in relation to 'collective *abulia*', in which 'a relationship between the psychopathological and the metaphysical' was fundamental to the regenerationism of the 'Generation of 1898' and the widespread perception of national decay.[27] Social or collective regeneration would come about, according to this view, not through economic change but instead through reforming the psychology of the individual and the resurgence of Will.

Fernando's art is an obvious expression of neurosis. In the opening chapters of *Camino de perfección*, the description of Fernando's painting *Horas de silencio* provides both a symbol and a product of the protagonist's anguished mental state. The figures of young people in mourning are set against background of the monstrous industrial city which will swallow up these aristocratic children who are so ill-prepared for life and are now abandoned in the wake of the deceased: 'Aquellos jóvenes enlutados, en el cuarto abandonado y triste, frente a la vida y al trabajo de una gran capital, daban miedo' (13). Once again, Baroja's novel echoes Nordau's theories of degeneracy in relation to the artist, who rejects beauty and morality in favour of an emotionally anguished, disturbing and menacing view of life. Fernando's drawings of the sick are described as 'figuras locas, estiradas unas, achaparradas las otras; tan pronto grotescas y risibles como llenas de espíritu y de vida' (8). These contorted, grotesque figures are in line with the absurdity, the rejection of morality and beauty of 'degenerate' art, and eschew realist and naturalist representation.

Fernando's artistic vision is symptomatic of his perceived degeneracy or psychopathology. As Fernando approaches Toledo at the height of his spiritual crisis, the landscape becomes a product of the physical inflammation of his eyes, in other words conjunctivitis: 'Las piedras blanquecinas, las tierras grises, casi incoloras, vomitaban fuego. Fernando, con los ojos doloridos y turbados por la luz, miraba entornando los párpados' (129). We recall that Nordau diagnosed degenerate artists as suffering from 'nystagmus, or a trembling of the eyeball'. According to this view, the retina of hysterical subjects are insensitive, leading to gaps in the field of vision and strange effects; this may be manifested by an absence of colour or alternatively the use of 'peripheral' colours: blue, yellow and red, all predilections for the hysterical.[28] Although Fernando does not display physical characteristics of degeneracy (or 'stigmata'), the temporary eye condition he suffers as he approaches Toledo combines with the sunlight to create a bleached, colourless landscape. This might, in fact, be deemed hypersensitivity rather than insensitivity. Fernando certainly suffers visual disturbances that are closely in line with the symptoms of hysteria and neurasthenia in a late nineteenth-century context. *En route* to Manzanares, Fernando is unsure whether the castle he sees is real or an optical effect: 'Debe ser un efecto de óptica — pensó Ossorio — , y se fué acercando con susto, como quien se aproxima a un fatasma que sabe que se va a desvanecer' (73). Elsewhere the landscapes created by Fernando's artistic vision constitute a panoply of colours.

In *Alma contemporánea* Llanas Aguilaniedo posited the mental degeneration of the artist, who suffers from hypersensitivity and the prevalence of emotion over reason. As the artist seeks the goal of perfection, he is separated from the masses due to his spiritual and aesthetic elitism. According to this diagnosis, one that draws heavily (but not uncritically) on Nordau, acromatopsia — the inability to distinguish colours — is a symptom of the artist's degeneration and heightened nervous state. Neutral colours are offered as therapy for the degenerate artist.[29] In his *Navegar pintoresco* (1903), Llanas would delineate a trajectory of the artist towards alienation and mental collapse.[30] Unlike Nordau and Lombroso, however, for Llanas Aguilaniedo the artist's degeneracy is a mark of superiority. In Baroja's *Camino de perfección*, the language of therapy is couched both in symbolist and mystical language. For Baroja, as for Fernando Ossorio, the artist took precedence over the scientist.

Fernando's apparent degeneracy or sexual pathology is evidenced by his succession of dysfunctional relationships with women. Spurred by guilt, Fernando visits Ascensión, whom he raped during 'una época de furor sexual' (197). Plagued by 'recuerdos intensos gráficos de una pornografía monstruosa y repugnante' (195), Fernando is overcome by visions which merge religious imagery with carnivalesque symbolism: 'Vió ráfagas de luz, círculos luminosos y espadas de fuego' (196). Fernando's sexual behaviour is egotistical and impulsive; the memory of violence provokes mystical visions that draw on Catholic guilt, and echo Nordau's critique of the degenerate's morbid eroticism. Fernando's relationship with his lesbian Aunt Laura is defined by an aggressive sexuality. Laura is described in androgynous terms. As she takes control of their first sexual encounter, Fernando is emasculated in the wake of her dominant desire: 'A Fernando le parecía una serpiente de fuego que le había envuelto entre sus anillos y que cada vez le estrujaba más y más, y él iba ahogándose y sentía que le faltaba el aire para respirar' (44). In the context of Baroja's portrait of the *mujer serpiente* and threatening gender hybridity it is significant that Laura is rejuvenated by their relations, whilst Fernando develops symptoms of neuralgia. Fernando's decadence is not just personal but symbolic of the threat to a masculine culture in decline.[31]

In Toledo, the sight of a child's coffin provokes a nightmarish vision closely connected to Fernando's obsession with mortality. At the height of his psychological disturbance, the external world and Fernando's subjective state merge, to the point at which it is no longer clear what is 'real' (objective reality) and what is a projection of the protagonist's mind. Fernando believes he is verging on madness, and that this state is a product of heredity. Like the author, however, the protagonist considers opposing explanations for psychological disruption.

The vision of the 'Cristo momia' (52), or Christ-mummy, follows Fernando's sacrilegious kiss with Aunt Laura in Church. During this episode, the protagonist suffers convulsions, as well as visual and auditory disturbances, all in line with the physical symptoms of hysteria or neurasthenia as defined by late nineteenth-century medicine: 'Mil luces le bailaban en los ojos; ráfagas brillantes, espadas de oro. Sentía como avisos de convulsiones que le espantaban' (52). As Fernando's torment increases in the wake of this episode, 'unas veces veía sombras, resplandores de luz, ruidos, lamentos; se creía transportado en los aires o que le marchaba del cuerpo un brazo o una mano' (62). Interestingly, the protagonist visualizes himself losing limbs, a symbol once again of his lack of unity and wholeness and a powerful image of the loss of masculinity. Fernando, then, suffers hallucinations and mental instability in line with Nordau's influential conceptualization of degeneracy. Moreover, in the light of Fernando's suspected illegitimacy, it is interesting to note that paranoia, hallucinations, religious delusions and mania were commonly identified symptoms of congenital syphilis in the late nineteenth century.[32]

Fernando is uncertain whether the phenomenon of the *Cristo momia* was a supernatural apparition or a product of his unconscious. *Camino de perfección* expresses symptoms of neurosis in relation to the protagonist, but draws back from diagnosing the cause in conclusive terms. In other words, Baroja clearly hesitates in the narrative explanation of Fernando's vision of the Christ-mummy. He thereby balances hereditary and environmental determinism against the opposing possibility that this is a type of memory, a re-enactment of an earlier traumatic experience or legacy, in this case the pernicious influence of Catholic dogma, morality and sexuality. On one hand, this apparition constitutes a deterministic legacy in the context of the Catholic Church and Fernando's strict Jesuit education, one that replays deep-rooted teachings in his mind. On the other hand, the vision is the experience of a neurotic who suffers the consequences of a repetition of traumatic memory, a theory not dissimilar to the idea of *Nachträglichkeit*, or deferred action, in Freudian thought. Like Charcot, Freud viewed traumatic hysteria as the product of psychological rather than physiological developments, and as the consequence of psychic incubation. In *Studies on Hysteria* (1895), co-written with Josef Breuer, and 'The Aetiology of Hysteria' (1896), trauma thus constituted a memory or re-enactment, now experienced by the sexually mature adult. The episode of the *Cristo momia* in *Camino de perfección* merges the legacy of Catholic guilt with the dysfunctional development of Fernando's sexuality, through his incestuous and sadistic relationship with Aunt Laura and its expression through the kiss in Church.

Both the phenomenon of the *Cristo momia* and the vision of the cross can be interpreted as oneiric, nightmarish or hallucinatory visions that are produced by Fernando's mental state. They may be understood alternatively as evidence of degeneration, psychopathology or — more convincingly, in my view — Baroja's interest in psychic processes and the unconscious that has suggestive resonance beyond degenerationism. As Fernando reflects, 'unas veces se inclinaba a creer en lo inconsciente, otras suponía la existencia de fuerzas supranaturales, o por lo menos suprasensibles' (61). In this context, the *Cristo momia* episode constitutes an intuited representation of the psyche akin to the insight into the conscious resistance of the neurotic subject within psychoanalysis. The phenomenon is produced as the conflict between sexual desire and Catholic morality combine in Fernando's mind to produce this oneiric vision. The insight into Fernando's unconscious provided by these hallucinatory experiences centres on the memory of trauma, notably in relation to the death of his grandfather and the garrotting he witnessed as a child, as well as the psychological legacy of Catholic education and sexual guilt.

Fernando's trajectory provides evidence of mental, sexual and biological pathologies that is convincing to some extent within the meta-narratives of degenerationism. However, the development of Fernando's relationships with women also constitutes a search for the lost mother in psychodynamic terms. Dolores is a thinly disguised mother-substitute, who nurtures and provides a refuge for the protagonist through the application of maternal care to his fragile mental state. Within a simple model of psychological development, Fernando is thus construed as a child who seeks to define himself through interaction with others, thereby attempting to secure self-affirmation, acceptance and a solution to anxiety. As the primary object of identification, the absent mother is at the heart of this journey. Object Relations theory is particularly pertinent with regard to the mother–son relationship in *Camino de perfección*, as it is for the mother–daughter bond in *La casa de Aizgorri*.

Fernando Ossorio had already appeared in the earlier *Aventuras, inventos y mixtificaciones de Silvestre Paradox*, which provides supplementary information about his background not presented in *Camino de perfección*.[33] In *Silvestre Paradox*, Fernando's theories are even more overtly deterministic, and he identifies a sexual 'imbalance' which, according to the protagonist, affects nearly all his family. As he tells Silvestre: '¡Usted no sabe lo que es mi tía Laura! Es una mujer de un sadismo y de una perversidad inconcebible. En mi familia debe de haber algún desequilibrio sexual que se transmite de padres a hijos. Sólo mis dos tías han resultado castas; los demás, hombres y mujeres, de un desenfreno terrible, yo inclusive'.[34] Fernando's theories of sexual degeneracy are expressed in very similar terms of genetic transmission as alcoholism in *La casa de Aizgorri*. In *Camino de perfección* Fernando identifies a hereditary strain of deviancy in sexual behaviour: the transmission of degeneration from one generation to the next. Fictional characters allowed Baroja the means to explore such debates without authorial commitment to any single position.

Perhaps the most significant piece of information provided in *Silvestre Paradox*, and missing from the novel of 1902, is the inference that Fernando is in fact the half-brother of María Flora, whom his aunts wish him to marry, and not her cousin: 'María Flora y yo somos hermanos' (128). Furthermore, 'la madre de María Flora era tremenda, fuese pervirtiéndose hasta el extremo a que ha llegado...' (128). Fernando's psychological predicament is, in part, a manifestation of his anxiety about his origins and his mother's sexual behaviour. His parents' apparent rejection of him, we can deduce, is a consequence of his possible illegitimacy. According to Fernando, his mother abandoned him, and we infer that she is driven, like the rest of his family, by a promiscuous sexuality. The protagonist's dysfunctional relationships with women and his sexual trajectory, then, are key to the competing explanations of hereditary determinism and the effects of education, on one hand, versus internal psychic processes on the other. Given the rejection of biological explanation for neurosis in the earlier *La casa de Aizgorri*, it seems logical to suppose that Fernando's sense of abandonment by his mother in psychological terms is just as significant as any hereditary maternal strain of promiscuity. Once again, the suggestion of a delayed response to object-loss, through his perceived rejection by his mother, leads to problems in sexual development and maturity.

Nordau's theories were based on nineteenth-century scientific explanations of physiological, deterministic factors in human evolution. By the time Freud published *The Interpretation of Dreams* in 1900, the subjective truth of inner consciousness was now paramount. Like neurotic symptoms, Freud viewed dreams as the product of the conflict between unconscious and conscious impulses; as is well-known, analysing dreams would lead to their hidden unconscious elements and therefore shed light on neurosis. Baroja's attempts to capture the workings of the mind, even to render the unconscious through language, are evident intermittently in *La casa de Aizgorri* of 1900, but more decisively in *Camino de perfección*. In the former, the protagonist Águeda de Aizgorri dreams of her dead mother within a skewed Oedipal account of maternal loss. The latter includes direct references to 'lo inconsciente' (61) and 'la inconsciencia' (195), in a narrative that was highly original for its time.

Baroja's techniques for exploring the unconscious in *Camino de perfección* centre predominantly on the hallucinatory projections of repressed instinct. The narrator defines the function of dreams as the repository of what is repressed within daily and conscious experience: 'el sueño está preñado de vida, porque en las honduras de esa muerte diaria se vive sin conciencia de que se vive' (133). As Longhurst notes, the sequence of Fernando's night-time experience rests on an impossible chronology, and includes references to the sea in scenes that take place in Madrid, constituting obvious allusions to the unconscious mind and a persuasive indication that Fernando is dreaming.[35]

Most strikingly, Baroja appears to have intuited some of the ideas underpinning

Freud's exploration of the unconscious in novels that were closely contemporaneous with the publication of *The Interpretation of Dreams* in 1900, and *Three Essays on the Theory of Sexuality* in 1905. Freud's own commitment to degeneracy was problematic. In 1894 he analysed hysteria in childhood as a manifestation of degeneration, but he also argued in favour of the symptoms of traumatic experience, and expressed doubt about the validity of the adherence of French psychiatrists to the concept of degeneration.[36] In his early novels, Baroja's interest in hereditary determinism is interwoven by echoes of psychopathology. Whether or not this moves beyond biological explanation towards internal psychic processes is debatable. Certainly, Fernando suffers from delusions and hallucinations in *Camino de perfección* that can be aligned relatively simply with a diagnosis of mental degeneracy. These sequences, however, clearly demonstrate Baroja's understanding of the dialectic between conscious and unconscious states, dreams and subjective psychic processes. Indeed Fernando's feelings towards his mother lie more closely — I propose — within the realm of the psychodynamics of the family than determinism or degenerationism.

Baroja's interest in the spectral presence of the mother in *La casa de Aizgorri* and *Camino de perfección* presents a tantalizing but incomplete suggestion of the process of mourning and its pathological counterpart. This is constituted by the co-existence of love and anger towards the maternal figure as the child's first object of emotional identification and loss of this object through death or absence. Fernando's feelings towards his mother are evidently hostile, although they are only narrated briefly. Baroja's profound interest in early experience stems primary from his reading of Schopenhauer, and is clearly evident in the psychological representation of protagonists such as Águeda de Aizgorri and Fernando Ossorio. None the less, the tentative parallels with an Oedipal model and their uncertain anticipation of later Freudian works such as 'Mourning and Melancholia' (1917) are noteworthy, albeit incomplete.

Fernando's sense of having been rejected or slighted by his mother reinforce his attitude of ambivalence towards her through a process of unhealthy mourning. The loss of the object of identification or love, therefore, is transformed into ego-loss. Ambivalence is played out through Fernando's hostile treatment of a series of women, who act as replacement objects following abandonment by his mother. Within Freudian paradigms of melancholia, the object of love is not irretrievably lost as is the case in mourning for the death of a loved one. The effects of early experience for psychosexual development are not directly labelled in Baroja's early fiction, but they are just as powerful in their subtle exposition as the more overt discussion of biological paradigms.

In the context of Fernando's neurosis, *Camino de perfección* presents an original exploration of the workings of the unconscious. It is common knowledge that Baroja was sceptical about Freud and psychoanalysis, which he regarded as a pseudoscience, objecting in particular to the prominence given to the erotic and sexuality: 'En su teoría erótica, Freud no hace más que exagerar la nota vulgar' (*OC*, VII, 1310); Freud 'afirmará que todo es erotismo, sexualidad, tendencia libidinosa: algo poco idealista, pero ello no le impedirá sentirse un poco vate y sacerdote. [...] Yo en eso del psicoanálisis creo muy poco o nada' (*OC*, VII, 1310). Yet, despite his expressions of distaste both for Freud's theories and the avant-garde authors who attempted to write from the unconscious, Baroja's fiction demonstrates his keen interest in the influence of early experience, the manifestation of repressed impulse and — in my view — internal psychic processes that move significantly beyond deterministic paradigms.

Baroja's protagonist in *Camino de perfección* is clearly intended to be symbolic of the crisis of the nation at the end of the nineteenth century, and thus emblematic, too, of a degenerate Spain. The novel has often been read as a regenerationist critique of the state of the nation. The echoes of pathology culminate in Fernando's symbolic rebirth (or regeneration) on the shores of the Mediterranean, as he finds salvation in marriage to Dolores and the birth of their son.[37] Through his relationship with Dolores and the renunciation of art, at the end of *Camino de perfección* Fernando is able to achieve a partial reintegration of his personality. Following the imagery of fertility in the natural world that accompanies their honeymoon, Dolores gives birth to a baby girl who dies. Fernando's sense of guilt indicates that he perceives the child as a product of his lack of wholeness, the sick product of a diseased consciousness. This interpretation indicates not a deterministic legacy, but a symbolic one: 'Al contemplar aquella pobre niña engendrada por él, se acusaba a sí mismo de haberle dado una vida tan miserable y tan corta' (331). Two years later, however, their healthy and robust baby son is seen as the culmination of the protagonist's repossession of strength and his salvation in nature.

Echoing the ideas of Ganivet and Unamuno, the trajectory of Baroja's protagonist suggests that national regeneration stems from the modification of individual psychology, rather than social change or the external milieu.[38] For Ganivet, *aboulia* is a disease that is revealed in 'el influjo de las perturbaciones mentales sobre las funciones orgánicas'.[39] In the diagnosis and cure of *aboulia*, the need to remedy the human intellect thus takes precedence over influential nineteenth-century models of biological evolution, determinism and positivistic thought. Most significantly for the analysis in this chapter, Unamuno saw the artist-genius as the catalyst for regeneration and a cure for the spiritual ailments of the nation. As Cardwell notes, in Baroja, Azorín and other contemporary Spanish authors, 'the "degenerate" artist is the single possible hope for mankind since he is the most evolved'.[40]

At the end of the novel, Fernando wishes to keep his son away from the disturbing ideas of art and religion, and will bring him up 'en el seno de la Naturaleza' (334), far from the frenzy of urban life. Yet, this reintegration is only partly achieved. As his mother-in-law sews a page of the Gospel into the baby's sash, Fernando's desire to protect his son is undermined by the grandmother's perpetuation of the norms and values of society in the next generation. The protagonist's partial recovery from the symptoms of degeneration and pathology provides a characteristically ambivalent ending. By contrast to the *modernismo* of Juan Ramón Jiménez and others in which the abnormal and degenerate are construed ideologically as natural and regenerating, in *Camino de perfección* the process is one of contradictory normalization and incomplete cure through a return to the natural world.

In sum, Baroja's degenerate artist participates in a cultural vogue at the turn of the century, one so powerfully evoked by Nordau. Through his representation of Fernando Ossorio in *Camino de perfección* Baroja debates the role of hereditary determinism in the development of the protagonist's neurosis. However, the positivist ideas raised by Fernando's trajectory are undermined by ambivalence, and by the end of the novel the artist's regeneration is incomplete. His rebirth constitutes an optimistic outcome, but one that is countered by prevalent social norms, bourgeois morality and particularly the pernicious influence of the Catholic Church. Determinist explanation in this novel is undermined — or at least accompanied — by Baroja's tentative interest in subjectivism and psychic processes. The echoes of degenerationism and Nordau's artistic theories in *Camino de perfección* are powerful but incomplete. Baroja debates hereditary determinism in his exploration of the artist's mind, but fails to adhere convincingly to its premises. Regenerationism is evoked in abstract terms through the symbolic role of Fernando's rebirth, but is not accompanied by any practical foundation. To further explore the pathology and degeneracy of the artist, and by association his wife and muse, I now turn to the exposition of hysteria in Blasco's *La maja desnuda*, its representation of visual art and the female body.

La maja desnuda

Blasco's *La maja desnuda* has frequently been dismissed as one of the author's popular works and a failed attempt at the psychological novel.[41] There are few existing critiques of this novel. One exception is the critical introduction by Facundo Tomás to the 1998 Cátedra edition of this work, which focuses on Blasco's engagements with the artistic sphere in his representation of Mariano Renovales.[42] Tomás's wide-ranging survey examines parallels with nineteenth-century French realism and naturalism (Balzac and Zola) and the influence of Spanish visual art. By contrast, my own study explores the myriad echoes of late nineteenth-century theories of art as the product of mental degeneracy in *La maja desnuda*, with a particular focus on the ways in which these ideas inform Blasco's portrait of the artist Mariano Renovales. I consider the treatment of the female body through ekphrastic representation of Goya's *maja desnuda* from which the novel takes its title, and contend that the medical diagnosis of neurasthenia and hysteria potently echoes — but does not fully sustain — the symptoms of degeneracy in Renovales's wife and muse, Josefina.

In the trajectory of Josefina's physiological decline, Blasco offers pseudo-scientific explanations, both moral and physical, for her nervous crises. This disorder of the female body and mind provides a suggestive point of comparison with the symptoms of male hysteria in *Camino de perfección*. My reading of the degenerationist elements of Blasco's *La maja desnuda* therefore offers a new approach to contextualizing an often neglected example of popular fiction of the period. I emphasize the resonant commonalities with Baroja, a primary figure of the 'Generation of 1898' authors, and their shared incorporation of cultural narratives prominent at the turn of the century. My study thereby seeks to problematize further this traditional literary label, its frequent emphasis on autochthonous models, male subjectivity and cultural elitism.

La *maja desnuda* is Blasco's most lengthy treatise on the plastic arts, as Facundo Tomás has pointed out, and incorporates some of the ideas expressed in his lecture 'La pintura española' which he delivered in Buenos Aires in 1909. By the time Renovales returns from Italy, he paints, like the Impressionists, 'al aire libre; aborrecía la luz convencional del estudio, la estrechez de su ambiente' (244–45), and finds inspiration and subject matter in the environs of Madrid. Now, in place of the large-scale painting of his early success, at the 'Exposición' he presents small canvases in a daringly realist style: 'lienzos pequeños, estudios confiados al azar de un buen encuentro, pedazos de Naturaleza, hombres y paisajes, reproducidos con una verdad asombrosa y brutal que escandalizaba al público' (245). It is commonly accepted that Renovales's art is based on the 'luminism' and quasi-impressionism of Blasco's fellow-Valencian, Joaquín Sorolla, whom Blasco greatly admired. Renovales's work is praised for its naturalism and its use of light: 'le alababan sus obras por la exactitud con que cautivaba el natural, por el brillo de la luz, el color indefinible del aire y el exterior de las cosas' (192). The ekphrasis of Renovales's portrait of the Condesa de Alberca, too, was inspired by Sorolla's recently executed portrait of Blasco's lover, Elena Ortúzar, of 1906.[43]

The pictorialism of *La maja desnuda* was obviously influenced by contemporary developments in the plastic arts.[44] Blasco's esteem for Sorolla is evident (as elsewhere) in his 1923 Preface to *Flor de Mayo* in which he recounts seeing the painter on the beach 'reproduciendo mágicamente sobre sus lienzos el oro de la luz, el color invisible del aire, el azul palpitante del Mediterráneo'.[45] Blasco certainly did not share Nordau's wholesale rejection of modern art as symptomatic of degeneracy and unhealthy decline. However, he does incorporate pervasive contemporaneous ideas in the fictional portrait of Mariano Renovales that echo Nordau's critique of artists as mentally unstable and degenerate. Within Nordau's theoretical model of degeneracy, hysteria and neurasthenia characterize the diseased mind of the artist. Renovales espouses traits of ego-mania and vanity characteristic for Nordau of the French decadents and symbolists and, by the end of the novel, he produces an example of expressionist art characteristic of the excessive emotionalism and excitability of the degenerate. Alongside this portrait, the artist's wife Josefina displays a nervous and physiological disorder that appears — superficially at least — to be symptomatic of hysteria and the organic decline of degeneracy.

Popular myths about the degenerate artist propel the trajectory of Blasco's protagonist. In particular, the association between art and degeneracy prevalent at the turn of the century implicitly underpins Josefina's objections to sexualized subject matter. For Renovales, the nude female form is not decadent or the object of depravity, but constitutes instead 'la obra definitiva de la Naturaleza' (188). Renovales, then, equates the nude in art with nature and life itself. The ekphrasis of Goya's *La maja desnuda* in the opening scenes of Blasco's novel, as Renovales walks through the Prado and is arrested by the striking luminosity of the naked figure, underscores the daring originality and eroticism of a work that would inspire Blasco's novel a century later:

> Era la mujer pequeña, graciosa y picante; la Venus española, sin más carne que

la precisa para cubrir de suaves redondeces su armazón ágil y esbelto. Los ojos ambarinos, de malicioso fuego, desconcertaban con su fijo mirar; la boca tenía en sus graciosas alillas el revuelo de una sonrisa eterna. (186–87)

In this succinct ekphrasis of the painting, there is little reference to representation or artistic technique; rather, the inscription of the body is wholly dominant, almost as if the figure were flesh and blood: Renovales looks at 'aquel cuerpo' (186) and not 'aquel cuadro'. This is key to the controversy provoked by the painting: the *maja*'s appeal to the male onlooker as an object of sexual fantasy. Goya was investigated by the Inquisition in 1815 for obscenity in relation to the pair of portraits, *La maja desnuda* and *La maja vestida* (*c.* 1805).[46] The figure's blatant nudity placed the portrait in the realm of erotica for private consumption in Manuel Godoy's *gabinete de desnudos*. Furthermore, as Rebecca Haidt has argued, the painting opposed contemporary norms which asserted that the predominance of whiteness denoted 'lujuria' or 'sensuality'.[47] From the beginning of the novel, Blasco explores bourgeois resistance or prudishness towards the female nude that fuels Josefina's objections to her husband's paintings. The novel therefore rests on popular representations of 'mojigatería' that echo *fin-de-siglo* conceptions of decadent or immoral artistic subject matter.

When Renovales visits Goya's painting at the Prado, members of the public (notably middle-class women) are outraged by the representation of the female nude, reacting to the portrait as a shocking example of moral indecency: 'Era el odio al desnudo, la cristiana y secular abominación de la Naturaleza y la verdad, que se ponía de pie instintivamente, protestando de que se tolerasen tales horrores en un edificio público poblado de santos, reyes y ascetas' (188). The ekphrasis of Goya's painting can thus be read in the context of contemporary bourgeois attitudes from the perspective of 1906 to morality and sensuality in art. Indeed Goya's *maja* was of great interest to the turn-of-the-century public imagination; by 1924 the painting would also inspire a short story by Carmen de Burgos, *La que quiso ser maja*.[48]

In *Degeneration*, Nordau alludes to late nineteenth-century views of Goya's paintings through the character of Des Esseintes in Huysmans's *À rebours* (1884), explaining that the opinion of the decadent artist in this novel is deliberately the opposite of that of the crowd. As Goya's works gained popular admiration, the degenerate artist suffers from 'a mania for contradiction' (opposing the prevalent view), as Des Esseintes's carefully cultivates his dislike for the works.[49] In Blasco's *La maja desnuda* the process is the reverse: Renovales admires the nude portraits against the current of popular disapproval among the audience at the Prado. The middle-class public objects with prudish distaste to Goya's *maja*. Renovales by contrast is captivated. For Nordau, emotion and pleasure form the true source of artistic creation; however, art must demonstrate both beauty and morality in order to avoid charges of sensuality and degeneration. From the outset, Renovales is framed in relation to contemporary ideas about the dissolute mind of the artist, whose obsession with eroticism was deemed indicative of mental instability. Later in the novel, as he sinks into insanity, Renovales conforms increasingly closely to Nordau's notion of the mentally diseased degenerate.

Zola's own portrait of the artist in his novel *L'Œuvre* (1886) depicts the public outcry over the production of artist Claude Lantier, commonly accepted as a fictional representation of Paul Cézanne. This focuses notably on his incongruous representation of the female nude in a fictional painting widely thought to be based on Manet's *Le Déjeuner sur l'herbe* (1863). Following the death of his son, Claude paints the dead body before he descends into a state of obsession and insanity, an influential model for Blasco's own portrait of the degenerate artist.[50] By 1910, Enrique Gómez Carrillo, an enthusiastic proponent and disseminator of French Decadence in Spain, would expose what he termed the hypocrisy of Nordau for failing to understand the literary sensibilities of Baudelaire, Verlaine, and the symbolist poets brutally critiqued by *Degeneration*.[51]

By presenting the painting through the eyes of Renovales, Blasco represents the *maja* indirectly through the gaze of a specific male onlooker who observes the painting 'con delectación', in other words, with visual and sensual pleasure. Yet in the figure's direct, challenging, even confrontational gaze, Goya's *maja*, it has been suggested, embodies a 'nude who transgresses her idealized locus within the painting to confront the viewer'.[52] This reading of resistance by the nude figure, seemingly displayed as an erotic spectacle, challenges the act of scopophilia (the drive for pleasurable viewing) and thus voyeuristic appropriation as it does in the case of *Olympia*. The *maja*'s gaze, of such prominent interest in modern criticism of Goya's masterpiece, is emphasized by Blasco's representation of the figure, in which the eyes gleam with 'malicioso fuego' (187). This is not an indication, in other words, of passive submission. As Robert Hughes has observed, Goya's *maja* does not constitute 'a passive and receptive appeal to male fantasy, like almost any other eighteenth-century nude you might care to name'.[53] The *maja*, then, resists containment by confronting the male gaze and drive for sexual possession.

As a result of vehement objections to her husband's use of nude models, Josefina is demonized within Renovales's imagination as both a threat to his artistic ambitions, and more generally to order and rationality. Josefina's condition is referenced in contradictory terms in the novel. It constitutes both a nervous malady and progressive physical debility; the root cause is identified both as pathological jealousy and the physical effects of childbirth and motherhood. Her condition is diagnosed by Renovales as the result of 'celos inmensos, mortales, anonadadores' (254) and by the doctor as neurasthenia, as she is consumed by this 'desarreglo nervioso' (254). The novel, then, points directly to a moral source of her decline: 'Su enfermedad tenía un origen moral: era neurastenia, honda tristeza' (250). The pseudo-scientific explanations of the novel include 'nerviosidades de la pobre Josefina' (268) and more tellingly 'los desarreglos del sexo' (291).

The narrative compounds physiological and neurological explanations for Josefina's symptoms, which stem obviously from a menstrual disorder that destroys her health. Certainly, her illness is narrated as a process of wasting away from within: 'Adelgazaba como si la consumiese un fuego oculto; derretíase en interna combustión el grasoso almohadillado que rellenaba su cuerpo con graciosas ondulaciones. Comenzaba a marcar el esqueleto sus agudas aristas y obscuras oquedades bajo la piel pálida y flácida' (249). The explanations of her physical decline are therefore signalled in contradictory terms: it is a nervous disorder, jealousy, moral decay, or neurasthenia. In other words, the novel echoes the prevalent association between the uterus and emotional disturbance, thereby confusing physiological with emotional explanation in its diagnosis of the female body and mind.

Her decline is narrated in strikingly physical or bodily terms, with descriptions of 'su cuerpo enflaquecido por la enfermedad' (255) and her 'delgadez esquelética' (255). Yet, the narrator resorts almost immediately to an emotional or neurological counterbalance, suggesting that her physical self-combustion is due to jealousy: 'La atormentaban incesantemente los celos, amargando su pensamiento, devorando su vida' (255). Thus, Blasco's engagement with contemporary discourses of degeneration blends popular understanding of feminine psychology with resounding echoes of hysteria and biological degeneration that had seeped into the public imagination during this period. The diagnosis of Josefina as pathologically jealous echoes pseudo-scientific explanations of emotionalism as evidence of hysteria and a nervous system weakened by (in this case moral) degeneration. However, it also draws on the dominant nineteenth-century view of hysteria as a disorder of the female body through its association with physiology and the uterus, merging this with its subsequent classification as a neurological condition. The diagnosis of biological decay in relation to moral or emotional debility is far from consistent or convincing, but none the less alludes in schematic terms to powerful contemporary ideas about organic inheritance. The latter is demonstrated by Renovales's view of his daughter Milita, who embodies robust health and a biological legacy that eschews her mother's debility: 'con ella no se extinguía la raza' (258). The future of the nation depends on the strength of the female body for reproduction, yet Milita's youthful vigour contrasts with Josefina's decline.

The narrative emphasis on Josefina's jealousy is the primary motivation emphasized by earlier criticism. Within this psychological portrait, Gascó Contell affirmed that: 'sería difícil hallar en ninguna novela una descripción mejor de los estragos progresivos de este sentimiento en un alma femenina'.[54] According to this reading, Renovales is turned mad by his love for the dead Josefina, after suffering 'la tiranía de una mujer histérica, enemiga de su arte'.[55] By critics at least, Josefina is cast as castrating female, hysterically jealous and intent on destruction of the male artist. By the doctor, she is diagnosed as the neurotic, neurasthenic artist's wife. In other words, Blasco employs a fictional medic to interpret her plight through the language of degeneracy and pseudo-scientific explanation.

Josefina's response to Renovales's creation of female nudes demonstrates the problematic identity of the genre on the boundaries of obscenity or indecency. The cultural understanding of the female body, its interpretation and its susceptibility, is demonstrably dependent on cultural narratives. The process of Josefina's ageing and decline is not defined as a physical process, but is instead explained through recourse to the cultural implications of pathology. Whether through jealousy, hysteria or physiological disease, Josefina represents a threat to the attempted containment of the female body both through its artistic depiction as nude and its interpretation via medical authority. As Josefina ages and succumbs to illness, the representation of her body in the narrative is of her disappearing, or even of dissolution: 'Su demacración era espantosa, no encontraba límites [...] como si tras la desaparición total de la carne fuese liquidándose el mísero esqueleto' (382). In this passage, Josefina becomes the embodiment of physical degeneration: from neurasthenia and a nervous disorder, her health declines through organic decay.

It must be acknowledged that the novel's treatment of degeneration is far from consistent. Blasco's portrait of Renovales interacts with contemporary conceptualizations of the artist, including (but not limited to) the work of Nordau and its influence on cultural meta-narratives. Blasco's interest in the cultural understanding of degeneracy contrasts with Baroja's formal medical training. None the less, in *La maja desnuda* the discourses of degeneration that implicitly underpin the representation of art in the novel culminate in the final stage of Renovales's artistic development through expressionism. For Nordau, the degenerate artist 'scarcely appreciates or even perceives the external world, and is only occupied with the organic processes in his own body. He is more than egoistical, he is an ego-maniac'.[56] The weakness of Will of the degenerate person makes it impossible to suppress these obsessions. Thus objective phenomena (as in the case of Fernando Ossorio) become subordinate to subjective vision and excessive emotionalism, a position echoed by the final trajectory of Renovales at the end of Blasco's portrait of the artist.

The ekphrasis of Renovales's last painting of Josefina displays a rejection of realism and move instead towards abstraction. The artist's remorse for his treatment of Josefina and his impossible desire to be reunited with her lead to the creation of his final, definitive — and monochrome — portrait of his deceased wife. In the painting, Renovales eschews realistic representation, instead moving towards a primarily expressionist style:

> [...] un lienzo gris en su mayor parte, sin otro color que el del preparado, y sobre éste rayas confusas y entrelazadas delatando cierta indecisión ante los diversos contornos de un mismo cuerpo. [...] Saltaba a la vista la inverosimilitud de los rasgos, la rebuscada exageración: los ojos enormes, monstruosos en su grandeza; la boca diminuta como un punto; la piel de una palidez luminosa, sobrenatural. (437–38)

Through the 'mancha de colores' (437) and the predominance of grey, the artist rejects conventional norms of beauty and representation, giving pre-eminence instead to the expression of emotional experience. The reproduction of recognizable physical reality is rejected in favour of the subjective and interior vision. Exaggeration replaces verisimilitude, as proportions are deformed, and the figure's pale skin becomes unreal to the point that it is 'sobrenatural' (438). The body — 'una desnudez divina' (438) — has yet to be painted and is delineated instead through 'rayas confusas y entrelazadas' (437). Finally, in this painting, the body is no longer controlled and ordered; rather, the figure of Josefina transgresses a unified form, and is represented though hallucinatory or supernatural techniques. Renovales's art has progressed from naturalism to expressionism and the breakdown of representation, exemplifying the creative product of the degenerate artist, whose emotionalism and susceptibility are paramount.

Renovales's recourse to abstract art is the logical product of his descent towards insanity in the context of popular paradigms of the artist's degeneracy. It echoes the attempt of expressionism to represent a different form of reality, through the emphasis on emotion and subjective expression. Furthermore, the expressionist painting of Josefina presents an antithesis to the 'magical regulation of the female body' within classical forms of art.[57] Josefina, then, finally escapes the containment of the earlier nude portrait she so vehemently attacked, as the final portrait confirms the excessive emotionalism and excitability of the artist, and constitutes a product of his unbalanced mental state.

In the execution of this painting, Renovales at last conforms to the stereotype of the 'mad', degenerate artist, shutting himself away for days in a frenzy of artistic creation. And stereotypically, too, his reacquisition of his ability to paint stems from the angst he now feels for the irreparable loss of Josefina. In other words, the artist's talent is finally connected to his alienation and difference. As Renovales sinks into a state of near delirium caused by his feelings towards his dead wife, he becomes increasingly an object of ridicule as he searches out perceived 'doubles' of Josefina among the prostitutes and actresses of sickly appearance in Madrid. His talent as an artist is now seen to be intrinsically linked to 'madness'. Only the torment of his personal life can propel him towards artistic creation in the definitive portrait of Josefina. By the end of the novel, the echoes of Nordau's degenerate artist are striking if not wholly complete: the artist's difference is cast in the context of egomania, one of the cardinal marks of degeneration. For the degenerate, the external world does not exist: reality is a creation of the mind. This is reflected by the delirious or hallucinatory state in which Renovales operates, fuelled by obsession with his dead wife, and symptomatic of mental disturbance.

In Blasco's novel contemporary conceptions of hysteria and insanity resoundingly inform the portrait of the artist and his reluctant muse, Josefina. Renovales's descent towards insanity leads to the production of abstract art, a primary object of Nordau's critique of degeneracy. Renovales's sensuous or immoral art and the obsession with the female nude, as well as his final portrait, echo to some extent cultural myths about the degenerate artist during the *fin de siglo*. The artist's increasingly outlandish behaviour culminates in the final scene of the novel in which he prepares to paint 'la Bella Fregolina', employed as a singer at a 'teatrillo de los barrios bajos' (462), for her perceived likeness to Josefina. Confronted with what in the artist's mind is the reincarnation of Josefina, Renovales discovers that he has lost the ability to paint. Yet, the vital quality of art is such that it can even revive the dead: 'La muerta no había muerto; rodeábale, resucitada por su mano' (412). The novel has frequently been read as the triumph of the deceased Josefina over the protagonist: the first English translation of the novel in 1920 was entitled *Woman Triumphant*.[58] At the end of the novel the artist is confronted by the reality of the loss of his wife, and the impossibility of creating a definitive work of his subject, as he contemplates his own mortality — 'la garganta de voraces negruras... la muerte' (475) — in a state of near insanity. Renovales finally embodies the mythical figure of the tormented artist.

By December 1910, the date of Roger Fry's exhibition 'Manet and the Post-Impressionists' in London, the adherents to Lombroso's and Nordau's school of degenerationism were still vocally present. One cast the exhibition as 'degeneracy, lunacy and gross subjectivism' against 'natural truth and scientific fact'.[59] The portrait of Renovales in *La maja desnuda* reinforces the persistent (if not entirely persuasive) association between the artist and morbid eroticism, pathology and insanity. By the time Nordau published *Degeneration*, Lombroso had already concluded from his work on the skull that artists were insane: artistic genius was cast as a form of criminality and insanity.[60] At the turn of the century, however, Nordau's theories were under attack. George Bernard Shaw refuted the claims of the Austro-Hungarian journalist in his article 'A Degenerate's View of Nordau' (1895). Havelock Ellis would later point (in 1936) to the 'not very scientific doctrine of "degeneration" then floating in the air and applying it to contemporary men of letters and art'.[61] There is little evidence in either *Camino de perfección* or *La maja desnuda* that the flamboyant myths of degeneration expressed by Nordau are accepted uncritically by the two authors. Each author engages with the idea of the degenerate artist in the portrait of his unbalanced or neurotic painter, but neither subscribes fully to Nordau's premises or the irredeemable trajectory of degeneration.

The madness of the artist was a fashionable idea at the turn of the century, a cultural myth that drew on notorious figures such as Van Gogh, who was loudly proclaimed a lunatic, and an embodiment of pathology by the continuing proponents of degenerationism. In both *Camino de perfección* and *La maja desnuda*, the artist suffers from psychological instability that affects his ability to create art. For Fernando, the reintegration of his personality means that he can no longer paint. For Renovales, the death of Josefina, 'la burguesita', leads not to artistic freedom, but to inertia, and the (temporary) paralysis of artistic endeavour. At the end of *Camino de perfección* Fernando Ossorio eschews both art and religion in order to seek regeneration. *La maja desnuda* ends, by contrast, with a portrait that embodies the symptoms of the degenerate artist through the primacy given to emotional expressionism and abstraction. It thereby represents the artist's subjectivism: in the language of degeneration, his ego-mania.

Blasco's engagement with theories of degeneration in *La maja desnuda* rests predominantly on resonant popular and cultural myths about the artist. These dominant narratives provide a key foundation for the popular psychology (rendered through examples of *style indirect libre*), rather than any socio-cultural analysis of artistic atavism. Freud distanced himself from degeneracy, moving instead towards the concept of traumatic memory within psychopathology. Baroja's novel interweaves these influential turn-of-the-century debates through his fictional portrait of the vision of the neurotic artist in *Camino de perfección*. In the next chapter I look back to two novels of 1900 in order to extend the comparison of Baroja's and Blasco's turn-of-the-century literary representations of degeneration, pathology and sexuality.

Notes to Chapter 1

1. Nordau, *Degeneration*, p. 43.
2. Nordau, *Degeneration*, p. 13.
3. See Greenslade, *Degeneration, Culture and the Novel*, pp. 123–24.
4. Paul-Maurice Legrain, *Du Délire chez les Dégénérés* (Paris, 1886), p. 11; cited by Nordau, *Degeneration*, p. 22.
5. Lombroso, 'Nordau's *Degeneration*: Its Value and Its Errors', *Century Illustrated Monthly Magazine*, October 1895, pp. 936–37 (p. 936).
6. Cardwell, 'Oscar Wilde and Spain', pp. 43–49.
7. Glyn Hambrook, 'Baudelaire, Degeneration Theory and Literary Criticism in *Fin de siècle* Spain', *Modern Language Review*, 101.4 (2006), 1005–24 (p. 1017).
8. Emilia Pardo Bazán, *Obras completas*, 4 vols (Madrid: Aguilar, 1973), III, 1174–75.
9. Miguel de Unamuno, 'Sobre la erudición y la crítica', *La España Moderna*, December 1905, pp. 5–26 (p. 22).
10. Hambrook, 'Baudelaire', p. 1018.
11. Pompeyo Gener, *Literaturas malsanas* (Madrid: Fernando Fe, 1894), p. 5.
12. Cardwell, 'Deconstructing the Binaries of *enfrentismo*', p. 161.
13. Nordau, *Degeneration*, p. v.
14. Nordau, *Degeneration*, p. vi.
15. Oscar Vázquez, 'Regenerating the "Man-Beast"'. By the same author, see also *The End Again: Degeneration and Visual Culture in Modern Spain* (University Park: Pennsylvania State University Press, 2017).
16. George Mosse, Introduction, *Degeneration*, p. xxii.
17. Nordau, *Degeneration*, p. 31.
18. Pick, *Faces of Degeneration*, p. 24.
19. James Strachey, 'Sigmund Freud: A Sketch of his Life and Ideas', in Sigmund Freud, *On Sexuality: Three Essays on the Theory of Sexuality and Other Works* (London: Penguin, 1991), pp. 13–26 (p. 19).
20. Pick, *Faces of Degeneration*, pp. 228–30.
21. Nordau, *Degeneration*, pp. 35–39.
22. Baroja, *Camino de perfección (Pasión mística)* (Madrid: Caro Raggio, 1993), p. 20. All subsequent references are to this edition.
23. Flint and Flint, *Pío Baroja: 'Camino de perfección'*, p. 26.
24. Janet Beizer, *Ventriloquized Bodies: Narratives of Hysteria in Nineteenth-Century France* (Ithaca, NY: Cornell University Press, 1994), pp. 1–12.
25. Catherine Jagoe, 'Sexo y género en la medicina del siglo XIX', in *La mujer en los discursos de género*, ed. by Catherine Jagoe, Alda Blasco and Cristina Enríquez de Salamanca (Barcelona: Icaria, 1998), pp. 305–48 (p. 341).
26. Pedro Felipe Monlau, *Estudios superiores de higiene pública y epidemiología (curso de 1868 a 1869: lección inaugural)* (Madrid: M. Rivadeneyra, 1868), pp. 18–20.
27. Donald L. Shaw, 'More about *Abulia*', *Anales de la literatura española contemporánea*, 23.1/2 (1998), 451–64 (pp. 453–58).
28. Nordau, *Degeneration*, pp. 27–28.
29. Cardwell, 'Deconstructing the Binaries of *enfrentismo*', p. 162.
30. Cardwell, p. 163.
31. On this broader context, the reader is referred to *Culture and Gender in Nineteenth-Century Spain*, ed. by Lou Charnon-Deutsch and Jo Labanyi (Oxford: Clarendon, 1995).
32. See Stannard, *Galdós and Medicine*, p. 128.
33. C. A. Longhurst, '*Camino de perfección*: hacia la novela del inconsciente', *Insula*, 665 (May 2002), 20–23 (pp. 20–21).
34. Baroja, *Aventuras, inventos y mixtificaciones de Silvestre Paradox*, *Obras completas*, II, 7–150 (p. 128). All subsequent references are to this edition.
35. On Baroja's techniques for rendering the workings of the psyche, the reader is referred to Longhurst, '*Camino de perfección* and the Modernist Aesthetic', pp. 193–95.

36. Josef Breuer and Sigmund Freud, *Studies on Hysteria, 1893–1895* (Harmondsworth: Penguin, 1974), pp. 146–47.
37. William O. Deaver asserts that Dolores represents matriarchal authority and a female voice at the centre of the text. 'Una deconstrucción feminista de *Camino de perfección*', *Crítica Hispánica*, 18.2 (1996), 267–73. It should be noted, however, that Fernando is unable to conceive of a relationship beyond a mother-substitute figure.
38. On the inversion by Ganivet and Unamuno of the accepted evolutionary model which posited that changes in the environment would affect biological development, see Gayana Jurkevich, 'Abulia, 19th century Physiology and the Generation of 1898', *Hispanic Review*, 60 (1992), 181–94 (p. 192).
39. Ángel Ganivet, *Obras completas*, ed. by Melchor Fernández Almagro, 2 vols (Madrid: Aguilar, 1961), I, 286.
40. See Richard Cardwell, 'The Mad Doctors', pp. 182–85.
41. Gerald G. Brown, *Historia de la literatura española: el siglo XX* (Barcelona: Ariel, 1974), p. 106.
42. Vicente Blasco Ibáñez, *La maja desnuda*, ed. by Facundo Tomás (Madrid: Cátedra, 1998). All subsequent references are to this edition. Introduction, pp. 9–150.
43. Tomás, ed., *La maja desnuda*, p. 265 n. 59.
44. Javier Pérez Rojas, 'Un período de esplendor: la pintura valenciana entre 1880 y 1918', in *Centro y periferia en la modernización de la pintura española (1880–1918)*, intro. by Carmen Pena (Barcelona: Ambit, 1993–94), pp. 162–98 (p. 170) and Norris, 'Visión azoriniana del paisaje español'; quoted in Gayana Jurkevich, *In Pursuit of the Natural Sign: Azorín and the Poetics of Ekphrasis* (London: Associated University Presses, 1999), p. 233 n. 16.
45. Blasco Ibáñez, *Obras completas*, 4th edn, 3 vols (Madrid: Aguilar, 1961), I, 396.
46. Robert Hughes, *Goya* (London: Harvill, 2003), pp. 331–32.
47. On the private consumption of erotic images and literature in the late eighteenth century see Rebecca Haidt, '*Los besos de amor* and *La maja desnuda*: The Fascination of the Senses in the *Ilustración*', *Revista de Estudios Hispánicos*, 29 (1995), 477–503.
48. My thanks to Rocío Rødtjer, PhD candidate at King's College London, for alerting me to this connection.
49. Nordau, *Degeneration*, pp. 306–07.
50. On these intertextual connections, the reader is referred to Tomás, Introduction, *La maja desnuda*, pp. 97–104.
51. Cardwell, 'Deconstructing the Binaries of *enfrentismo*', p. 167.
52. Janice Tomlinson, *Goya in the Twilight of Enlightenment* (New Haven, CT: Yale University Press, 1992), p. 120.
53. Hughes, *Goya*, pp. 242–43.
54. Gascó Contell, *Genio y figura*, p. 95.
55. Gascó Contell, p. 95.
56. Nordau, *Degeneration*, p. 254.
57. Lynda Nead, *The Female Nude: Art, Obscenity and Sexuality* (London: Routledge, 1992), pp. 2–7.
58. *Woman Triumphant (La maja desnuda)*, trans. by Hayward Keniston (New York: Dutton, 1920).
59. S. K. Tillyard, *The Impact of Modernism, 1900–1920: Early Modernism and the Arts and Crafts Movement in Edwardian England* (London: Routledge, 1988), p. 92.
60. Cesare Lombroso, *The Man of Genius* (London: Walter Scott, 1891), p. 9.
61. Reprinted as G. B. Shaw, 'The Sanity of Art' (1907), in *G. B. Shaw: Major Critical Essays*, ed. by Michael Holroyd (Harmondsworth: Penguin, 1986), pp. 309–60 and Havelock Ellis, *From Rousseau to Proust* (London: Constable & Co., 1936), p. 276.

CHAPTER 2

Trauma and the Origins of Neurosis: From Degeneration to the Unconscious in Two Novels of 1900

This chapter puts forward new readings of two contemporaneous novels, their partial assimilation of meta-narratives of degeneration, and the interactions of degeneration theory with psychodynamic paradigms of trauma, sexuality and madness. Published in 1900, Baroja's *La casa de Aizgorri* and Blasco Ibáñez's *Entre naranjos* share resonant points of comparison — I propose — in their contradictory response to degenerationism and the representation of the female psyche. My opening chapter addressed the figure of the degenerate male artist in the wake of Nordau's infamous approach to decadent artistic production and the corrupting immoral environment of the city. Chapter 2 examines the rural reach of degenerationism through the generational legacy of alcoholism in *La casa de Aizgorri* and the sexual morality of the Valencian *huerta* in *Entre naranjos*. Urban space was a prominent locus of middle-class fears about crime, prostitution, and the primitive behaviour of the masses. The cultural narratives of degenerationism, however, were not unique to the city.

Baroja's keen interest in the workings of the unconscious is notably demonstrated by his turn-of-the-century works, *Vidas sombrías*, *La casa de Aizgorri* and *Camino de perfección*. Blasco's own interweaving of determinism, symbolism and psychological development in *Entre naranjos* locates him as markedly closer to Baroja's own literary development in 1900 than the conventional division between the 'Generation of 1898' and popular fiction attests. The analysis of these two novels exemplifies the literary transposition of degenerationism and its combination with theories of the unconscious as a salient example of the cultural assimilation of ideas that permeated the spectrum of artistic production of this period.

Baroja's first novel was profoundly concerned with questions of biology and degeneration, preoccupations that are brought into narrative focus through the representation of neurosis in relation to the female protagonist, Águeda de Aizgorri. Her dilemma centres on the rejection of marriage and maternity according (it is implied) to her destructive fear of producing degenerate children. This anxiety stems from her belief in the biological legacy of alcoholism. Whether or not Baroja shared these deterministic concerns is a key question that my chapter seeks to address. The anxieties of French *dégénérescence* that posited the resonant influence of generational pathologies, including alcoholism, within mental decline provide a fertile foundation in Baroja's *La casa de Aizgorri*. Morel's influential treatise predicated a model of hereditary alcoholism that was assimilated and modified by his successors in France, views that would later inform the moral stance of hygienic medicine in late nineteenth-century Spain. *La casa de Aizgorri* reflects these concerns but — I contend — ultimately subverts the deterministic principles Baroja has debated over the course of the novel. It does so through a curious anticipation of Freudian paradigms in the representation of Águeda's psychological trajectory.

On the surface, Blasco's *Entre naranjos* appears to deal less directly with the pseudo-scientific discourses of degeneration than Baroja's novel. Heredity and environmental determinism obviously inform the representation of psychology and behaviour, but they are debated in relatively straightforward ways. More significantly, however, the promiscuous sexuality of Leonora Moreno in *Entre naranjos* is configured in striking relation to the Amazon, a prominent figure within sexology at the turn of the century, and a trope of keen interest within *fin-de-siècle* paradigms of degeneration and female deviance. Like Baroja's Águeda de Aizgorri, Blasco's Leonora is characterized with reference to a traumatic experience that produces neurotic or pathological symptoms. Each author interweaves naturalist and determinist paradigms with an (albeit tentative) exploration of the unconscious mind in relation to the female psyche, and each focuses on the figure of the absent mother in the representation of psychological models and processes. Without it being necessary to posit a paradigm of direct influence, both authors took an obvious interest in the effects of early experience and family structures in the development of human behaviour. This chapter traces the salient echoes of both degenerationism and psychoanalytic models in the representation of the female subject in *La casa de Aizgorri* and *Entre naranjos*.

As Sander Gilman has argued, the concept of degeneration is inseparable from human sexuality, not least because the scientific study of sexuality was based on pathology and the concept of deviancy.[1] Sexology and psychoanalysis are pertinent contexts for the analysis of degeneration and its relevance to gender ideologies at the turn of the century. In 1844 Heinrich Kaan had defined a universal or ubiquitous concept of sexual pathology based on childhood deviancy through an analogy between primitive man and children.[2] Within this model, pathology was based on an atavistic return to a primitive stage of evolution. Later in the nineteenth century, degeneration was fundamental to Freud's work, not least because his theories of the unconscious were based on a biological scientific foundation. None the less, in his 1894 essay on neurosis Freud wrote about degeneration in a neurological context as distinct from his physical or biological understanding of hysteria in relation to childhood: 'Hysterical children are very frequently precocious and highly gifted; in a number of cases, to be sure, the hysteria is merely a symptom of a deep-going degeneracy of the nervous system which is manifested in permanent moral perversion'.[3]

Freud eventually rejected the biological concept of degeneracy, moving instead towards the role of trauma in the development of psychopathology, and eventually towards degeneracy as a 'disease of civilization' within the sphere of political rhetoric and pseudo-science.[4] As Gilman observes in relation to Freud's work, 'degeneracy can be the inheritance of behaviour patterns from one generation to another. The existence of such earlier psychological structures played a major role in Freud's recasting of the moment of degeneracy from prenatal influence to early childhood experience'.[5] The Oedipus complex accounted for the survival of the primitive human race, a theory developed in *Totem and Taboo* (1913), with its resonant subtitle: *Some Points of Agreement between the Mental Lives of Savages and Neurotics*. In the primal horde, Freud argued, the devouring of the father by the sons accomplished the process of identification with him through the cannibalistic or oral stage of libidinal development.

Freud is a key figure in the theorization of psychic trauma because he famously underscored the trauma of sexual assault in his seduction theory. Originally a term for surgical rupture of the protective encasement of the body provided by the skin, trauma was transposed to psychology and psychiatry, a linguistic and conceptual adaptation that was popularized by the work of Freud and others.[6] In 'Heredity and the Aetiology of Neuroses' (1896), Freud argued that all neuroses originated in sexual life. He attempted to explain adult neuroses in relation to childhood experiences — specifically the trauma of sexual assault — that had affected the individual. Freud's concept of traumatic sexual history within his seduction theory, and its psychic repetition within memory, provides a resonant point of reference for the legacy of Leonora's experience of sexual abuse during adolescence in Blasco's novel of 1900.

It is widely thought that by 1897 Freud rejected his seduction theory and began instead to explain neurosis as originating in the psyche, via an Oedipal model. However, the relationship between internal and external processes was not a straightforward process of cause and effect within his approach to trauma. Like Charcot, Freud saw traumatic hysteria as the result of psychological (not physiological) incubation. Trauma was thus construed as the re-enactment through memory and mature understanding of an earlier experience.[7] However, he continued to reject a causal relationship between external actions such as assault and the development of trauma: the latter was the result of the interaction between experience and the meaning lent to it by the individual subject. He thereby rejected external trauma as direct cause, instead emphasizing psychosexual origins and the interiorization of trauma through the re-enactment of earlier desires and fantasies.[8] In other words, neuroses derived from internal sexual drives and not external trauma. In *Beyond the Pleasure Principle* (1920) Freud would later define the dreams of traumatic neuroses as arising from the compulsion to repeat, as a memory of the psychic traumas of childhood.

In the representation of Águeda and Leonora, childhood and pre-adolescent experience has profound importance in the legacy of trauma implicit in each character's mental predicament. In both novels the female psyche is construed in relation to pathology and models of degeneration through the representation of neurosis, insanity and deviance. These problems stem — I argue — not from genetic inheritance but instead from the overbearing role of Águeda's alcoholic father in *La casa de Aizgorri* and sexual violence in *Entre naranjos*. Baroja's novel resonates with Freud's theorisation of the Oedipal model as the origin of neurosis. Blasco's has more in common with Freud's earlier seduction theory and the experience of abuse. In each case, however, the death of the mother, and thus the absence of maternal protection, provides the catalyst for the experience of psychopathology or trauma. In *La casa de Aizgorri*, neurosis is evidenced through symptoms such as visions, nightmares, or more specifically *pavor nocturnus* (night terrors) implicit in the description of Águeda's 'terrores' (37). For Leonora, repressed impulse is evidenced by sexual abstinence that follows her history of promiscuity. These symptoms have obvious correlations to degenerationism, as well as the notion of psychic memory (or revival of past experiences), in *fin-de-siglo* medical and psychiatric discourses.

In France Morel's biological model of degeneration was posited on a complex interaction between hereditary factors and environmental determinants. His early career was defined through his interest in cretinism which exemplified his conceptualization of human degeneration and the belief that 'degeneration can be congenital or acquired, complete or incomplete, susceptible of improvement or incurable'.[9] His influential *Traité des dégénérescences physiques, intellectuelles et morales de l'espèce humaine* identified the transformation of pathological processes across generations, a development of hereditary paradigms. Madness for Morel was biological in origin, a view echoed in Spain by the psychiatrist José María Escuder whose volume *Locos y anómalos* (1895) identified the seed of insanity as germinating in the womb.[10] The anxiety within French *dégénéresence*, which posited that degeneration would culminate in the eventual sterility and extinction of the human race, drew particularly on fears about the declining birth rate in France. In a Spanish context, the anxieties that fuelled regenerationism were posited instead on beliefs regarding national decline and the need for reform, whether political, educational, or spiritual. Baroja's early novels are informed to some extent by these calls for renewal in biological and scientific terms. In Blasco the representation of un-maternal and sexually precocious women, epitomized by Leonora in *Entre naranjos* and Neleta in *Cañas y barro*, respond in resonant terms to prevalent fears about human reproduction. In neither case, however, does the fictional representation fully sustain degenerationist discourses or ideologies.

As Pick observes, phrenology was of limited appeal to Morel's concept of degeneration which 'was far more complex than such a popular taxonomy of images, or such a dream of finding "the signboard" of criminality'. The superficial features of degeneracy (bodily stigmata) accompanied 'a mysterious and hidden world of pathology'.[11] Instead, *dégénéresence* identified the abnormal and dangerous elements of society in a period of urban expansion and social inequality, a reality that has obvious resonances with Baroja's clinical approach to urban deprivation in Madrid novels such as *La busca*. Unlike Morel, however, Baroja does not advocate a solution to this problem in the guise of social medicine; degenerationists such as Morel, alongside social hygienists in Spain, viewed the removal of these dangerous elements of society as a necessary obstacle to contagion. Social problems, including crime, alcoholism and prostitution, were treated according to scientific theories of heredity and pathology through a powerful biological model that extended well beyond French national borders. By contrast, Baroja's early novels explore and debate prominent questions of determinism and degeneration without ascribing to any eugenicist model of practical reform. Similarly, Blasco's turn-of-the-century fiction represents female deviancy in relation to morality and sexuality, but does not fully sustain the premises of degenerationism in a determinist or positivist context.

La casa de Aizgorri

Baroja's first novel, *La casa de Aizgorri: novela en siete jornadas*, originated as a play, retaining its dialogue form virtually throughout. The overtly naturalist themes are evident from the beginning of the novel: the alcoholism of Águeda's father and the factory workers, poverty and harsh rural conditions. Don Julián, the village doctor, diagnoses the psychological state of Águeda's father in unambiguously deterministic terms: 'El daño que hace en el padre se manifiesta en el hijo o en el nieto [...]. Así, los hijos nacidos, desequilibrados y enclenques, pagan las culpas de los padres, por esa fatalidad inexorable de la herencia' (21). For Don Julián, physical and psychological damage are biological in origin and are passed down through the generations, clearly echoing French models of *dégénérescence*. Águeda's anguished predicament is, then, a direct consequence of her belief that she will likewise suffer the perceived degeneracy of her family, manifest already in the physical condition of her father, Don Lucio, and half-brother, Luis, who spends his days in an alcohol-fuelled state of inertia and lack of Will. Her fears are predicated on an overwhelming belief in hereditary degeneration, and particularly inherited alcoholism, a widespread concern among Spanish hygienists of the late nineteenth century. As Longhurst argues, the arrival of Águeda's half-brother Luis when she is fourteen is key to understanding her neurotic symptoms and rejection of marriage to Mariano: 'ella pertenece a una familia de degenerados, y si contrae matrimonio su descendencia lo será también'.[12]

Baroja's *La casa de Aizgorri*, of course, deals not with an urban environment but a rural Basque setting based on the author's visit to Pasajes, near San Sebastián. The location is defined by the distillery inherited by Don Lucio de Aizgorri. The distillery has belonged to several generations of his family and — according to the village doctor, Don Julián — bestows a legacy of alcoholism within the local community. It is thereby thought to be poisoning the entire village of Arbea through a process of degeneration and generational inheritance, as the doctor Don Julián comments to Águeda: 'Vino tu abuelo y puso la fábrica, excitado por el lucro, y poco a poco el alcohol fue infiltrándose y la degeneración cundió por todas partes. [...] Ese es el aspecto más triste de los efectos del alcohol; no mata, pero hace degenerar a la descendencia, seca las fuentes de la vida'.[13] Distilled spirits were widely regarded by hygienists of the period as more dangerous and more likely to lead to chronic alcoholism that wine or beer.

Furthermore, as Sosa-Velasco has argued, the Basque setting for *La casa de*

Aizgorri allows the author to debate questions of nation and degeneration through an evaluation of the superiority of the Basque people over Spanish inheritance: 'Baroja cree que la regeneración de la nación española se encuentra en la raza vasca'.[14] According to this scholar, Águeda's recovery of energy and Will at the end of *La casa de Aizgorri* demonstrates her superiority to the Spanish María Aracil, the female protagonist of *La ciudad de la niebla* (1909) and *La dama errante* (1908).[15] My own reading of the novel problematizes this straightforward solution to degeneration. Baroja certainly emphasized the superiority of Basque lineage. One might note, however, that both Águeda de Aizgorri and María Aracil take refuge in a very similar bourgeois solution of marriage and domesticity. This is represented through a resurgence of Nietzschean vitalism in the case of Águeda versus María's sedentary apathy at the end of *La ciudad de la niebla*. None the less, I propose that the conclusion of *La casa de Aizgorri* in fact contests a deterministic and racial paradigm, instead positing (or at least implying) the primary role of internal psychological factors in the recovery of the female protagonist. These centre on Águeda's emotional recovery from the death of her mother, through which she eventually overcomes the absence of a maternal role model on which to base her own process of marriage to Mariano. This marriage is the foundation for having her own children, a terrifying prospect as long as she continues to believe that her offspring will inherit the intergenerational tendency for alcoholism of the Aizgorri lineage. In other words, the resolution for Águeda at the end of the novel is not found in inherited or biological strength, but instead the death of her father which provides a catalyst for her psychological recovery in Freudian terms.

Águeda's father, Don Lucio, is an alcoholic, as evidenced by physical symptoms including pain, tremors and eventually delirium. According to the doctor, his alcoholism is exacerbated by the noxious influence of the distillery: 'no bebía mucho, es cierto; pero había bebido. Además, respiraba continuamente los vapores del alcohol' (20). His son Luis suffers physical symptoms that were strongly associated during this period with hereditary alcoholism, such as 'facciones borrosas e inexpresivas, la mandíbula desarrollada, los labios belfos, y los ojos [...] parecen entontecidos, y sólo se animan con ráfagas de cólera' (6). These symptoms are an implied consequence of his father's biological legacy. Luis suffers from neurasthenia and mental instability and is designated by his father as an idiot, a product of inherited insanity: '¿Educarle? ¡Si es idiota! Es de familia; en la mía ha habido muchos locos [...]. He conocido lo menos seis o siete, entre locos y suicidas, en mi parentela. [...] Antes había locos en la familia, y ahora son idiotas' (14–15). Sent away from home under mysterious circumstances, Luis is implicitly designated as the illegitimate offspring of Don Lucio. In the context of deterministic paradigms and the apparent degeneration of her half-brother, the sanity of Águeda's mother is even more important for her daughter's own biological inheritance and mental stability.

Morel's influential studies predicated two laws: that of double fertilization (or double jeopardy: the risk of psychological inheritance from both parents) and that of progressivity, in which each successive generation was thought to evidence a greater measure of degenerate characteristics through hereditary transmission. The inevitable and destructive transmission posited by Morel would eventually lead to the extinction of the family lineage, through the generational modification of a nervous temperament. This would be exacerbated in the second generation as disorders of the nervous system and in the third as insanity.[16] The thesis had wide-ranging implications for social psychiatry and subsequent studies of hereditary insanity in France and elsewhere. Of course the concept of degeneration was predicated on particular biological, moral and cultural perspectives which by the early twentieth century would be crucial to critical debate about its validity.

In 1884 the American psychiatrist John P. Gray concluded that disease could not be inherited and was instead the product of external factors.[17] By the turn of the twentieth century, the new science of heredity began to cast light on questions that had not as yet been resolved by contemporary biology. In 1900 blood groups were discovered; in the early 1880s chromosomes were first described, and by 1901 thirty-four chromosomes in pairs had been identified, one set maternal, the other paternal.[18] These scientific breakthroughs had a significant impact on contemporary approaches in psychiatry which had been dominated by the biological models of Darwin and Spencer. By the 1920s, genetic theory would reconstruct Darwin's doctrine of natural selection, as Jean Gayon has documented.[19] The development of genetic theory would thus cast light on the role of hybridization (or crossing of species) in evolution, which presented unresolvable problems for Darwin.

As a model of environmental biology, Morel placed particular emphasis on alcoholism, although he also included other toxins such as opium, hashish and tobacco. From the 1890s, the role of hereditary alcoholism was underscored by hygienists in Spain in the wake of late nineteenth-century French studies of degeneration. According to these theories, alcoholism was the cause of biological alterations to the nervous system; the descendants of alcoholics were predisposed to epilepsy, hysteria, madness and so on, views echoed to some extent by the presentation of Don Lucio's family in *La casa de Aizgorri*. As Campos indicates, the anti-alcohol propaganda of late nineteenth-century Spain exemplifies the expression of degeneration theory in relation to biology and heredity. Alcoholism was the focus of both the moral stigma associated particularly with the working classes and powerful arguments in favour of the intervention of social hygiene.[20] In 1896, for example, Rafael Cervera Barat emphasized the role of heredity in the development of alcoholism, arguing that 'los estragos del alcoholismo se van acumulando de una generación a otra, hasta que se extinguen por completo las familias'.[21] The influence of Morel's thesis of progressivity, and that of his French successors such as Legrain, on Cervera Barat's statement hardly needs to be underscored. Within three generations (the same number identified by Morel in his subsequent volume *Traité des maladies mentales* of 1860), he argued that mental disorders were passed on through a paradigm of 'degeneración mental' which would lead progressively to the demise of the family line.[22] The Spanish nation and the species itself were at stake through the effects of this inheritance, which was the root cause of numerous social disorders, including criminality.

In the context of nineteenth-century psychiatry, there are suggestive echoes of Esquirol's concept of monomania in the representation of Águeda's emotional condition, particularly her obsessive preoccupation with the generational legacy of madness. According to this thesis, an *idée fixe* produced derangement in an otherwise sound mind. Despite being widely discredited in forensic psychiatry, Spanish alienists of the 1870s and 1880s continued to use the term *monomanía*. Giné y Partagas, for example, advocated the *tratamiento moral* of those suffering from 'monomanías sensoriales o aluncinatorias — cuando el delirio de las ideas, sin ser difuso, sino manteniéndose circunscrito en una órbita más o menos extensa, está sostenido por sensaciones alucinatorias'.[23] He considered the effects of heredity to be most common in mental disease.[24] Like Morel, he posited a biological or organic predisposition in the development of neurological disturbances. Morel's study of mental illness, however, challenged Esquirol's notion of monomania because it construed madness as both hidden and progressive. By 1881 Galdós's *La desheredada* would echo these psychiatric and medical theories of the day, in the portrait of insanity of Tomás Rufete, and the representation of Isidora's macrocephalic son, Riquín, an example of pathological or morbid heredity.[25]

However, the crossings and counter-crossings between determinist paradigms and internal psychic processes that define the development of mature sexuality in *La casa de Aizgorri* are not straightforward. The novel explores the psychological symptoms from which Águeda suffers, including night terrors and visions. The village doctor proposes a biological argument as an explanation for Águeda's neurosis. Don Julián is just one of the many fictional echoes of Baroja's medical vocation in his early novels, and obviously a figure who represents scientific authority of the day. Baroja did not necessarily concur, however, with his fictional doctor, and instead employs Don Julián to put forward a possible explanation founded on hereditary paradigms. Alongside Baroja's exposition of heredity in this novel is an interest in the maternal and paternal figures that diverts in subtle but compelling ways from biology. Certainly Águeda's predicament is richly suggestive of unconscious motivation and internal psychic processes, as demonstrated by the significance of her dreams or visions of her dead mother. A close reading provides evidence of Baroja's interest in the psychodynamics of the family that counters the biological determinism of Don Julián's medical narratives. In a persuasive analysis of the novel, Longhurst has already identified an Oedipal (or more accurately Electra) paradigm in *La casa de Aizgorri*.[26] I seek to extend this critical reading through the application of a feminist perspective that problematizes the straightforward transference of a Freudian model of male development to female sexuality. I thereby underscore both the innovative exposition of female psychic development in *La casa de Aizgorri* and its tentative rejection of degenerationism, despite the novel's highly traditional ending.

The protagonist's own profound fears or imaginings (evidence of her suspected degeneracy) are expressed in a central passage, replete with symbolic imagery, in which her mother appears as the primary focus:

De noche, sola, sin el amparo de mi madre, ya muerta, veía sombras que se echaban sobre mí y dos alas negras a la cabecera de mi cama. Unas veces, aquellas alas oscuras me arrastraban por las nubes y me paseaban por encima de

> tierras negras, de lagos también negros, con olas turbias e intranquilas. Otras veces, en medio de las tinieblas, veía una luz blanca, muy blanca, y en medio de aquella luz se dibujaba una figura, la de mi madre, y me sonreía dulcemente y me llevaba en sus brazos a ver regiones llenas de luz y de flores. (25)

Águeda's dreams are a well-rehearsed arena for the repetition of a painful experience that provides a key to understanding her symptoms of neurosis: the loss of her mother, a primary figure of emotional identification within Object Relations theory. Furthermore, Águeda's visions of her mother provide evidence of an unresolved emotional response to her death. For Freud, of course, melancholia, depression and guilt were the pathological counterparts of mourning.[27]

It has already been implied in the same passage that the protagonist's belief in inherited degeneracy is itself a primary source of her psychological predicament, as Don Julián acknowledges: 'Esa compañía eterna de la razón con una idea cansa, cansa mucho, y puede llegar hasta perturbar el cerebro' (24). The appearance in Águeda's visions of her deceased mother, surrounded by a 'luz blanca' (25), is a clichéd image of maternal protection, an example of the rather straightforward moral lines drawn in this early work: she is idealized, above all, because she is absent. However, beyond the basic symbolism of the passage, Águeda's anxiety that she has inherited a strain of madness from her father exacerbates the process of mourning for her lost mother.

In *La casa de Aizgorri* the death of her mother, with whom Águeda identifies, represents a profound source of fear. Águeda's experience of loss moves beyond a natural process of mourning the death of a loved one because it also has significant implications for her relationship with Don Lucio. Her father represents degeneration and psychological instability, but his role can also be explained in relation to the sublimation of unconscious or repressed motives, as Longhurst concludes: 'la neurosis de Águeda se fundamenta en las figuras inquietantes y perturbadoras del padre y el hermano tras la muerte de su madre'.[28] If we apply an Oedipal model, however, this explanation of neurosis and psychoanalytic paradigms casts Águeda's predicament as evidence of a problematic relationship with her father through an assumed transference of the Oedipus Complex, a model based on the development of boys, directly to the female child.

My own reading interprets these echoes of psychoanalysis through an alternative lens based on the protagonist's continuing identification with her mother. While Freud favoured the Oedipal model in which the father's intervention between mother and son instigates their separation, feminist theory has emphasized the pre-Oedipal period, and the daughter's 'long continuation of her pre-Oedipal attachment to her mother, and of her embracing the Law of the Father [the prohibition against incest] so much less enthusiastically than the son'. The female child's identification with the parent of the same sex does not, therefore, necessitate the rejection of her mother, because 'there is for the daughter no Oedipal "crisis"'.[29] This process seems to be supported, at least partially, by *La casa de Aizgorri*.

Don Lucio's disdainful identification of Águeda's likeness to her mother — 'Has salido a tu madre. Eres, como ella, ñoña y sentimental' (11) — reveals the negative and overbearing role of her father. His daughter serves as an uncomfortable reminder of his unfair treatment of his deceased wife, whom the protagonist energetically defends. Águeda expresses only love and not hostility towards her deceased mother: there is no evident ambivalence in her response to the lost object of attachment. Instead, Águeda appears to be caught in a circular process of mourning. Her inability to move on from love for her dead mother through marriage to Mariano is an indication of pathology or 'melancholia'. Whether or not her 'visions' are accurately suggestive of an Oedipal paradigm, Baroja's interest in heredity is mitigated and challenged persuasively by a pseudo-Freudian exposition of the psychodynamics of the family.

Confronted by her father's hostility, the protagonist continues to identify with her mother, and invokes the feminine through her calls for protection and comfort: '¡Madre! ¡Madre! Siento que tu alma me rodea y vela por mí. ¡Oh! ¡Protégeme! Lleva algún consuelo a mi pobre cabeza trastornada' (35). Águeda has lost a maternal role model on which to base her sexual and behavioural development on the threshold of adulthood, the point at which (we surmise) her mother dies. This is supported by Mariano's admiring observation that 'si muchas veces he llegado a pensar que *no es usted mujer*' (12; my italics). This statement unwittingly underlines her lack of 'embodiment' within a physical relationship as she fends off her suitors: the threatening Díaz, but also Mariano whom she loves. Regardless of this association, the observation refers directly to Mariano's symbolic perception of her as 'una sustancia [...] esa idea luminosa y profunda que forma su alma' (12): an abstract, but radiant, substance that constitutes her spiritual foundation.

The epilogue completes the implicit references to the maternal in *La casa de Aizgorri*. Águeda's entrance to Mariano's home is narrated in terms of a return to childhood and to a surrogate who fills the place of her own absent mother. The protagonist's acceptance of Mariano, then, signals a resurgence of the traditionally feminine, which is accompanied by water imagery as the protagonist escapes Arbea by overcoming her fears and crossing the waters of the dyke at night and alone. She gains a mother-substitute, who dreams of grandchildren and domesticity. Águeda is no longer 'unwomanly', taking charge of the accounts of the distillery in place of Díaz, nor the 'mujer valiente' (43) helping to forge the iron 'volante' in Mariano's factory in a proto-masculine role. She is now reborn as a 'muchacha' who companionably helps her new mother to make up her bed with 'sábanas, que huelen a sol' (49), as a new day dawns. In marriage, Águeda finds freedom and a release from her undisclosed (repressed) feelings, not least sexuality and maternity. *La casa de Aizgorri* concludes with a highly traditional solution for women through bourgeois domesticity.

The paradigms of degeneration and neurosis are debated in both a biological and psychological context. Águeda expects the death of her father to plunge her into insanity. This experience of terror stems from the fear that she will inherit a strain of madness from her father. When her father dies, she begins to overcome these 'fantasías enfermas' (37) and unhealthy visions, she gathers her energy and Will, and defeats the spectre of psychological breakdown. The protagonist frees herself from the legacy of the paternal in psychodynamic, not deterministic, terms: 'ante lo inexplicable y ante la muerte, su espíritu se recoge y se siente con energía y, victoriosa de sus terrores, entra con lentitud en la alcoba de su padre, se arrodilla junto a la cama y reza largo tiempo por el alma del muerto' (37). In other words, Águeda's neurosis was a product of the unhealthy influence of her father, one that has driven a healthy process of mourning towards pathology. The protagonist overcomes this neurosis and she emerges victorious from the experience of terror, her fear of insanity and degenerate visions. Thus, the dutiful daughter remains at her father's side, but symbolically turns away from her father's influence. Significantly, it is following her father's death and the disappearance of her brother that she is able to accept marriage to Mariano. If we accept the novel's simultaneous — and inherently contradictory — implication of a Freudian model and the continuing attachment to her mother, then Águeda must free herself from the legacy of her father. His dominant presence has impeded psychological growth because it has implicitly forbidden a relationship beyond himself.[30] As she accepts the man she loves, she initiates self-definition. By the end of La casa de Aizgorri there is no rejection of her mother, whether conscious or unconscious. According to my reading, Águeda's recuperation is dependent on the memory of maternal love. Thus the trajectory of Baroja's protagonist both parallels and simultaneously subverts Freudian paradigms.

In the mid-nineteenth century Jacques Joseph Moreau de Tours put forward a hereditary role in mental illness, hysteria and alcoholism. By 1900 psychopathological studies in both neurology and psychiatry identified psychic as well as physical stigmata, including insanity, *pavor nocturnus*, moral delinquency and sexual perversion.[31] In sum, Águeda's predicament is demonstrably not the consequence of insanity or degeneracy, and neither is it biological in origin. Instead, her experience of terror and 'degenerate' visions are by implication the product of psychological trauma in the wake of her mother's death. They represent the obstacles to a healthy development of adult sexuality provided by problematic family relationships, including an overbearing and alcoholic father, and an apparently degenerate half-brother. Her neurosis is not biological or inherited, but is instead the product of psychodynamic models of development, in which she must build an adult feminine identity and free herself from the psychic (rather than hereditary or organic) legacy of paternal influence.

By the end of the novel, Baroja's adherence to determinist paradigms in La casa de Aizgorri is rejected through the protagonist's Nietzschean recuperation of Will. A belief in heredity and familial transmission is expressed by the voice of the village doctor as medical authority, but this model is ultimately rejected by the novel's ending. Águeda finally accepts marriage, maternity and the domestic sphere, an ending that represents the assuaging of social anxieties that focused on the female body and its perceived responsibility for the health of future generations. Baroja's first novel subverts naturalist premises of hereditary determinism but in doing so resorts to a traditional solution of marriage that allows social order to re-establish itself. La casa de Aizgorri debates alcoholism and insanity in the light of existing models of biological determinism and emerging theories of the unconscious mind, providing evidence of the author's fundamentally contradictory and complex approach to cultural theories of degeneration at the turn of the century.

Entre naranjos

Written in the autumn of 1900, *Entre naranjos* was Blasco Ibáñez's fourth novel. Existing criticism has frequently identified a naturalist formula in the author's Valencian novels such as *La barraca* (1898) and *Cañas y barro*. Medina, for example, asserts that *Cañas y barro* demonstrates 'the fullness of Blasco's acceptance of the naturalists' deterministic philosophy. Man's struggle against the bestiality of his own instincts and the powerful forces of nature is again shown to be a futile one'.[32] *Entre naranjos* debates a relatively simple deterministic thesis that explores the influence of heredity and environment in relation to the protagonist Rafael and his father, the deceased *cacique* Ramón Brull. The determinism of the novel, however, fails to amount to a fully fledged doctrine, despite its superficial appeal.

Doña Bernarda's exasperation that Rafael has apparently inherited his father's promiscuous libido draws obviously on a straightforward biological model of heredity. Her statement reinforces her fierce moral disapproval of her son's relations with Leonora: ' — ¡Lo mismo que tu padre! — exclamó iracunda doña Bernarda — . No puedes negar su sangre: mujeriego, amigo de las perdidas, capaz, por una cualquiera, de comprometer la suerte de la casa'.[33] Likewise, at the end of *Entre naranjos*, eight years after Rafael's abandonment of her, Leonora sums up the impossibility of their relationship in the context of their contrasting education and family background, and thus their opposing and incompatible destinies as the product of heredity and cultural lineage: 'Somos de diferente raza. Tú naciste burgués, yo llevo en las venas el ardor de la bohemia. El amor, la novedad de mi vida, te deslumbraron; batiste las alas para seguirme, pero caíste con el peso de los afectos heredados. Tú tienes los apetitos de tu gente' (203). Positioned in the concluding pages of the novel, the statement appears to represent the conclusion to the novel's rather disjointed exploration of hereditary determinism. The question of 'race', however, is interpreted in social and moral, rather than biological terms. Like the statement of Doña Bernarda above, Leonora's protest is shaped by anger and emotion, rather than science. The paradigm of hereditary determinism, in any case, is far from consistent. Rafael's 'carácter débil e irresoluto' (129) contrasts markedly with both his father's imposing authority and his mother's strong Will. As in *Cañas y barro*, genetic models are at best contradictory.

Leonora's behaviour stems more obviously from childhood sexual trauma than biological determinism. The cultural influence of Freud's seduction theory is a pertinent context here. Her statement that 'en el fondo odio a los hombres: he sido siempre su más terrible enemiga' (80), belies her traumatized response to sexual abuse. This emotional response is rooted in adolescence, when her father's lack of vigilance allowed her music tutor, an old man with an apparently paternal air, to rape her. The loss of maternal protection through the absence of her mother who died following childbirth is also significant in this context. Educated in 'un ambiente libre de escrúpulos' (109), Leonora confides in Rafael that 'creo que no he sido nunca inocente' (107), suggesting that she internalizes blame for her sexual desirability and precocious knowledge. The effects of early experience are interpreted falsely by Leonora as innate characteristics. According to Rafael's family mentor Don Andrés, she inherited her father's notoriously unconventional, bohemian perspective at an early age: 'esa muchacha salió idéntica al doctor; tan chiflada como él: su mismo carácter' (52). Contradictory hereditary explanation masks the traumatic legacy of abuse during adolescence to produce Leonora's promiscuous sexuality in adulthood. Thus, 'su naturaleza sensual' (111), her essential nature, is interpreted within the narrative as responsible for the ensuing period of sexual abuse by Boldini, her singing teacher. An alternative reading of this experience, however, would be a traumatic repetition of her sexual history in Freudian terms. The deterministic leanings of *Entre naranjos*, alongside other Valencian novels, are also mitigated to some extent by elements of Romanticism, 'chance and the occurrence of the improbable', as Anderson notes in relation to *Cañas y barro*.[34]

Entre naranjos engages with degeneration theories less directly than *La casa de Aizgorri*. However the novel is obviously informed by bourgeois standards of morality, sexuality and assumptions regarding both normative parameters of social behaviour and their transgression. Leonora's promiscuity and physical desirability are the motivation for her social marginalization as *femme fatale*, the object of desire and potent threat for the weak-willed protagonist. Her initial rejection of Rafael only fuels her definition as an Amazon, in line with her display of physical violence and sexual assertiveness. However, the story of Leonora's personal history lends itself directly — I contend — to an incipient, psychoanalytic reading that positions her promiscuity and subsequent abstinence as a developmental reaction to earlier abuse. In *Studies on Hysteria* (1893–95), Freud and Josef Breuer argued that the symptoms of hysteria could only be understood through the analysis of trauma, and 'specifically early experiences of sexual "seduction" or assault'.[35] The memory of traumatic experience (whether external or internal in origin) is particularly significant, according to this thesis, because it continues to be revived within the patient's psyche for many years after the event. Freud's seduction theory therefore provides a persuasive context and contemporaneous reference for the reading of Leonora's development following sexual assault during adolescence. Certainly Blasco Ibáñez's portrait of women frequently has recourse to stereotypical iconography of the *fin de siècle*, including moral degeneration. The portrait of Leonora's transgressive sexuality, however, can be interpreted in the light of psychological models current during the period that move beyond a straightforward model of biological determinism or indeed degenerationism.

Leonora is construed as a *femme fatale*, the dangerous object of male desire for whom a Russian lover and 'un muchacho de Nápoles' (90) have already died. Her expression of hatred for men belies unconscious motives, including a self-destructive sexuality. This is evidenced by her elopement with Salvatti, an ageing baritone who exploits her for financial gain. If we apply a popular — if not wholly accurate

— reading of Freud's seduction theory, her behaviour is a logical consequence or mature re-enactment of adolescent trauma. Leonora's return to Alcira, the environment of early childhood, marks her new-found celibacy, in which she rejects a sexual relationship with Rafael, at least temporarily. As in the case of Águeda in *La casa de Aizgorri*, elective celibacy provides evidence that repressed fear, anxiety or trauma are continuing to be re-enacted by the mature adult. In any case, Leonora's predicament provides more convincing evidence of psychosexual development than a hereditary paradigm. The representation of Leonora sustains curious, incipient parallels with a popularized version of contemporary theories of trauma and sexual pathology, although these models are not fully developed.

In a similar way, the frequent insistence on Leonora's role as mother-substitute for Rafael presents a suggestive anticipation of Freudian theories of sexual development. When Rafael impulsively sets out to rescue Leonora (unnecessarily) from the flood, she indulges him with 'cierta superioridad maternal, como una mujer bondadosa que cuida a su hijo después de una travesura que la llena de orgullo' (73), a motif that is repeated numerous times. The antithesis of convention, Leonora represents an exotic and worldly 'otherness', and an object of fantasy and desire. Thus, the female protagonist moves from domineering mother-substitute (who rejects him) to lover, a process indicative of Rafael's temporary overcoming of excessive dependence on his mother through her substitution. Rafael positions his lover as rival to maternal love. Sexual maturity, and the replacement of the mother by an external object of desire, however, is not fully achieved by Rafael in his relationship with Leonora. In the struggle with his mother, there are striking Oedipal overtones, even if they are not fully developed or consistently applied. Without wishing to posit any direct influence, in 1899 Freud published his *Interpretation of Dreams*, and in 1905 *Three Essays on the Theory of Sexuality*, in which he expressed the view, so shocking to his contemporaries, that children (both male and female) are sexual beings. Rafael's desire for Leonora can be read according to a basic psychological model that emphasizes early experience, and its consequences for subsequent relationships beyond the biological family unit, as echoes of those original family structures. According to this paradigm, Rafael's relationships with women are evidence of his search for a replacement mother-figure according to the expression of gender clichés, whether through an erotic object of desire (Leonora) or a domineering wife (Remedios).

Alongside these Freudian and developmental traces, the referencing of Leonora as an Amazon positions her obviously as a *mujer fatal* in the context of female deviancy. Earlier in the novel, when Rafael attempts to assert 'la autoridad del sexo' (129) through force, Leonora is cast as castrating female, 'la walkyria dominadora' (88), who fends him off with physical strength. Accompanied by the '¡hojotoho!' of her war cries, her would-be lover is pinned to the floor, 'oprimido por el pie de la viril amazona' (138). Gender roles are reversed, as Leonora physically defeats Rafael in 'una lucha brutal, innoble' (134). The latter pursues Leonora in futile and frustrated desire: an inexperienced 'bebé travieso' (81), and an object of ridicule amongst the townsfolk. Indeed, it is the shameful thought of emasculation if his lover were to leave Alcira alone, leaving him 'triste e inerte como una doncella a la que abandona su amante' (164), that provokes the reassertion of Rafael's Will: 'Él era un hombre' (164). Remedios, the wife chosen for Rafael, is coldly authoritarian, bearing his children, but denying him both affection and passion. The ending of the novel exposes the monotony of his conventional, bourgeois existence, and his marriage to a younger embodiment of his mother in the novel's conclusion. Irony is a dominant aesthetic mode in *Entre naranjos*, as Azorín remarked.[36]

Leonora's deviance from an acceptable feminine (and marriageable) identity situates her obviously within the realm of moral and sexual degeneracy. The figure of the Amazon appeared in numerous turn-of-the-century paintings that were fascinated by the masculine warrior bodies of the primitive woman. As Nicholas Francis Cooke warned in 1870, the virago was 'a sort of mistake of Nature. [...] These masculine women nearly always ally themselves with blanched males, weak physically and mentally'.[37] The depiction of the weak male versus the dominance of Leonora does not entail any genuine reversal of power, since these stereotypes are steeped in late nineteenth-century misogynist discourse. A prominent trope of *fin-de-siècle* European art and literature, the construction of woman as savage or primitive was already present in the analysis of sexual degeneracy in relation to the Amazon in J. J. Bachofen's *Mother Law* (1870). Bachofen traced the movement from the age of promiscuity to matriarchy and finally patriarchy as evidence of the development of society. The violence of the Amazon was identified in this work as 'savage degeneration', in which the female warrior unnaturally dominated the male.[38] This view presupposes the development of human sexuality towards the advanced stage of the white male, with women and non-Europeans signified as a primitive or savage Other who displays traits of sexual degeneracy beyond normative cultural models.

In other words, degeneration was believed to signal a return to primitive forms of evolution, and was exemplified by the figure of the promiscuous and violent female. According to anthropological theory of the second half of the nineteenth century, matriarchy was primitive and patriarchy was evidence of the evolution of civilization, as Freud would later emphasize in his study of the Primal Horde. The 'natural' matriarchy of primitive societies was therefore superseded by civilized patriarchy, in which women were commodified as private property.[39] It is worth noting that Henry Maudsley's works on psychiatric medicine and mental illness were translated into Spanish in the early 1880s, notably *The Pathology of Mind* (1867) and *The Physiology of Mind* (1876).

Alongside the visual objectification of the *femme fatale* as a sexual fantasy, Leonora both underlines and simultaneously resists the male gaze in her role as the Wagnerian Valkyrie, the Amazonian warrior and castrating female who returns Rafael's gaze in a threatening fashion. Viewed almost consistently through Rafael's perspective, Leonora is cast primarily as an object of desire, a perspective underlined by his observation of the album of her past as 'un prodigioso *fetiche*' (89; my italics). When they first meet at the hermitage, Rafael 'devoraba con sus ojos los contornos de aquella mujer' (39). Later, he observes her eating an orange, indicative of the symbiotic relationship between Leonora and the orange groves, as her natural environment to which she retreats to recuperate from the excesses of her past: 'Crujían los gajos entre sus dientes, y el líquido de color de ámbar rezumaba, cayendo a gotas por la comisura de sus labios carnosos y rojos' (92). As Laura Mulvey explains in her study of narrative cinema, 'the woman as icon displayed for the gaze and enjoyment of men, the active controllers of the look, always threatens to evoke the anxiety it originally signified. The male unconscious has two avenues of escape from this castration anxiety': either voyeurism, or 'fetishistic scopophilia', that is 'turning the represented figure itself into a fetish so that it becomes reassuring rather than dangerous'.[40]

In her negation of passive submission to male fantasy, Leonora represents an engulfing threat to the protagonist. Her assertive gaze subjects Rafael to 'una nueva mirada de aquellos ojos verdes; pero esta vez fría, amenazadora, algo así como un relámpago lívido reflejándose en el hielo' (44). Leonora's intense passion is such that it threatens to consume her lover, evidence of the danger of female desire for the weak-willed Rafael: 'Te devoraría [...]. Siento impulsos de comerte, mi cielo, mi rey, mi dios' (154). The representation of Leonora echoes *fin-de-siècle* anxieties about the vampiric or castrating woman. Despite her reversal of the archetypal male gaze, the representation of Leonora is steeped in misogynist iconography of the period, notably the devouring female. Her initial resistance to Rafael's advances is demonstrably referenced according to the primitive or savage identity of the promiscuous and violent female. As the 'virile' or masculine Amazon defeats her male victim, she thereby emasculates him.

The literary representation of violent women was key to the commercial success of late nineteenth-century sensation fiction, not least because they embodied a pronounced trait of moral degeneracy. The threat is not just individual, but derives from a feminine force that gains momentum as a collective body. As Huyssen argues, the illegibility of the *femme fatale* signals 'male fears of an engulfing femininity': 'in Le Bon's study [of the crowd], the male fear of woman and the bourgeois fear of the masses become indistinguishable'.[41] In Blasco's earlier *La barraca*, the crowd acquires a collective identity as a violent mob with primitive emotions, played out notably by women and children. The 'fuente de la Reina' is a noisy gathering point for over thirty young women who go to collect water on Sundays. The women include Batiste's daughter, Roseta, who works at the cigarette factory and becomes the physical target of the hostility of the people of *la huerta* towards the family they marginalize. Significantly, violence against Roseta is perpetuated by the feminine crowd: 'Sin acuerdo ni palabra previos, [...] todas cayeron a un tiempo sobre la hija del Batiste' (97).[42] Roseta escapes dishevelled, scratched and bleeding. The anonymous feminine collective resorts to primitive violence as a response to the economic threat to established hierarchies that Batiste's family represents, thereby perpetuating the cycle of social disruption embodied by the working-class masses.

Physical aggression by the mob eventually culminates in the death of the youngest child of the family, five-year-old Pascualet, at the hands of other boys. In *La barraca* two central scenes of violence against the family employ women and children as the perpetrators of dangerous aggression. These episodes engage closely with contemporary theories of the crowd, in which primitive violence and degeneration are foregrounded in evolutionary terms: in other words, the return to ancestral savagery. Within this anthropological system, infanticide held powerful association with uncivilized, tribal behaviour, a trope that culminates in the neonaticide of *Cañas y barro*. Degenerationism informs feminine violence, sexuality and the failure to protect the youngest members of society in Blasco's Valencian novels, even if the degenerationist paradigm is not fully developed or sustained.

In *Entre naranjos* the crowd represents likewise a primitive force of uncontrolled emotion and instinct, embodying 'el fervor de la muchedumbre' (63). This primitivism is a powerful source of emotional contagion for the whole town, including men, women and children. On the night of the flood, the inhabitants of Alcira struggle against the forces of nature, as their torches illuminate the faces of 'la vociferante multitud. [...] Pasaban por las calles con el estrépito y la violencia de un pueblo amotinado, bajo el continuo gotear del cielo y los chorros de los aleros' (58–59). The masses are characterized by emotion and violence, anticipating the behaviour and psychology of the crowd in the exposition of the degenerate urban masses in Blasco's Madrid novel *La horda*. In *Entre naranjos* the revolutionary potential of the crowd is represented in a rural context. Here the author draws powerfully on the water imagery so common in the nineteenth-century novel in relation to its symbolic referencing of the dissolution between public and private boundaries. During the flood, the natural torrent merges with the human inundation of the street by the impoverished population who seek survival through fervent prayers for deliverance.[43]

There are few critical studies of *Entre naranjos*; existing articles critique the novel in uncertain terms as a combination of turn-of-the-century elements. Theodore A. Sackett, for example, describes the text as 'esta extraña novela, mezcla de naturalismo, modernismo y noventaiochismo'.[44] Cardwell's analysis of the earlier *La barraca* rests on naturalist pre-determinism, in which 'man acts at the bidding of an all-powerful nature'.[45] This paradigm is evidenced to some extent in *Entre naranjos* by the intoxicating and aphrodisiac effect of the orange groves on the two lovers, evidence of the dominant influence of environment. Yet, as we have seen, Rafael's own struggle as the self-indulgent 'príncipe heredero' (34) against the expectations of his family ultimately fails to sustain any coherent deterministic thesis. Indeed, the novel privileges symbolist and impressionist elements alongside a partial adherence to naturalism, not least in the sensual, lyrical and fantastical descriptions of landscape: 'Los naranjos, cubiertos desde el tronco a la cima de blancas florecillas con la nitidez del marfil, parecían árboles de cristal hilado; recordaban a Rafael esos fantásticos paisajes nevados que tiemblan en la esfera de los pisapapeles' (141). Mood and sensation are paramount. Here, as elsewhere, the combination of sense impressions in the many descriptions of the countryside surrounding Alcira — the sounds, the perfume of the orange blossom, the changing light, and panoply of colours — contribute to the pictorial impressionism and 'plasticity' of *Entre naranjos*. The luminous Valencian landscapes of Blasco's novels, in particular the sensual atmosphere of *Entre naranjos*, are reminiscent of Sorolla, who gave one of his paintings the same title. Similarities have also been drawn between the Sorolla's 'quasi-impressionism' and the 'chromacity' of Blasco's *La barraca*.[46]

Beyond the obvious decadence associated with Leonora who seeks 'la belleza hasta en la muerte' (77), and the romantic plot, there is little existing analysis of the often-cited symbolist or *modernista* foundation of *Entre naranjos*. These aspects of the novel — its emphasis on sensuality, impressionism and musical form — are closely allied to the context of degenerationism. When Rafael sets out to rescue Leonora from the flood, her voice is described in synaesthetic terms through its association with visual imagery and colour. He is received in the darkness by 'aquella voz ligeramente burlona, que parecía poblar la obscuridad de mariposas de brillantes colores' (72). The multiple sense impressions that sustain the sentimental theme recall the works of Gabriele d'Annunzio. Throughout the novel, Leonora's sexual appeal is symbolized by the repeated references to her green eyes, cascade of golden hair, and sonorous voice that recall poetic or musical refrains. This technique approximates to some degree a tentative musical structure in *Entre naranjos* through the use of the Wagnerian *leitmotif*, or unending melody: 'los ojos verdes, grandes, luminosos' (40); 'grandes ojos verdes, luminosos y burlones' (99); 'sus verdes ojos brillaban con reflejos metálicos' (134).[47] When Leonora and Rafael finally consummate their relationship amidst the heady atmosphere of spring, the orange groves represent not an all-powerful Nature in which the individual struggles for survival, but 'el triunfo de la Naturaleza y el Amor' (146) in celebration of Wagner. The novel's uncertain adherence to naturalism and inconsistent determinism are tempered by its debt to symbolism and its relation to musical form.

The symbolist musical and poetic refrains of *Entre naranjos* implicitly evoke the principle of aesthetic synthesis, the 'total art-work' that constituted Wagner's ideal. Azorín claimed that *Entre naranjos* was the first Spanish novel to embody 'tan fervorosa exaltación de Wagner [...] en los espléndidos naranjales de Alcira.'[48] This statement refers to the co-existence of musical and visual qualities within the novel's evocation of landscape, as well as the *fin-de-siècle* vogue for the German composer. *Entre naranjos* approximates, albeit to a limited degree, the interconnections between the arts expressed by the symbolists in the late nineteenth century, which in turn drew on the literary or associative synaesthesia of French poetry and particularly Baudelaire's *Les Fleurs du mal* (1857). *Entre naranjos* represents not a wholehearted espousal of hereditary and environment, but a combination of naturalist, impressionist and symbolist elements. Blasco's incipient interest in unconscious impulses in this novel draws on the individual emotional experience and fleeting sensations of symbolism.

Nordau of course listed Richard Wagner as the epitome of the degenerate artists and musicians of the *fin de siècle*. Nordau dubbed Wagner a 'crazed graphomaniac', due to the 'incoherence, fugitive ideation, and a tendency to idiotic punning' in his writings, as well as his display of persecution mania, megalomania and mysticism.[49] For Lombroso, the stubborn adherence to a single idea was symptomatic of graphomania. In *Degeneration*, Nordau parodied Wagner's art-work of the future, which advocated the fusion of arts, through its exaggeration as a poetic drama of music and dance, within a landscape painting framed by an architectural structure. In this sense, the total art-work constituted not progress, but retrogression to a primeval or pre-human stage.[50] Above all, Nordau objected to the 'shameless sensuality' and degenerate sexuality of works such as *Tristan und Isolde* which evidence the 'erotic madness' from which Wagner suffered. In the degenerate, mysticism accompanied eroticism, as evidence of morbid sexuality.[51] If we apply these theories to Blasco's turn-of-the-century Valencian novels, his tragedies of passion invoke a reckless sensuality that was considered symptomatic of degeneration within symbolist and mystical art. They draw too on the endless melody or *leitmotif* of Wagnerian art that was evidence (apparently) of graphomania. *Entre naranjos* thereby conforms to the criteria for decadent or degenerate art that proved so distasteful to Nordau.

What is variously termed the symbolist or lyrical novel was exemplified by Huysmans and Dujardin by the 1880s, when Émile Zola opportunistically declared the repetition in his Rougon-Macquart novels as musical pattern. The genre depended on the discovery of a new form: 'expanding symbols' or the 'accumulation of image and symbolic device', and Dujardin's 'monologue intérieur' that would represent an 'uninterrupted movement of consciousness'.[52] In the symbolist elements of Baroja's *La casa de Aizgorri* and Blasco's *Entre naranjos*, we are of course closer to E. M. Forster's 'pattern and rhythm'[53] than to the 'hieroglyphic density'[54] of high modernism. None the less, an experimental example of interior monologue is evident in the epilogue to *La casa de Aizgorri*. As Mariano's mother dreams of grandchildren, external, objective reality becomes fused with subjective reflection through the internalization of sensory experience. The shouts and gunfire become the evil spirits from which the grandmother must protect her descendants, in a passage reminiscent of fairy-tale.

Each author expressed his perception that art and literature derived from the subconscious in strikingly analogous terms. In 1899 Baroja claimed that 'el arte actual nace de lo subconsciente e impresiona también lo subconsciente' (*OC*, VIII, 851). In a letter, Blasco made a very similar statement in relation to the process of writing: 'Una sensación, una idea, no buscadas, surgidas de los limbos de lo subconsciente, sirven de núcleo, y en torno de ellos se amontonan nuevas observaciones y sensaciones almacenadas en ese mismo subconsciente, sin que uno se haya dado cuenta de ello'.[55]

In conclusion, *La casa de Aizgorri* and *Entre naranjos* reveal a comparable fusion of late nineteenth-century literary modes that demonstrate their inconsistent adherence to naturalism alongside an experimental, incipient interest in contemporaneous approaches to the workings of the psyche. Both novels are rooted in debates about heredity and environment, but they simultaneously distance themselves from determinist precepts through their forays into symbolism and the unconscious mind. In late nineteenth-century Europe, it is well known that naturalist fiction played a significant role in the dissemination and debate of degeneration theories by Maudsley, Morel, Lombroso, Nordau and others. As Seltzer argues, the premise of the naturalist novel is the 'aesthetic of genesis as degeneration'.[56] *La casa de Aizgorri* clearly debates notions about hereditary disease and generational legacies within the

Aizgorri family, a prominent concern of literary naturalism. Alcoholism of course is the dominant focus of Zola's *L'Assommoir* (1877), a novel that famously depicts poverty in the working-class districts of Paris through its deterministic portrait of Gervaise Macquart.[57] Although they express a seemingly naturalist theme, *La casa de Aizgorri* and *Entre naranjos* demonstrate an ambivalent approach to biological and hereditary paradigms. Both novels are strongly informed by naturalism, even if the influence is ultimately a negative one. Alcoholism and insanity are construed not as hereditary problems that Águeda de Aizgorri will pass on to her offspring through a process of degeneration, but instead familial problems that become an obsession in psychological terms through the overbearing role of her father. Similarly, Leonora's position as *femme fatale* is not evidence of inherited pathology, but a consequence of the combined weight of nature and nurture, and more persuasively the memory and re-enactment of sexual trauma in adolescence.

In *La casa de Aizgorri* Baroja addresses the question of biological degeneration in response to his medical interest in hereditary alcoholism, but ultimately subscribes to an intra-psychic development of neurosis in relation to his female protagonist. By contrast, Blasco Ibáñez's invocation of cultural paradigms of degeneration in *Entre naranjos* rests on contemporary concepts of social and moral deviancy that coexist alongside Freudian echoes of psychic trauma. In the next part of the book I turn from rural to urban Spain in order to examine degeneration in two city novels, Baroja's *La busca* and Blasco's *La horda*, and their naturalist representations of early twentieth-century Madrid.

Notes to Chapter 2

1. Sander L. Gilman, 'Sexology, Psychoanalysis, and Degeneration: From a Theory of Race to a Race to Theory', in *Degeneration: The Dark Side of Progress*, ed. by J. Edward Chamberlin and Sander L. Gilman (New York: Columbia University Press, 1985), pp. 72–96 (p. 72).
2. Heinrich Kaan, *Sexual Pathology* (1844); see Gilman, 'Sexology', p. 73.
3. 'Hysteria' (1888), *The Complete Psychological Works of Sigmund Freud*, I, [1886–1899] (1966), p. 52.
4. Gilman, 'Sexology', pp. 81–86.
5. Gilman, 'Sexology', p. 82.
6. Ruth Leys, *Trauma: A Genealogy* (Chicago, IL: University of Chicago Press, 2000), p. 19.
7. Leys, *Trauma*, pp. 19–20.
8. Leys, *Trauma*, pp. 19–21.
9. Morel, 'An analysis of a treatise on the degenerations, physical, intellectual and moral of the human race, and the causes which produce their unhealthy varieties with notes and remarks by the translator Edwin Wing M.D.', *Medical Circular*, 10–12 (1857–58), p. 268. Cited by Pick, *Faces of Degeneration*, p. 41.
10. Escuder, *Locos y anómalos*, p. 43.
11. Pick, *Faces of Degeneration*, p. 52.
12. Longhurst, 'Entre el naturalismo y el simbolismo', p. 21.
13. Pío Baroja, *La casa de Aizgorri*, in *Obras completas*, 1 (1946), pp. 1–49 (p. 21). All subsequent references are to this edition.
14. Sosa-Velasco, *Médicos escritores*, p. 96.
15. Sosa-Velasco, p. 68.
16. Eric T. Carlson, 'Medicine and Degeneration: Theory and Praxis', in *Degeneration: The Dark Side of Progress*, ed. by J. Edward Chamberlin and Sander L. Gilman (New York: Columbia University Press, 1985), pp. 121–44 (p. 122).

17. Carlson, 'Medicine and Degeneration', p. 138.
18. Carlson, 'Medicine and Degeneration', p. 139.
19. Jean Gayon, *Darwinism's Struggle for Survival: Heredity and the Hypothesis of Natural Selection*, trans. by Matthew Cobb (Cambridge: Cambridge University Press, 1998).
20. R. Campos Marín, *Alcoholismo, medicina y sociedad en España (1876–1923)* (Madrid: CSIC, 1997).
21. Rafael Cervera Barat, *Alcoholismo y civilización* (Valencia: A. Cortés, 1896), p. 22. Cited by Campos et al., *Los ilegales*, p. 167.
22. Cervera Barat, *Alcoholismo y civilización*, p. 23.
23. Juan Giné y Partagas, *Tratado teórico-práctico de freno-patología o estudio de las enfermedades mentales* (Madrid: Moya y Plaza, 1876), p. 449.
24. Giné y Partagas, *Tratado teórico-práctico*, p. 221.
25. See Stannard, *Galdós and Medicine*, pp. 112–14.
26. Longhurst, 'Entre el naturalismo y el simbolismo'.
27. Sigmund Freud, 'Mourning and Melancholia', in *Standard Edition*, XIV, 243–58.
28. 'Entre el naturalismo', p. 21.
29. Margaret Homans, 'Representation, Reproduction, and Women's Place in Language', in *Literary Theory: An Anthology*, ed. by Julie Rivkin and Michael Ryan (Oxford: Blackwell, 1998), pp. 650–55 (pp. 652–54).
30. The daughter's Freudian desire for the father is accompanied by the father's own seduction: because he 'refuses to recognize and live out his desire, *he lays down a law that prohibits him from doing so*'. Luce Irigaray, *Speculum of the Other Woman*, trans. by Gillian G. Gill (Ithaca, NY: Cornell University Press, 1985), p. 38.
31. Carlson, 'Medicine and Degeneration', pp. 127–28.
32. Jeremy T. Medina, *The Valencian Novels of Vicente Blasco Ibáñez* (Valencia: Albatros, 1984), p. 80. Existing studies of naturalism include among numerous others the pioneering article by Katherine Reding, 'Blasco Ibáñez and Zola', *Hispania* (USA), 6 (1923), 365–71; Rafael Conte's positioning of Blasco as a successor to naturalism in 'Vicente Blasco Ibáñez: lecciones de un centenario', *Cuadernos Hispanoamericanos*, 72 (1967), 507–20; and Cardwell's *Blasco Ibáñez: La barraca* (London: Grant and Cutler, 1973). More recently the extent of the influence of Zola and French naturalism on Blasco has been assessed by Christopher L. Anderson's *Primitives, Patriarchy, and the Picaresque in Blasco Ibáñez's 'Cañas y barro'* (Potomac, MD: Scripta Humanistica, 1995) and Cardwell's 'Blasco Ibáñez ¿escritor naturalista radical?', in *Vicente Blasco Ibáñez, 1898–1998: la vuelta al siglo de un novelista*, ed. by Joan Oleza and Javier Lluch, 2 vols (Valencia: Biblioteca Valenciana, 2000), I, 349–74.
33. Vicente Blasco Ibáñez, *Entre naranjos* (Buenos Aires: Austral, 1950), p. 83. All subsequent references are to this edition.
34. Anderson, *Primitives, Patriarchy, and the Picaresque*, pp. 148–49.
35. Leys, *Trauma*, p. 20.
36. Azorín praised *Entre naranjos*, in which Blasco 'narra con ímpetu, rapidez y color', and identified its frequent recourse to a refined position of irony. 'Una cuestión', *ABC*, 2 September 1954, p. 31.
37. Nicholas Francis Cooke, *Satan in Society* (Cincinnati, OH: C. F. Vent, 1876 [1870]), p. 280.
38. *Myth, Religion, and Mother Right: Selected Writings of J. J. Bachofen*, trans. by Ralph Manheim (Princeton, NJ: Princeton University Press, 1967), p. 105.
39. Labanyi, *Gender and Modernization*, p. 45.
40. Laura Mulvey, 'Visual Pleasure and Narrative Cinema', in *Literary Theory: An Anthology*, ed. by Julie Rivkin and Michael Ryan (Oxford: Blackwell, 1998), pp. 585–95 (p. 591).
41. Andreas Huyssen, *After the Great Divide: Modernism, Mass Culture, Postmodernism* (Bloomington: Indiana University Press, 1986), pp. 52–53.
42. Vicente Blasco Ibáñez, *La barraca* (Madrid: Alianza, 2004), p. 93.
43. Labanyi, *Gender and Modernization*, p. 110.
44. In 'Blasco Ibáñez y el IV centenario', *Hispania*, 75.4 (October 1992), 897–905 (p. 905).
45. Cardwell, *Blasco Ibáñez: La barraca*, p. 15.
46. Nancy Ann Norris, 'Visión azoriniana del paisaje español', *Cuadernos de Aldeeu*, 1.2–3 (1983), 373–83 (p. 382).

47. An obvious musical analogy is likewise evident in Baroja's use of the *ritornello* in short stories such as 'La melancolía' and 'La muerte y la sombra'.
48. Azorín, 'Wagnerismo', *ABC*, 5 April 1952, p. 3.
49. Nordau, *Degeneration*, pp. 171–73.
50. Nordau, *Degeneration*, pp. 173–76.
51. Nordau, *Degeneration*, pp. 182–88.
52. Melvin J. Friedman, 'The Symbolist Novel: Huysmans to Malraux', in *Modernism: A Guide to European Literature, 1890–1930*, ed. by Malcolm Bradbury and James McFarlane (London: Penguin, 1991), pp. 453–66 (pp. 453–55).
53. E. M. Forster, *Aspects of the Novel* (Harmondsworth: Penguin, 1990), pp. 134–50.
54. Friedman, 'The Symbolist Novel', p. 465.
55. Quoted in Gascó Contell, *Genio y figura de Blasco Ibáñez*, p. 92.
56. Mark Seltzer, 'The Naturalism Machine', in *Sex, Politics, and Science in the Nineteenth-Century Novel*, ed. by Ruth Bernard Yeazell (Baltimore, MD: Johns Hopkins University Press, 1986), p. 133.
57. For a comparison of Baroja and Zola, including *L'Assommoir*, the reader is referred to Otis, *Organic Memory*, pp. 75–92.

PART II

Urban Degeneration in the Naturalist Novel

CHAPTER 3

Prostitution and Criminality in Turn-of-the-Century Madrid: Baroja's *La busca* (1904)

Although not unique to the urban sphere, degenerationism was to a large extent a response to industrialization and the rapid growth of cities in the nineteenth century, and provided a ready narrative with which to diagnose the endemic problems of the metropolis. Degeneration was commonly positioned in relation to urban centres, the outcome of the stress of modern life and the development of new technologies: the flourishing press, greater rapidity in transport, the noise and productivity of industrial society. The critics of modernity and bourgeois supporters of the social status quo configured the urban environment as a locus of degenerative disease, a perspective that was invigorated by Nordau's diagnosis of the toxic environment of the city. In Zola's *La Bête humaine* (1890), the railway system drives the narrative of degeneration, connecting Paris to terminus towns, and providing a metaphor for the unstoppable forces of heredity. Modernization was thereby construed not as progress but instead a powerful channel for degeneration and pathology. Middle-class fears about the public visibility of women in the urban sphere within social discourses of the period, as well as profound concerns about the dangers of prostitution, alcoholic mothers, and the working-class masses, reinforced these retrogressive approaches to the metropolis.

Part II of my book recuperates the parallel trajectories of Baroja and Blasco Ibáñez by analysing their city novels through a new lens. Existing critiques of Baroja's Madrid trilogy *La lucha por la vida* have focused predominantly on the documentary veracity and historical validity of the works.[1] More recently, Carlos-Alex Longhurst has addressed poverty, criminality and marginalization in an article that presents an illuminating comparison of low-life in Baroja's *La busca* and Blasco Ibáñez's *La horda*.[2] I seek to extend this incipient pairing through an original analysis of the relationship to degenerationism evidenced by the two authors' Madrid novels of 1904–05, with a new focus on the literary representation of urban prostitution and the feminine horde. The next two chapters analyse the influence and assimilation of compelling, gendered aspects of degeneration theory in the urban landscapes of *La busca* and *La horda*, alongside a discernible scepticism on the part of both authors towards these received cultural narratives. My readings develop and take forward previous scholarship through their contextualization of the genealogy of gender and degeneration in Baroja's and Blasco's city novels and their specific emphasis on women in turn-of-the-century Madrid.

Each author's representation of the metropolis focuses notably on urban indigence, the primitivism of the masses, and criminality. Each places a particular emphasis on the occupation of public space by women, whether through the exposition of prostitution and criminal anthropology in Baroja's *La busca*, or the violence of the feminine crowd in Blasco's *La horda*. Dominant gendered paradigms of criminal anthropology, social hygiene and bourgeois politics underpin both texts. Neither author, however, assimilates the meta-narratives of degenerationism in uncritical terms. This central section of my book offers an original analysis of the close commonalities between Baroja's and Blasco's Madrid novels through my assessment of each author's contradictory responses to urban degeneration, its relationship to naturalist fiction, and the perceived threat posed by women in the public spaces of the metropolis. Countering Baroja's vocal claims at the time of publication that Blasco had mimicked *La busca* in his own novel *La horda* that appeared the following year, I seek instead to illuminate the common cultural narratives that inform and shape both works. The two novels share significant ground in their social, political, ideological and literary approach to the Spanish metropolis.

Following the evocation of the Basque Country as the setting for early works such as *La casa de Aizgorri*, Baroja turned his attention to naturalist representations of the capital city in *La busca*, the first part of his *La lucha por la vida* trilogy. Dominant contemporary theories of criminal anthropology, both Spanish and European, obviously inform the depiction of the criminal underworld in *La busca*. Cesare Lombroso's well-known treatise *Criminal Woman* (1893) is a particularly pertinent context for Baroja's representation of urban prostitution. In Spain, Bernaldo de Quirós and Llanas Aguilaniedo published their influential *La mala vida en Madrid* in 1901, an autochthonous study of criminology in the capital city. The social and anthropological concerns of *La busca* would later be developed in Baroja's trilogy *La raza* and its final novel *El árbol de la ciencia* through the referencing of biological paradigms of national development.

My purpose in this chapter is to explore the extent to which *La busca* adheres to naturalist and positivist discourses of atavism and criminality through my close focus on prostitution within the novel's representation of the marginalized underworld of Madrid. By the turn of the century, Lombroso's conceptualization of the criminal was still loudly resonant. The Italian brand of criminal anthropology had caught the public imagination and continued to travel with ease across national borders, a momentum sustained despite vociferous scientific opposition to his views. In *La busca*, I contend, Baroja's assimilation of the positivist and deeply misogynist foundations of Lombroso's criminal anthropology is partial but demonstrably incomplete.

The influence of the language of degeneration in Baroja's exposition of social pathologies is noteworthy. However, the novel belies a deep-rooted scepticism towards the certainty of cause and effect upheld by scientific positivism. Both realism and naturalism underscored the assumption that social control was the result of observing and describing society.[3] The scientific neutrality to which Émile Zola optimistically aspired is thereby undermined by the ideological consequences of both the social and literary diagnosis of pathology. Baroja certainly accumulates observed data through the depiction of the urban landscape in *La busca*. By contrast with the attempts of deterministic systems to predict particular social and biological outcomes, however, the novel refuses to offer any consistent formulation of the laws governing the observed facts. Baroja exposes the poverty and degradation of the urban masses in *La busca*, but offers little by way of practical reform.

Despite obvious echoes of atavism in the portrait of urban poverty and prostitution, *La busca* ultimately fails to endorse the anthropological and gendered premises of *Criminal Woman*, or indeed the eugenicist legacy of Lombroso's work. Instead, Baroja's novel of 1904 demonstrates a complex combination of hereditary and environmental factors that places the author's exposition of social and national concerns more convincingly as a successor to Morel and French *dégénérescence* than to Italian criminology. The novel's portrait of the indigent masses in turn-of-the-century Madrid is memorable for its panoramic perspective on the sheer scale of degradation: moral, physical and social. Alcoholism constitutes a particularly potent fuel for endemic corruption. Prostitutes and criminals, however, are more readily portrayed as the victims than the source of poverty and disease. Furthermore the urban landscape of Madrid is as frequently pictorial as it is scientific. In *La busca* there is little evidence of the detachment of the neutral observer or indeed the objective scientific viewpoint sought by Zola's brand of literary naturalism.

Science none the less informs the panorama of pathology in the *barrios bajos* of *La busca*. Baroja's representation of the delinquent and criminal in turn-of-the-century Madrid draws obviously on prominent theories of phrenology and physiognomy that continued to grip the public imagination across much of Western Europe in the late nineteenth century. The character of el Bizco is a straightforward representation of the born criminal, whose innate propensity for amorality and violence is evidenced by cranial and physiognomic features. Of particular interest for my analysis is Lombroso's identification of the 'born' prostitute. It is well-known that his study *Criminal Woman* construed female sexuality as inherently deviant and was a key influence in the cultural and social recourse to 'scientific' evidence in pathologies of the female body put forward by late nineteenth-century discourses.

Lombroso's criminal anthropology offered a diagnosis and a potential cure for ingrained social problems through its dubious foundations in medicine and science. His doctrine was the subject of increasing controversy among doctors and criminologists in the late nineteenth-century, and sustained intensifying critique from foreign scientists from the 1880s onwards. In 1892, Havelock Ellis wrote in a letter that 'nothing too severe can be said of Lombroso's lack of critical judgement and historical insight and accuracy; one forgives it all because he has opened up so many new lines of investigation and set so many good men to work'.[4] Despite the mounting opposition to his theories, their enduring cultural legacy rests on the influence they exerted within the popular imagination both within and beyond Italian borders, and their construction through 'scientific' discourse. In Spain, as across Western Europe, the degenerate criminal was a powerful object of fascination and revulsion in a socio-cultural context. Lombroso had a profound influence on *fin-de-siglo* Spanish intellectuals, as Luis Maristany attests.[5] The impact of his theories on the Spanish naturalist novel was likewise widespread.[6]

Baroja was, of course, well acquainted with Lombroso's work. The library at his house 'Itzea' in Vera de Bidasoa contains a copy of French translations of Lombroso's *L'Homme criminel* and *L'Homme de génie*, as well as Nordau's *Degeneración* in Spanish translation.[7] The references to Lombroso in Baroja's essays are at best equivocal. In relative terms Baroja regarded Lombroso more favourably, for example, than Letamendi, the scientist who attempted to apply mathematics to biology: 'En el sentido del aparato y de la oquedad, no llegaba tampoco a la altura de los Lombroso y de los criminalistas italianos, que dejaron, al menos, datos' (*OC*, VII, 592). Lombroso's criminal anthropology was based on the assumption of empirical evidence and upheld by positivist certainty. Baroja, by contrast, profoundly undermined the belief system of positivism in his fiction and essays through sardonic comments about quack pseudo-science and an ironic approach to *cientifismo*. In *Aventuras, inventos y mixtificaciones de Silvestre Paradox* the accumulation and explanation of observed data as a scientific method is roundly undermined through the mockery of Silvestre's taxidermy and pseudo-scientific systems. For Baroja, Lombroso worked on a system of data, but one that was essentially flawed.

Commonly accepted as the founder of criminal anthropology, Lombroso was among the first theorists to apply scientific methods to the study of crime in which he claimed to have discovered the 'born' criminal. Lombroso's work attempted to match the physical stigmata of degeneration or abnormality with human behaviour on a systematic basis, and drew on influential theories of physiognomy and phrenology. Facial features and physical gestures had already been placed within a typology of deviance and normative cultural signifiers, as nineteenth-century science assimilated earlier studies of physiognomic representation. Most obviously these include the influential *Essays on Physiognomy* by Johann Caspar Lavater.

Lombroso's own work set out to define a criminal typology, based on head shapes and cranial abnormalities in the skulls of criminals. According to Lombroso, these physical deviations were inherited and present from birth, and products of the phenomenon of atavism, the reversion to a primitive stage of evolution. In fact, Lombroso did not distinguish consistently between the concept of atavism (with its Darwinian emphasis on selection and regression) and degeneration in its sociocultural or environmental context, and frequently used the terms interchangeably. French *dégénérescence*, by contrast, drew on the belief in hereditary degeneration, but stressed the profound effects of social pathologies in relation to generational legacies. The proponents of *dégénérescence* pointed to a complex interaction between biological and environmental agency within potent theories of racial decline.

In *L'uomo delinquente* (1876), translated as *Criminal Man* (1891), Lombroso describes the 'nature of the criminal — an atavistic being who reproduces in his person the ferocious instincts of primitive humanity, and the inferior animals':

> Thus were explained anatomically the enormous jaws, high cheek-bones, prominent superciliary arches, solitary lines in the palms, extreme size of the orbits, handle-shaped or sessile ears found in criminals, savages, and apes, insensibility to pain, extremely acute sight, tattooing, excessive idleness, love of orgies, and the irresistible craving for evil for its own sake.[8]

Positivist criminology was an important resource within post-unification Italy and late nineteenth-century national debates. Later, of course, it potently informed fascist rhetoric of the 1920s and 1930s. For Lombroso criminality constituted primitive evidence of nature within a more advanced (or evolved) society. The positivist study of criminology created a science that would defend the state against the unproductive elements of society, namely the criminal and atavist.[9] The eugenicist solution was to remove, contain or eliminate these delinquent individuals in order to prevent their negative influence from continuing to affect the evolution of society.

The relevance of these theories of post-unification Italy to the *fin-de-siglo* Spanish context is complex but extremely compelling. In Spain, as in Italy and elsewhere in Europe, degeneration was a cultural response to formidable social threats in relation to class, economics and gender. In late nineteenth-century Madrid, great disparities in wealth and a rigid class system underpinned the bourgeois fear of the rebellious and impoverished underclass. Working-class women were a primary object of ideological discourses that expressed such middle-class fears because they represented the epitome of the subordinate Other beyond the realm of the private. By occupying a public space through work — in factories, as prostitutes — lower-class women subverted the domestic impetus of the *ángel del hogar* as an ideology of control. The regenerationist agenda of turn-of-the-century Spain is of particular significance in this regard, since it provided momentum for the reinvigoration of cultural recourse to the myths of degeneration. In the wake of the 1898 'Disaster', the social fabric was under threat from events abroad (the loss of the last remnants of Spain's New World Empire) and from within, through the internal divisions represented by communism, anarchism and feminism.

In Spain the interpretation of the Italian positivist school had resounding impact on theories of criminality. As Campos Marín has noted in his study of Spanish psychiatry of this period, in the 1880s and 1890s Lombroso and his disciples propelled degenerationism to an international sphere, by uniting it to the widespread *fin-de-siècle* preoccupation with criminality. The work of Lombroso generated intense debate in Spain among both its proponents and detractors, and was undoubtedly one of the main routes for the assimilation of degenerationist theories from abroad.[10] The dominant influence of Lombroso and Italian criminology was disseminated extensively both within the clinical world of psychiatry and also through popular debate.

It is commonly accepted that regenerationism cannot be understood without reference to degeneration as its corollary. In Spain the 'Disaster' of 1898 led to a widespread examination of national decadence, degeneration and decline. This recourse to biological explanation for the state of the nation emphasized heredity in the proliferation of criminals and individuals suffering from mental illness and abnormalities, with profound implications for psychiatry, social and hygienic medicine.[11] In any case, the concept of decline was inseparable from that of progress. The Darwinian model posited social evolution as the consequence of the survival of those who adapted most successfully to a physical environment. For Herbert Spencer, the environment consisted of the collective 'social state' as well as the physical elements of Darwinism. The welfare state thus posed a serious danger by preserving weak individuals with consequences (disease, mortality, criminality) for future generations.[12] Within degeneration theories, criminals, prostitutes and alcoholics would weaken the social milieu through corruption of healthy individuals.

Baroja's *La lucha por la vida* trilogy was inspired by his experience from 1896 managing the bakery inherited from his maternal aunt, Juana Nessi y Arrola, in Madrid. The first novel of the trilogy, *La busca* follows the fortunes of Manuel Alcázar as he moves around the capital in search of work and the means to meet his basic needs for survival. According to this structuring principle, Baroja depicts the poverty and misery of the lower echelons of society: the beggars, criminals and prostitutes of Madrid. Yet the descriptions of the city and its inhabitants are frequently as pictorial as they are naturalistic. The narrative adopts an intermittently lyrical tone, and Baroja's social criticism is punctuated by painterly renderings of Madrid that demonstrate his literary interest in the use of spatial form. Picasso was fascinated by the work, and began to illustrate its initial serialized publication. The Caro Raggio edition of *La busca*, as with various other novels by Baroja, is illustrated by etchings by Pío's brother, Ricardo Baroja, a painter and engraver.

La busca and *Mala hierba* were published in instalments in *El Globo* (March–May 1903), and then revised substantially for publication in volume form by Fernando Fe (1904).[13] When *La busca* first appeared, critical reception focused particularly on the perceived impersonality of narrative style, its detachment and apparent objectivity.[14] Certainly the narrator makes dubious claims to the role of impartial chronicler of Madrid society through his direct emphasis on 'los deberes del autor, sus deberes de cronista imparcial y verídico' (10). Julio Caro Baroja extends these debatable declarations of objectivity and truthful documentation in his Prologue to the novel, stating that the trilogy does not constitute 'una denuncia pública, sino un documento informativo' (p. xiv). These assertions cannot be accepted uncritically since the author's moral demand for social change is abundantly evident in the trilogy. Although his regenerationist agenda was limited in practical terms, Baroja's early novels document vividly the cultural legacy of a backward and dogmatic Spain. The objects of national critique in his novels of the first decade of the twentieth century include political systems, bourgeois morality and institutions, the Catholic Church, and an anti-progressive society. *La busca*, however, does not propose any applied programme of reform. The trilogy as a whole explores the potential of socialism and anarchism to effect change, but fails to subscribe to the premises of any concrete ideological system.

In *La busca* the protagonist, Manuel Alcázar, acts as a structural device by which

Baroja offers a panorama of the *barrios bajos* of Madrid. Manuel's movements map the poverty and squalor, 'tristeza e incultura' (53) of the poor quarters of the city near the Manzanares. Male violence, immorality and criminality in the urban setting are exposed *par excellence* through the figure of *el Bizco*, the criminal, rapist and thief of the Madrid underworld. Strikingly reminiscent of Lombroso's simian atavist, the character resembles:

> una especie de chimpancé, cuadrado, membrudo, con los brazos largos, las piernas torcidas y las manos enormes y rojas. [...] La cara del *Bizco* producía el interés de un bicharraco extraño o de un tic patológico. La frente estrecha, la nariz roma, los labios abultados, la piel pecosa y el pelo rojo y duro, le daban el aspecto de un mandril grande y rubio. (69)

The physical portrait of *el Bizco* rests particularly on the atavism of the criminal through regression to a state of primitivism and animalism. Likewise, his facial features (reminiscent of the mandrill) are in keeping with Lombroso's physiognomic categorization of the criminal and his ape-like appearance. Physical and moral degeneracy go hand in hand, as *el Bizco*'s violent actions — rape, crime and murder — are documented.

The description above draws obviously on racial distinctions that were fundamental to the myths of degeneration. The racial typologies inherent within Baroja's referencing of criminal degeneracy draw in schematic and highly problematic terms on the erroneous myth of the immoral Negro, and his association within this classification system with the ape. Discourses of criminal degeneration thereby upheld the cultural myth of white Europeans as the epitome of civilization and black people as Other, a typology emphasized by Baroja's description of the atavistic criminal.[15] Compounding these complex issues was the frequent slippage in the use of racial terminology by the proponents of degenerationism to designate variously the human race, anxieties about the future of European nations and racial 'inferiority' or decadence. The referencing of racial paradigms thereby encompassed the perceived threat posed both by the degenerate Other beyond Western borders and the degenerate within.

In the portrait of *el Bizco*'s brutal and instinctive criminality, Baroja's interest in physiognomic classifications that sustained criminal anthropology could hardly be clearer. *El Bizco* is a born criminal, unthinking, unintelligent, ape-like and brutal, and is placed in counterpoint to Vidal, whose intelligence allows him to use criminality as a chosen means of economic sustenance. The passage cited above provides evidence of a relatively straightforward assimilation of the premises of criminal anthropology, through the echoes of Lombroso's categorization of skull shapes, craniology and phrenology in the characterization of *el Bizco*. Elsewhere in *La busca*, however, Baroja's depiction of criminality rests much more strongly on environmental determinism and the social effects of poverty than on hereditary models. This city novel, I suggest, provides evidence of a contradictory process of assimilation and detachment from dominant biological models of generational pathologies in favour of complex environmental interactions, social and familial relationships.

By the turn of the century, of course, Lombroso's theories were already being widely discredited. Opposition to Lombroso's work among criminologists and doctors, which increased from the mid-1880s onwards, was based on critiques of its adherence to biological determinism in the assumed hereditary nature of the criminal type and its posited atavism. These assumptions were anathema to those who argued for the significance of environmental factors in the development of criminal behaviour. As Greenslade argues, 'throughout the period during which the criminal was the object of such professional scrutiny, Lombroso had paradoxically managed to fix the born criminal type into the popular imagination — quite in defiance of the drift of expert opinion and the empirical evidence'.[16] Havelock Ellis's work *The Criminal* (first edition 1890) identified environmental factors in the production of atavistic behaviour in children, women and criminals, who were grouped together as 'primitive peoples': 'The criminal acts like the savage [...] because a simple and incomplete creature must inevitably tend to adopt those simple and incomplete modes of life which are natural to the savage. It is not a real atavism, but mainly, it is probable, only a pseudo-atavism'.[17] Within this discourse, women were classified and defined through deviant behaviour and criminality, as atavistic throwbacks to primeval development. Despite an increasing distancing from Lombroso's criminal anthropology in late nineteenth-century theories of behaviour, essentialist constructions of women as intellectually inferior and primitive persisted.

Lombroso's theories of anthropological criminality extended beyond the nature of the criminal to a pervasive cultural model of deviance and atavism, and encompassed the artist, the genius and the prostitute. His co-authored work with Guglielmo Ferrero, *La donna delinquente, la prostituta e la donna normale* (1893), was translated into English in 1895 as *The Female Offender*, a modification in the emphasis of the original title. This study famously construed female sexuality as deviant and as delinquent. The arguments were illustrated by visual representations of physical deformity and anomalies in numerous portraits of women. In their well-known introduction to *Criminal Woman*, Rafter and Gibson argue that the book's ongoing dominance 'led to the long-term emphasis on female crime as biological in nature. It led, as well, to a particularly heavy stress on sexual and psychological factors in explanations of female crime'.[18] In fact, the concept of deviance in *La donna delinquente* does not just denote criminal women, but encompasses all women in the classification of pathology. Likewise, the prostitute (a common example of the female born criminal) is a term that variously denotes women who are paid for sex, but at other times refers to married women who commit adultery. For Lombroso, prostitution denoted a return to a primitive stage of evolution and was the female equivalent of male criminality. The term prostitute thereby becomes a rhetorical device, indicating all women considered to be beyond the definition of 'normality'.

In Lombroso's study, female offenders are classified into two main groups: criminals and prostitutes, and a number of secondary categories, including suicides, insane criminals and hysterical offenders. At the crux of Lombroso's argument is the idea that the lower number of female criminals than male is an additional sign of women's inferior evolution. Women are therefore classed as 'big children' with latent 'evil tendencies'.[19] Atavistically, the female criminal is — according to this study — nearer to her primitive origin than men, but the relative scarcity of anomalies is (apparently) due to the lesser rate of variations than in the male. Female born criminals are exceptions, and are created by living conditions which have 'brought out' the innate immorality of all women, 'even the normal ones' (225).

The longevity of Lombroso's theories about female criminality may be explained through their appeal to the deeply ingrained association of women with nature and biology, the equation of female deviance and sexuality, and perhaps most powerful of all, his scientific underpinning of these assumptions.[20] For Lombroso, all women represent deviation from the male, civilized norm. The clear distancing of Baroja's representations of women in *La busca* from the innately criminal and deviant conceptualization of prostitution in Lombroso is particularly significant for our understanding of gendered paradigms in the novel. Although there are undeniable echoes of atavism, I propose that Baroja's depiction of prostitutes does not rest in any consistent way on the notion of innate vice or moral insanity. Instead, for Baroja environmental factors and economic necessity are paramount. *La busca* puts forward, none the less, a moral and ideological perspective that goes well beyond a neutral stance of documentation or exposition of the indigent masses of the capital, and certainly does not remain impartial.

The extent to which Baroja's novel sustains or conversely contradicts the dominant referencing of poverty within contemporary social, political and hygienic discourses as the source of disease and contamination is revealing. Neo-Malthusian arguments for population limitation were loudly promoted by certain strands of the anarchist movement during this period in Spain, as evidenced by anarchist reviews such as the Catalan journal *Salud y Fuerza* (1904–14). Despite Baroja's sympathy for anarchist ideals, however, the author would conclude that socialism and anarchism could offer little by way of practical reform. In his essay 'Contra la democracia' (1899), Baroja associated liberty with conscience, and socialism with stomachs (*OC*, VIII, 864). The author expressed suspicion of the masses, and depicted the indigent hordes of Madrid in *La busca* as a breeding ground for crime and disease. However, he was also sceptical about the route to reforming these problems through anarchism or socialism. *La busca* does not in any case place responsibility for the symptoms of poverty on the lowest echelons of society and neither does it proffer a eugenicist perspective for containing, limiting or eliminating social problems. Positivist solutions for reform are not the aim of Baroja's urban exposition.

The boarding house of Doña Casiana, which is only one step removed from the status of the neighbouring brothel, provides detailed scope for Baroja's exposure of prostitution in the daily struggle for economic survival in *La busca*. The most obvious example is the illicit occupation of Irene, who is only fifteen or sixteen years old when she becomes pregnant through her work as a prostitute. This activity provides meagre support for herself and her grandmother. The incident causes squalid comedy at Irene's expense among the lodgers at the boarding house, and ends with a back-street abortion. The prostitute's moral and physical damage is patched up as she reverts to an irreparably squalid model of femininity.

The narrator adopts a characteristically ironic tone towards Irene's display of feminine abjection. The priest comments that 'tiene cara de infanticida' (36); the narrator observes that she dances *sevillanas* 'con menos gracia que un albañil' (37). These voices of moral conservatism are sardonic rather than sententious. The root causes of her predicament include a lack of education and a family model of social degradation (one that is learnt not inherited) in the depiction of three generations of prostitutes: the former courtesan, Doña Violante, her daughter Celia and granddaughter Irene. The description of the room shared by the three women revels in naturalist squalor, dirt and unhygienic smells: 'entre la falta de aire y la mezcolanza de olores que allí había, se formaba un tufo capaz de marear a un buey' (33). Here, the narrative of *La busca* sustains — albeit fleetingly — the dominant association in public health discourses of the late nineteenth century between prostitution and foul odours, between physical and moral squalor. The prostitute was frequently construed during this period as a primary source of degeneration and a pressing object in the drive for social sanitation. Baroja's own interest, however, remains personalized and individualized. Irene's sexual history is the object of ironic description, rather than a case study of collective moral reform or urban sanitation.

Following the expansion of the capital in the second half of the nineteenth century, by the turn of the twentieth century prostitution in Madrid had reached proportions of overwhelming concern to social commentators and health experts. This social question was of particular interest to hygienists and criminologists, as well as prominent novelists such as Galdós. In 1899, there were over 2000 official prostitutes registered in Madrid. The figures for clandestine prostitution in the city, however, were much higher, and were estimated in 1900 to be around 15,000.[21] In 1900, 133 deaths from syphilis were recorded in the Spanish capital.[22] As Bernaldo de Quirós and Llanas Aguilaniedo indicated in 1901, prostitution was 'una de las labores más propias del sexo femenino' undertaken by 'un número considerable de mujeres de todas las edades, de todos los estados, de todas las profesiones y de todas las clases de la sociedad'.[23] Clandestine prostitution included servants and factory workers whose pay was insufficient, and ranged across social classes, including middle-class women.

One of the fundamental contentions of Lombroso's work on female criminality is the idea of the 'born' prostitute. Most pertinently, Lombroso ascribes the motivation for prostitution to psychology and innate immorality, rather than socio-economic factors. According to this view, prostitution originates psychologically, 'not in lust but moral insanity' (213). Although poverty figures in the list of identified causes of prostitution, for Lombroso the specific causes are 'only apparent, with the fundamental cause lying in individual degeneration'. He concludes that 'prostitution is nothing more than the female form of criminality' (221). According to his study, the immediate causes of prostitution are secondary to the innate immorality of the women, and include: poverty; the death of parents or abandonment; to support aged or infirm parents; to raise orphaned siblings; widows or abandoned women, trying to raise a numerous family; servants seduced and fired by employers; concubines who have lost their lovers and have no other means.[24] Lombroso adds the lack of maternal feeling, theft, blackmail and alcoholism to the list of the vices of the 'born' prostitute.

According to Lombroso's study, economic necessity and social factors were profoundly subordinate to women's innate tendency to vice. As evidence of the lure of the pathological, for Lombroso prostitution constituted a refusal to work for a living, a common concept also among health experts in the late nineteenth century. Honourable work represented self-discipline, order and virtue. By contrast, vice was associated with idleness and aversion to labour. Employment, then, was a source of reform for the idle and the criminal, including fallen women. In 1901 the Spanish criminologists Bernaldo de Quirós and Llanas Aguilaniedo echoed Lombroso's view of innate apathy as the common denominator among prostitutes, asserting that: 'Todos los autores que han estudiado a las mujeres dedicadas a este triste oficio, afirman que los hábitos psicológicos en ellas son la pereza, el ocio, el horror a toda clase de trabajo metódico y continuado, la apatía más completa'.[25]

In the wake of industrialization and urbanization, discourses on public hygiene focused particularly on the spread of venereal disease, notably syphilis. This disease provoked fear in the collective public sphere, beyond the realm of the private and individual. Syphilis, then, became a symbol of the degenerate sexuality of the prostitute and the contamination of wider society through her innate deviance. Contemporaneous discourses about the prostitute (including that of Lombroso) centred on the notion of inherited degeneracy, a position supported to some extent by Freud's view of inherited nature in sexuality. Deviant women, it was thought, had an inherent disposition for prostitution that was not genuinely caused — but merely provoked — by severe economic need to provide for themselves, their families and children.[26]

In public health discourses the prostitute was identified as the source of disease, and was represented frequently through images of filth, decomposing waste, and drains, as Teresa Fuentes has shown.[27] Through her role in the spread of vice, as a source of both physical and moral infection, the prostitute was considered to pose a threat to the social fabric. Venereal diseases were commonly perceived during this period as the consequence of sexual deviance or transgression, in other words, the result of innate immorality. In the *Revista de España*, Philiph Hauser advised in 1884 that syphilis was 'uno de los agentes debilitantes y degenerativos de la raza humana'.[28] Hauser was one of many contemporary hygienists to view syphilis as one of the primary causes of racial degeneration, and believed that it could both be passed on through direct contact and inherited. The battle against syphilis undertaken by social medicine placed at stake the very evolution of the human race.

In the late nineteenth century, in the light of urban epidemics and cholera infections, prostitution was construed by social commentators in Spain as a 'social plague, a torrent of flooding waters that invades society, and a malignant virus secretly undermining generation after generation'.[29] In other words, pathological definitions of the female body and sexuality construed the prostitute as a source of plague, infection and filth. In their turn-of-the-century study of criminality *La mala vida en Madrid*, Bernaldo de Quirós and Llanas Aguilaniedo configured the female legions of prostitutes in relation to germ theory. This volume, incidentally, was republished with illustrations by Ricardo Baroja.[30] The armies of female nightworkers were depicted as an 'inmenso cultivo de microbios o de bacterias patógenas ... suspendido en un ambiente saturado de estímulos sexuales y que entonces aparece como el polvo que flota en el ambiente cuando le cruza, rasgándole, un rayo de luz solar'.[31] According to turn-of-the-century criminology and social hygiene in Spain, prostitutes represented a widespread source of infection of society and urban space. The female body becomes the site of decomposition, one that gives birth to a degenerate legacy, a process that reflects contemporary anxieties about human reproduction, moral and biological decline in a national context. More specifically, urban women were considered susceptible to promiscuity and prostitution due to the seductive appeal of material goods.

Speaking of Paris, Walter Benjamin famously remarked that the modern city is a public space in which people and consumer goods become available as a spectacle.[32] The modern city is thus characterized by visual display, exemplified by the public visibility of the prostitute. Galdós's *La desheredada* and *La de Bringas* posit prostitution and adultery as symbols of excessive consumerism.[33] Ángel Pulido's advice to women in his manual *Bosquejos médico-sociales para la mujer* (1876) denoted the health risk posed by prostitution as 'la publicidad del pecado', the public visibility of wrongdoing.[34] Labanyi's analysis of *La desheredada* rests on its representation of excess and waste. The figure of the prostitute is 'a luxury in that she represents surplus sexuality, and a waste-disposal unit in that contemporary medical theory — obsessed with the healthy circulation of fluids in the body [...] insisted on the need for the efficient elimination of surplus flow, including semen, which if blocked would rot and pollute the system'.[35] According to this model, prostitution became associated with sewage systems. For Pulido, prostitution was a 'llaga depuratoria del organismo social'.[36] The referencing of the margins of the city in *La desheredada* anticipates the urban periphery of Blasco's *La horda* in which the working classes depend on recycling the refuse of consumer society. By contrast to the prostitute who recycles and endlessly trades the same commodity of her body through her receipt of bodily fluids, the rag-and-bone man represents the productive recycling of society's consumer cast-offs. Both represent 'efficient drains [...] for they recycle the national wealth'.[37]

In Baroja's trilogy, the numerous metaphors of filth, rubbish and disease are allied not just to prostitution but to a wider portrait of criminality and poverty that emphasizes female degradation. References to sewage, rubbish and foul odours abound, as demonstrated by the description of the 'barrio de las Injurias' in *Mala hierba* as an environment of human waste: 'Era una basura humana, envuelta en guiñapos, entumecida por el frío y la humedad, la que vomitaba aquel barrio infecto. Era la herpe, la lacra, el color amarillo de la terciana, el párpado retraído, todos los estigmas de la enfermedad y de la miseria' (*OC*, I, 461). By the time Baroja published *El árbol de la ciencia* in 1911, he applied metaphors of sanitation much more specifically to prostitution and the treatment of syphilis, tropes that are repeated through the often indiscriminate transposition of semi-autobiographical material from his novel back to autobiography in his Memoirs. In *Desde la última vuelta del camino: familia, infancia y juventud* (written in the 1940s), Baroja describes the notorious San Juan de Dios hospital as a human dunghill. This well-known Madrid institution that treated women infected with syphilis is a rotten environment of disease: 'Ver tanta desdichada sin hogar, abandonada en una sala negra, en un estercolero humano, comprobar y evidenciar la podredumbre que acompaña la vida sexual, hizo en mí una angustiosa impresión' (*OC*, VII, 596). Despite the author's compassionate tone, the passage none the less sustains the common association during this period between syphilis, prostitution and social infection.

In the context of the bourgeois agenda of contemporary hygienists to sanitize the city through the control of prostitutes, Baroja's *La busca* exposes the scale of poverty and degradation evident in the *barrios bajos* of Madrid. At the mercy of extreme poverty, disease and alcohol, prostitution is not construed by Baroja as an innately criminal (or indeed, sexually deviant) activity on the part of the women, but primarily a means for economic survival in an environment where few alternatives are fostered. The possibilities of economic sustenance for working-class women were limited predominantly to domestic service, begging and prostitution, feminine occupations that are all documented in the novel's panorama of Madrid's poor. Even domestic service, an honourable alternative, is portrayed in relentless terms through *la Petra*'s exhausting physical labour at the boarding house and her lonely death in humble circumstances. As seamstresses, *la Justa* and *la Salomé* demonstrate a further typical occupation for working-class women. In the second part of the trilogy, *Mala hierba*, *la Justa* becomes a prostitute following rape, demonstrating the pervasive moral corruption of the urban environment.

In the numerous depictions of prostitutes in *La busca* there are salient echoes of atavism and degenerationism, and an emphasis both on hereditary and environmental factors. The 'golfas viejas' embody the physical ravages of a lifetime of prostitution. The primitive animalistic state and expression of *la Paloma* is produced by her forty-year entrapment in poverty and prostitution. The group of four adolescent prostitutes, *la Mellá, la Goya, la Rabanitos* and *la Engracia*, all aged between thirteen and eighteen, present various forms of physical degradation and deformity: 'De las cuatro muchachas la más fea era la *Mellá*; con su cabeza gorda y disforme, los ojos negros, la boca grande con los dientes rotos, el cuerpo rechoncho, parecía la bufona de una antigua princesa' (242). *La Mellá* arguably displays the physiognomy and physical stigmata of degeneration, and the wayward sexuality of criminal women, demonstrated by her uneven head shape, broken teeth and thickset, dwarfish body. Furthermore, the atavistic characteristics of the four prostitutes are clearly demonstrated by their incorrect (primitive) use of grammar: 'Hablaban todas de manera tosca; decían *veniría, saliría, quedría*; en ellas el lenguaje saltaba hacia atrás en curiosa regresión atávica' (241). Baroja's description overtly echoes the assumptions of criminal anthropology that the prostitute bears a strong atavistic resemblance to the primitive woman.

The novel does not directly analyse the causes of prostitution, but the author's position in *La busca* is far from neutral. Alongside the referencing of atavism and physical anomalies which accompany moral corruption in the representation of these women, the narrative highlights above all social determinants: poverty, lack of education and opportunities, and a milieu of endemic degradation. Physical deformities and disease are both the cause and the consequence of prostitution. *La Rabanitos* is described as physically and emotionally infantile and her growth is stunted, she has blue patches around her mouth and nose, her body is thin and diseased, and she coughs up blood. This is a common symptom of tuberculosis, one of the commonly accepted causes — alongside syphilis and alcoholism — of degeneration. The majority of the women demonstrate a moral corruption that is the product of their degradation and vulnerability. Whether this is innate or acquired is not the primary object of Baroja's urban exposition. The narrative evidence, however, points overwhelmingly to the social and environmental determinants in the formation of young prostitutes, and the inability of women to escape the cycle of poverty.

La Engracia is characterized as worldly and cynical; she lacks intelligence and education, and her language is described as pornographic. Her moral code represents feminine abjection or monstrosity: 'hablaba poco, y cuando hablaba era para decir algo muy bestial y muy sucio, algo de un cinismo y de una pornografía complicada. Tenía la imaginación monstruosa y fecunda' (244). She became a prostitute at the age of nine, and observes that she earned more money as a child prostitute than as an adolescent. In this respect she embodies the sexual precocity of Lombroso's criminal woman, who — despite a lack of interest in sex — turns to the profession of prostitution at an early age due to an (apparently) innate propensity for vice. Yet Baroja's interest in *La busca* focuses abundantly on examples of social marginalization and neglect, as well as the illiteracy and lack of education that sustain both poverty and prostitution. These elements are awarded much more attention than any reinforcement of a born predisposition to vice. Once again we find a direct engagement with social discourses of poverty of the period with a particular focus on prostitution and the female body, and once again Baroja's approach is to identify and expose social problems and their consequences for the individual. In the case of *la Paloma*, the experience of sexual degradation has produced a monster. Her language is bestial and her face expresses emotion in animalistic terms: 'sus ojos, negros y brillantes, tenían expresión de melancolía puramente animal' (243–44). In *La busca* deterministic models are evoked through the interaction between heredity and environment, between biology and the urban milieu. However, the novel fails to sustain the biological premises of degeneration and the inevitable decline of the nation through hereditary legacies alone.

Like poverty, prostitution is portrayed as a social disease in *La busca*. In this context, Baroja's novel echoes to some extent the observation of Austrian doctor, Philiph Hauser, in relation to social medicine in Madrid at the turn of the century: 'La prostitución es una enfermedad social que participa de los defectos de la organización de la sociedad en que vive y a expensas de la que se nutre'.[38] We might distinguish here between the individual prostitute and the collective social role of prostitution. *La busca*, however, does not overtly condemn the prostitute as a social parasite or source of corruption, although her role in the spread of disease is undeniable. For Baroja, the poverty-stricken masses and the legions of prostitutes are the embodiment rather than the root cause of urban disease: social, moral and physical. By 1911, the social ills of the capital city would be evoked even more forcefully in Baroja's representation of prostitution and social medicine in *El árbol de la ciencia*. Even here, though, the author's vision would remain agnostic and metaphorical rather than absolute.

The concept of eugenics, a term coined by Francis Galton in 1883, in its relation to population control and the reproduction of the poor sectors of society at the turn of the century is a pertinent context for *La busca*. The high rates of disease among the poverty-stricken masses and the city's prostitutes are the central focus of the novel. Gregorio Marañón's later study of biology and feminism in 1920 discussed high rates of infant mortality through recourse to biological essentialism, in a statement that echoes some of the social problems raised by Baroja's panorama of the city in *La busca*: 'Casi todos estos hijos numerosos desaparecen antes de ser hombres o mujeres útiles, porque la madre no ha podido engendrarlos fuertes, ni cuidarles luego su debilidad o sus enfermedades; porque la escasez del hogar no alcanza a alimentarles suficientemente; porque el Estado, en fin, no suple con una acción protectora la miseria familiar'.[39] The title of Baroja's trilogy, *La lucha por la vida*, provides an obviously Spencerian reference to natural selection. *La busca* places the pathological body, its reproduction and degradation, at the heart of this struggle for life.[40]

The legal regulation of prostitution, enshrined in the Reglamento of 1865, was accompanied by a broader range of reformatory practices, including institutions for the regeneration of prostitutes, and philanthropy. The regulation of prostitutes is alluded to fleetingly in *La busca* through the women's fear of being sent by the Guardia Civil to the 'Convento de las Trinitarias', officially the Asilo de la Santísima Trinidad. In turn-of-the-century Madrid there were a number of institutions for fallen women, many of which employed disciplinarian practices to educate and reform prostitutes. In Baroja's novel, the four adolescent prostitutes accept the exchange of sex for economic survival because they fear the alternative of the convent as a means of social reform. This institution is a futile punishment for prostitution because the adolescent prostitutes regard abandonment in the street perversely as a form of freedom. In *La busca*, the convent is briefly represented as a means of disciplinarian social control and regulation of the prostitutes' wayward sexuality. In practice, the disciplinary techniques of such reformatory institutions were founded on the instilment of a work ethic, and particularly the skills required for domestic service, in other words, accepted feminine roles. Ironically, the assumed 'innate' immorality of prostitutes could therefore be corrected, in theory, through social reformatory practices. This environmental solution for a hereditary problem provides an interesting contradiction in dominant bourgeois ideology, as Fuentes notes.[41] In other words, prostitutes — like the poor — were condemned for embodying the conditions of degradation to which society abandoned them. Innate vice was a convenient narrative by which middle-class morality could judge the working classes as a marginalized and dangerous Other.

Within bourgeois ideologies, women were not just perceived as a source of vice but conversely as the domestic guardians of morality and social stability according to their identity as the *ángel del hogar*. This moral stance was closely intertwined in the late nineteenth century with hygienic discourses that commented on sanitation and prostitution, poverty and alcoholism. In this context, the environmental vulnerability of children to the physical and moral degradation of their parents and the community into which they have been born is carefully underscored by Baroja. At the Casa del Cabrero (a group of lowly hovels) the degenerate environment is powerfully evoked. This community is dominated by alcohol and criminality, of which women and children are the principal victims (rather than the source) of degenerate crime. As the men and women smoke and sleep half-dressed, the children are left to fend for themselves in a physically, sexually and morally dangerous milieu. *El Bizco* boasts openly that he has raped some of the pre-adolescent girls of the neighbourhood. Social environment, rather than atavism, is the most significant factor in Baroja's exposition of urban pathologies and generational legacies.

At the 'taberna de la Blasa' the ageing prostitutes are accompanied by their degenerate offspring in a community that feeds the masses with more alcohol:

> Entre la fila de viejas había algunas chiquillas de trece a catorce años, monstruosas, deformes, con los ojos legañosos; una de ellas tenía la nariz carcomida completamente, y en su lugar, un agujero como una llaga; otra era hidrocéfala, con el cuello muy delgado, y parecía que al menor movimiento se le iba a caer la cabeza de los hombros. (113)

These adolescent girls bear the physical marks of parental alcoholism in their deformities and bleary eyes. One has a missing nose; one is hydrocephalic and can barely hold her head up. In this context, it is impossible not to question the assertion of Julio Caro Baroja that the novel offers a 'documento informativo' rather than constituting a 'denuncia pública'. Baroja's portrait of urban low-life in *La busca* is quite obviously not limited to a stance of detached neutrality. Instead, the novel openly represents the moral and physical degradation of the poverty-stricken lower-class masses, and their vulnerability to corruption and disease. Despite the echoes of atavism and anthropology, Baroja's primary interest in the novel is an exposition of environmental squalor, the city's underbelly of degradation, criminality and corruption. The obvious subtext of the novel is the abandonment of the lower classes by society and the state. As a clinician, Baroja does not propose a socio-political remedy for this situation, but instead presents a damning portrait of disease in the capital city: physical, moral and national.

The prostitute *la Paloma* holds a thin and pale child three or four years old, the damage to whose nervous system is demonstrated by his constant blinking, and to whom she gives a glass of brandy. Within this marginalized environment of poverty and prostitution, alcohol is omnipresent. The effects of alcohol wreak damage both within the womb and through the environmental normalization of the consumption of brandy by a small child. Baroja starkly exposes alcoholism as a prevalent source of physical and mental damage for the poverty-stricken masses, and an endemic problem among the urban poor. The effects of alcoholism and generational damage, more frequently and convincingly environmental than hereditary, are documented throughout *La busca*. At the tavern, *el Pastiri* exemplifies the nefarious effects of alcohol through his mutism (or 'afonía'), one of the common symptoms of hysteria in the late nineteenth century. The ageing beggar, *la Muerte*, is frequently observed in a state of drunken delirium and embodies numerous physical ravages of alcoholism.

The momentum of degenerationism was inextricably bound to urbanization in nineteenth-century Spain as across Europe and, with the expansion of cities, gained new credibility at the moment at which criminological atavism was losing its legitimacy. Late nineteenth-century French theories of degeneration posited the assumption of hereditary alcoholism and, through the explanation of social pathologies, the eventual sterility and extinction of the 'race' or nation. This terminology placed at stake specifically the future of Western Europeans. Both Morel and Lombroso believed that urban life in the industrial age was leading to physical and moral decline. For Nordau, the progress of civilization was leading to greater 'effort of the nervous system and a wearing of tissue', in other words an 'enormous increase in organic expenditure', and therefore the fatigue and exhaustion of the human body.[42] Following Morel's earlier doctrine, in 1895 the French doctor Legrain identified 'the slow but fatal brutalization of the individual; intellectual and physical sterilization of the race with its social consequences: the lowering of the intellectual level and depopulation, indubitable causes of the decline of civilized nations'.[43] Morel's *Traité des dégénérescences* had already identified inherited patterns of degeneration in relation to deviations from normality, and incorporated a vast range of physical and moral 'abnormalities'. For Morel, *dégénérescence* indicated pathological transformations both in individuals (in physical and moral terms) and society. This model was drawn from the biologist Jean Baptiste Lamarck, in which changes in heredity followed adaptation to conditions in the environment.

Within degenerationism and social medicine, French theories of alcoholism were highly influential in Spain during the *fin de siglo*, as Campos et al. have demonstrated.[44] Through the distressing appearance of the prostitutes' degenerate offspring in *La busca*, Baroja underscores the interaction between biology and the urban milieu. This combination is much more closely aligned with the findings of Morel and French *dégénérescence*, and the complex interactions between heredity and environment, than with Italian criminal anthropology. The purpose of my argument in favour of these commonalities, however, is not to suggest the predominance of a direct influence by one particular set of ideas on Baroja. Instead, the potent traces of degenerationism in *La busca* indicate the author's interest in competing scientific theories by the turn of the century. The stark panorama of the novel is perhaps more straightforward. As a former physician, for Baroja the symptoms of poverty and degeneration in the urban environment were as tangible as they were theoretical, and of immediate concern for the nation's collective health and its future.

El Corralón becomes a microcosm of the city, in which poverty, vice and alcoholism are exposed in an indictment of the deterministic consequences of an environment of mass indigence. In a community defined by squalor and hunger, a full spectrum of poverty is visible. The women work harder than their male counterparts, they are unkempt and constantly angry, whilst the men — 'entontecidos y bestiales' (82) — spend all their earnings on alcohol. Within this febrile microcosm of poverty, hunger and alcoholism, theft and prostitution are added to the long list of different means to survive 'la eterna e irremediable miseria' (80). Poverty is not simply a state but becomes a psychology of apathy and passive resignation for the masses who have no hope of salvation. Even this community, however, is one step removed from the abject poverty of the men, women and barefoot children who beg at the Corte de los Milagros. Here Baroja ironizes the ineffective charity of the Doctrina, where the nuns distribute sheets to the beggars and paupers of the capital, a futile gesture towards those who are near starvation. The novel references the premises of hereditary determinism and hereditary alcoholism intermittently, but not convincingly. Instead Baroja's depiction of the cycle of poverty rests predominantly on an understanding of social and environmental influence, not biological essentialism. In short, *La busca* exposes the stark realities of mass indigence in the Spanish capital, but fails to condemn its victims. The institutions that claim to help the vulnerable members of society — the hospital and the convent — are ineffective. If environment is the principal cause, then the problems of the metropolis are endemic but not intractable. The novel's conclusion suggests that the remedy lies not in positivist systems, but instead the individual's conformity to middle-class values.

The metaphors of sanitation that recur throughout the description of the poor districts of Madrid in *La busca* culminate in Manuel Alcázar's incipient regeneration at the end of the novel. The protagonist sees himself as part of the detritus expelled from the city: 'aquella tierra, formada por el aluvión diario de los vertederos; aquella tierra [...] le parecía a Manuel un lugar a propósito para él, residuo también desechado de la vida urbana' (256). His symbiotic relationship with the urban landscape becomes a metaphor for his path towards salvation and his dreams of modest resolution through work, a humble home, and a wife who loves him. Influenced by the common sense of the intellectual rag-and-bone man, Señor Custodio, and his daughter *la Justa*, the protagonist's rehabilitation into society commences through his renewed interest in productivity and normativity. By the end of the novel, Manuel envisions his reincorporation into society through his desire for a traditional family model and economic productivity. The weak-willed protagonist, an *abúlico* with a disinclination for work, is now revived through the promise of social stability and the rejection of criminal activity. Eventually, then, it is Manuel Alcázar and not the prostitutes of *La busca* who is rehabilitated through a model of honest work and humble living. The narrative effects the reform of the male protagonist, rather than the deviant female body and mind of the prostitute. In other words, Manuel's rehabilitation takes place through a process of self-reform of the petty criminal.

By the end of the trilogy, Manuel finds refuge (both physical and symbolic) in the arms of *la Salvadora* and his work as a printer. The reform — indeed regeneration — of the delinquent and degenerate criminal is achieved through conventional bourgeois solutions of marriage and honest work. In any case, Manuel's regeneration provides evidence that environmental corruption is not an inevitable marker of degeneration: apathy and petty criminality are both resolved at least on an individual and symbolic scale. Neither heredity nor milieu constitutes the sole predictor of human behaviour and social outcomes.

The exposure of poverty and human degradation in *La busca* is punctuated and to some extent alleviated by the novel's salient pictorialism. When Manuel approaches Madrid, his emotional reaction of fear is accompanied by a painterly description of the cityscape. A bloodshot sunset illuminates Manuel's passage through the poor and sordid districts of the suburbs as the train draws in to the Estación de Mediodía: 'un crepúsculo rojo esclarecía el cielo, inyectado de sangre como la pupila de un monstruo; [...] pasaba por delante de las barriadas pobres y de casas sórdidas' (21). Baroja avoids the typology, categorization and claims to scientific detachment of both Italian criminal anthropology and Zola's brand of naturalism.[45] Pointing to the 'graphic, almost pictorial language' of Baroja's *La busca* and Blasco's *Cañas y barro*, Longhurst underscores both authors' departure from naturalism on the basis that the root causes of these 'harsh environments' are not explained.[46] Similarly, despite the obvious overtones of Baroja's title *La lucha por la vida*, the trilogy does not demonstrate a straightforward or reductive adherence to the premises of evolutionary theory.

Baroja's descriptions of the poor sectors of Madrid society stem from direct observation through his work at the family bakery in the Calle de la Misericordia which adjoined the Convento de las Descalzas Reales. The author's portrait of the Madrid underworld was based on his empirical observation of the city's inhabitants and poor districts. However, his interest in urban low-life was also inspired by literary influences in Spain and beyond. These include his enthusiasm for Charles Dickens' famous depictions of London and Eugenie Sue's Paris in the *feuilletons*.

To conclude, *La busca* provides a stark description of poverty, social degradation and disease in early twentieth-century Spain. The implicit underpinning by the ideas of French *dégénérescence* (Morel, Legrain) accompanies the echoes of autochthonous discourses of public hygiene in Spain, and their focus on prostitution, alcoholism and poverty in the capital city. In *La busca* Manuel Alcázar serves as structural device, inconsistent moral barometer, and participant in petty criminality, before he is expelled to the outskirts as moral waste in need of social rehabilitation. In the second half of the nineteenth century in Europe, degeneration came to be seen not as a consequence of poverty, 'but as a self-reproducing force; not the effect but the cause of crime, destitution and disease'.[47] Baroja both draws on these cultural myths and resists subscribing to this paradigm through his exposure of environmental determinants in poverty, disease, criminality and prostitution in turn-of-the-century Madrid. *La busca* exposes the shortcomings of society that creates squalid conditions for the working classes to inhabit, and then condemns them for embodying this squalor. I now turn to Blasco's panorama of the social disorder of the urban masses in *La horda* through my focus on crowd theory and the national question in Spain, Blasco's ardent Republicanism and democratic principles. I do so in order to compare the multiple engagements with naturalism and degenerationism in Baroja's *La busca* and Blasco's Madrid novel of 1905.

Notes to Chapter 3

1. Herbert Ramsden, *Baroja: La busca* (London: Grant and Cutler, 1982), Carmen del Moral, *La sociedad madrileña fin de siglo y Baroja* (Madrid: Turner, 1974) and Soledad Puértolas Villanueva, *El Madrid de la 'lucha por la vida'* (Madrid: Helios, 1971).
2. Longhurst, 'La mala vida en Madrid'. The naturalist elements of Baroja's urban trilogy and Blasco's rural novel *Cañas y barro* are the subject of the same scholar's 'Representations of the "Fourth Estate"'.
3. Labanyi, *Gender and Modernization*, p. 87.
4. Havelock Ellis, 1892 letter to John Addington Symonds, cited by Nicole Hahn Rafter and Mary Gibson in their Introduction to Cesare Lombroso and Guglielmo Ferrero, *Criminal Woman, the Prostitute and the Normal Woman* (Durham, NC: Duke University Press, 2004), p. v.
5. *El gabinete del doctor Lombroso (Delincuencia y fin de siglo en España)* (Barcelona: Anagrama, 1973).
6. See Pura Fernández, *Eduardo López Bago y el Naturalismo radical: la novela y el mercado literario en el siglo XIX* (Amsterdam: Rodopi, 1995) and 'Orígenes y difusión del naturalismo: la especificidad de la práctica hispana', in *Revista de Literatura*, 58.115 (1996), 107–20.
7. José Alberich, 'La biblioteca de Baroja', *Revista Hispánica Moderna*, 27.2 (1961), 101–12 (p. 107).
8. *Criminal Man according to the Classification of Cesare Lombroso* (New York and London: G. P. Putnam's Sons, 1911), p. xv.
9. See Pick, *Faces of Degeneration*, p. 126.
10. Campos Marín, 'La teoría de la degeneración', p. 198.
11. Campos Marín, 'La teoría de la degeneración', p. 203.
12. Robert A. Nye, 'Sociology: The Irony of Progress', in *Degeneration: The Dark Side of Progress*, ed. by J. Edward Chamberlin and Sander L. Gilman (New York: Columbia University Press, 1985), pp. 49–71 (p. 57).
13. See OC, VII, 752–53.
14. Julio Caro Baroja, Prologue to Pío Baroja, *La busca* (Madrid: Caro Raggio, 1997), p. ix. All subsequent references are to this edition.
15. Stepan, 'Biological Degeneration', p. 113.
16. Greenslade, *Degeneration, Culture and the Novel*, p. 96.
17. Havelock Ellis, *The Criminal* (London: Walter Scott & Co., 1890), pp. xv–xvi.
18. Rafter and Gibson, Introduction, p. 4.
19. *Criminal Woman*, ed. by Rafter and Gibson, p. 183, p. 185. All subsequent references are to this edition.
20. Rafter and Gibson, Introduction, p. 27.
21. Rafael G. Eslava, *La prostitución en Madrid: apuntes para un estudio sociológico* (Madrid: Vicente Rico, 1900), p. 92 and Moral, *La sociedad madrileña*, p. 136.
22. Philiph Hauser, *Madrid bajo el punto de vista médico-social*, 2 vols (Madrid: Establecimiento Tipográfico Sucesores de Rivadeneyra, 1902), II, 147.
23. Constancio Bernaldo de Quirós and José M. Llanas Aguilaniedo, *La mala vida en Madrid* (Madrid: B. Rodríguez Serra, 1901), p. 235.
24. Lombroso, *Criminal Woman*, p. 220.
25. Bernaldo de Quirós and Llanas Aguilaniedo, *La mala vida en Madrid* (1901 edn), p. 59.
26. Gilman, 'Sexology', p. 85.
27. On the control of prostitution in *Fortunata y Jacinta* and *Nazarín*, the reader is referred to Fuentes, *Visions of Filth*, Chapter 2. The gynaecologist Ángel Pulido described syphilis in metaphorical terms as 'un monstruo misterio que se desenvuelve y conserva en el seno de la prostitución, como el miasma en el agua cenagosa, y como el veneno en la cabeza de la víbora'. In addition

to the images of sanitation in references to stagnant water and draining (Fuentes, p. 45), Pulido's description of syphilis obviously engages with the Biblical imagery of the serpent and the Fall of Eve in order to draw moral conclusions.

28. Philiph Hauser, 'El siglo XIX considerado bajo el punto de vista médico-social', *Revista de España*, 101 (1884), 202–24, 333–58 (pp. 214–15).
29. Eslava, *La prostitución en Madrid* (1900), pp. 61, 80, 89; cited by Noël Valis, 'On Monstrous Birth: Leopoldo Alas's *La Regenta*', in *Naturalism in the European Novel*, ed. by Brian Nelson (Oxford: Berg, 1992), 191–209 (p. 203).
30. C. Bernaldo de Quirós and J. María Llanas Aguilaniedo, *La mala vida en Madrid: estudio psicosociológico con dibujos y fotografías fotograbados del natural* [1901], ed. by J. Broto Salanova (Huesca: Instituto de Estudios Altoaragoneses, 1998).
31. Bernaldo de Quirós and Llanas Aguilaniedo, *La mala vida en Madrid* (1901 edn), pp. 252–53.
32. Walter Benjamin, *Charles Baudelaire: A Lyric Poet in the Era of High Capitalism* (London: Verso, 1989), p. 50.
33. Labanyi, *Gender and Modernization*, p. 113.
34. Ángel Pulido y Fernández, *Bosquejos médico-sociales para la mujer* (Madrid: Imprenta a cargo de Víctor Saiz, 1876), pp. 113–14.
35. Labanyi, *Gender and Modernization*, p. 117.
36. Pulido y Fernández, *Bosquejos*, p. 116.
37. Labanyi, *Gender and Modernization*, p. 120.
38. Hauser, *Madrid bajo el punto de vista médico-social*, II, 143.
39. Gregorio Marañón, 'Biología y Feminismo', *Conferencia pronunciada en la Sociedad Económica de Amigos del País*, Sevilla, 21 February 1920 (n.p. [Madrid]: Sucesor de Enrique Teodoro, 1920).
40. On eugenics and birth control in early twentieth-century Spain, the reader is referred to Raquel Álvarez Peláez, 'La mujer española y el control de natalidad en los comienzos del siglo XX', *Asclepio*, 2 (1990), 175–200.
41. Fuentes, *Visions of Filth*, pp. 67–68.
42. Nordau, *Degeneration*, p. 39.
43. M. Legrain, *Hérédité et alcoolisme: étude psychologique et clinique sur les dégénérés buveurs et les familles d'ivrognes* (Paris, 1889), p. 59; cited by Pick, *Faces of Degeneration*, p. 51.
44. Campos Marín et al., *Los ilegales*, Chapter 4, on 'La medicina social y la degeneración'.
45. On Baroja's dislike of Zola and French naturalism, see *OC*, VII, 745.
46. He concludes that 'the label Naturalist, if we were to ascribe anything approaching a genuinely Zolaesque value to the term, would clearly be misleading and unsatisfactory'. Longhurst, 'Representations of the "Fourth Estate"', p. 95.
47. Pick, *Faces of Degeneration*, p. 21.

CHAPTER 4

Crowd Psychology and the Urban Masses: Blasco Ibáñez's *La horda* (1905)

It is by now a commonplace that rapid urbanization in the nineteenth century lent powerful momentum to the cultural appeal of degeneration theories. Echoing a common trope of French naturalism, Blasco's *La horda* configures the urban masses in relation to social pathologies and, in particular, the primitive violence of the crowd as a source of contagion. *La horda* represents prevalent sociological problems of widespread concern during the period: namely mass population, indigence and criminality. Both crowd psychology and eugenic discourse construed the city as a febrile site of pathology and degeneration. Fuelled by the uneven development of modernity, the city was frequently posited as the site of infection and squalor: biological, social and political. Like the urban landscape of Baroja's *La busca*, Blasco's Madrid novel *La horda* drew profoundly on late nineteenth-century cultural, scientific and social discourses that exerted a fascinating appeal in Spain as in other parts of Europe. This chapter assesses the extent to which Blasco both incorporates and challenges these theories.

Following *La catedral*, *El intruso* and *La bodega*, *La horda* was the last of four social novels that Blasco published between 1903 and 1905. Written whilst he served as a politician in Madrid, the material for *La horda* was based on Blasco's observation of the outskirts of the city. The author commented in the 1925 prologue that 'ninguna de mis obras tiene una base tan amplia en la realidad'.[1] Just one year after Baroja's panorama of Madrid in *La busca*, *La horda* provides a similarly broad exposition of poverty, hardship and disease in an urban milieu. Baroja claimed loudly that Blasco's 1905 novel was directly inspired by his own depiction of urban poverty and vice in the preceding year, and dismissed *La horda* as an inferior offshoot of *La busca*.[2]

Degeneration in Blasco's novel is rooted obviously in social concerns, although family genealogies play an inconsistent deterministic role within this environment of degradation. The most obvious exposition of degenerationism in *La horda* is found both in the representation of criminality, treated with morbid fascination by the popular press of the period, and urban indigence. More specifically, Blasco's representation of the primitive survival of the masses echoes partially — but not wholeheartedly — the recourse to popular science that underpinned Zola's brand of naturalism. *La horda* provides resonant echoes of Morel's research on heredity and pathology, Lombroso's physiognomic categorization, and especially Gustave Le Bon's analysis of the atavistic regression of the crowd.

In Spain the cultural myths of degeneration drew particular strength from middle-class fears about social instability and the rebellion of the working classes. These anxieties were driven by marked disparities in wealth, a rigid class system, and the growth of political movements such as socialism and anarchism. Blasco's treatment of urban poverty in *La horda* is the product of an obviously ideological viewpoint (the author's fervent Republicanism) and a preoccupation with the revolutionary potential of the crowd.

In *La busca* Baroja exposes urban disease and indigence, with a dominant focus on the figure of the prostitute. In *La horda*, Blasco's interest in human reproduction in an environment of overwhelming poverty provides a significant point of comparison. The collective panorama of poverty is humanized through the trajectory of the protagonist Isidro Maltrana, his relationship with factory worker Feliciana and the birth of their son. Feli's death following childbirth responds implicitly to the context of degenerationism because the female body becomes emblematic of the struggle for social control and the debilitated social body. Baroja's early novels are specifically informed by a clinical understanding of theories of hereditary and biological decline, even if this paradigm is ultimately rejected. By contrast, Blasco's fiction of this period offers a more populist incorporation and transmission of cultural narratives of degeneration. This statement is not intended to blindly support Baroja's own view that *La horda* was a poor imitation of *La busca*. The widespread debates about mass urban poverty by politicians, criminologists, psychologists, hygienists and legal practitioners had already provided ample material for realist and naturalist representations of urban filth during the period, not least the well-known Madrid novels of Galdós. Indeed, despite the authors' divergent backgrounds, *La busca* and *La horda* offer a comparable cultural engagement with degenerationist tropes across the traditional hierarchies of canonical and popular fiction alike.

By the 1890s the urban environment provided a focus for newly invigorated theories of cultural degeneration at the point at which the concepts of psychiatric degeneration and criminal atavism were losing credibility. Late nineteenth-century theories of the crowd in France centred not on the primitivism of the rural but instead on mass society in the cities. Gustave Le Bon defined the crowd ('la foule') as an ominous force that signified inevitable regression to a primitive state: the crowd organism evinced in evolutionary terms 'the atavistic residue of the instincts of the primitive man'.[3] Blasco's choice of title, *La horda*, is particularly significant in this context. Le Bon's interest in craniology provided a foundation for a hierarchy of intelligence in which Western Europeans, men and scientists were seen as superior to 'savages', women and workers, an argument predicated on evolutionary theory.[4] Criminal anthropology had already pointed to dubious scientific evidence for women's supposedly inferior intellectual and evolutionary development.

Between 1845 and 1870 the population of Madrid doubled, despite elevated urban death rates due to typhus, which was endemic in the southern suburbs, and cholera epidemics. High levels of emigration from the provinces created a surplus labour market beset by poverty, creating an impoverished underclass that fed middle-class fears about social instability. As Bahamonde notes, 'la burguesía teme la radicalización de los antagonismos de clase, fruto del proceso de proletarización de la sociedad madrileña'.[5] Social inequality produced volatile conditions for civil disorder and unrest. In this unstable environment, degeneration theory would respond in apparently scientific terms to social problems, through diagnosis of the marginalized, indigent population of the city. Public health experts were at the forefront of these discourses as social hygienists took a vital role in the prevention of the spread of disease and degeneration. Alcoholism was perceived as a particular threat to the health of the nation and its children, and strongly informed the degenerationist approaches of hygienic medicine. For the physician Philiph Hauser, who had practised under Claude Bernard in Paris, alcoholism (like syphilis) was 'una enfermedad [...] degenerativa de la raza humana'.[6]

Working-class women were seen as a dangerous element of the impoverished urban masses, not least because they transgressed the division between the public and private sphere that sustained the bourgeois ideology of the *ángel del hogar*. In the context of Revolution, women became the iconographic embodiment of political anarchy through the feminization of the crowd, even one made up of men. As the French crowd theorist, Gabriel Tarde, stated: 'by its routine caprice, [...] its credulity, its excitability, its rapid leaps from fury to tenderness, from exasperation to burst of laughter, the crowd is woman, even when it is composed, as almost always happens, of masculine elements'.[7] The tendency to imitation, rapid changes in emotion and violence within the crowd were designated as feminine characteristics and feminine in origin. Within these theories, the revolutionary crowd was denoted as both threatening and castrating. The leader-hypnotist was allied to the violent and degenerate woman, who inspired the atavism of the crowd, as exemplified by the French *pétroleuses* of 1871.[8]

In Leopoldo Alas's *La Regenta* (1884–85), a group of working-class women attempts to stone to death a Protestant pastor, echoing contemporary fears of the primitive, castrating and frenzied force of the female crowd, as well as the anti-Protestant sentiment that accompanied revolutionary fervour. Republican rhetoric in Spain employed the term 'clases desheredadas' with reference both to women and the masses. The access of both groups to the public sphere, particularly the street as a space that did not belong to civic society, was a source of acute anxiety. The street, none the less, integrated figures such as the vagrant and the prostitute into a market economy through a model of circulation and consumption.[9] The term 'mujer pública' referred to the prostitute's inhabitation of the public space of the street.

Late nineteenth-century 'science' of the crowd pointed to the savagery and violence of women. As Lombroso observed in *Criminal Woman*:

> During revolutions, women become terribly enraged once they are set in motion. Many of the reported examples of female cruelty concern collective cruelty. [...] Women participated in the Paris Commune of 1870 with the greatest of violence. They were the most bloodthirsty heroes in the assassination of priests (which a woman initiated) and in the executions of hostages, surpassing in cruelty men themselves, whom they rebuked for knowing too little about killing.[10]

Within the crowd, women were perceived as a castrating force, posing danger to human reproduction not individually, but rather in a national context. More broadly they represented, therefore, the descent towards (anticipated) collective sterility and extinction. Women's violence in the crowd was seen as a key signifier of degeneration, because it subverted their domestic role and duty to reproduce healthy children for the future of the nation. Lombroso's observations above are overtly reminiscent of the violence and cannibalism of the Amazon or female warrior.

In Spain as elsewhere in Europe, the lower-class woman in the public sphere ultimately embodied the potential for the incitement of an emotional and violent crowd in the context of Revolution. Degenerationism developed as a particularly middle-class ideology that privileged male authority and the social status quo. In his study of Galdós, Stannard has argued that the 'theory of degeneration provided a means of condemning the social vices popularly associated with the *masa obrera* while, at the same time, offering a distancing, intellectual security that bolstered the identity of middle-class professionals'. As demonstrated by the case of the bourgeois artist, however, the middle classes were not immune to their own forms of degenerative disease and vice.[11]

In the context of industrialization and urban poverty in Spain, diseases such as tuberculosis, alcoholism and syphilis constituted a dangerous threat to social stability and the status of the governing bourgeoisie. Degeneration theory provided an ideological means to explain and control threatening social ills, through the privileging of scientific knowledge. It could also be invoked in a more immediate and practical sense to remove degenerates from society through their institutionalization in hospitals, asylums and prisons.[12] Degeneration theory was the product of middle-class medical professionals, hygienists and psychiatrists. However, it was infinitely useful as a method of explanation and diagnosis, as demonstrated by its widespread application to social and political problems on a pan-European scale. Degeneration theory sought to explain and control the threat of the Other, according to race, class, education, wealth and gender. The diseased, the deviant and the subversive were thus a combined object of examination, control, marginalization and ultimately removal by the respectable classes.[13] The dangerous proliferation of mass culture was commonly regarded as a metaphor for the mobilization of the working classes, as Sieburth has argued. In Spain, as elsewhere, mass-produced fiction thereby drew on fears of 'engulfment by the large crowds of the modern city — crowds where strangers may touch each other in sensual or contaminating ways'.[14] For the socialist Juan Bou in Galdós's *La desheredada* (1881), only the workers constitute the 'pueblo', a worker's State in which money and wages would be replaced by the exchange of labour. In this novel, the Paseo de la Castellana is referenced as a 'torrent' and a 'bonito mareo', images that symbolically configure the circulation of wealth in a world of commodities.[15]

La horda opens with an atavistic representation of the crowd as primitive or 'pre-historic', echoing the evolutionary and anthropological premises that inform the urban representation of *La busca*. Describing the awakening of the city, the population of Cuatro Caminos begins to make its way to market to sell food and goods: 'Pasaban y pasaban jinetes y carros, como una horda prehistórica que huyese llevando a la espalda el hambre, y delante, como guía, el anhelo de vivir'.[16] As in Baroja's novel, pictorial description accompanies the rendering of desperate poverty and alcoholism. Blasco likewise extends the metaphor of rubbish and 'residuos' in relation to the marginalized poor. Poverty is thus configured, through evolutionary premises, as regression to a primitive stage of existence. The rag-and-bone man, Coleta, embodies the dominant symbiosis of poverty and alcoholism through his symbolic association with urban filth.

Given the novel's emphasis on dirt, rubbish and lack of sanitation, it is no coincidence that *la Isidra*, Maltrana's mother, becomes a washerwoman at the peak of poverty and dies after catching pneumonia washing clothes in freezing conditions at the river. The metaphor of sanitation (expressed here through fluid) is strongly sustained in relation to the endemic sickness of the urban poor. Isidro Maltrana's father drinks and beats his mother, an archetypal combination of alcoholism and domestic violence. Following the death of his father in an accident (recalling the death of Manuel's alcoholic father in *La busca*), Isidro is sent to live at the Hospicio. This charitable institution provides education, discipline and an impersonal ethos for destitute children of the city who resign themselves to the poorhouse and its stigmatizing grey uniform through a process of dehumanization: they respond 'con una pasividad automática de soldado, como si les atrajese la obscura boca de la portada monumental' (30). The army of poor mothers, made up of washerwomen, widows, beggars, and other forms of abandoned womanhood, make emotional weekly visits to see their offspring, engendered as a futile distraction from hunger.

The scene in question presents the problems of the poor in implicit relation to over-population, alongside the overt referencing of the instinctive behaviour of the indigent masses as a collective. The fate of the 'asilados' may be read in the light of the economic theory of Malthus (1798) who believed that charity, feeding the poor and curing their illnesses had negative social consequences because these activities maintained an overpopulation that could never escape poverty.[17] Early twentieth-century theories of eugenics were based on the control of reproduction, not through regulating the numbers of children through restraint rather than artificial methods (Malthus) but through the selection of high-quality parents. By contrast, as Álvarez Peláez explains, many anarchists opposed birth control according to their belief in the universal right to have healthy, robust, well-fed and educated children and the view that birth control favoured the bourgeoisie.[18] None the less, the debate for some anarchists moved from an overriding concern about population growth towards greater personal welfare, including control over reproduction. As Cleminson observes, anarchist neo-Malthusians promoted, for example, the use of contraceptive devices in debates over questions of population that would lead to the anarchist eugenics of the 1920s and 1930s.[19] Birth control in nineteenth-century England was promoted on the basis of individual freedom, the avoidance of abortion and infanticide, and the raising of existing children.[20] In Blasco's *La horda* the futile efforts of the institutions of social containment for the indigent masses (the orphanage, the hospital and the prison) and the overpopulation of the poor districts and slums of Madrid are of primary concern.

La horda addresses a number of the same social questions as Baroja's *La busca* in its exposition of the sickly offspring of the urban poor in terms of heredity and biology. Blasco's narrative treatment of these issues draws on determinism in schematic but contradictory terms. Abandoned to abject poverty and a solitary existence, Isidra merely compounds her situation when she shacks up with a kindly neighbour and falls pregnant with Pepín, a hydrocephalic and weak infant who displays 'una cabeza enorme sobre un cuello delgado; un cuerpecillo débil que anunciaba una fealdad igual a la suya' (32). The protagonist Isidro Maltrana is intelligent and bookish. His half-brother Pepín, a child who runs riot in the neighbourhood, 'pertenecía a otra raza: la de su padre' (34). Genetic inheritance is superficially referenced in physical and behavioural terms in relation to the reproduction of the poverty-stricken masses. Pepín, however, inherits none of the honest work ethic espoused by his father, José. The overwhelming evidence of the novel in relation to deterministic paradigms is environmental. Isidro Maltrana's social 'transplantation' through the protection of his benefactor is short-lived; his academic dreams are cut short by the realities of poverty and his mother's sudden illness and death, once again echoing Manuel Alcázar's experience in *La busca*. As in Baroja's urban panorama, environmental determinants hold the trump card over heredity and innate characteristics.

Blasco's novel is less uniformly concerned with the narrative exposition of disease and physical deformity than Baroja's depiction of the urban poor. None the less, *La horda* debates hereditary models, often with inconsistent conclusions. Both Isidro and his *novia* Feliciana are portrayed as suffering from hereditary anaemia, reflecting a literary interpretation of biological decline that echoes in popular form Baroja's more direct concern with hygienic and social medicine, as well as organic degeneration. As a child, Isidro presents 'una palidez anémica' (26); as young women, Feliciana and a fellow-worker embody a fleeting liberation from the 'anemia hereditaria' (17) that is their inevitable destiny. *Aboulia* is also configured in relation to collective health. Like Manuel Alcázar, Isidro Maltrana is characterized obviously as an *abúlico* and symbol of his generation: 'él reconocía su gran defecto, el mal de su generación, en la que un estudio desordenado y un exceso de razonamiento había roto el principal resorte de la vida: la falta de voluntad. Era impotente para la acción' (12). He reads voraciously and spends his time on philosophical and political dreams, rather than practical work for the paper which would allow him to earn money to support himself. As the embodiment of anaemia, fatigue, lethargy and futile intellectualism, and described repeatedly as 'feo', Isidro Maltrana is a suggestive symbol of generational decline.[21] As in the case of Baroja's Manuel, however, his regeneration at the end of the novel overturns this degenerationist paradigm in favour of the individual's potential to overcome his circumstance.

La horda is punctuated by references to atavism and primitivism which centre particularly on the representation of the urban masses and the indigent population who turn to criminality to avoid starvation. Feliciana's father, *el Mosco*, is defined as an example of atavistic regression to primitive survival. This is evidenced not by physiognomic stigmata or disease as in Baroja's novel, but instead through dangerous criminal activity. By contrast to the portrait of the homicidal *el Bizco* in *La busca*, the poacher *el Mosco* reacts to the urban environment through the revival of atavistic and primitive instincts, 'como si lejanos atavismos tirasen de él, arrastrándolo a la existencia del hombre primitivo' (56). His predilection for illegal hunting draws on an ancestral inheritance that constitutes an anachronism in modern urban society. El Mosco is a primitive throwback, but his energy and virile masculinity contrast with Isidro's own lack of Will and his impractical intellectualism. These apathetic elements together fuel Isidro Maltrana's further descent into pauperism over the course of the novel.

La horda sustains and develops the dominant association found in Baroja's novel between poverty and filth, through its renderings of the Northern suburbs of Madrid: Cuatro Caminos, las Carolinas, Tetuán, Bellasvistas and Chamartín, an area with which Blasco was familiar during his walks from the Paseo de la Castellana. Viewed from a distance, this area of Madrid seems to be built on waste itself: 'Parecía de lejos un montón de escombros y basura' (84). The extended shack of Zaratustra (*tío Polo*), with whom Isidro's grandmother (Eusebia) lives in an unofficial 'marriage', is a 'mansion' built on the refuse and detritus of the city and which exudes a smell of putrefaction: 'Todos los despojos de la villa habían sido empleados en la edificación; [...] botes de conserva, latas de petróleo, cafeteras, orinales' (86–87). Interestingly, the metaphor of refuse does not reflect the decomposition or disintegration of the dwelling, but instead the squalid expansion and reconstruction from waste, a process of recycling of which *tío Polo* is ironically proud. The masses survive on this process of salvaging of scraps and rags, the hoarding and recycling of other people's waste, demonstrated by the numerous 'traperos' of the novel and Eusebia's 'treasure' which consists entirely of cast-offs. None the less, metaphors of sanitation abound in *La horda*. The noise and restlessness of the Rastro, with its 'infernal estrépito' (142), is described as a dunghill, 'un estercolero' (146). The Madrid poor build their lives on a foundation of manure, itself a metaphor for organic decline typical of *dégénérescence*. In *La horda*, however, the dunghill constitutes a powerful metaphor for social hierarchies, rather than inevitable biological decadence. The recycling of second-hand goods at the Rastro, none the less, was regarded by health experts of the period as a source of contagion.[22] More broadly, in Blasco as in Galdós, ragpickers become a metaphor for the recycling and circulation of the excess and waste of consumer society.

Within this environment of degradation and filth that provides the breeding ground for the poor, Feliciana represents for Isidro Maltrana cleanliness and moral purity, and embodies a common occupation for working-class women at the 'fábrica de gorras'. She is characterized, through Isidro's perspective, in relation to youth and 'limpieza' (92). Among the many references to the foul-smelling poor quarters of Madrid, Feliciana's innocence delays her inevitable decline. Her naivety and youthfulness contrast with the squalor of her surroundings. Later Feliciana is both physically and emotionally transformed by maternity, anticipating Baroja's descriptions of Lulú in *El árbol de la ciencia*, as nervous emotion overcomes her equilibrium: 'La maternidad trastornaba su débil organismo. La invadía una intensa tristeza, atormentando su imaginación' (193). In this environment, reproduction is a risky undertaking, amply demonstrated when Feliciana succumbs to puerperal eclampsia, the eventual cause of her death following childbirth.

Through the focus on reproduction of the masses within the overpopulated slums and poor districts of Madrid, *La horda* presents an urban landscape that was regulated to some extent through social sanitation, hygienic medicine and the removal of undesirable elements who were contained instead within institutional settings. As a highly politicized and popular form of scientific discourse, eugenics aimed both to improve the population and slow its perceived decline. It took many varied forms across different scientific and social groupings, ideologies and nations, and had particular resonance in Spain in relation to fears about national decline, degeneration and regenerationism in the early twentieth century. In the urban sphere, eugenics provided scientific explanation for social problems such as overpopulation, alcoholism and unhygienic living conditions. Yet, as Richard Cleminson explains, the causes of degeneration in urbanized, industrialized Europe were sought, not in 'social structures or political-economic organisation' but rather 'in mental and physical attributes; in short, in the body politics of the nation'. Eugenics identified the presence of 'rogue elements — either poor social or economic organisation, or more often than not, degenerate and diseased populations'.[23]

Galton's eugenics emphasized good breeding as the path to a strong race. According to the premises of social hygiene, rogue elements and individuals — including the criminal and the prostitute — needed to be removed from society through institutions of reform or containment, such as the convent or the prison to prevent contamination of wider society. As Greenslade notes, Darwin's acceptance of Spencer's formulation 'the survival of the fittest' (in its original sense of adaptation to the process of natural selection) did not anticipate the subsequent interpretations of the notion of 'fitness' in terms of value judgement and in the context of social fears and ideological application. In the late nineteenth century, as social Darwinism drew attention to 'competition and conflict', '"fitness" became purposive; it had an end — complete with strategies to direct the conduct of individuals, groups, populations, races'. Society was failing to eliminate unfit individuals who were reproducing at an alarming rate.[24]

In this context, the union of the weak-willed Isidro Maltrana (no longer demonstrably a 'ser superior' but instead the embodiment of moral weakness) and the frail Feliciana might reasonably be expected to lead to the production of sickly offspring. By contrast to *El árbol de la ciencia* in which mother and baby both die during childbirth, however, their son is born healthy and survives, implying a process of regeneration through the rebirth of Will at the end of *La horda*. As a drain on resources, Feliciana is thus sacrificed for the future of father, son and nation, as Isidro resolves to work for the child's future, a resolution described in terms of evolution and social hierarchy: 'Ya que el mundo estaba organizado sobre la desigualdad, que figurase su hijo entre los privilegiados, aunque para ello tuviese que aplastar a muchos' (297). The protagonist's hopes for the next generation are symbolic of the potential health of the nation. Regeneration and rebirth depend on the overcoming of circumstances by the individual in the face of an urban panorama of socio-economic injustice. For both Baroja and Blasco, *aboulia* can be surmounted by the individual, a potentially Nietzschean solution that further problematizes the ideological perspective of each author.

The ending of *La horda* in which Isidro redeems himself overturns, to some extent, the premises of hereditary and environmental determinism through the individual's overcoming of poverty through self-reform. This resolution, however, represents a failure of idealism: Isidro Maltrana will strive to support his son not within any socialist vision of equity and justice, but through writing for financial gain at the expense of the indigent masses. As Iturrioz declares in *El árbol de la ciencia*: 'Que la vida es una lucha constante, una cacería cruel en que nos vamos devorando los unos a los otros'.[25] The works of Herbert Spencer were well known in late nineteenth-century Spain thanks to the proliferation of translations from the 1880s. It is common knowledge that Spencer's economic model of society was strongly influenced by degeneration theory, which itself drew momentum from Darwin's view that regression or racial deterioration was the accompaniment to evolution. According to social Darwinism, the struggle for life in the urban sphere was leading to overpopulation that signalled an excessively successful adaptation within the degenerate state of the unfit species which retains atavistic characteristics. In 1883 Francis Galton wrote that 'those whose race we especially want to have, would leave few descendants, while those whose race we want to be quit of, could crowd the vacant space with progeny'.[26]

Neither *La lucha por la vida* nor *La horda*, however, sustains a reductively Darwinist reading of their exposition of urban degradation or indeed a eugenicist approach to the problems of urban indigence and overpopulation. Criminal anthropologists and social hygienists focused on the figure of the degenerate and criminal as the source of disorder. Removing the disturbed and dangerous elements of society, such as criminals, prostitutes and anarchists, was key to protecting society from the ravages of degeneration and decline. In fact, Blasco depicts the institutions of containment — namely the orphanage, the hospital and the prison — as both damaging and futile. The preceding chapter discussed the use of reformatory organizations, such as the convent, in the regulation of prostitution. In a similar way, the control of criminality in *La horda* is represented through the threat of prison as the locus of disciplinary order.

According to the social historian Pedro Trinidad Fernández, the Restoration witnessed a proliferation of reformatory institutions in Spain, including the establishment of prisons, penitentiaries and madhouses, as well as laws against vagrancy and other forms of social disorder. These measures and institutions permitted 'el control de todos los que no aceptan la normativa social': in other words the regulation of marginal groups.[27] In *Discipline and Punish: The Birth of the Prison* (1975), Foucault traces the punishment of the deviant individual from the eighteenth century, as the body became the locus of control and reform.[28] In the early nineteenth century, the soul and mind replaced the body as the primary source of punishment through the birth of the modern prison. State or beneficent institutions of social control (the prison, the convent, the orphanage) thus depended on the removal and reform of deviant individuals. Discourses on public hygiene, medicine and gender intersected closely in their construction of digressions from social norms in order to regulate the existence of prostitutes, criminals and other groups deemed to constitute a social threat.

During the Restoration, the Krausists addressed social reform in relation to the theory of 'natural law'. They did so through the belief in education as a means of converting the masses into responsible individuals; conversely, their liberal belief in freedom was dependent on the reduced role of the State.[29] As Labanyi notes, the Krausists rejected a social Darwinist model of a 'free' society. However, like Spencer, their view of society was based on a biological model in which the various organs contribute to the functioning of the social body as a whole. Within this system of nationhood, the family functioned as model for wider society, due to its vital role in the teaching and inculcation of civic values. The mother, in particular, was responsible for the welfare and citizenship of the family as an alternative to State intervention, a role that blurred the division between the private and public spheres.[30] With the growing professionalization of medicine from the mid-nineteenth century in Spain, medical experts performed a central role in the regulation of problematic elements of society, namely the working classes and women.

By contrast to Krausist values, hygienic medicine (or 'medicina social') drew on a predominantly positivist foundation that provided doctors with the role of regulating and preventing sickness in society. In 1865 Claude Bernard's *Introduction à l'étude de la médecine expérimentale* denoted this experimental science as the study of a sick society that would restore the health of the social body. As Labanyi notes, 'the new medical experts' conversion of society into a giant controlled laboratory experiment is what permitted Zola to make Claude Bernard's book the basis of literary naturalism. [...] Hence Zola's insistence on the novelist as social reformer'.[31] Public hygiene included the treatment of the insane and the criminal, through management of asylums and prisons, as key aspects of social health; it also incorporated sanitation, urban poverty and prostitution. The regulation of prostitution in Madrid in the 1870s and 1880s included the use of licensed brothels, and the medical inspection and hospitalization of prostitutes. Degeneration theory had a particular impact in Spain through criminology and the widespread public debate of Lombroso's classifications in the 1880s and 1890s.

Blasco's *La horda* moves its attention beyond the language of pathology and disease to the juridical. Within its analysis of transgression and punishment, what Foucault termed the 'carceral society' comes under scrutiny, according to a model of power based on binary oppositions: normal versus abnormal, healthy versus diseased. Isidro Maltrana's half-brother, Pepín el *Barrabás*, provides the motive for the salient description in *La horda* of the Cárcel Modelo, the ironically named jail to which both adults and juvenile delinquents are sent for reform. In reality the prison serves as a breeding ground for crime. Pepín is fourteen years old when he is sentenced to time at the Cárcel Modelo for theft, a disgrace that horrifies his father José.

There is no simple hereditary system of cause-and-effect in the portrait of juvenile criminality; Blasco's attention centres much more prominently on the environment of poverty and degradation from which Pepín attempts to escape through crime. The social structure of the prison, however, provides a fertile environment for a budding gift for criminal leadership.

The description of the jail is undertaken through Isidro Maltrana's perspective and is represented through morbid imagery of cemeteries and tombs: 'vio de un golpe las naves enormes, las galerías superpuestas, y en ellas las puertas de las celdas con gruesos cerrojos. [...] Las filas de puertas recordaban a Isidro las tramadas de nichos de un cementerio' (179). Pepín, by contrast, is much less awe-struck by his surroundings; he finds his own niche in the boys' section of the jail and becomes the leader of the adolescent and pre-adolescent delinquents through his natural affinity with crime: 'se erguía con la arrogancia fanfarrona de un gallo joven, estremeciéndose todo su cuerpo linfático y desmedrado, con esa ruindad física de los homicidas por instinto' (183). In this environment of poverty and delinquency, Pepín is deemed unlikely to escape his innate instinct for criminality.

Reform, in other words, is an unlikely outcome of prison, and will not overcome either hereditary or environmental factors. Like the asylum, the Cárcel Modelo functioned in reality as a form of social containment and exclusion, rather than a means of reintegration or reform. The question of criminality in Spain was widely debated in the popular press during this period, and lent ample material for sensationalist treatment, as Soledad Puértolas has shown.[32] In 1902, for example, the newspaper *Nuestro Tiempo* published an article by Dorado on the causes of crime, and the inefficacy of the penal system, a commentary that presents a similar view to the perspective of *La horda*: 'El que es recluido en [nuestros establecimientos penitenciarios] por primera vez, sin haber perpetrado un delito que arguya verdadera perversidad, difícilmente se sustrae de perniciosos ejemplos y deja de aprender las malas artes del delincuente'.[33] Blasco's *La horda* portrays the prison system as dysfunctional and profoundly ineffective, and configures in obvious terms its failure to reform criminality in young men.

In the description of the child delinquents, there are strong echoes of criminal anthropology, although this does not amount to a concerted attempt at scientific classification in Blasco's novel. The boys' heads are shaved and reveal strange cranial configurations; some are marked by the scars of scrofula and smallpox: 'Había testas enormes, que parecían temblar por su peso sobre el cuello delgado y débil; otras presentaban por detrás un ángulo recto, un corte radical, que denunciaba la anulación de gran parte de la masa encefálica' (180). In this environment of male adolescent subversion and posturing, the decision of Levita's father to send him to prison to correct his crime in stealing is clearly ironizado. *El Machaco* has already been in prison twenty-three times. The intelligent Pepín is a hardened criminal in the making. *El Viruelas* bears the physical signs of criminality: 'era un monstruo de fealdad, con las facciones roídas, la nariz aplastada, los ojos casi ocultos bajo las cejas colgantes, y un hedor nauseabundo que surgía al mismo tiempo de su boca y su piel' (181). The causes of crime are multifaceted, and are entrenched by reformatory institutions. There are obvious references to criminal physiognomy in these descriptions, but social determinants take precedence over heredity; indeed the boys present a disturbing picture of disease as the physical legacy of poverty. The urban exposition of injustice and inequality in *La horda* is a powerful expression of Blasco's use of the social novel as an ideological tool. As Caudet argues, his fervent adherence to Republicanism was the product of intellectual, rather than sentimental, conviction. Blasco's political convictions rested on the rejection of Capitalism, Church and State, the 'trilogía nefasta',[34] ideological foundations that profoundly informed his editorial work and social novels.

In the second half of the nineteenth century, Madrid and Barcelona grew exponentially, each city reaching half a million inhabitants by 1900.[35] The consequences of urbanization are reflected in both *La busca* and *La horda* through the focus on the beggars and vagrants of the capital, and in the latter through the manual labour provided by the construction of public buildings for urban expansion, including the Gran Vía from 1905. Isidro Maltrana's father and stepfather are both building labourers, representing the largest sector of Madrid's working classes. The description of the crowd at the funeral of Isidro's stepfather, who dies at work when a building collapses, starkly reflects Blasco's exposition of social injustice and the corruption that defines the wealthy and powerful. In doing so, the passage draws on a common social metaphor of degeneration in the novels of Zola and other naturalist authors: the violence of the mob.

An aggressive crowd of alcohol-fuelled women has already been witnessed in the Bakhtinian pursuit of Isidro during *Carnaval*: 'Al ver a Maltrana habían vuelto a enmascararse, y se agitaban en torno de él, empujándolo, cogiéndole por las solapas, gritando, con una algazara semejante al cloquear de un gallinero: "¡No me conoces! ... ¡No me conoces!"' (96). The anonymous feminine crowd hunts down Isidro, an episode that ends with Feliciana declaring love for the weak-willed protagonist. She views the bookish Isidro Maltrana, ironically, as 'un ser superior' who will transplant her from the primitive existence into which she was born. In the descriptions above, the notion of imitation or suggestibility within the collective behaviour of the women is apparent, reflecting contemporary theories of crowd psychology as a social organism vulnerable to contagion. For Le Bon, for example, the crowd is susceptible to suggestion by the leader-hypnotist, the individual who would captivate the horde through a process of mass replication or mimicry.[36]

In his famous analysis of crowd behaviour, *Les Lois de l'imitation*, Gabriel Tarde viewed imitation and envy as characteristic of modern consumer society, because imitation constitutes a democratizing force. For Tarde, the metropolis provided the power of attraction on which modernity was created: chronic hypnotism thereby provided the large-scale imitation of the modern nation. His ideas were disseminated in Spain from the 1880s, and he became known particularly for his writings on Lombroso; *Les Lois de l'imitation* was translated into Spanish in 1907.[37] More broadly, the excitability of the crowd, inspired by hypnotic leaders, drew momentum from the immediate threat of mass politics, anarchism and socialism. The science of crowds and the biological and cultural regression that they denoted were bound in complex ways to these contentious social questions. Blasco's invocation of degenerationism, therefore, presents complex contradictions with his overt aim to expose social injustice. Like women, the indigent masses embodied both revolutionary potential and a dangerous threat to established middle-class values.

If the working classes were responsible, according to a bourgeois perspective, for their own plight, then urban poverty — alongside alcoholism, madness, crime and prostitution — was a social pathology in which social and political instability were rooted. In the second half of the nineteenth century, the *cuestión social* in Spain referred particularly to the problem of how to deal with the working classes. Yet the exclusion of women from civil society aligned them with the status of the proletariat, blurring the distinction between the bourgeoisie and the working classes in relation to the woman question. The representation of the Revolution of September 1868 — the *Gloriosa* or *Septembrina* — in Pardo Bazán's *La Tribuna* (1883) provides a suggestive point of reference in this context, most notably in its depiction of working-class women as a threat to social stability and a source of political volatility. In the Prologue, Pardo Bazán openly condemns the folly of embracing an unfamiliar model of government; that of a Federal Republic. The novel portrays the reaction of Amparo and her fellow-workers at the tobacco factory of Marineda to events that took place in Madrid between the *Gloriosa* and the advent of the First Republic.

In her 'Apuntes autobiográficos', Pardo Bazán commented on the women of the tobacco factory of La Coruña and their support for the Republican cause: 'aquellas mujeres, morenas, fuertes, de aire resuelto, había sido las más ardientes sectarias de la idea federal en los años revolucionarios'.[38] Amparo's political fervour, exacerbated by the performance of reading aloud contemporary events in the newspaper to her fellow-workers, is inspired particularly by fantasies of physical danger and her self-designation as 'una heroica pitillera', rather than any real understanding of Republicanism or political systems: 'Por todas partes fingía su calenturienta imaginación peligros, luchas, negras tramas urdidas para ahogar la libertad' (*OC*, II, 141). In *La Tribuna*, Pardo Bazán exposes the optimistic, ingenuous belief of Amparo and her co-workers that Republicanism would fulfil both personal fantasies (political fervour and social ascent through marriage) and resolve the *cuestión social* on a national scale. Instead of empathy with lower-class women, Pardo Bazán provides a satirical response to the political consequences of the Revolution of 1868 through her representation of the female urban proletariat.

Returning to *La horda*, the excessive behaviour of the female crowd takes place during *Carnaval*, a period in which the order of everyday life (including the rules and categories of gender) is temporarily suspended. *Carnaval* thus becomes both an emblem of consumer spectacle and social dissolution, anticipating the revolutionary fervour of the masses. At the funeral procession, the nature of the masses is emphasized through a specific focus on the women in the angry crowd railing against social injustice which sacrifices the poor in order for the rich to increase their wealth: 'Las mujeres vociferaban en torno del féretro, iracundas, llorosas, como si el rudo sol del verano mordiese con agresiva demencia sus cabezas despeinadas. [...] Y las mujeres eran las primeras en avanzar, en agarrarse a las puntas del féretro, empujando a los portadores para que rompiesen las filas de la fuerza pública' (209–10). The angry mob, then, takes on a collective identity, as the crowd ('la muchedumbre') advances and the young men throw missiles at the police. As the crowd gathers momentum in its vocalization and expression of an obviously political and social viewpoint, the revolutionary power of mass urban society, demonstrated through the primitive force of collective emotion, is repelled by the brutal response of the police and more broadly a corrupt justice system. Women are at the forefront of this proletarian might of aggressive and unrestrained emotion. The revolutionary female crowd was frequently denoted within degenerationist discourses as a hysterical and castrating force.

In the context of Revolution, the potential violence of the mob is described by Georges Clemenceau and Gustave Le Bon as the 'blood lust' of 'wild beasts', driven by primeval emotion. In Blasco's novel, the violence expressed by the crowd at the funeral dissipates in the face of near starvation and police brutality, a commentary on the submissive posture of Spanish society that embraces a potentially more radical position than Baroja's social regenerationism in *La busca*. For Clemenceau, the atavism intrinsic to crowd psychology was a product of industrialization and rapid urbanization, and constituted the disastrous consequence of mass society.[39] For Le Bon, collective psychology provided insights into social illnesses and pathology within a model of racial anthropology that posited the primevalism of the crowd as an anachronistic throwback within modern, civilized society to 'primordial sentiments embedded in the primitive heritage of the race'.[40] Blasco's implicit engagement with Le Bon's conservative and anti-democratic perspective is revealing.[41] The model of society as a biological organism, that informed the theories of Auguste Comte and Herbert Spencer, is expressed by Le Bon through the notion of mental contagion within the collective, and according to which the socialist hordes were seen to represent a decline into decadence.

In his essay 'Lejanías' (published in *Revista Nueva* in 1899), Baroja identifies the revolutionary potential of the oppressed masses: 'Producen una fuerza ordenada, nacida del desorden; un despotismo nacido de una anarquía. Nada hay tan reaccionario como el ejército que forman, nada tan revolucionario como las masas en donde nacen' (*OC*, VII, 860). In 'Espíritu de subordinación' (1903), however, Baroja refers to the impotence of the people to rise up against injustice.[42] Baroja, then, is pessimistic about the revolutionary capacity of the people for effective action and, in his short story 'Patología del golfo', points to the deficiencies of a society that abandons its poor.[43] The anarchist ideals explored in *Aurora roja*, the final novel in Baroja's trilogy, are ultimately rejected as an ineffective political solution to social injustice.

The ending of Blasco's *La horda* alludes to the possibility of revolutionary change and greater social equity. However, the primitivism of the crowd, it is implied, stands in the way of achieving this potential. Just as Baroja's delinquent is reformed at the end of *La busca* and returned to the bourgeois status quo, similarly the promise of rebellion by the angry mob at the end of *La horda* is overwritten by an ambivalent bourgeois resolution for Isidro Maltrana: 'Y las gentes felices temblarían de pavor ante las caras amenazantes, las vestiduras miserables, las miradas de famélico estrabismo, los anhelos locos y criminales de destrucción' (296). The ending of each novel, *La busca* and *La horda*, obviously fails to support the inevitable outcome and validity of the premises of degenerationism or indeed an unequivocal ideological stance.

Neither Blasco nor Baroja offers a resolution to the plight of the indigent masses, who are condemned by passivity to remain in poverty and squalor. Juan's anarchist ideals are defeated at the end of *Aurora roja*. The revolutionary potential of the crowd likewise fails to materialize in the closing pages of *La horda*. For Isidro Maltrana's stepfather, José, neither socialism nor anarchism will provide a solution to social inequalities. When his son is sent to prison, social organization is unable to provide military discipline: 'No; la sociedad no era un ejército; era más bien un rebaño triste y manso, que los malos pastores obligaban a pastar en campos de desolación, reservándose para ellos las mejores tierras' (177). Blasco's revolutionary appeal to the masses at the end of *La horda* is defeated by the failure of idealism and the reassertion of bourgeois order.

Zola's representation of the moral implications of Nana's social ascent is of interest as a point of comparison for the social injustice exposed by Baroja's and Blasco's city novels. The eponymous anti-heroine of *Nana* (1880) both fails to reproduce offspring and represents the destruction of male victims. She leaves a train of devastation in her wake, symbolizing social upheaval and biological degeneration.[44] Descended from several generations of alcoholics, Nana is an embodiment of social ascent as a disruptive force: 'She had grown up in the slums, in the gutters of Paris; and now, tall and beautiful, and as well made as a plant nurtured on a dung-heap, she was [...] a ferment of destruction, unwittingly corrupting and disorganizing Paris between her snow-white thighs'.[45] Nana overcomes her lowly origins but retains a degenerative influence of moral corruption. In Madrid too the poor are conceived and raised on a dung-heap of unsanitary and toxic conditions, both physical and moral, amidst hunger and alcoholism. Pathological models of heredity and degeneration inform the urban novels of Baroja and Blasco, but ultimately fail to sustain their representation of social inequity.

In *La horda* Feli's admission to hospital is accompanied by a description of the repulsive illnesses of poverty-stricken men, women and children, and the grotesque scabs and abscesses that accompany them: 'cegueras purulentas, costras roedoras, abcesos que desfiguraban sus miembros, retorciéndolos' (277). The death of Feliciana is narrated through the cynical detachment of the young and impassive doctor Nogueras who both mistakes the date of her demise and announces to Isidro Maltrana the final ironic indignity. Feli has been buried in a common grave for the poor following the medical dissection of her body for research. Her corpse thus embodies the symbiosis between refuse and poverty according to the exploitation of the indigent classes by the wealthy and powerful. The dissecting room provokes a vision of the inequalities of a hierarchical society that devours the poor: 'una humanidad horriblemente superior pervertida por la antropofagia, donde los fuertes se alimentasen con los despojos de los débiles' (288). Like the orphanage and the prison, the hospital becomes a breeding ground rather than a solution for human degradation, a predicament symbolized by Feli's demise as a lowly victim of the predatory rules of power and authority.

Even in death, Feli does not escape the position of weakness and exploitation conferred by poverty. Moreover, the metaphor of recycling that defines the poor quarters of Madrid, the *Rastro* and indigent consumerism is now applied through anthropophagy to Feli's physical remains. Just as the ragpickers recycle the waste of consumerism, thereby circulating goods according to a capitalist model, Feli's body becomes an expendable waste product for social medicine. The dissection of her body does not cast any specific light on her illness. Rather, her death as a pauper without the protection of wealthy loved-ones exposes her to ultimate indignity as an anonymous specimen for medical research. Blasco does not neglect the common metaphor of Spain as a diseased society prevalent in the works of early twentieth-century authors. In this case, however, the medic is part of a hierarchical system that employs its authority to abuse the economically vulnerable classes.

La horda ends with a description of the city that rests on the culmination of the metaphors of filth, expulsion and sanitation that characterize the impoverished hordes. Blasco employs vocabulary that is strikingly similar to Baroja's in his representation of the marginalized poor as apparently atavistic or primitive beings who procreate offspring in an environment of over-population and waste. Blasco's rendering of the city, however, differs from Baroja's in two fundamental ways. Firstly, the description of the urban poor in final section of *La horda* contributes to a stark ideological message about class and privilege. The capital city is 'dominadora y triunfante' (296), and takes a powerful position as it watches over the sufferings and privations of the impoverished masses: 'No veía la muchedumbre famélica esparcida a sus pies, la horda que se alimentaba con sus despojos y suciedades, el cinturón de estiércol viviente, de podredumbre dolorida' (296). Blasco, then, takes a more obviously political stance on the deprivation and marginalization of the poor.

Julio Caro Baroja points (in not unbiased terms) to the contrast between *La horda* and *La busca* on the basis of Blasco's greater reliance on moral doctrine and Baroja's greater subtlety.[46] Certainly Blasco's novel appears to offer a more direct political and social perspective than Baroja's. In reality, however, the ideological stance of each author is blurred by contradictions. In Blasco's *La horda* the final panoramic visions of the city and propagandist message that accompanies them offer a stark exposition of the capitalist exploitation of the proletariat and the power of the ruling classes. The revolutionary desire of the crowd, however, is inseparable from the primitivism and atavism of degeneration, epitomized by the public visibility of the working-class woman. Bourgeois prejudices inevitably inform the exposition of social injustice, despite Blasco's idealism.

The inevitable outcome of Isidro Maltrana's misplaced expectations of success accompanies repeated references to his lack of Will: 'Su voluntad desplomábase, vencida, falta de fuerza para luchar: quería morir. [...] El mundo estaba frío, sin alma y sin piedad. [...] No podía más: era un vencido' (261–62). The protagonist regrets his transplantation from poverty to education and the expectation of a better life following the charity of his benefactress. Darwinian overtones are clearly evident in this social engineering from the expectation of manual work to intellectual life, which has left him weak and unable to support himself or his family: 'Carecía de vigor físico para trabajar como un hombre; era un enclenque debilitado por el estudio,' (271). *Aboulia* is not inherited from his father, the physical labourer, but acquired from intellectual pursuits and aspirations, a mental and spiritual draining of vitality that fails to extract him from the poverty of his origins. As in *La busca*, the novel's conclusion witnesses the regeneration of the weak-willed protagonist: 'Caía hecha polvo la herrumbre de su voluntad. Era otro hombre: su audacia consideraba con desprecio todos los obstáculos' (298). The protagonist determines to overcome his biological inheritance in order to change the fortune of a son born in his own image: 'feo, con su misma fealdad y la de aquel pillete que estaba en la cárcel entre los rateros menores. La misma cabeza enorme, que parecía moldeada por las manos de la desgracia' (280). If we are to believe Isidro Maltrana's recuperation of strength and vitalism, the ending of *La horda* represents the symbolic overcoming of corroded willpower, debility and generational pathologies.

Blasco's reputation as 'el Zola español' was cemented early in the twentieth century according to the observations of critics such as Ernest Mérimée in 1903 following the publication of the French translation of *La barraca* and the author's own openly expressed enthusiasm for the French novelist. Even in a relatively recent volume of essays on Blasco, the author continues to be defined by naturalist models.[47] However Zola's brand of naturalism aimed to apply scientific method to literary representation; his Rougon-Macquart novels set out the inherited effects of pathologies such as alcoholism, and their role in crime and prostitution. In *La horda* we find little of the conscious scientific detachment of the empirical observer characteristic of French naturalism. By the end of Blasco's *La horda*, both hereditary and environmental determinism (the baby's birth into squalor, poverty and an environment of alcoholism) find the potential for resolution through the trope of regeneration. In this novel there is little attempt to attain either the objectivity or neutral omniscience of naturalism, and the inconsistent appeal to hereditary determinism in the novel does not ultimately amount to any credible thesis. Naturalism is certainly present in Blasco's Madrid novel of 1905, but is moderated by the appeal of other forces: political, individual and symbolic.

Early twentieth-century programmes of medical and mental science in Spain (including discourses of hygiene, degeneration and evolution) were propelled by the increasing centralization of the state, the uneven experience of modernity, and the growth of the city as a site of disease, whether social, biological or ideological.[48] Baroja's and Blasco's representations of turn-of-the-century Madrid emphasize the abject poverty and primitivism of the masses, and the reproduction of humanity in an environment of squalor and alcoholism. The solution for Blasco as for Baroja, it is implied, is the spiritual regeneration of the individual and bourgeois values. For Morel and his successors, *dégénérescence* was leading inevitably to sterility and extinction. This idea is undermined by the tentative regenerative promise at the end of both *La busca* and *La horda* in which Manuel Alcázar and Isidro Maltrana achieve an ambivalent bourgeois salvation. In the final part of my book, I analyse moral deviance and infanticide in Blasco's *Cañas y barro*, and paradigms of pathology and nation in Baroja's *El árbol de la ciencia*. The next two chapters explore the authors' common focus on maternity and human reproduction in the context of degenerationist debate.

Notes to Chapter 4

1. Blasco Ibáñez, Prólogo, *La horda* (1925); Casa-Museo Blasco Ibáñez archive.
2. In his Memoirs, Baroja remarked that 'siguiendo de lejos las novelas mías de vida pobre madrileña, hizo Blasco Ibáñez su novela *La horda*' (*OC*, VII, 870). According to José Luis León Roca, the antipathy between the two authors was fuelled by Baroja's claim that *La horda* was evidence of plagiarism: *Vicente Blasco Ibáñez* (Valencia: Prometeo, 1967), p. 334.
3. Gustave Le Bon, *Psychologies des foules* (Paris: Allan, 1896), p. 39.
4. Robert A. Nye, *The Origins of Crowd Psychology: Gustave Le Bon and the Crisis of Mass Democracy in the Third Republic* (London: Sage, 1975), p. 33.
5. Ángel Bahamonde Magro and Jesús Martínez, *Historia de España: siglo XIX* (Madrid: Cátedra, 1994), p. 44.
6. Hauser, 'El siglo XIX', p. 209.
7. Gabriel Tarde, *L'Opinion et la foule* (Paris: n.pub., 1901), p. 195.
8. Pick, *Faces of Degeneration*, pp. 91–94.
9. Labanyi, *Gender and Modernization*, p. 105.
10. Lombroso and Ferrero, *Criminal Woman*, p. 66.
11. Stannard, *The Theme of Degeneration*, p. 14.
12. Stannard, *The Theme of Degeneration*, p. 54.
13. Greenslade, *Degeneration*, p. 23.
14. Stephanie Sieburth, *Inventing High and Low: Literature, Mass Culture, and Uneven Modernity in Spain* (Durham, NC: Duke University Press, 1994), pp. 6, 16.
15. Labanyi, *Gender and Modernization*, p. 107.
16. Vicente Blasco Ibáñez, *La horda* (n.p.: CreateSpace, 2013), p. 4. All subsequent references are to this edition.
17. R. Malthus, *An Essay on the Principle of Population, as it Affects the Future Improvement of Society* (1798); cited by Raquel Álvarez Peláez, 'La mujer española' (p. 178) in relation to the theories and practice of birth control in early twentieth-century Britain and Spain.
18. Álvarez, 'La mujer española', p. 182.
19. Richard Cleminson, *Anarchism, Science and Sex* (Oxford: Peter Lang, 2000), Chapter 3. This study assesses manifestations of eugenics in Spain through analysis of three anarchist reviews: *Salud y fuerza*, *Generación Consciente* and *Estudios*.
20. Álvarez, 'La mujer española', pp. 178–81.
21. On Isidro Maltrana as an *abúlico* and a *déclassé*, transplanted temporarily out of poverty, see Claire-Nicolle Robin, 'La horda (1905) de Blasco Ibáñez: del "naturalismo" a la militancia', in *Vicente Blasco Ibáñez, 1898–1998: la vuelta al siglo de un novelista*, ed. by Joan Oleza and Javier Lluch, 2 vols (Valencia: Generalitat Valenciana, Conselleria de Cultura i Educació, 2000), I, 472–81.
22. Hauser, *Madrid bajo el punto de vista médico-social*, p. 320.
23. Cleminson, *Anarchism, Science and Sex*, pp. 40–42.
24. Greenslade, *Degeneration, Culture and the Novel*, pp. 36–37.
25. Baroja, *El árbol de la ciencia* (Madrid: Cátedra, 1989), p. 130. All subsequent references are to this edition.
26. Francis Galton, *Inquiries into the Human Faculty and its Development* (London: Macmillan, 1883), p. 318.
27. 'La reforma de las cárceles en el siglo XIX: las cárceles de Madrid', *Estudios de Historia Social*, 22–23 (1982), 69–188 (p. 166).

28. Michel Foucault, *Discipline and Punish: The Birth of the Prison* (Harmondsworth: Penguin, 1991), pp. 25–26.
29. Labanyi, *Gender and Modernization*, pp. 54–55.
30. Labanyi, *Gender and Modernization*, pp. 59–60.
31. Labanyi, *Gender and Modernization*, pp. 66–67.
32. Puértolas quotes widely from the press on the pressing issue of crime in her book *El Madrid de la 'lucha por la vida'*; see particularly pp. 67–79.
33. *Nuestro Tiempo*, 17 May 1902, p. 812.
34. Francisco Caudet, 'Reivindicación de Blasco Ibáñez frente a la crítica', in *Vicente Blasco Ibáñez, 1898–1998: la vuelta al siglo de un novelista*, ed. by Juan Oleza and Javier Lluch, 2 vols (Valencia: Generalitat Valenciana, Conselleria de Cultura i Educació, 2000), II, 680–99 (pp. 682–83).
35. Puértolas, *El Madrid de la 'lucha por la vida'*, p. 18.
36. Nye, *The Origins of Crowd Psychology*, p. 69.
37. Labanyi, *Gender and Modernization*, p. 210.
38. Emilia Pardo Bazán, *Obras completas*, 3 vols (Madrid: Aguilar, 1973), III, 725.
39. Nye, *The Origins of Crowd Psychology*, p. 2.
40. Nye, *The Origins of Crowd Psychology*, p. 62.
41. Nye, *The Origins of Crowd Psychology*, p. 14.
42. Baroja, 'Espíritu de subordinación', *El Globo*, 22 March 1903 p. 1.
43. Baroja, *Cuentos: Vidas sombrías* (Madrid: Caro Raggio, 1991), p. 192.
44. Pick, *Faces of Degeneration*, p. 85.
45. Emile Zola, *Nana*, trans. by George Holden (Penguin: Harmondsworth, 1979), p. 221.
46. Julio Caro Baroja, Prologue, *La busca*, p. xvi.
47. Peter Vickers traces the application of the naturalist methods of Blasco's Valencian cycle in the social novels, including *La horda*: 'fiel al naturalismo, se asegura de que su argumento se desarrolle según las fuerzas determinantes que actúan sobre él'; 'Blasco Ibáñez y las novelas "sociales", 1903–1905', in *Vicente Blasco Ibáñez, 1898–1998: la vuelta al siglo de un novelista*, ed. by Joan Oleza and Javier Lluch, 2 vols (Valencia: Generalitat Valenciana, Conselleria de Cultura i Educació, 2000), I, 464–81 (p. 468).
48. Cleminson, *Anarchism, Science and Sex*, p. 57.

PART III

❖

Pathologies of Body and Mind, Gender and Nation

CHAPTER 5

Adultery, Infanticide and Sensation Fiction: The Morality of Reproduction in Blasco Ibáñez's *Cañas y barro* (1902)

Adultery and criminality feature prominently in the nineteenth-century realist and naturalist novel, not as a valid measure of their frequency or veracity but instead an indication of their disproportionate status in social consciousness. Echoing these dominant narrative tropes, Blasco Ibáñez's turn-of-the-century novels present memorable portraits of the fictional adulteress in the guise of Dolores in *Flor de Mayo* (1895) and Neleta in *Cañas y barro*. Adultery was commonly positioned as a symptom of moral degeneration because it represented a potent threat to bourgeois social norms, class and the containment of the female body for reproduction. In *Cañas y barro* adultery leads to neonaticide and suicide, both markers of degeneration in Tonet, Neleta's lover. By contrast the survival of the anti-heroine is an unexpected narrative outcome of her transgressions that casts suggestive light — I contend — on the economic influence of Blasco's literary market and women readers.

Blasco's portrait of adultery and infanticide in *Cañas y barro* draws richly on popular conceptions of moral degeneration and criminality at the turn of the century. The local community of El Palmar is defined by apparently pathological characteristics and immoral actions: Neleta's sexual transgressions, the physical excesses of her husband Cañamèl, and the greed of local vagabond Sangonera, whose over-consumption of food and alcohol causes his death. Finally, it is Tonet's susceptibility to *aboulia* that proves the undoing of four generations of his family, the Paloma clan. However, the claims of environment far outweigh the legacy of heredity in this novel. *Cañas y barro* echoes the moral and social paradigms of degenerationism, and implicitly references hereditary legacies in schematic terms, but does not transpose the actions of the adulteress to a persuasive model of national decline. At the time of their publication the Valencian novels, notably *La barraca* and *Cañas y barro*, were greeted as a compelling demonstration of Blasco's adherence to the paradigms of Zola's narratives and the epitome of Spanish naturalism.[1] Naturalist concerns are certainly present in *Cañas y barro*. In place of scientific detachment, however, the novel draws predominantly on popular models of sensation fiction and melodrama, both of which relied heavily on exaggerated portraits of femininity. In Blasco's novel of 1902, I propose, the adherence to literary naturalism is effectively mitigated through appeal to these genres.

Blasco's interest in the tropes of pathology and deviance stemmed obviously from his close acquaintance with French naturalist fiction, which was serialized by the *folletín* section of *El Pueblo*. Zola's *La Débâcle* was published, for example, in 1900; *Vérité* was serialized in *El Pueblo* in 1902. Blasco particularly admired the French writers Victor Hugo and Émile Zola, although he denied any close resemblance with the latter's naturalist doctrine (*OC*, I, 15). The publishing house he founded with his friend Francisco Sempere issued Blasco's own works, but it also contributed to the dissemination of foreign scientific, philosophical and literary works in Spain, including Darwin, Nietzsche, Nordau, Spencer and Zola. Blasco was obviously acquainted with prominent evolutionary and degenerationist theories of the period. Cures for tuberculosis and syphilis, among other diseases, featured frequently in the advertisements of his newspaper *El Pueblo*.

Both the sensationalist and pathological elements of Blasco's early fiction would prove commercially lucrative for an author whose modest inheritance had been spent on subsidizing the costs of *El Pueblo*.[2] Portrayed in sardonic terms by Baroja and other members of the so-called 'Generation of 1898' as a populist political interloper in the serious world of art and literature, Blasco's financial gains were the source of ill-disguised sour grapes by the intellectual establishment. However the author's commercial success has been defended by many critics who point to the predominantly ideological aims of his cultural ventures, a guiding philosophy that outweighed economic motivation. Laguna Platero observes that Blasco promoted mass media for Republican goals: 'El fin no fue el dinero, sin la política'.[3] Through his journalistic and editorial work, he harnessed popular media in order to support the cultural and political education of the masses, a position central to his Republican ideology. Blasco's imprint with Sempere (later Editorial Prometeo) aimed to educate by selling books for one peseta. Equality and justice were the overt aims of his social novels, although their practical value lay predominantly in testimony and exposition, rather than any genuine achievement of social change. It is ironic, then, that lucrative commercial success through the appeal to middle-class audiences of his literary and cinematic output would be the eventual outcome of democratizing goals to expand cultural literacy among the masses. In Blasco's early twentieth-century literary fiction, the popular resonance of sensationalism and social deviance would prove particularly effective.

Sensationalism in Blasco draws both on the pathological foundations of naturalism and the emotional force of Romanticism, without full adherence to either. In *Cañas y barro* the treatment of the controversial subject matter of infanticide (or more accurately neonaticide) echoes deep-rooted socio-cultural anxieties at the turn of the century through its rejection of an idealized model of motherhood. Criminal anthropology had already diagnosed and categorized both wayward female sexuality and deviance from maternal instinct. Lombroso's analysis of female criminality foregrounded the phenomenon of infanticide, a crime that was recognized (under some circumstances) as the product of social pressures, as well as moral insanity or innate criminality: 'infanticide is most frequent where illegitimacy is rarest. When illegitimacy is treated with enormous severity, infanticide becomes more frequent, for the fear of dishonour pushes women into crime. [...] In sum, some crimes of passion are caused by public opinion and prejudice'.[4] For Lombroso, adultery was a tell-tale mark of the female born criminal. He thereby explained that laws are harsher towards women who commit adultery than men, because 'woman is naturally and organically monogamous and frigid'. Adultery, therefore, is insignificant when committed by men, but is for women 'the gravest of crimes'.[5] Social and cultural factors are subordinated to explanations of women's innate monogamy and lack of sexual desire, in accordance with their perceived inferior physical sensitivity.

The representation of Neleta draws implicitly on prevalent popular conceptions of degeneration. Most obviously, she is an adulteress and therefore a source of moral and physical danger. She marries Cañamèl for financial gain and cheats on her ageing husband through an affair with her childhood sweetheart, Tonet. In addition to this evidence of immorality, she is the landlady of the local tavern which provides alcohol to the population of El Palmar, thereby embodying once again a source of communal degeneration. Women's work in an environment corrupted by alcohol provides a dangerous milieu for pregnancy, a situation only exacerbated by the child's illegitimacy. In this context, the representation of Neleta is aligned closely with the *mujer fatal*, the apparent source of the downfall and death of two male generations of the Paloma clan, through the infanticide and suicide committed by Tonet. Adultery thus draws in powerful ways on discourses of degeneration. The physical symptoms or stigmata of degeneracy in *Cañas y barro* are confined to passing references to alcoholism and physical excess in Tonet, Cañamèl and particularly Sangonera. By contrast, social deviancy and marginalization define the figure of the adulteress, in accordance with Neleta's position as an outsider, both morally and congenitally.

This chapter considers Blasco's treatment of infanticide in the context of historical accounts of the phenomenon and high infant mortality rates in the late nineteenth century. The contemporary fascination with this 'unnatural' crime is noteworthy in relation to its association with degeneration. The union of Neleta and Tonet becomes aligned to some extent with that of an Amazonian society, in which matriarchal power upturns patriarchal structures. Their partnership culminates in the neonaticide of the male heir and suicide of the male lover, both constituting particularly emotive crimes within Blasco's sensationalist plot. *Cañas y barro* interweaves a contradictory naturalist model of organic pathologies through the exposition of social deviancy. This key trope draws on a number of inconsistent explanations of hereditary and environmental determinism, none of which provides a coherent model of degeneration in organic terms, but instead echo in popular form the Biblical role of Eve, or the *mujer serpiente*, in man's downfall. The death of the child in *Cañas y barro* is the result of moral, rather than physiological, degeneration. None the less, pathology (social, sexual, moral) is implicitly referenced both by the *aboulia* of Tonet and the transgressive immorality of Neleta.

The figure of the Amazon was a prevalent trope of turn-of-the-century visual art, in which masculinized women warriors wielded power over weak men, thereby 'leading to further degeneration'.[6] The Amazonian woman was allied particularly with the violent infanticide of male offspring and the lack of maternal feeling. These paradigms have obvious resonance in the plot of *Cañas y barro* in which Neleta is made culpable by the Paloma family for the untimely death of her son and lover. J. J. Bachofen's *Mother Law* (1870) constructed a view of history based on the development of human sexuality, and posited 'the movement from the hetaeristic age, of the age of exploitative promiscuity through matriarchy to eventual domination of the patriarchy as proof of the maturation of human society'. The violence of the Amazon is thus identified by Bachofen as 'savage degeneration': 'the state of the Amazon, the cruel and unnatural domination of the male by the woman warrior, was a sign of an aberrant but necessary stage in human development'.[7] Kleist's *Penthesilea* (1808) and other nineteenth-century representations depicted the female warriors murdering their male offspring. According to Hegel's *Lectures on the Philosophy of Religion* (1832), Amazon women were reputed to drive away the men and pound their sons to death.

As a *mujer fatal* Neleta dominates her husband and lover, using sexual desirability to wield financial control. She overcomes maternal instinct and instructs Tonet to abandon the newborn child to protect her hard-won inheritance. Blasco, however, ultimately reverses the model of maternal violence, thereby referencing infanticide not through the murderous actions of the mother, but instead the weak-willed father. The extent to which Neleta is construed as culpable for the novel's infanticide is significant in this regard. Most obviously, the novel's conclusion distorts the popular conception of infanticide as the product of female psychopathology.

For Lombroso, adultery was evidence of the degenerate sexuality of women. The most advanced stage of human sexuality was seen as that of male European adults. Women, black people and children were seen as the embodiments of primitive development. Homosexuality, promiscuity, adultery and prostitution were thereby construed as forms of deviant and degenerate sexuality.[8] Within this framework, women were innately categorized as the Other. As an adulteress, Neleta's desire for her lover provides evidence of wayward sexuality according to the norms of degeneration theory. In other words, the narrative recourse in *Cañas y barro* to prevalent *fin-de-siècle* misogynist representations of women (as the *mujer fatal* and *mujer serpiente*) draws on dominant social and moral discourses of degeneration, which situated feminine desire as aberrant outside the confines of heterosexual marriage.

Blasco's representation of Neleta echoes this paradigm, but ultimately subverts the model. His portrait of the *femme fatale* to some extent reinforces contemporary paradigms of bourgeois morality. However both Neleta's survival and the preservation of her financial independence at the end of the novel resist the almost inevitable demise of the *mujer fatal* in male-authored fiction of the period.[9] In *Cañas y barro* the anti-heroine is morally transgressive but not irredeemably degenerate, and neither is she punished for her actions by the novel's conclusion. Instead she survives with her inheritance intact, an ending that at best contains a contradictory moral message that does not sustain either the premises or outcomes of degenerationism. In recent years, a strand of critical interest in *Cañas y barro* has turned its attention to gendered paradigms, but no existing studies to my knowledge address the intriguing issues of degeneration and deviance in relation to Neleta's sexuality, Tonet's *aboulia* or indeed the novel's infanticide.[10]

From the sirens of Homer's *Odyssey* to the vampires of Bram Stoker, the *femme fatale* is not of course unique to the late nineteenth century. It is well known, however, that the figure was reconstructed across European literatures and art in this period, and became a cultural phenomenon of the *fin de siècle*. In simple terms, the *femme fatale* is defined by her sexuality which is threatening or fatal to her male partners, as demonstrated by abundant literary and visual representations of women that drew on religious and mythological archetypes including Eve, Lilith, Salome and Medusa.[11] In Spain, the figure is exemplified by the exotic allure of Valle-Inclán's Niña Chole and in visual art by the decadent women of Ramon Casas's paintings. *Sífilis* (Fig. 1.2) depicts a prostitute wrapped in a shawl upon which a snake uncurls. An obvious symbol of the fall of Eve, the serpent demonstrates the iconographic representation of the woman as perilous temptation or feminine 'maldad'. The trope occurs frequently in Blasco's turn-of-the-century fiction, notably *Flor de mayo*, *Entre naranjos* and *Cañas y barro* through the visual referencing of woman as serpent common in late nineteenth-century European art and literature. Bram Dijkstra's influential study of European *fin-de-siècle* art traces the contradictory representation of women as sexual innocence and threat to provide evidence of the 'virulent misogyny [that] infected all the arts' during this period.[12]

Blasco's 'ficción de masas' relied heavily on feminine consumption. Both the author's representations of women and the commercial popularity of his novels may be interpreted productively in the light of recent research by Sharon Marcus, who posits a new relationship between the image and the spectator in nineteenth-century England. Reframing existing assumptions about Victorian women as sexless angels defined only by male desires, Marcus argues that fashion plates, among other objects and images of the period, 'assumed a female gaze'.[13] Women played a central role as the represented subject, but also as readers and spectators with active agency. Of interest in this regard is Blasco's well-known friendship with Carmen de Burgos, who expressed particular admiration for his fiction. Blasco's works are widely thought to have provided inspiration for a number of her own short novels, including *La indecisa* (1912) and *La que quiso ser maja* (1924). The latter was published in *La Novela Pasional*, a collection of erotic short novels. Significantly, however, her protagonist refuses to shed any clothes, an ironic response to Blasco's *La maja desnuda*.[14] The iconographic representation of women in Blasco's novels engages obviously with traditional stereotypes that reinforce the binary categories of dangerous versus submissive women. In *Cañas y barro*, however, I suggest that these divisions are subordinate to the transgressive appeal of Neleta's actions as she prioritizes financial independence above maternity and imposed morality. The representation of Neleta is by no means a feminist portrait. I argue, however, that it can be read instead as a model of vicarious pleasure for women readers beyond the didactic censure of degenerate female sexuality.

In the context of the literary reception and readership of Blasco's novels, the author's motivation for the infanticide of *Cañas y barro* is particularly intriguing. Of course the sensationalist elements of plot in Blasco's turn-of-the-century novels, encompassing notably female adultery (Dolores, Leonora, Neleta), female rivalry and fighting, and the deaths of children, had particular significance for Blasco's popular success. The original *Casa Editorial Sempere* editions of *Flor de Mayo* and *Arroz y Tartana* were priced at one peseta per volume, although they barely sold 500 copies.[15] The publication of the bestseller *La barraca* in 1898, however, would mark a change in Blasco's fortunes, selling 15,000 copies by 1904. The popularity of this novel depended to a large extent on its famous representation of a hostile environment and collective psychology. These naturalist elements coexist alongside the tragic inevitability of the *desenlace*, the downfall of Batiste's family and the death of his son Pascualet, elements that respond more readily to Romanticism. Blasco's decision to place *El Pueblo* and later the novels published through his editorial work with Sempere within the financial reach of the working classes provides evidence of his ideological and political intention to reach a mass public. His Republicanism, however, did not preclude the striking accumulation of wealth and property.

The notoriety of the author's Valencian novels rested to a large extent on their obviously sensationalist elements. *Cañas y barro* draws inspiration from prominent contemporary moral debates and social phenomena that were disseminated by the popular media. Infanticide was a particularly emotive crime during this period. Nineteenth-century sensation fiction was a popular genre that commonly portrayed women who were predisposed (according to contemporary psychology) to acts of crime and insanity. It drew on scandals of the period through exaggeration, and was fuelled by feminine violence.[16]

In late nineteenth-century Spain, *inclusas* (or foundling hospitals) were established to admit illegitimate children in order to reduce rates of infanticide by providing mothers with an alternative solution for avoiding dishonour. As Revuelta Eugercios documents in her study of La Inclusa de Madrid, in 1902 the institution admitted over 1300 abandoned children.[17] Historically, foundlings were also abandoned to the mercy of 'kind strangers' in the countryside or the care of relatives. These alternative possibilities for the moral and financial dilemmas of the birth of illegitimate children raise the obvious question of why Blasco Ibáñez chose for the actions of his central characters to culminate in infanticide. His plot discards the alternative for Tonet to abandon the baby in the doorway of a Church in Valencia as instructed by Neleta.

In the wake of childbirth, Neleta is terrified by the risk of discovery and discounts the idea of finding a woman in the countryside to wet-nurse her son: 'Nada de llevar la criatura a un pueblo inmediato a la Albufera, buscando una mujer fiel que lo criase. Había que temer las indiscreciones de la nodriza, la astucia de los enemigos. [...] Había que abandonar al recién nacido, fuese como fuese'.[18] Despite the power she exerts over Tonet, who becomes infantilized in the face of her determination, at no point does she raise the possibility of killing the child. In *Cañas y barro* neonaticide was guaranteed to grip the reader's imagination much more effectively than mere abandonment. The latter, however, was by no means an assurance of survival. Foundling hospitals for abandoned children in Spanish cities were associated with high infant mortality rates due to the poverty of the mothers, disease and poor nutrition. In 1880 the paediatrician Manuel Tolosa Latour identified the infant mortality rate at Madrid's La Inclusa as reaching 85 per cent.[19]

In early nineteenth-century France, J. E. D. Esquirol considered pregnancy to be a volatile condition that could cause psychological disorder in women.[20] The British historian Daniel Grey argues that by the end of the nineteenth century, infanticide was popularly regarded as 'the crime of a single (and probably young and working-class) woman driven mad by the shame of her situation and the pain of childbirth'.[21] The prevailing image of the 'typical' infanticidal woman in the press was that of the working-class servant girl. By the 1860s, public outcry about the high incidence of infanticide peaked. Infanticide was seen as a largely female crime and was often ascribed in Britain to 'puerperal insanity' in the immediate weeks following childbirth.[22] In 1865, the *British Medical Journal* claimed that 'puerperal mania' could sometimes cause women to suffer an 'uncontrollable impulse' to 'destroy her own offspring', and asked: 'Does such a woman (becoming a murderess) deserve our deepest sympathy; or ought she to be handed into the hangman's hands?'[23]

Pregnancy and childbirth were, according to these medical views, potentially explosive conditions that could provoke a latent form of madness in some women: myths of maternal violence were intrinsically constructed upon concerns of national development, including social class and reproduction. In 1902, Havelock Ellis cited a French article by Audiffrent which argued that the impulse to commit neonaticide is not confined to the human female, but is also found in the natural world. Infanticide by women was construed as animalistic, and needed to be controlled by a civilized society.[24] The theory supports contemporaneous theories of atavism and criminology in the positioning of female reproduction as allied to savage behaviour, as Kramar and Watson note: 'Criminality was thus deemed the result of degeneration, amounting to biological pathology, occurring within the borders of civilized societies'. For Audiffrent as for Lombroso, 'human deviance (of which neonaticide is an example) is evidence of a retreat from civility and biological degeneration understood in quasi-Darwinian evolutionary terms'.[25]

In the context of contemporary European debates about criminality and atavism, infanticide and neonaticide were construed predominantly as actions perpetrated by women in response to pregnancy and childbirth. The causes were deemed to be both psychopathological and socio-economic. In fact the neonaticide of *Cañas y barro* fails to conform to these popular stereotypes. Following the birth of her illegitimate child, Neleta's response is defined not by emotionalism or insanity but financial logic. Rather it is Tonet (the virile *guerrillero* turned *abúlico*) who commits infanticide and subsequently suicide in the gruesome ending of the novel. The dangerous 'symptoms' thought to be associated with puerperal insanity (infanticide and suicide) are embodied in *Cañas y barro* not by the mother but instead the father.

In Blasco's novel, recourse to neonaticide is driven wholeheartedly by the demands of the plot, and its recourse to a popular blend of sensationalism and Romantic tragedy. Neleta gives away her child, but she does not conform in any persuasive sense to the violent degeneracy of the Amazon.

In Spain the establishment of *inclusas* points to the social, moral and juridical acknowledgement of the common existence of infanticide in the late nineteenth century, with particular relation to illegitimate children. Blasco's treatment of the event is characterized by grotesque naturalistic detail, as Tonet is horrified to encounter the evidence of his crime floating in the water. The baby is now 'algo lívido y gelatinoso erizado de sanguijuelas: una cabecita hinchada, deforme, negruzca, con las cuencas vacías y colgando de una de ellas el globo de un ojo; todo tan repugnante, tan hediondo' (260). The neonaticide of *Cañas y barro*, together with the morbid description of the dead baby, picks up on a phenomenon common in the nineteenth-century Spanish press: the public's obsession with crime. Reviews such as *La España Moderna* published articles by leading criminologists which educated readers about crime in response to widespread European debates on degeneration and particularly the theories of Lombroso. In his fictional depiction of neonaticide, Blasco engages with the common sociological phenomenon of illegitimate births. The novel draws on a public fascination with a crime commonly associated with feminine violence, but subverts the paradigm. *Cañas y barro* toys with popular versions of deviant sexuality through its representation of the figure of the adulteress, but refuses ultimately to condemn Neleta as essentially degenerate.

According to the ideology of the *ángel del hogar*, women were construed as dutiful models of morality within the family unit. The slow but steady incorporation of women into the workforce during the Restoration, as Campos et al. have noted, was due to a number of complex socio-economic factors, most notably the need for cheap labour, and led to intense controversy about women's work during this period. Doctors and hygienists drew attention to the effects of women working in factories and workshops for the health of both women and children, and also the moral and practical guardianship of the home. The harmful consequences for reproduction and lactation due to the constitution of the female body, considered weaker by nature than that of the male, were emphasized: 'El incremento de abortos, partos prematuros, el nacimiento de niños "desmediados e incompletos", el aumento de la mortalidad infantil en el medio proletario eran algunas de las consecuencias nefastas de la actividad extradoméstica femenina' (1914).[26] These arguments within scientific and pseudo-scientific discourse posited the ideal of the domestic angel, or *ángel del hogar*, in which the woman's role was in the home. There she was required for 'el cuidado de sus hijos, para su crianza, para su educación, [...] al calor de los besos de una madre'.[27] In the wake of Darwinism and evolutionary theory, the economy of the body and the social effects of reproduction gained even greater currency.[28]

It is significant, in this context, that Neleta inherits her public role and wealth from both the illicit activities of Cañamèl and the *taberna* they run in El Palmar. Neleta's role as landlady of the local tavern can therefore be analysed in response to the discourses of hygienists and conservative morality at the turn of the century that focused on the toxic effects of alcoholism, both for the poor population and future generations. According to this view of heredity, the strong connection between alcoholism and degeneration led to madness and criminality. In *Cañas y barro* Blasco traces pathologies in moral and social rather than biological and national terms. The corrupting source of alcohol is none the less implicit in the trajectory of the adulterous couple.

Blasco focuses much more clearly on moral decadence than the physical transmission of deviant characteristics. As Campos, Martínez and Huertas indicate, the low population growth rate, the role of women in the education of her children, the moral environment in which they grew up, and the perceived harmful effects of women's work lent increasing momentum to the attempts to explain and eradicate degeneration: 'Entre las causas principales del nacimiento de niños entecos, malformados o viciosos estaba el trabajo femenino'.[29] Both reproduction and children's education were the justification for the containment of women's activities and identities. In order to preserve the structures and bourgeois values of late nineteenth-century society, the question of national development became emotively allied to the social and medical regulation of maternity and women's bodies.

Neleta's deviancy from the ideology of domesticity (through adultery and material gain at the expense of her child) positions her by implication as the prime source of moral degeneration. In Neleta, however, there are no signs of the physical ravages associated with a life of excess. Furthermore, her son is robustly healthy, defying his mother's persistent efforts to provoke miscarriage by applying quack remedies and punching her stomach in desperation: 'la salud de Neleta se burlaba de todo. Aquel cuerpo, en apariencia delicado, era fuerte y sólido' (210). Neither mother nor baby embodies the inherited physical traits of degeneracy which signified, according to scientific discourse of the period, the exhaustion of the race.[30] Moral degeneracy is a different matter, at least from the point of view of contemporary ideologies.

In *Cañas y barro* the echoes of degenerationism can be understood in the context of class, gender, hereditary and environmental determinism. Despite the poverty of her background and maternal lineage, Neleta is 'la muchacha más guapa de la Albufera' (87). Her physical beauty and desirability are presented as a surprising triumph over her lowly origins and environment, as she grows up in the midst of poverty 'como una flor rara, contrastando su hermosura con la pobreza física de las otras hijas del Palmar' (75). The other girls of El Palmar apparently resemble the eels that form their main source of nutrition: 'su perfil anguloso, la sutilidad escurridiza de su cuerpo y el hedor de los zagalejos les daba cierta semejanza con las anguilas' (36). Here an idiosyncratic form of environmental determinism is at work, through the eminently questionable assumption that a poor diet causes the physical unattractiveness of the local women.

By contrast, Neleta with her red hair and green eyes is an exotic outsider. These physical descriptions, which place Neleta in a different category from the other local girls, insinuate covertly that she herself is illegitimate and that her father must be of more privileged class and descent. Her beauty is, by implication, the product of immorality. Whether for reasons of nature or nurture, her pregnancy by Tonet is a repetition of her mother's own history. Her father is not present and her mother leads a 'vida anormal' (55) selling fish at the market in Valencia to earn money. Neleta is of different biological and class lineage from the other girls of the Albufera. This factor underpins both her apparent sexual and moral deviance, but also her economic and social success.

Neleta has traditionally been interpreted by critics as the fatal woman, the incarnation of avarice, and the source of destruction of male characters: firstly of Cañamèl, and finally Tonet and her baby, the last two generations of the Paloma clan. She is listed by Jeremy Medina among Blasco's 'masculine or domineering women' and represents, according to this perspective, 'feminine avarice, as well as the force and fecundity of nature herself. [...] She is individualized only by her sexual frustration and an occasional suggestion of real affection for Tonet'.[31] In an early review published in *El Liberal* in 1903, Murga referred to her as 'una concepción perfecta dentro del mal'.[32] Neleta represents, according to these readings, a source of temptation as the seductive and dangerous *mujer fatal*.

Neleta is not defined by maternity or domesticity, but instead by ambition. The adulterous relationship with her childhood sweetheart betrays the terms of marriage to Cañamèl as a traditional contract of financial and sexual exchange. Later she renounces her child in order to preserve the financial inheritance accorded by Cañamèl's will. By the closing pages, she is free from ties of maternity, matrimony or financial dependence: 'Neleta era la única mujer del Palmar que, con su acostumbrada dulzura, hacía frente al rudo vicario. [...] No necesitaba hombres' (204–05). Blasco's anti-heroine is not contained within the domestic sphere as the nurturing, self-sacrificing wife and mother, the *ángel del hogar* or *madre abnegada* of nineteenth-century discourse. She faces the hostility of the inhabitants of El Palmar for her moral decadence beyond these confines.

The most significant transgressions of feminine norms are found in the expression of Neleta's sexuality and her determination to overcome maternal instinct. She embodies robust health, sexual desire and fertility, characteristics that align her with *voluntad*, the Schopenhauerian Will-to-live. Following Tonet's long absence from El Palmar and her marriage to Cañamèl, the childhood *novios* are drawn together 'con los ojos fijos, como si se devorasen' (128). Neleta reveals the coexistence of reason and Will that allows her survival in a patriarchal world, although this is achieved fundamentally through the traditional exchange of economic privilege for sexual relations. There is no genuine attempt in the novel to pathologize the lack of priority given to maternal feeling, despite obvious flaws in her character. Neleta is above all the embodiment of rational judgement and sanity as she preserves her inheritance at the expense of the survival of her lover and baby.

Mirroring to some extent the novels of Galdós, adultery is configured as a marker of excess and the commodification of the female body beyond the domestic sphere. By contrast to the death through excessive consumption by Cañamèl, Tonet and Sangonera (through sex, alcohol and food respectively), however, Neleta in fact contains both emotion and sexual desire in order to protect her economic inheritance. She denies Tonet entry to her bedroom, for example, during her husband's illness in Ruzafa. In the case of Cañamèl, his excessive capitulation to physical drives and immoral financial earnings is accompanied by infertility, a symbolic marker of physical and moral decline. By contrast to Galdós's Rosalía de Bringas, who commits adultery for money, Neleta undertakes marriage in exchange for economic gain and engages in adultery to satisfy unfulfilled desire. According to this model, adultery represents surplus desire and the breaking of a contract of ownership, ending in a lack of productivity symbolized by the death of the child. Like the prostitute, the adulteress blurs the boundaries between the private and public spheres.

Neleta is characterized fairly bluntly through the trait of avarice. The narrative provides some justification for this flaw by emphasizing the poverty and hunger of her childhood years as motivation for her refusal to marry Tonet because this would necessitate surrendering her inheritance: 'La avaricia de la mujer real se revelaba en Neleta con una fogosidad capaz de los mayores arrebatos. Despertábase en ella el instinto de varias generaciones de pescadores miserables roídos por la miseria' (205). Both hereditary and environmental factors are at play here within the narrator's explanation. Neleta has inherited the instinct of generations of poor ancestors, a reaction exacerbated by her own experience of childhood poverty. In the absence of her father, her mother sold fish at the market in Valencia and she relied on Tonet's mother to feed her. Both the poor role model provided by her mother and financial insecurity are catalysts for Neleta's manipulations; her instinct for survival however, is (apparently) inherited. In the context of naturalism, Blasco's exploration of determinism is schematic rather than compelling.

Neleta's personal sacrifices during her marriage to the ageing and unwell Cañamèl, a union that secures her financial future, necessitate a controlled masquerade. When she discovers that *la Samaruca* (Cañamèl's sister-in-law) has accompanied her dying husband in Ruzafa in order to manipulate his will, Neleta banishes the mask of femininity: 'Se mostró tal como era. Su vocecita mimosa, de dulzonas inflexiones, se tornó ronca' (196). As she initiates a physical fight with *la Samaruca*, Blasco's representation of the adulteress as viper echoes the popular iconography of the *mujer serpiente* typical of *fin-de-siècle* (misogynist) constructions of women: 'Neleta, con su sonrisita dulce y su voz melosa, ocultaba una vivacidad de víbora, y mordía a su enemiga en la cara con un furor que la hacía tragarse la sangre' (197). Similar imagery is found in the exotic representation of Valle-Inclán's Niña Chole and other vampiric representations of women prevalent in Rubén Darío and authors of *modernismo*. Referenced as both Salammbô and Lilith, Niña Chole's beauty is identified as 'la gracia serpentina', and is simultaneously a source of attraction and horror for the male in the opening chapter of *Sonata de estío*.[33] In Blasco's *Flor de Mayo* the alluring Dolores is described by her mother-in-law as the 'hermoso culebrón' (115), a perilous combination of sexual instinct and danger.

Maternal instinct is not absent in Neleta. After four years of marriage to Cañamèl, no pregnancy materializes, despite 'sus fervientes deseos' (91). It could be argued, therefore, that her adulterous relationship with Tonet is a manifestation of both sexual and unfulfilled maternal desire. Biological instinct, however, is subordinate to her hard-won financial and social status. When she falls pregnant by Tonet, she rejects aggressively her impending maternity and tries to abort the baby: 'odiaba con furor salvaje el ser oculto' (210). As her pregnancy progresses, she embarks on an almost impossible mission to hide the pregnancy from the view of the townsfolk and *la Samaruca*, driven only by her insuperable strength of Will which increasingly inspires fear in Tonet. Through a monumental effort, she continues to work in the *taberna* until the day of the child's birth, strapping up her body by means of a corset to hide the growing baby. Realism, clearly, was not Blasco's priority in composing the narrative plot of *Cañas y barro*.

According to existing critical readings, Neleta's deviation from expected norms of feminine conduct culminates in the destruction of two generations of the Paloma clan. She insists that they must abandon the baby in Valencia, as her fierce resolve takes precedence over Tonet's weakness: 'Tonet la oía aterrado. Intentó resistirse, pero la mirada de Neleta impuso cierto miedo a su voluntad siempre debil' (216). Confronted by his lover's prodigious determination to overcome any sentimental weakness, or the resurfacing of latent maternal instinct, he obeys at first but recognizes his impotence to fulfil the task: 'Reconocíase impotente para cumplir su promesa' (232). Neleta's dominance results in the symbolic castration of Tonet. Reversing the earlier and repeated emphasis on his masculinity, symbolized by his moustache — an 'adorno viril' (92) — , he is unmanned apparently by Neleta's authority and determination. Yet the debility of his resolve and his own moral vacuum have been apparent from the beginning of the novel. This characteristic weakness is evidenced both by his dislike of hard work and the violent treatment of his adopted sister, a foundling named *la Borda*, whom he beats 'como a una bestia sumisa' (82).

The presentation of Tonet engages obviously with theories of degeneration still current at the turn of the century, particularly in relation to adultery, criminality and suicide. As parents Tonet and Neleta both display emotional incapacity, evidence of moral decadence according to degenerationists. Familial lineage or heredity is significant, although sporadically referenced by Blasco. The absence of Will is particularly influential in this regard. The many children of Tonet's grandfather, *tío Paloma*, were all 'seres blancuzos y enfermizos' (32). The death of all these children except for Tono represent the generational debility of the Paloma clan. As the idle progeny of the hardworking *tío Tono*, Tonet lacks interest in working the land as his father has done before him, and instead escapes to become a Civil Guard in Cuba. He is an *abúlico*, the degenerate offspring of the Paloma lineage. Upon his return to El Palmar, he helps his father 'con el ardor momentáneo de los seres de escasa voluntad' (95). If avarice defines Neleta, the loss of Will that characterizes Tonet symbolizes a common trope in turn-of-the-century Spanish fiction: the lack of masculine volition needed to revitalize the nation.

There are two notable elements in this presentation. Firstly, Tonet embodies a contradictory form of determinism, not least because his father Tono is the epitome of hard-working masculinity: the latter is 'el hombre más hombre de toda la Albufera' (33), 'siempre serio y pronto para el trabajo' (34). Tonet's dislike of hard work, in other words, is not inherited from his father, although other characteristics appear to intensify through the different generations. In this regard, the traits of pathology and madness may be latent in one generation, and reappear in the next. For Morel, criminal and insane tendencies, for example, could lurk undetected in the body, incubated by parents and later developed by their descendants. Like his grandfather, Tonet is characterized as virile and audacious, but his demise is propelled by 'su instinto de muchacho perezoso' (51), an innate quality reinforced repeatedly by the narrative. By contrast to *tío Paloma*, 'lo que su nieto odiaba, con una repulsión instintiva que ponía de pie su voluntad, era el trabajo' (48). Hereditary determinism is frequently present but fails to constitute a coherent thesis in *Cañas y barro*. Prior to the infanticide, Tonet's reasoning draws on hereditary determinism as a justification for the crime he is about to commit: 'sentía resucitar en él la dureza de los viejos Palomas, la cruel frialdad de su abuelo, que veía morir sus hijos pequeños sin una lágrima' (233). He shares certain characteristics with his grandfather but not others; here, the legacy of family traits proves a useful recourse for faulty reasoning.

Against the advice of his father and grandfather, Tonet seeks refuge from hard work in constant heavy drinking or alcoholism. Morel posited that children could inherit the alcoholism of their parents, leading to the intensification of alcoholism in later generations and eventually racial exhaustion, a theme central to Galdós's earlier *Angel Guerra* (1890–91).[34] In *Cañas y barro* Blasco does not depict the physical ravages of alcoholism in naturalist terms; neither does he subscribe in any meaningful way to paradigms of hereditary alcoholism. Although Sangonera becomes an alcoholic like his father, the models of heredity proffered sporadically by Blasco remain unconvincing. After years spent as a vagabond and drunkard, Sangonera eventually dies of 'una apendicitis mortal' (252), the result of extraordinary abuse of his body through over-consumption of food and alcohol. His father, in turn, died of alcoholism, a form of physical excess that was considered symptomatic of degeneration within hygienic medicine. The trajectory and gruesome demise of this minor character, however, hardly constitutes a fully conceived set of beliefs on the part of the author.

Cañas y barro has commonly been regarded as the epitome of Blasco's naturalism, written by the natural Spanish successor to Zola's scientific determinism. Medina, for example, argues that in the Valencian novels 'Blasco's point of view is one of objectivity and neutral omniscience', a position in line with the aims of French naturalism.[35] More recently some critics have begun to revise this view.[36] Hereditary determinism is not a primary force in the novel. Environmental determinism is rendered more insistently by Blasco, given the powerful description of setting that dominates the novel, but even here his naturalism is far from wholehearted, scientific or objective. *Cañas y barro* evokes the abject poverty and struggle for survival in the harsh setting of El Palmar and the Albufera, an environment characterized by filth, squalor and foul odours. The naturalist aspects of the novel, however, are frequently mitigated by recourse both to sensationalism and Romantic irony that undermines a convincing comparison with the scientific determinism of Zola.

In sum, *Cañas y barro* toys with the exposition of both hereditary and environmental determinism, but fails to sustain any coherent or scientific approach in line with the architects of literary naturalism. Neleta is neither the violent Amazon of degeneration theory and sexology nor the perpetrator of infanticide. None the less, an interest in both determinism and degeneration sustains the narrative plot, albeit with limited adherence to a consistent thesis. The contradictions within Blasco's exposition are exemplified by the demise of Cañamèl who, as a smuggler and moneylender, represents a lack of morality. As an outsider, however, he embodies more robust inherited characteristics than the inhabitants of El Palmar. He is 'viejo y enfermo, pero de raza fuerte' (173), and his physical decline is caused not by any consistent application of hereditary determinism but environmental damage: alcohol, overeating, and an obsessive desire for Neleta. Blasco's description revels in grim physical details: 'Cañamèl se agravaba en sus dolencias. [...] Su salud estaba quebrantada; pero al verle cada vez más grueso, más hinchado, desbordando grasa, la gente declaraba con gravedad que iba a morir de exceso de salud y buena vida' (187). Cañamèl fails to father a child, a role fulfilled instead by his younger rival, Tonet, who kills the child due to his lack of *voluntad*. In Blasco's novel of 1902, *aboulia* ultimately causes the demise of a family line, a potential symbol of regional decline but one that is not fully exploited. Although there is no consistent thesis regarding inherited characteristics, the descriptions of the illness and demise of both Cañamèl and Sangonera are none the less aligned with hygienic medicine of nineteenth-century Spain, which posited a strong link between illness and excess, whether caused by lust, gluttony, ambition, or envy.[37] In Blasco's representation of the pathologies of El Palmar a degenerationist model is incipient, but not fully developed.

The dead baby becomes the victim not just of Neleta's lack of maternal protection, but also the moral degeneration of the Paloma line which ultimately results in its eradication. The child becomes 'el último vástago maldito de una famosa dinastía de pescadores' (271). In the wake of his actions, and haunted by the spectre of the child he has drowned in the Albufera, Tonet justifies his actions and makes his lover culpable (through the narrator's use of *style indirect libre*) for his actions: 'Él no era malo. Tenía la buena sangre de su padre. Su delito era el egoísmo, la voluntad débil, que le había hecho apartarse de la lucha por la vida. La perversa era Neleta' (264). Extending Blasco's engagement with the iconography of the *mujer serpiente*, Tonet identifies Neleta with Sancha, the serpent of local folklore. This perspective interprets her sins (sexuality) as responsible for his downfall as a latter-day Adam, through her fatal embrace: 'Él era como el pastor de la leyenda: había acariciado de pequeña a la serpiente, la había alimentado, prestándola hasta el calor de su cuerpo, y al volver de la guerra asombrábase viéndola grande, poderosa, embellecida por el tiempo, mientras ella se le enroscaba con un abrazo fatal, causándole la muerte con sus caricias' (265). Neleta is construed as the source of the downfall and degeneration of the male by the subjective judgement of a fictional character.

Blasco's unconventional anti-heroine does not function, however, as a successful moral warning. Tonet and the male child die, whilst the adulteress survives with her inheritance intact. The moral lesson is at best dubious. Certainly Neleta appears to have held powerful appeal for contemporary readers. A favourable contemporary review of *Cañas y barro* by Eduardo Gómez de Barquero, published in *La España Moderna* (Madrid) in 1903, emphasizes the author's strong characterization and his ability to convey 'la feroz codicia y la inhumana insensibilidad de Neleta'.[38] Her resolve is apparently inhuman, but it is certainly also memorable. In the context of degenerationism, she is equipped physically but not morally to engender the next generation. In symbolic terms, her role as genetic outsider is not enough to remedy Tonet's *aboulia* or lack of volition. Furthermore she refuses to accept passively the demands of maternity at any cost. The representation of Neleta simultaneously sustains the norms of contemporary morality, and subverts its logic. This may well have proven a strong element of the novel's appeal for a readership so frequently construed as the uniform and passive recipients of an accepted feminine morality.

By the end of the novel Neleta shows no remorse for the death of her son and lover. In fact her reaction is one of fear that *tío Paloma* will give away her secret. Blasco's representation of the adulteress and *mujer fatal* rests on a combination of competing narrative perspectives. As a morally reliable witness, Tono describes her earlier in the novel as a scatterbrain: 'una casquivana' (98), a term that hardly reflects the later emphasis on her almost inhuman resolve. Tonet labels her 'la perversa'. *La Samaruca* dubs Neleta the 'mujer mala [...] haciendo perder la calma a los hombres' (112), viewing her as the manipulative fortune-seeker who wrests Samaruca's own rightful occupation of her dead sister's position. Cañamèl cannot resist her 'gracia felina' (88), and is consumed by insatiable sexual desire that, according to popular legend, destroys his health and eventually takes his life. *Tío Paloma* deems her to be 'la perdición de una familia' (268); 'aquella Neleta resultaba una perra ardorosa que había perdido al muchacho' (270). Paloma blames her powerful sexuality for the downfall of his family. The author's presentation of Neleta is less obviously judgemental. Above all she survives, revealing no remorse for her actions. Just as significantly, she remains independent financially, and free from the ties of marriage and maternity. At the end of *Flor de Mayo*, Dolores desperately grieves the death of her son at sea, the outcome of her adultery with her husband's brother. Overwhelmed by an unrelenting 'lamento de dolor' (243), she mourns her unbearable loss: 'Fill meu! ... fill meu!' (243). In this earlier novel, maternal anguish provides a stark moral warning for the consequences of female adultery. Unlike the fate of Dolores, the loss of Neleta's lover and child at the end of *Cañas y barro* does not lead to the grief of repentance or any coherent moral lesson.

Among the women of the Valencian novels, Neleta functions as the most developed embodiment of the *femme fatale* with reference to her powerful sexuality, her implication in the deaths of Cañamèl, Tonet, her baby, and her quest for financial status. As Dijkstra argues: 'By 1900 the vampire had come to represent woman as the personification of everything negative that linked sex, ownership, and money'.[39] Doane identifies the construction of the feminine body in relation to excess in late nineteenth-century art and literature: 'the *femme fatale* is represented as the antithesis of the maternal — sterile or barren, she produces nothing in a society which fetishizes production'.[40] Neleta produces a baby but fails to ensure his survival, thus embodying an unacceptable version of womanhood. Symbolically, however, the infanticide denotes sterility in terms of reproductive success; the outcome of moral deviance through adultery is the failure of reproduction. The infanticide is carried out according to the social motivation and moral bankruptcy of the novel's characters, but its primitivism denotes regression in anthropological terms. Tonet rationalizes an act undertaken to protect an inheritance; its primitive quality is underlined by the grotesque descriptions of the child. In the language of degenerationism, infanticide becomes the inevitable outcome of the *abúlico*'s innate apathy and the racial weakness of the people of the Albufera. For the purposes of plot in *Cañas y barro*, however, the representation of infanticide taps into a public fascination rather than a convincing biological paradigm.

In the late nineteenth century, Galdós famously depicted women's struggle against the entrapment enshrined by the institutions of marriage and family in novels such as *Tristana* (1892). Pardo Bazán proposed new models for male and female roles in *Memorias de un solterón* (1896). By contrast, Blasco Ibáñez returns to the delineation of woman as temptation, ensnaring her unsuspecting male victims, thereby constructing woman as a symbol of a destructive sexuality. Blasco's refusal to kill off his female characters or contain them within a domestic solution does not negate the frequently conservative treatment of gender in his novels. Neleta, however, occupies a contradictory position, embodying both the misogynist representations of fatal women of the *fin de siglo*, but also a transgressive figure of identification for women readers. As Marcus argues, the nineteenth-century novel was 'one of the most important cultural sites for representing and shaping desire, affect, and ideas about gender and family'.[41]

The representation of the adulteress and the infanticide of *Cañas y barro* demonstrates, I contend, that Blasco's novels were mediated, as is the case of nineteenth-century realism, by the expectations and desires of his readership. The power of the literary market and its effect on the composition of fiction is something that famously preoccupied influential contemporary authors such as Galdós and Unamuno. In this context, the economic triumph of the *mujer fatal* at the end of *Cañas y barro* is significant. From a lowly background of poverty and illegitimacy, Neleta is the outsider and entrepreneur who overcomes the deterministic legacy of her social education. That this figure is a woman is a telling indication of Blasco's eye to his literary market.

Following the success of his Valencian novels, Blasco would later become an international celebrity, both in recognition of his literary works and even more pertinently their adaptation as Hollywood films. In 1926 Greta Garbo would make her screen debut in Monta Bell's *Torrent*, the United States film adaptation of *Entre naranjos*. It is interesting, in this context, that Blasco emphasized both the salient female component of his film audience, and associated the feminization of mass culture with degradation and degeneration, as David George argues in his analysis of the film adaptation of *Sangre y arena*.[42] Similarly, as Alda Blanco explains, the mass appeal of the *folletín* — and particularly the class and gender composition of its audience — led to its critical reception as a 'degraded form', revealing fears about the perceived 'feminization' of culture in the nineteenth century.[43] Having published his early novels in the *folletín* of *El Pueblo*, Blasco applied this successful formula to the representation of Neleta and sexual plot in *Cañas y barro*.

Crime, suicide, alcoholism and adultery were posited as social pathologies that endangered European nations, because they were manifestations of an internal process of degeneration. *Cañas y barro* makes literary capital from its sensationalist treatment of social issues that underscored the need to contain the female body: adultery, illegitimacy and infanticide. It references popular understanding of symptoms of degeneration: *aboulia*, alcoholism and moral deviance through its representation of the crimes of adultery, neonaticide and suicide. *Cañas y barro* represents the failure of maternal instinct. Paternity is also at stake through the progressive generational legacy of *aboulia* as demonstrated by the demise of Tonet and his male lineage. Although it lacks the philosophical momentum of the dominant emphasis on *voluntad*, fatigue and loss of volition in Unamuno, Azorín or Baroja, *aboulia* is none the less a recurrent trope in Blasco's early fiction. In *Cañas y barro*, however, the social status quo is at risk, rather than the survival of the species. Developing my analysis of dysfunctional maternity and paternity in *Cañas y barro*, I dedicate my final chapter to the reproductive legacy of a diseased nation explored by Baroja's *El árbol de la ciencia*.

Notes to Chapter 5

1. In 1903 following the French translation of *La barraca*, Ernest Mérimée emphasized Blasco's 'admiration pour les naturalistes français': 'Blasco Ibáñez et le roman de mœurs provinciales' *Bulletin Hispanique*, 5.3 (1903), 272–300 (p. 299). In 1909 Andrés González Blanco identified Blasco as the Spanish adherent to Zola and French naturalism: *Historia de la novela en España desde el romanticismo a nuestros días* (Madrid: Saenz de Jubera, 1909), p. 582, a view endorsed by Eduardo Zamacois in 1910: *Mis contemporáneos: V. Blasco Ibáñez* (Madrid: Librería Sucesores de Hernando, 1910), pp. 22–26. The influence of naturalism remains a dominant question in studies of Blasco's Valencian and social thesis novels. See Cardwell, 'Blasco Ibáñez ¿escritor naturalista radical?'.
2. In the prologue to *Flor de Mayo* Blasco Ibáñez describes the exhausting work of editing the paper alongside writing his serialized novels (Madrid: Cátedra, 1999), pp. 59–61. All subsequent references are to this edition.
3. Laguna Platero, *El Pueblo: historia de un diario republicano, 1894–1939* (Valencia: Institució Alfons el Magnànim, 1999), p. 123. Caudet expresses a similar defence of Blasco's motivation in 'Reivindicación de Blasco Ibáñez', p. 681.
4. Lombroso and Ferrero, *Criminal Woman*, pp. 203–04.
5. Lombroso and Ferrero, *Criminal Woman*, p. 61.
6. Cooke, *Satan in Society*, p. 280.
7. Gilman, 'Sexology', p. 75.
8. Gilman, 'Sexology', p. 87.
9. A recent reading of the television adaptation of *Cañas y barro* likewise underscores that Neleta's transgression of traditional feminine roles does not lead to her death. Laura Mancheño, 'Maternidad y familia en *Cañas y barro* y su adaptación televisiva: el caso de Rosa y Neleta', *Bulletin of Spanish Studies*, 87.2 (2010), 177–94 (p. 179).
10. For further analysis of feminine roles in the novel, the reader is referred to Anderson, *Primitives, Patriarchy and the Picaresque*, Chapter 3, pp. 75–114 and Mancheño, 'Maternidad'.
11. Rebecca Stott, *Fabrication of the Late Victorian Femme Fatale: The Kiss of Death* (Basingstoke: Macmillan, 1992).
12. Dijkstra, *Idols of Perversity*, p. viii.

13. Sharon Marcus, *Between Women* (Princeton, NJ: Princeton University Press, 2007), p. 112. The book casts new light on existing studies of the visual and literary representations of women, an approach that could usefully be applied to the Spanish context.
14. My thanks to Rocío Rødtjer, PhD candidate at King's College London, for bringing this connection to my attention.
15. As listed in the original volume editions of *Flor de Mayo* (Valencia: Sempere, 1895) and *Cañas y barro* (Valencia: Sempere, 1902). I am indebted to the Biblioteca de Valencia for allowing me access to these editions.
16. On sensationalism and melodrama in nineteenth-century Spanish fiction, the reader is referred to Susan Kirkpatrick, 'Fantasy, Seduction, and the Woman Reader: Rosalía de Castro's Novels', in *Culture and Gender in Nineteenth-Century Spain*, ed. by Lou Charnon-Deutsch and Jo Labanyi (Oxford: Clarendon, 1995), pp. 74–97 (pp. 74–75). On gender paradigms in British sensation fiction, including theories of female insanity, see Andrew Mangham, *Violent Women and Sensation Fiction: Crime, Medicine and Victorian Popular Culture* (Basingstoke: Palgrave Macmillan, 2007), p. 5.
17. Bárbara A. Revuelta Eugercios, *Los usos de la Inclusa de Madrid, mortalidad y retorno a principios del siglo XX (1890–1935)* (unpublished doctoral thesis, Universidad Complutense de Madrid, 2011), p. 88.
18. Blasco Ibáñez, *Cañas y barro* (Madrid: Alianza, 2003), p. 215. All subsequent references are to this edition.
19. Manuel Tolosa Latour, *El Niño* (Madrid: La Gaceta Universal, 1880). In 1881 he published *La protección médica al niño desválido*.
20. Jean Étienne Dominique Esquirol, *Des Maladies mentales, considérées sous les rapports médical, hygiénique et médico-légal* (1838); trans. by E. K. Hunt, *Mental Maladies: A Treatise on Insanity* (Philadelphia, PA: Lea and Blanchard, 1845), p. 392.
21. Daniel Grey, 'Women's Policy Networks and the Infanticide Act 1922', *Twentieth Century British History*, 21.4 (2010), 441–63 (p. 454).
22. Cath Quinn, 'Images and Impulses: Representations of Puerperal Insanity and Infanticide in Late Victorian England', in *Infanticide: Historical Perspectives on Child Murder and Concealment, 1550–2000*, ed. by Mark Jackson (Aldershot: Ashgate, 2002), pp. 193–215 (p. 193).
23. Anon., 'Law and Insanity', *British Medical Journal*, 1 (1865), 275–77 (p. 275).
24. Havelock Ellis, 'Précis of "Considerations on Infanticide" [Quelques Considérations sur l'Infanticide]. (Arch. d'Anthropol. Crim., January 18th, 1902) Audiffrent', *The Journal of Mental Science*, 48 (1902), 366.
25. Kirsten Johnson Kramar and William D. Watson, 'The Insanities of Reproduction: Medico-legal Knowledge and the Development of Infanticide Law', *Social Legal Studies*, 15.2 (2006), 237–55 (p. 243).
26. J. González Castro, *El trabajo de la mujer en la industria. Condiciones en que se efectúa y sus consecuencias en el porvenir de la raza. Medidas de protección necesaria* (Madrid), pp. 23–24. Quoted in Campos et al., *Los ilegales*, p. 176.
27. N. Fernández Cuesta y Porta, *La vida del obrero en España desde el punto de vista higiénico* (Madrid: Valentín Tordesillas, 1909), p. 116. Quoted in Campos et al., *Los ilegales*, p. 176.
28. Pick, *Faces of Degeneration*, p. 6.
29. Campos et al., *Los ilegales*, p. 174.
30. In Galdós's *La desheredada* Isidora's son is born with rickets, a disease considered to be a consequence of inherited degeneracy and alcoholism. On the diagnosis of degeneracy, mental illness and criminality on the basis of physical traits, the reader is referred to Campos Marín et al., *Los ilegales de la naturaleza*, pp. 32–40.
31. Medina, *The Valencian Novels*, pp. 79–80.
32. Alfredo Murga, '*Cañas y barro*: novela de V. Blasco Ibáñez', *El Liberal*, 1 April 1903, p. 1.
33. Lily Litvak, *Erotismo fin de siglo* (Barcelona: Bosch, 1979), p. 145.
34. See Fuentes, *Visions of Filth*, pp. 109–31.
35. Medina, *The Valencian Novels*, p. 87.
36. Anderson notes that the 'deterministic impetus' is mitigated by the Romantic element of

chance, 'as opposed to the [...] scientifically inevitable bent of French Naturalism'. *Primitives, Patriarchy, and the Picaresque*, pp. 148–49. Similarly, for Longhurst: 'in a novel that at certain earlier moments seemed to be developing in the direction of Naturalist experimenting with environmental determinism, Blasco eschews any kind of deterministic thesis', 'Representations of the Fourth Estate', pp. 89–90.
37. On the concept of excess, see Alison Sinclair, 'Luxurious Borders: Containment and Excess in Nineteenth-Century Spain', in *A Companion to Spanish Women's Studies*, ed. by Xon de Ros and Geraldine Hazbun (Woodbridge: Tamesis, 2011), pp. 211–26 (p. 215).
38. *La España Moderna*, 1/2/1903, 'Crónica literaria', pp. 173, 175.
39. Dijkstra, *Idols of Perversity*, p. 351.
40. Mary Ann Doane, *Femmes Fatales: Feminism, Film Theory, Psychoanalysis* (London: Routledge, 1991), p. 2.
41. Marcus, *Between Women*, p. 8.
42. David George, 'Cinematising the Crowd: V. Blasco Ibáñez's Silent Sangre y arena (1916)', *Studies in Hispanic Cinemas*, 4.2 (2007), 91–106.
43. Alda Blanco, 'Gender and National Identity: The Novel in Nineteenth-Century Literary History', in *Culture and Gender in Nineteenth-Century Spain*, ed. by Lou Charnon-Deutsch and Jo Labanyi (Oxford: Clarendon, 1995), pp. 120–36 (p. 128).

CHAPTER 6

Eugenics and National Decline: The Failure of Maternity in Baroja's *El árbol de la ciencia* (1911)

Baroja's deep-rooted concern with biology and the nation, present from his earliest fiction, culminates in *El árbol de la ciencia*, the final part of his *La raza* trilogy, through the focus on heredity and failed reproduction. The novel draws on autobiographical memory in relation to Baroja's own experience as a medical student in Madrid from 1887: he received a degree in Medicine in 1893. *El árbol de la ciencia* echoes widespread social fears about degeneration through its treatment of national decline, a concept with which Baroja was by this time profoundly familiar. Indeed the novel expresses powerful concerns about the future of an apparently hysterical and neurotic 'race' through the exposition of *aboulia*, a narrative focus that has particular significance for the representation of the female body and its reproduction. The stillborn child produced at the end of *El árbol de la ciencia* is commonly interpreted as a symbolic exposition of the decline of the Spanish nation and evidence of a deeply pessimistic approach to the country's future. My final chapter seeks to problematize this dominant critical perspective by emphasizing Baroja's profound agnosticism and irony as the two most salient characteristics of his fiction.

El árbol de la ciencia is the culmination of Baroja's preoccupation with heredity that was fundamental to his early novels. The fictional doctor Iturrioz categorizes both the protagonist Andrés Hurtado and his wife Lulú as biologically and mentally unfit to have children. Iturrioz expresses a eugenicist perspective that echoes medical discourses of the period, through his advice that the couple (both neurotics) should not conceive children. Baroja's exposition of hygienic medicine is developed through the narrative focus on Andrés Hurtado's medical training in Madrid, notably his experience of the Hospital San Juan de Dios, where prostitutes were treated for venereal disease. Furthermore, the novel's focus on prostitution as a source of disease in both social and biological terms reinforces the strong association between women and the working classes as a political threat so common in the early twentieth century.[1] Like other key figures of modernism, Nietzsche ascribed feminine characteristics to the masses, pointing to the decline and feminization of culture in the late nineteenth century.[2] Racial discourses in early twentieth-century

Spain were fuelled by contemporary bourgeois concerns about declining birth rates and the infertility of the middle classes compared with the alarming reproduction of the lower-class masses.[3]

Baroja fails to offer a solution to social ills in the guise of a Nietzschean overcoming of determinism in *El árbol de la ciencia*, as he does through the tentative conclusion presented by his earliest novels such as *La casa de Aizgorri*. I argue that his novel of 1911 offers an agnostic approach to exposing rather than resolving the contemporary predicament of the Spanish nation through its resonant engagement with a Schopenhauerian model of knowledge. The compelling philosophical foundations of *El árbol de la ciencia* are interwoven with contemporary discourses of nation, heredity and degeneration. For Sosa-Velasco, in *El árbol de la ciencia* 'la raza española muestra su degeneración al transmitirse de padres a hijos'.[4] Countering existing critical studies, I contend that the generational paradigm debated over the course of the trilogy is not sustained by the novel's conclusion. My own reading emphasizes Baroja's characteristic scepticism in philosophical and ideological terms. Baroja was profoundly concerned by the pressing question of heredity in the context of the nation's future, but the novel ultimately resists a coherent biological model.

The theories of race expressed by Baroja in his later essays are found in incipient form in his novel *El árbol de la ciencia*. These ideas are vocalized by fictional characters, allowing the author to avoid committing to a single viewpoint, by contrast with his non-fiction writing. Baroja would later explore the association between race, culture and degeneration in his collection of essays *Ayer y hoy* published in 1939, in which he wrote that:

> La cuestión de la herencia resuelta sería la clave de la historia [...] Se podría averiguar si hay razas verdaderas o no las hay, qué es lo que pasa en un país cuando decae, qué es lo que falla en *una civilización que degenera*, por qué muchas naciones históricas de gran importancia no pueden recuperar, por esfuerzos que hagan, su antiguo esplendor [my italics].[5]

In other words, for Baroja the question of inherited characteristics and generational legacies was key to assessing the decline or degeneration of nations and civilizations. From the perspective of 1939, theories of race and biology were fundamental to explaining national character, a view that is in line with both Zola and Morel.

However, in his essay 'La raza y la cultura' of 1938, Baroja had already argued that: 'La raza debe de tener algo que ver con el carácter de la cultura y con el idioma; pero, por ahora, esta relación científica no se ha encontrado. [...] La cultura se transmite por vías distintas a las que siguen los caracteres zoológicos y raciales' (*OC*, VIII, 941–42). In other words, in relation to culture, Baroja resisted simplistic theories of inherited characteristics: cultural characteristics were more than a question of biological transmission. Race, in any case, was a problematic and ill-defined term, as demonstrated by the author's statement in 'Las razas nobles' of 1936: 'La raza es un concepto oscuro, mal definido, de carácter biológico, naturalista' (*OC*, V, 952). As Laura Otis has argued in her study of organic cultural memory, Baroja remained sceptical about the crude association of culture with race or biology.[6] At the time he wrote his early novels, and in the context of hereditary determinism, however, Baroja was profoundly interested in contemporary biology and the legacy of Ribot, Darwin, Haeckel, Spencer and Bernard, among others.[7] In *El árbol de la ciencia* Baroja chose to explore a number of contemporary theories in fictional form, not least the potential for the biological transmission of degenerate characteristics to subsequent generations. It thus represents the culmination of his contradictory engagements with degeneration theories in his early fiction.

The trajectory of Andrés Hurtado as angst-ridden anti-hero is well documented in accordance with the dominant critical focus on male subjectivity in Baroja.[8] My analysis in this chapter, by contrast, offers an original examination of the treatment of hereditary pathology in *El árbol de la ciencia* through a specific focus on the female body and mind. In her eschewal of traditional gendered roles and domesticity and the narrative emphasis on her lack of fitness for maternity and reproduction, Lulú is aligned not with the biological function of motherhood, but instead androgyny and intellectualism. The central female character of Baroja's novel of 1911 is asexual, unconventional, and demonstrably unfit for childbearing. 'Una mujer cerebral, sin fuerza orgánica y sin sensualidad, para quien todas las impresiones son puramente intelectuales', Lulú is defined by cerebral qualities.[9]

Elaine Showalter has argued in an Anglophone context that in the late nineteenth century 'the women who aspired to professional independence and sexual freedom were denounced as case studies in hysteria and degeneration'.[10] A consequence of her purported asexuality or hypersexuality, her search for economic independence and the rejection of maternity, the New Woman was a key source of anxiety in relation to discourses of degeneration and the healthy reproduction of the human race.[11] Female emancipation was feared, in this context, as a rapid path to degeneration; similarly, the regressive women who failed to conform to ideal womanhood were identified as atavistic throwbacks in evolutionary terms.[12] In *The Sexual Question* (1906) the Swiss psychiatrist and eugenicist August Forel echoed this prevalent view, arguing that 'the modern tendency of women to become pleasure-seekers, and to take a dislike to maternity, leads to degeneration of society'. Construed as 'a grave social evil', this problem 'rapidly changes the qualities and power of expansion of a race', and must be cured in order to preserve the dominion of white Europeans. For Forel, the 'fundamental weakness of the feminine mind' was similar to that found in the 'inferior races', underscoring the perceived superiority of the white male as the epitome of evolution, and the grouping of women, children and non-Europeans as primitive Other within turn-of-the-century discourses of degeneration.[13]

Associated with femininity in nineteenth-century medicine, however, hysteria has become synonymous with female rebellion and protest in contemporary feminist theory. In her analysis of Sarah Grand's *The Heavenly Twins* (1893), Ann Heilmann explains that in the late nineteenth century 'hysteria was associated with unrestrained female sexuality as well as with sexual resistance to marital intercourse'.[14] Symptomatic of both excessive sexuality and asexuality, hysteria was a token of social disorder or disruption produced by the female body and mind. Baroja's *El árbol de la ciencia* draws on a number of turn-of-the-century medical discourses of degeneration, including the hereditary legacies of neurotic parents and hysteria in both men and women. Lulú represents a potentially threatening model of womanhood through the failure of maternity, exemplified by the haemorrhage that causes the death of both mother and baby during childbirth at the end of the novel. This abrupt outcome is a powerful narrative symbol of social disruption, but not convincingly, in my view, of national degeneration.

Of course, at the heart of the moral and biological approach to the degeneration of the unconventional woman (with its obvious echoes of the Biblical Fall) in the late nineteenth and early twentieth centuries is the perceived social, moral and physical responsibility of the female body to reproduce healthy offspring. Anxieties about changing women's roles at the turn of the century fuelled the cultural myths of degeneration, which were presented so powerfully in the guise of science. Nineteenth-century anthropologists, including Lombroso, used an apparently scientific basis to establish the intellectual inferiority of women and to emphasize instead the biological function of human reproduction.

In a national context, the domestic role of women was considered fundamental to the survival of the 'race' and the future of society. Spanish social medicine of the early twentieth century provided stark warnings about the dangers of women working for the production of healthy offspring in biological and moral terms:

> En el aspecto familiar y social, el daño es también de gran importancia, y va directamente contra la salud y el vigor del pueblo y de la raza. La permanencia de la mujer, durante todo el día, en el taller o en la fábrica destruye el hogar doméstico. [...] Consecuencia de este abandono son la desidia, el despilfarro, la enfermedad, la disipación; en suma, la ruina material y moral de padres e hijos.[15]

The absence of the mother from the home was, according to this perspective, the source of degeneration of society, criminality, infant mortality, and moral dissipation. The quotation above provides a striking example of gendered directives within social medicine of the period.

Biological models of degeneration thus became an ideological tool in the context of women's roles and identities and the preservation of traditional social values. Women's work outside the home was posited as both physically and morally damaging to the family unit and children's wellbeing within broader discourses of racial degeneration and eugenics. Within a social model of degeneration, women's work was cast in similar terms to alcoholism, which also kept mothers away from their children and prevented the dissemination of good models of behaviour. Physical work by women was seen as environmentally damaging to the foetus during pregnancy, and morally risky.

Baroja's naturalist representation of the Madrid underworld in the earlier novel *La busca* had already focused on the exposition of both criminality and prostitution. In *El árbol de la ciencia* the author would develop his critique of the clinical treatment of prostitutes through the representation of the protagonist Andrés Hurtado as medical student and 'médico de higiene' in the Spanish capital. At the Hospital de San Juan de Dios, Andrés observes first-hand the ravages of syphilis in the prostitutes of the capital. This aspect of the novel draws on autobiographical experience as a medical student in Madrid. Similarly, the death of the protagonist's brother Luisito was based on the death of Baroja's eldest brother Darío from tuberculosis in 1894. Andrés's practice as a village doctor in Alcolea del Campo drew obvious inspiration from Baroja's own brief experience as a provincial doctor in Cestona in 1894–95.

Andrés Hurtado's visit to the Hospital de San Juan de Dios provokes an exposition of the problems of poverty, criminality and prostitution through the language of social disease: 'Espectador de la iniquidad social, Andrés reflexionaba acerca de los mecanismos que van produciendo esas lacras: el presidio, la miseria, la prostitución. [...] El pueblo evolucionaba a la inversa, debilitándose, degenerando cada vez más. Estas dos evoluciones paralelas eran sin duda biológicas' (267). Influenced by the theories of his Uncle Iturrioz, Baroja's protagonist explains the existence of criminality, poverty and prostitution with direct reference to biological evolution and degeneration. Later in the novel, Hurtado witnesses the degradation and alcoholism of the mass of prostitutes of Madrid, and their mistreatment by owners of the brothels who refuse medical attention for the women: 'duermen en cualquier rincón amontonadas, no comen apenas; les dan unas palizas brutales; y cuando envejecen y ven que ya no tienen éxito, las cogen y las llevan a otro pueblo sigilosamente' (272). Nature and nurture are inextricably entwined in the plight of the prostitutes.

Hurtado's understanding of the unsanitary conditions and cruelty to which the prostitutes are exposed places an emphasis on social responsibility for the spread of disease. The narrative thus echoes contemporary discourses of social hygiene which cast the prostitute as the source of venereal disease, and therefore a danger to the health of the urban masses. The protagonist's impression of San Juan de Dios confirms the association between prostitution, filth and lack of sanitation through the image of the human dunghill: 'Las enfermas eran de lo más caído y miserable. Ver tanta desdichada sin hogar, abandonada, en una sala negra, en un estercolero humano; comprobar y evidenciar la podredumbre que envenena la vida sexual, le hizo a Andrés una angustiosa impresión' (82). Baroja's fictional physician, however, takes a humanitarian approach, stating that prostitution 'es una cosa brutal, imbécil, puramente económica, sin ningún aspecto novelesco' (273). The cause of prostitution for Andrés Hurtado is economic and not (as criminologists claimed) an innate disposition to vice. The alternatives for women living in poverty in Madrid and who needed to earn an income were limited, as Carmen del Moral has documented in her analysis of the documentary realism and veracity of Baroja's Madrid novels.[16] Lack of education for women was a major obstacle to escaping a life of prostitution; according to Eslava, seventy-five per cent of prostitutes in Madrid at the turn of the century were illiterate.[17]

In the light of the unprecedented scale of prostitution in the Spanish capital, and the threat posed by the high incidence of syphilis, the regulation of prostitution was a controversial topic. Only official prostitutes could receive treatment for venereal diseases at the Hospital de San Juan de Dios. Clandestine prostitutes had to seek treatment at private clinics, evidence that the regulation of prostitution would not be an effective means of reducing the scale of sexually transmitted disease: 'al reconocer y reglamentar la prostitución el Estado pasaba a protegerla y estimularla, sin con ello evitar ninguno de los riesgos e inconvenientes que para la higiene y moral pública suponía'.[18]

The representation of prostitution in *El árbol de la ciencia* is therefore contradictory. It posits critical social factors in the cycle of poverty and exploitation, but it also draws to some extent on positivist science and the terminology of social sanitation that sought to protect the urban masses from the spread of disease and moral corruption. Hurtado's experience in Madrid induces both a pessimistic (Schopenhauerian) view of life, but also 'anarquismo espiritual, basado en la simpatía y en la piedad, sin solución práctica ninguna' (84). Without wishing to ignore the narrative distance between author and character, Hurtado's analysis of social injustice is not predicated on any programme of practical reform. Like Baroja, the protagonist adopts a critical, but ultimately detached and ironic stance.

Baroja was well aware of the brutality and degradation of a life of prostitution. The prostitutes of the capital are both the victims and the catalysts for moral and biological degeneracy. They embody vice and disease, but above all ignorance or 'inconsciencia', and are trapped by their own sense of dishonour, the national obsession of 'una raza de fanáticos' (274). As Baroja documents in *El árbol de la ciencia*, the medical treatment of prostitutes in turn-of-the-century Madrid was far from humane or effective. For one of the doctors who worked at the hospital, San Juan de Dios was 'un hospital-cárcel y un centro de demoralización'.[19] Andrés Hurtado's experience reinforces the depiction of an institutional model that removes social problems via 'una mezcla de manicomio y de hospital' (81). Baroja's clinical experience as a medical student proved fertile material for the fictional representation of urban pathologies and the inscription of the female body as the site of disease.

El árbol de la ciencia presents a stark portrait of the female underworld of the capital through the exposition of prostitution and degradation. In the light of this urban setting, my analysis of degenerationism turns now to the representation of Lulú as the embodiment of scientific discourses that focused on maternity and the suitability of the female body and mind for engendering healthy offspring. Contesting traditional critical readings of Baroja's representations of women, Trueba Mira recuperates the salient participation of Lulú, alongside her male counterpart Andrés Hurtado, in the philosophical inspiration of *El árbol de la ciencia*: Schopenhauer's *The World as Will and Representation*. Contrary to Schopenhauer's own identification of women with biology and propagation, Lulú is caught in a similar conflict between intellect and Will as Hurtado.[20] Thus, when nature and biological instinct reassert themselves in the form of Lulú's desire for a child, maternity represents the culmination of the imposition of 'life' over intellect. Trueba concludes that, by the end, 'su propia naturaleza femenina', as well as society, impedes the development of her personality, thereby destroying the intellect that also defines her.[21] My own analysis draws on this reappraisal of Lulú's key significance in the philosophical foundation of *El árbol de la ciencia*. I do so not to perpetuate critical debate about the competing trajectory of male and female characters in this novel, but instead to argue that Baroja's representation of failed maternity both echoes and ultimately rejects dominant discourses that sought explanation in hereditary pathologies and generational decline.

The Schopenhauerian conflict between reason and Will is significant in this context, since both Lulú and Andrés suffer from *aboulia*, a frequently cited symptom of degeneration. Both the prostitutes of San Juan de Dios and the character of Lulú embody, in different ways, unacceptable models of womanhood that pose a threat to social order and the status quo. The prostitutes are marginalized according to their perceived incapacity for work, poverty, and the threat they pose to the health of the urban population. Lulú's ideological modernity and disruptive sexuality present a different but equally powerful danger to successful propagation. She resists both a heterosexual relationship and maternity, before she succumbs with Andrés to the conventional, bourgeois trappings of marriage and motherhood.[22] In other words, the portrait of prostitution in the novel informs my reading of Lulú's unconventional identity, since both representations of femininity draw strongly on contemporary theories of race, reproduction and degeneration in a moral and biological context.

Schopenhauer's mordant views about women are found most obviously in his essay 'On Women', in which he states that women are 'big children [...]: a kind of intermediate stage between the child and the man, who is the actual human being, "man"'. He adds that 'fundamentally women exist solely for the propagation of the race and find in this their entire vocation'.[23] The dormant instinct for maternity is represented through Lulú's transformation from cerebral and unconventional 'non-woman' to hysteria during pregnancy. None the less, in relation to the conflict between the intellect and the Will (if not to parenthood), her psychological trajectory — even by the end of the novel — is very similar to Andrés's own. On this aspect my reading diverges from that of Trueba Mira. Will reasserts itself in Lulú's desire for a child. By the end of the novel, therefore, her trajectory resumes a parallel path to that of Andrés, both in philosophical and psychological terms.

Clearly Baroja chose to dispense with both Lulú and Andrés at the end of the novel, underscoring the incapacity for survival of the neurotic pair and their weak offspring. In symbolic terms, Lulú's death also potentially emphasizes the risk she poses for the nation's future through her apparent physical and mental degeneracy. By contrast with Blasco's Neleta, she thus exemplifies the typical destruction of unconventional women in male-authored fiction of this period.[24] *El árbol de la ciencia* demonstrates Baroja's most direct engagement with dominant narratives of national decline and degeneration of his early novels. However, the racial metaphors do not amount to a convincing adherence to positivist ideologies that he rejected in his earliest fiction. Even the vivid demise of Lulú and her baby in childbirth at the end of the novel does not constitute an irredeemable symbol or inevitable biological outcome. For Baroja the cultural exposition of Spanish society was more than a question of heredity.

Lulú is presented from the outset as an exception to socio-cultural expectations of femininity, as the initial description of her attests: 'le faltaba el atractivo principal de una muchacha: la ingenuidad, la frescura, la candidez. Era un producto marchito por el trabajo, por la miseria y por la inteligencia. Sus dieciocho años no parecían juventud' (97). Her intellectual capacity, together with her position as the poor daughter of a widow, has prematurely aged her. At the age of eighteen, she lacks the ingenuous quality of youth. In this description Baroja hints at popular paradigms of degeneration in both psychological and physiological terms: she is 'withered' by work, poverty and intelligence. She lacks the expected feminine quality of innocence. The description above implicitly alludes to the hidden disease of tuberculosis, commonly attributed as a symptom of degeneration. It would later be replicated indiscriminately as autobiography in Baroja's memoirs, based on a woman with whom the author was acquainted during his time as a medical student in Madrid and who later died from tuberculosis (*OC*, VII, 1324–25). The description of Lulú, however, is influenced as much by cultural norms as it is by science.

Lulú is presented as unfeminine, even sexless. The lack of importance she assigns to sexuality accompanies her professed indifference to convention, evident in the ambivalence she expresses both to marriage and, by implication, maternity: 'Decía que si un hombre la pretendía, y ella viera que la quería de verdad, se iría con él, fuera rico o pobre, soltero o casado. Tal afirmación parecía una monstruosidad, una indecencia a Niní y a doña Leonarda. Lulú no aceptaba derechos ni prácticas sociales' (114). Her mother doña Leonarda and sister Niní deem this social deviancy to be monstrous. Lulú's unconventionality places her beyond social norms, a liminal space emphasized by her sexual ambivalence and the blurring of gender boundaries. Through the family's descent to poverty after the death of her father, and the necessity for the sisters (*las Minglanillas*) and their mother to make a living amidst 'un ambiente de miseria bastante triste' (96), Lulú is set outside the domestic realm, and expects neither to marry nor to become a mother.

Lulú's androgynous traits are indicative of her marginal status, beyond the established norms of society. Ortega y Gasset's designation of this character as 'una extraña y simpática mujercita' covertly implies her social abnormality alongside the appealing qualities of empathy and intelligence.[25] Androgyny, however, is also a key symptom of degeneracy because effeminacy in men and virility or masculinity in women were seen as evidence of racial exhaustion. Both Darwin and Spencer equated progress with sexual difference, and regression with sexual indifferentiation. The predominance of intelligence over Will (Schopenhauer's blind force underlying the universe) continues to define Lulú. The complementarity of Lulú and Andrés encompasses the gender-imposed norms to which each fails to conform through her eschewal of domesticity and his rejection of work outside the home. Thus, the comparable move towards indifferentiation embodied by each character can be interpreted as a symptom of regression within degenerationist paradigms: in other words, a regressive outcome of modernization in social terms. It is significant to note in this context that the narrative voice is in fact consistently positive in its presentation of Lulú. When Andrés is bemused by her unconventionality, the narrator points to shortcomings in his limited experience of women: 'Andrés

Hurtado trataba a pocas mujeres; si hubiese conocido más y podido comparar, hubiera llegado a sentir estimación por Lulú' (114).

Indeed Andrés and Lulú are framed as intellectual and spiritual counterparts, a pairing reinforced by their similar trajectory in philosophical terms. Both characters seek refuge from the world of suffering identified by Schopenhauer, and in each case, the intellect predominates over Will. Lulú professes both an absence of sexual desire and an indifference to life itself. This lack of Will is ascribed by the narrator to her precocious development: 'sin duda supo lo que eran la mujer y el hombre en una época en que su instinto nada le decía, y esto le había producido una mezcla de indiferencia y de repulsión por todas las cosas del amor' (114). Again, there is a suggestion here of moral, mental and physical degeneration, although this is not accompanied by narrative censure in direct terms. Andrés offers an alternative diagnosis, one that is based on biology. To cure this 'miseria orgánica' (114), he prescribes fresh air and nourishing food as a cure for her *aboulia*. At this point, the lack of Will is more powerful than the remedies provided by hygienic medicine.

However Lulú's rise to economic independence is emblematic of temporary regeneration at least in social terms, as she capitalizes on her intellect in order to overcome the legacy of poverty and physical debility. Following the death of his brother Luisito, and his experience as a village doctor in Alcolea del Campo, Andrés returns to Madrid towards the end of the novel. Lulú is now running her own business, the dressmaking shop, originally financed by her brother-in-law Don Prudencio, and has attained both economic security and independence, marking a significant shift in her social identity and status.

The eventual union between the pair is not based on a conventional model of economic exchange, but instead their intellectual and spiritual compatibility as the descendants (apparently) of a neurotic 'race'. As Andrés explains to Iturrioz, it is a marriage between an 'hombre artrítico, nervioso' (287) and 'una novia, antigua amiga suya, débil y algo histérica' (287). Andrés, then, diagnoses the weakness of his own nervous system, and the tendency towards hysteria of his future wife. Echoing contemporary medical discourse, Iturrioz's advice is that the couple should not have children: 'El delito mayor del hombre es hacer nacer. [...] Se tienen hijos sanos, a quienes se les da un hogar, protección, educación, cuidados..., podemos otorgar la absolución a los padres; se tienen hijos enfermos, tuberculosos, sifilíticos, neurasténicos, consideremos criminales a los padres' (287–88).

In 1889, Dr José María Esquerdo, head of the mental section of Madrid's Provincial Hospital, published an article entitled 'De la locura histérica', which warned against hysterics marrying.[26] For Iturrioz, 'la única garantía de la prole es la robustez de los padres' (288). This statement echoes the language of French *dégénérescence* in the mid-nineteenth century, and the view expressed by Philippe Buchez's well-known *Introduction to Science* (1842) that robust parents produced robust children; correspondingly, the nervous ailments of parents would be passed on to their descendants. Like Morel, Buchez employed science to confirm the theory of original sin. In other words, the science of degeneration of Buchez drew on a religious foundation for the explanation of biological and environmental damage to progress in social, moral and physical terms.²⁷ In a similar way, in Morel's pessimistic study the individual embodied the sins of the fathers, a view echoed by *El árbol de la ciencia*. Baroja's title obviously denotes the Biblical Fall through the danger posed by Eve's ingestion of knowledge. For Hurtado, however, religion is a 'mentira vital', or life-sustaining lie. By the end of the novel, his faith in knowledge or science is also undermined, casting the Biblical reference of the novel's title in resoundingly ironic terms. The third-person narrative follows Andrés's perspective as Lulú moves from the role of spiritual companionship towards the resurgence of Will and her desire for a child. Whilst Andrés attempts to maintain a state of intellectual detachment from biological impulses, the reproductive force in Lulú provokes a nervous, animalistic dependency that, according to the narrator, contains the roots of their destruction.

Baroja's fictional scientist in the novel, Iturrioz, express a strongly eugenicist perspective that the possibility of engendering unhealthy offspring is enough to provide a deterrent to reproduction: 'El perpetuar el dolor en el mundo me parece un crimen' (288). In discussion with Andrés, Iturrioz echoes the eugenicist doctrine of 'artificial selection'. The progressive degeneration of the human race could be countered by birth control not, as Malthus argued at the end of the eighteenth century, by reducing the quantity of children, but instead by seeking higher quality parents for procreation through the study of health, pathology and family history.²⁸ Francis Galton and others proposed the prevention of the mentally ill, those suffering from epilepsy, tuberculosis and syphilis, as well as criminals and vagrants from becoming parents. Galton advocated confinement; the solution imposed by his followers in the United States was enforced sterilization.²⁹ In Spain, pre-marriage medical certificates were devised as a practical means of seeking healthy reproduction. Tuberculosis was seen as a particular danger for healthy reproduction and the future strength of the nation: the subject of a conference in San Sebastián in 1912. In order to safeguard 'los robustos derechos de la especie', the prevention of those suffering from tuberculosis from marrying was seen as a necessity.³⁰ The portrait of Andrés and Lulú in *El árbol de la ciencia* engages closely with contemporary debates in social medicine that discussed the future health of the nation in alarmist terms.

Iturrioz expresses warning about the degeneration of the 'race' in line with contemporary science. In particular he advises against the consequences of the reproduction of the masses who display the effects of alcohol:

> Yo te confieso, para mí nada tan repugnante como esa bestia prolífica, que entre vapores de alcohol va engendrando hijos que hay que llevar al cementerio o que si no van a engrosar los ejércitos del presidio o de la prostitución. Yo tengo verdadero odio a esa gente sin conciencia, que llena de carne enferma y podrida la tierra. (288)

For Iturrioz, there is no merit in fathering 'abundante y repulsiva prole. [...] No, no debe ser lícito engendrar seres que vivan en el dolor' (288–89). The trope of social infection through the immoral engendering of sick children — depicted through the image of rotting flesh — is key to the doctor's social theories. Iturrioz's brand of eugenics is summed up by his ideas about the reproduction of the masses: 'La fecundidad no puede ser un ideal social. No se necesita cantidad, sino calidad. Que los patriotas y los revolucionarios canten al bruto prolífico, para mí siempre será un animal odioso' (289). Fertility should not be a universal aspiration; society requires quality rather than quantity in the production of future generations.

The question of reproduction for Andrés and Lulú obviously debates contemporary fears about generational decline so pertinent in Spain during this period. Lulú's rejection of traditional gender roles and boundaries is significant in this regard. She continues to work in her shop and, when Andrés struggles with his work at the hospital, their union dissolves the boundaries between the 'feminine' domestic sphere and the 'masculine' public sphere. Andrés gives up medicine and becomes a home-based translator, thereby distancing himself from the outside world. His marriage to Lulú provides a short-lived refuge, as he approaches the state of *ataraxia*, one that is disrupted by the force of biology. Lulú's desire for a child intrudes on this state of equilibrium, as her cerebral identity is destroyed by the 'amor animal' (299) that binds her to Andrés during pregnancy. When nature and biological instinct reassert themselves through her desire to reproduce, Andrés in contrast clings to rational motives against having a child: '¿Cómo decir a aquella mujer que él se consideraba como un producto envenenado y podrido, que no debía tener descendencia?' (298). Andrés Hurtado perceives his own degeneracy, and regards his wife's desire to have a child with profound fear, even terror.

The biological and emotional experience of Lulú's pregnancy echoes the common nineteenth-century association between hysteria and the uterus. Andrés Hurtado's response to news of his wife's pregnancy is one of anguish, whilst she becomes sentimental, dependent and possessive, as the following passage attests:

> El embarazo produjo en Lulú un cambio completo; de burlona y alegre, la hizo triste y sentimental.
> Andrés notaba que ya le quería de otra manera; tenía por él un cariño celoso e irritado; ya no era aquella simpatía afectuosa y burlona tan dulce; ahora era un amor animal. La naturaleza recobraba sus derechos. [...]
> Cuando adelantó el embarazo, Andrés comprobó que el histerismo de su mujer se acentuaba. (299)

From her original ambivalence towards marriage and maternity, nature now reclaims its rights through the assertion of the Will in Lulú. The once cerebral female protagonist is described as displaying 'manifestaciones histéricas' (299) during pregnancy, whereas Andrés is 'unbalanced' by the expectation of bringing a child into the world: 'Su cerebro estaba en una tensión demasiado grande, y las emociones que cualquiera podía sentir en la vida normal, a él le desequilibraban' (299). In response to Lulú's pregnancy, both characters display the symptoms of mental imbalance, hysteria or neurasthenia that were commonly understood as evidence of degeneration.

Hysteria had long been regarded as a psychological rather than a uterine disorder. However, its symptoms of emotional excess, instability and incoherence encouraged its continuing cultural and medical identification as a feminine malady, despite the recognition by nineteenth-century health experts that men could also be hysterics. According to Schopenhauer, sex and reproduction are the clearest and purest affirmation of the Will-to-life. This view is echoed by Andrés's view of love as a 'mentira vital': his statement that 'a través de una nube brillante y falsa, se ven los amantes el uno al otro, y en la oscuridad ríe el antiguo diablo, que no es más que la especie' (282). The male protagonist thus emerges from the negation of the Will through sexual desire, returning him to the world of suffering.

At first sight, the trajectory of the couple appears to take opposite directions, as Lulú moves from intellectual motivation to the assertion of the Will through maternity; Andrés, by contrast, clings to reason. Yet both characters suffer neurotic symptoms and emotional imbalance commonly accepted as signs of degeneracy. Furthermore, it is not abstract or philosophical theory that causes Andrés to take his own life at the end of the novel. Far from clinging to reason, he is unable to retreat into intellectualism, as the death of his wife and baby during childbirth propel him back to the world of the Will. The words of the anonymous doctor (a thinly veiled authorial appearance) suggest that nature (the tree of life) may have succeeded where medicine (the tree of science) failed:

> — Para mí — decía la voz desconocida — esos reconocimientos continuos que se hacen en los partos son perjudiciales. Yo no conozco este caso; pero, ¿quién sabe?, quizá esta mujer, en el campo, sin asistencia ninguna, se hubiera salvado. La naturaleza tiene recursos que nosotros no conocemos. (302)

Andrés's attempt to find refuge in science fails as he loses Lulú. His rational position is defeated as he faces the death of the woman he loves. It is not reason, but instinct and emotion that lead him to commit suicide, which is itself paradoxically an affirmation of the Will. In other words, the trajectory of the couple in relation to Schopenhauer's concept of Will, the philosophical foundation of the novel, follows a parallel path. According to this reading, both characters overcome *aboulia* through the resurgence of Will, not an indication in other words of an inevitable trajectory towards degeneration.

Furthermore, at the end of the novel the voice of male, scientific authority — that of the 'other' doctor — is employed to undermine the effectiveness of science and medicine. He suggests (questionably) that if Lulú had given birth with no medical intervention, perhaps she would have survived: nature may have succeeded where science failed. The privileging of medicine and biological science is finally undercut by the novel's ending. Here the author casts doubt over the ability of science to regulate the human body or the tree of life. This is an interesting position in relation to the debate about biological degeneration posed by *El árbol de la ciencia*, and a fundamentally ironic position on the part of an author who had himself abandoned a medical vocation.[31] In *La casa de Aizgorri*, Águeda's illness is diagnosed and interpreted both by the village doctor and her future husband Mariano, who suggest competing philosophies. The fictional doctor Don Julián positions her malady in the context of hereditary determinism, although he later recognizes the psychological root of her anxiety. By the novel's conclusion, Águeda's belief in her own neurosis is finally shown to be more powerful than inherited traits. Towards the end of his early period of novel-writing (1900–12), *El árbol de la ciencia* represents the culmination of Baroja's apparently pessimistic exploration of hereditary and biological legacies.

In *El árbol de la ciencia* the unwomanly Lulú dies in childbirth, and is thus refused her 'natural' maternal role, as nature defeats medicine or the tree of knowledge. The failed bids for independence of the women in Baroja's early novels, notably *La casa de Aizgorri*, *La ciudad de la niebla*, *El árbol de la ciencia* and *El mundo es ansí*, make the much-debated question of female nature at the turn of the century a pertinent context. Darwin's *Origin of Species* (1859) and more acutely *The Descent of Man, and Selection in Relation to Sex* (1871) underscored both biological determinism and the female role in heredity. These paradigms marked a shift from moral interpretations of sexuality to arguments that employed science to support theories of sexual difference in late Victorian England. Biological science perpetuated a particular set of moral values and cultural myths.

The Descent of Man was translated into Spanish in 1876, before the earlier *Origin of Species*, although both were already widely known. As Labanyi notes, 'from the start, Darwin's reception in Spain was tied to his biological theories of sexual difference'.[32] Similarly, medicine provided authority for theories of biological essentialism in early twentieth-century Spain. This transfer from religious authority to legitimization in medicine and science was not unique to Spain, but accompanies a similar shift across much of Europe and North America at the beginning of the twentieth century. Mary Nash has argued that 'biological essentialism rather than religion became a core feature in the construction of gender difference and the modernization of the notion of femininity in early twentieth-century Spain'. In Spain as elsewhere, medicine gave scientific legitimacy to 'ideological and cultural values, thus disguising cultural norms as objective, scientific facts'.[33] Biological science was subject to appropriation by a broader social and cultural agenda, in no small measure a response to anxieties around women's changing roles at the turn of the century.

It may be deduced that Lulú's inability to survive childbirth is the 'natural' consequence of Darwinian logic: her cerebral nature and lack of Will, evident in her pallor, gaunt appearance and sexless quality, that make her 'unnatural' for the maternal role. Yet, once again, male and female protagonists are paired in their unsuitability to a parental role in psychological and biological terms. Within the novel's rhetorical paradigm of heredity, the mother, father and child are all unfit to survive. But this, surely, is to simplify the novel's relationship to dominant sexual ideologies and scientific discourse. Indeed, the intervention of science in reproduction is, in fact, questioned by the appearance of the 'other' doctor, and his dubious interpretation of the resourcefulness of nature. In this regard, the Biblical reference of the novel's title is doubly ironic, as science and knowledge fail to overcome the irrational tree of life in Schopenhauerian terms.

Baroja's loose trilogy *La raza* is commonly accepted to be an exposition of the pessimistic outcome of the hereditary legacies that were so pertinent to the national 'problem' in the wake of 1898. In *La dama errante* Iturrioz, who features in the earlier novels of the trilogy, comments on the primitivism of the Spanish 'race' or nation as the following quotation attests: 'Este espíritu legalista ha producido en España una subversión completa de las energías. [...] Toda nuestra civilización actual ha servido para reducir al español, que antes era valiente y atrevido, y convertirlo en un pobre diablo' (*OC*, II, 253). Civilization has served to undermine the qualities of the Spanish people, through a process of reversion. Iturrioz identifies the destruction of Spanish culture and civilization through the imagery of organic degeneration: 'La vida española no tiene cuerpo, no es nada. [...] La península entera está gangrenada' (253–54). Spain is diseased and devoid of energy or Will, a process of degeneration that leads to emptiness or nothingness. According to this metaphor, the country is disembodied, and provides a morbid or sickly environment for the nation's future: 'Aunque hubiera aquí una invasión de raza joven, nueva, no podría resistir lo morboso del ambiente' (254).

Both Doctor Aracil and his daughter María are designated as neurasthenics. Despite her apparent energy, María is the product of a 'raza cansada'. For Iturrioz, 'nosotros somos viejos, nuestra raza ha vivido demasiado, y tenemos ya hasta los huesos débiles. [...] Estamos aplastados por siglos de historia que caen sobre nuestros hombros como una losa de plomo'.[34] At the end of *La ciudad de la niebla* María Aracil takes refuge in bourgeois respectability, marriage and maternity. Described by Iturrioz as 'un ensayo de emancipación que fracasa' (273), she returns to Madrid to marry Venancio, a resolution conveyed by the narrator's ambivalent pronouncement: 'Ha engrosado un poco y es una señora sedentaria y tranquila' (283). Indeed, her final conventional role is lamented, rather than prescribed. She submits to marriage and passive contentment in order to avoid the pitfalls of independence. At the end of *La casa de Aizgorri* Águeda overcomes a perceived legacy of degeneration. By contrast, María's pragmatic solution avoids the social disruption embodied by the (immoral) unmarried woman, but fails — apparently — to overcome the hereditary legacy of the Spanish 'race' or nation. None the less, at the end of *La ciudad de la niebla*, María produces a healthy son, an outcome denied by *El árbol de la ciencia* in 1911. Baroja presents generational paradigms in order to debate them in novelistic form through the opinions and beliefs of his fictional characters. In doing so, he avoids subscribing to any single set of theories or ideologies.

It cannot be denied that the discussion of heredity culminates in the final novel of the *Raza* trilogy. The demise of both Andrés and Lulú as neurotic parents who fail to produce healthy offspring provides a powerful literary response to contemporary debates about the nation's future. Whether Baroja's novel of 1911 provides an unquestioning exposition of the cultural myths of degeneration in positivist terms, however, is less certain. The inevitable outcome of hereditary determinism had already been undermined by his early novels, notably *La casa de Aizgorri* and *Camino de perfección*. In *La busca*, the representation of urban prostitution and criminality draws most forcefully on Morel's *dégénérescence* in the combination of innate and environmental factors. Yet even here, Baroja's conclusions are far from straightforward. French *dégénérescence* of the mid-nineteenth century was firmly rooted in history and a specific context, that of the 1848 Revolution and its legacy, and posited the accumulation of morbidity across generations. The fear that degeneration would eventually lead to collective sterility likewise reflected fears in France about the falling birth rate.[35]

Baroja's regenerationism was aligned in ideological terms to political, economic and spiritual reform. Yet in practical terms the manifesto of Azorín, Baroja and Maeztu ('los tres') of 1901 was of limited value, and demonstrates instead the demise of traditional values and an awareness of social problems at the turn of the century. Their regenerationist manifesto may be summarized by the following brief extract: 'Poner al descubierto las miserias de la gente del campo, las dificultades y tristezas de la vida de millares de hambrientos, los horrores de la prostitución y del alcoholismo, señalar la necesidad de la enseñanza obligatoria, de la fundación de cajas de crédito agrícola, de la implantación del divorcio como consecuencia de la ley del matrimonio civil'.[36] Rural and urban poverty, prostitution, alcoholism, education, agriculture and divorce laws are rapidly listed in sequence as areas for improvement, but with little strategy for implementation.

Baroja's scepticism about the straightforward association between heredity and the degeneration of nations and cultures in his essay of 1938 was cited at the beginning of this chapter. It suggests that his concept of race and national character went beyond a simplistic model of generational transmission. The ironic distance between the beliefs of the author and those of his fictional characters, including both Hurtado and Iturrioz, is of key significance in this regard. Neither character functions as the author's mouthpiece, although both discuss philosophical and physiological questions of concern to Baroja. The author explored anthropological approaches to degeneration and atavism in *La busca*, but remained sceptical about positivistic science, which he parodied alongside *cientifismo* in his novel *Aventuras, inventos y mixtificaciones de Silvestre Paradox*.

At the end of *El árbol de la ciencia* there is no Nietzschean overcoming of hereditary legacies; neither does Baroja propose an anarchist or eugenicist programme for reform. Despite the novel's powerful ending through the death of the protagonist, his wife and child, however, I argue that *El árbol de la ciencia* represents in fact an agnostic culmination of Baroja's exploration of degeneration in hereditary terms. It does so through an ironic reworking of the *dégénérescence* expounded in France by Morel and Buchez in the mid-nineteenth century and Biblical symbols of degeneracy or downfall. Although Andrés dies, he is a 'precursor': a representative of the uncertain future of the nation. The demise of Andrés and Lulú is not due to the impossibility of regeneration or the organic inevitability of degeneration. Instead they are precursors who struggle to overcome the social and cultural norms of their environment. The *aboulia* from which the couple suffers is fundamentally spiritual and metaphysical. It is neither inevitable nor hereditary, but dependent on environment. In other words, the neurotic protagonists symbolically represent the deep-rooted spiritual ailments of early twentieth-century Spain, and not the biological sterility that constitutes the unavoidable outcome of degeneration.

In the 1870s, both Hippolyte Taine and Théodule Ribot renewed the association between biological science and philosophical approaches to the study of the mind.

The narrative of *El árbol de la ciencia* is punctuated by naturalist descriptions that accompany Andrés Hurtado's experience as a 'médico de higiene' as he visits the syphilitic prostitutes at the city's Hospital de San Juan de Dios. These episodes emphasize the lack of sanitation, the inhumane treatment of the women, the implicit rendering of physical decay. Like Zola, Baroja was fascinated by the representation of generational pathologies and social health in naturalist terms, but in fact demonstrated a greater command of medical and scientific approaches to degeneration than Zola.[37] I diverge, however, from the existing critical view that 'Baroja uses Zola's paradigm that pathology can show heredity at work'.[38] Baroja debates hereditary paradigms in his early fiction, but ultimately moves beyond them through moderating and often sceptical approaches to biological determinism.

Baroja's exploration of physiology and psychopathology would appear — at least superficially — to situate his early fiction as a direct continuation of nineteenth-century naturalism, associated in Spain with Galdós, Clarín and Pardo Bazán. Baroja, however, did not consider himself a naturalist. In *El árbol de la ciencia* the hostile world inhabited by Andrés is a subjectively perceived environment, in which the pain and suffering that he witnesses in Madrid provide evidence that confirms his philosophical view. Like Unamuno, Baroja did not dismiss naturalism. He did, however, reject Zola's method of applying science to fiction and perceived the pressing needs of art and literature to have moved beyond the representational mode of naturalism by the late nineteenth century. In his essay 'Hacia lo inconsciente' of 1899, Baroja wrote that: 'El artista moderno no es, respecto a la Naturaleza, un espejo que trate de reflejarla: es más bien un instrumento delicado que vibra con sus latidos y amplifica sus vibraciones' (*OC*, VIII, 851). Baroja's early fiction does not convincingly sustain either naturalism or positivism, despite the key influence of these belief systems on his novels of the first decade of the twentieth century. Baroja was fascinated by heredity, but ultimately construed national character as more complex than a question of biology.

The term *aboulia* was popularized by Ribot's *Les Maladies de la volonté* (1883), prior to its appropriation by Ganivet and Unamuno in Spain to denote a collective psychological malady. In other words, as Shaw has demonstrated, the term was taken from psychopathology to denote a metaphysical condition.[39] In this context, the symptoms of *aboulia* may variously denote a Schopenhauerian conflict between Will and reason, a mental and moral disease, national and spiritual exhaustion. Baroja's novel explores a combination of these possibilities through the exposition of the limitations of medical science to explain or treat the human and social body.

My analysis has aimed to probe existing critical assumptions regarding the author's adherence to the premises of degeneration in the trilogy *La raza* through my account of Baroja's inconsistent approach to generational paradigms. In this regard, I conclude that in his Madrid novels he explored the concept of degeneration through a broad engagement with Morel's *dégénérescence*, a model that drew specifically on a mid-nineteenth-century French context, but one that exerted such a powerful influence within discourses of alcoholism and social hygiene in turn-of-the-century Spain. The biological transmission of inherited characteristics was of great interest to Baroja. The definition of race, nation and culture and their progress were not, however, reducible to a single theory. Baroja's early fiction, I propose, provides a powerful exploration of contemporary debates about the nation's future, but draws on the cultural narratives of degeneration and the literary naturalism that sustained them in fundamentally contradictory ways.

Notes to Chapter 6

1. Huyssen, *After the Great Divide*, pp. 50–52.
2. Friedrich Nietzsche, *The Case of Wagner* in *The Birth of Tragedy and the Case of Wagner*, trans. by Walter Kaufmann (Harmondsworth: Penguin, 1976), p. 161.
3. On the national birth rate in late nineteenth-century Spain, see Mercedes Granjel, *Pedro Felipe Monlau y la higiene española del siglo XIX* (Salamanca: Universidad de Salamanca, 1983), pp. 136–37.
4. Sosa-Velasco, *Médicos escritores*, p. 95.
5. Baroja, *Ayer y hoy* (Santiago: Ercilla, 1939), pp. 217–18.
6. Otis, *Organic Memory*, pp. 91–92.
7. On the influence of biologists on Baroja, see Otis, *Organic Memory*, p. 77.
8. See, for example, Soufas, *The Subject in Question*; and my own *Re-reading Pío Baroja*, in which I analyse the subjectively perceived and hostile environment inhabited by Andrés. Edward Inman Fox, 'Baroja y Schopenhauer: *El árbol de la ciencia*', in *Ideología y política en las letras de fin de siglo (1898)* (Madrid: Espasa-Calpe, 1988), pp. 157–75, mentions Lulú only as evidence of Andrés's pessimism.
9. Baroja, *El árbol de la ciencia*, p. 269.
10. Elaine Showalter, *The Female Malady: Women, Madness and English Culture, 1830–1980* (New York: Penguin, 1987), p. 146.
11. Of course the specific context of Spanish feminism, whose status as an organized movement occurred later than in the United States and other parts of Europe, must be emphasized in any attempt to transpose the term New Woman to Spanish fiction. On Spanish feminism, see Geraldine M. Scanlon, *La polémica feminista en la España contemporánea (1868–1974)* (Madrid: siglo veintiuno, 1976). On New Women in Spanish female-authored narratives, see Lou Charnon-Deutsch, *Narratives of Desire: Nineteenth-Century Spanish Fiction by Women* (University Park: Pennsylvania State University Press, 1994), Chapter 5.
12. See Dijkstra, *Idols of Perversity*, pp. 215–26.
13. August Forel, *The Sexual Question; A Scientific, Psychological, Hygienic and Sociological Study* [1906], trans. by C. F. Marshall (New York: Physicians and Surgeons Book Co., 1925), pp. 137–38.
14. On this question and its relevance to Victorian New Woman Fiction, see Ann Heilmann, 'Narrating the Hysteric: Fin-de-Siècle Medical Discourse and Sarah Grand's *The Heavenly Twins* (1893)', in *The New Woman in Fiction and Fact: Fin-de-Siècle Feminisms*, ed. by Angelique Richardson and Chris Willis (Basingstoke: Palgrave, 2002), pp. 123–35 (p. 128).
15. A. López Núñez, *La acción social de la mujer en la higiene y mejoramiento de la raza* (Madrid: M. Minuesa, 1915), p. 24.
16. Carmen del Moral, *La sociedad madrileña*, pp. 130–31.
17. Eslava, *La prostitución en Madrid*, p. 37.
18. Carmen del Moral, *La sociedad madrileña*, pp. 137–40.
19. Cited by Antonio Navarro Fernández, *La prostitución en la villa de Madrid* (Madrid: Ricardo Rojas, 1909), p. 247.
20. Virginia Trueba Mira, 'Lulú: el extraño personaje de *El árbol de la ciencia* de Pío Baroja', *Anales de la literatura española contemporánea*, 28.1 (2003), 183–202 (pp. 184–88).
21. Trueba Mira, 'Lulú', pp. 193–95.
22. Celaya Carrillo likewise construes Lulú as representative of the threat to the authority and selfhood of the bourgeois male posed by 'los cambios presentes y futuros en la situación social de la mujer'. *La mujer deseante*, p. 30.
23. Arthur Schopenhauer, 'On Women', in *Essays and Aphorisms*, trans. by R. J. Hollingdale

(London: Penguin, 1970), pp. 80–88 (pp. 81, 84).
24. On this common paradigm, the reader is referred to Stott, *Fabrication of the Late Victorian Femme Fatale*.
25. José Ortega y Gasset, 'Pío Baraja: anatomía de un alma dispersa', *Meditaciones sobre la literatura y el arte (La manera española de ver las cosas)*, ed. by E. Inman Fox (Madrid: Castalia, 1988), p. 119.
26. *Revista Clínica de los Hospitales*, 1 (1889), 1–9, 274–81, 337–40.
27. Pick, *Faces of Degeneration*, p. 64.
28. Álvarez Peláez, 'La mujer española y el control de natalidad', p. 182.
29. Álvarez Peláez, 'La mujer española y el control de natalidad', p. 182.
30. Campos et al., *Los ilegales*, p. 170.
31. Benjamin Fraser has likewise identified the novel's merging of binary opposites in relation to medicine and a contradictory approach to determinism in his article 'Baroja's Rejection of Traditional Medicine in *El árbol de la ciencia*', *Bulletin of Spanish Studies*, 85.1 (2008), 29–50.
32. Labanyi, *Gender and Modernization*, p. 356.
33. Mary Nash, 'Un/Contested Identities: Motherhood, Sex Reform and the Modernization of Gender Identity in Early Twentieth-Century Spain', in *Constructing Spanish Womanhood: Female Identity in Modern Spain*, ed. by V. L. Enders and P. B. Radcliff (Albany: State University of New York Press, 1999), pp. 25–49 (pp. 25, 35).
34. Baroja, *La ciudad de la niebla* (London: Nelson, 1932), pp. 272–73.
35. Pick, *Faces of Degeneration*, p. 51.
36. Luis Granjel, *Panorama de la generación del 98* (Madrid: Guadarrama, 1959), pp. 220–23.
37. Otis, *Organic Memory*, p. 77.
38. Otis, *Organic Memory*, p. 84.
39. Shaw, 'More about *abulia*', p. 451.

CONCLUSION

Readership and the Legacy of Degeneration Theory

In *Bodies of Disorder* the comparison of Baroja and Blasco Ibáñez, authors who have long been placed in altogether separate literary camps, has sought to illuminate significant parallels in their close engagement with discourses of gender and degeneration. This analysis raises the obvious question of reception and the response of contemporary readers to the literary representation of urban prostitution, immorality, degenerate minds and bodies. Women, of course, were considered particularly susceptible to emotionalism and the novelistic depiction of dubious morality. My Conclusion addresses the influence of the literary market, with particular emphasis on the consumer agency that women exerted over the production of literary fiction during this period. In the final section I examine the legacy and appropriation of degeneration theory in the early decades of the twentieth century in the context of each author's political convictions and ideological approach.

Female Readers and the Literary Market

The famous polemic between Baroja and Blasco Ibáñez was fuelled vigorously by the latter's commercial success. Baroja, of course, won the argument in relation to literary history, if not financial reward, and in 1934 was elected to the Real Academia Española, a position renounced by Blasco for political reasons.[1] The public hostility between the two authors echoed in resounding terms the contemporary debates led by Ortega and his contemporaries about high and low art, intellectual minority versus the masses. It was spurred on by collective resentment on the part of 'Generation of 1898' authors about the popularity and economic gains of Blasco's fiction. These bestsellers were dismissed as inferior to the elitist high culture of authors such as Unamuno and Ganivet, who perceived themselves as the new 'intelectualidad española', yet Blasco's economic gains were unrivalled by those of his modernist contemporaries.

Despite these factors, only limited critical attention has been paid to the literary market in turn-of-the-century Spain and, in particular, the considerable female readership that was attracted by the novels of this period. Late nineteenth-century representations of women in Spanish visual culture and literature have been analysed predominantly as responses to the male gaze. There is little scholarship on the agency of female readers and spectators in Spain, an area of reception studies that has gained increasing ground in scholarship of Anglophone literature in recent years.² Yet the question of the profitable literary market provided by women readers is fundamental to the creative tension present in both Baroja and Blasco Ibáñez between the fiction they wished to write and the audience on which they depended. My analysis below aims to contribute renewed attention to the significant but often neglected implications of readership in relation to the two Spanish authors under scrutiny, with particular emphasis on the agency and subjectivity of female readers.

Many years before achieving international fame, Blasco Ibáñez's novels were already enormously successful in Spain in commercial terms. In 1903, the first edition of *La catedral* was released with a print-run of 22,000 copies, a statistic that was not matched even by Felipe Trigo, one of the most widely read authors of this period.³ The publishing house Prometeo, established in 1914 by Blasco, Francisco Sempere and Fernando Llorca, was a key element in fostering the author's popularity. Editorial Prometeo commissioned distinctive book covers designed by Povo and others that were vital to the marketing of the author's fiction.⁴ Many of Blasco's novels enjoyed bestseller status, notably *Mare nostrum* (1917), *El papa del mar* (1925) and *A los pies de Venus* (1926). The whirlwind success of *Los cuatro jinetes del Apocalipsis* (1916) in English translation led to its Hollywood adaption in 1921 and made Blasco a millionaire.

Several of Blasco's early works — *Arroz y tartana*, *Flor de Mayo*, *La barraca*, *Sónnica la cortesana* and *Entre naranjos* — were published in the *folletín* of his Republican newspaper *El Pueblo* before their reappearance in volume form. It is commonly accepted that in the late nineteenth century a large number of readers were drawn both to the *novelas de folletín* (serialized in newspapers) and *novelas por entrega* (published separately in instalments) compared to novels published as volumes. As Ferreras and Botrel have shown, the readership for the *novela por entrega* was predominantly found in the cities where literacy rates were higher, among workers and the lower middle classes as groups which were economically more vulnerable and therefore attracted by the affordable regular expense of the *entrega*, and included a substantial proportion of women.⁵ In 1900 the male literacy rate was 44%; for women it was 29%, reflecting a still weak but increasing commitment to women's education. In Madrid female literacy at the turn of the century stood at 56.8%, well above that of the regions. However, within these figures levels of reading ability would have varied enormously. The circulation figures for the *folletines* in the late nineteenth century were considerably higher than for the *entrega*, in part because the price of the latter was five times that of a newspaper. In fact the frequently escapist, melodramatic and sentimental content of each form of serialized fiction was not necessarily dissimilar.⁶

Subsequent assertions of frustration on the part of male intellectuals such as Unamuno and Valle-Inclán regarding the disturbing influence of female consumers on the production of literature allow us some insight into the reception of turn-of-the-century fiction, particularly by a female audience. It is well known that

Unamuno expressed annoyance that his literary production was dependent on a frivolous literary market made up primarily of women, or rather 'señoras y señoritas' who, he claimed, avoided fiction of any depth.[7] Both the response of contemporary readers to Blasco Ibáñez's fiction, and more specifically the large female readership that his novels were likely to have attracted, are significant for our understanding of novelistic production during this period. This vital dynamic between created artefact and consumption — I contend — was fundamental to the narrative style and formula of novels such as *La barraca* and *Cañas y barro*, including sensationalist elements, suspense, and the appeal of unconventional anti-heroines. The transgressive behaviours of women in Blasco's novels offer the allure of illicit desire in a voyeuristic and imagined context: in other words, the textual fulfilment of desires proffered by fantasy. Both the specific appeal to women readers and the appropriation of sensation fiction and melodrama, I suggest, are important factors that sustain the uneasy position Blasco has long occupied in literary history.

The *folletín* was a key element of Blasco's Republican daily newspaper *El Pueblo*. As Laguna Platero observes, *El Pueblo* was established with the aim of extending its political propaganda to a large audience. It had an initial print run of between 5000 and 6000 copies, reaching a circulation of 13,000 copies by 1908, and functioned as a precursor to 'prensa de masas'.[8] Monthly subscription to *El Pueblo* cost 1.25 pesetas, making it the cheapest newspaper in Valencia from its inception in 1894. It should also be remembered that readership figures were doubtless considerably higher, given the likelihood of lending and multiple readings of one copy, as well as the common practice of reading aloud in groups. Two main elements are noteworthy in relation to the serialized publication of Blasco's early novels in the *folletín*. Firstly, the structure of novels such as *Flor de Mayo* was undoubtedly influenced by the requirement of fragmented publication for action at the end of each instalment, the drama created by adultery and a sexual plot, and simple characterization. The frequently sentimental, escapist, suspenseful nature of the *novela de folletín* in the second half of the nineteenth century is commonly acknowledged. Secondly, *novelas de folletín* were addressed particularly to women, providing evidence of the type of reading material perceived to be appealing to a popular and largely female audience.[9]

In late nineteenth-century Spain, women's access to reading as well as writing was defined in relation to morality, and above all the fear that they would be inherently susceptible to imitation through their high (and biologically driven) sensitivity. Women's consumption of melodrama, romance and sensationalism exacerbated the widespread anxiety that novels would contaminate their behaviour through seductive literary role models and the promise of passion and excitement that was absent from daily life. Of significance for understanding the reading habits of women in late nineteenth-century Spain is the common assumption that the moral degeneration of women was a product of reading or consuming the wrong type of fiction. This was namely sensationalist, violent and immoral literature that played on false romantic expectations or — even worse — provided a compelling role model for behaviour that was unacceptable by bourgeois standards. The sensation novels of the late nineteenth century, with their emphasis on adultery, disguise and crime, were of particular concern. In Britain, New Woman fiction of the 1890s would constitute an equally potent object of critique, for the undercutting of romantic expectations and moral standards of sexual purity. As Rita Felski argues, 'women's [assumed] emotionality, passivity and susceptibility to persuasion render them ideal subjects of an ideology of consumption that pervades a society predicated on the commercialization of pleasure'.[10]

The painting 'Una lectora impresionable' (printed in *La Ilustración Española y Americana* in 1884) presents a woman holding a book as she expresses an attitude of excitement and desire. As the commentator attests, she has just read a passage from *Faust*, 'y vagan en tropel por su exaltada mente "Ilusiones engañosas, / Livianas como el placer"'.[11] A similar posture, although less charged with intoxication, is Ramon Casas's *Joven decadente. Después del baile* (1899; cover image). As a sophisticated subject of higher society, the woman apparently poses little disruption to the social order. The book she holds open in one hand is evidence none the less of the agency of female desire on the part of the represented subject. As consuming subject, women readers constituted a potent threat to the social body, a visual trope underscored by the figure's languid, fatigued pose. The young decadent is as susceptible as any other woman to the perils of romantic or sentimental literature, as well as the corrupting force of intellectual development. *Joven decadente* provides a vivid variation on pervasive iconography of the period that represented the perceived strain on women's nervous systems of dangerous intellectual pursuits. Numerous visual depictions of fainting, languid women during this period emphasize social, intellectual and physical dangers for the delicate female body and mind.[12]

According to medical-scientific studies of the period, women had more sensitive nervous systems than men, and were therefore more prone to mental excitement.[13] Women were assumed to have an emotional and sentimental response to reading, as opposed to a rational one. In the light of this innate sensitivity, reading by women could (according to this view) provoke uncontrolled sexual desire and erotic pleasure, even the descent into prostitution and sexual depravation, particularly if the material were obscene. Within medical and pseudo-medical discourse, assumptions about women's greater susceptibility were commonplace, and rooted in biological difference, reproduction and the capacity for motherhood. In the second half of the nineteenth century, literary collections aimed particularly at women were established with the protection of feminine virtue in mind: *Biblioteca del Correo de la Moda*, *Biblioteca Perla*, *Biblioteca del Hogar*, *Biblioteca de la Mujer*, *Biblioteca Moral y Recreativa* and, in the 1870s, the *Biblioteca de señoras*.[14]

The profitable trade in books aimed at middle-class women is illustrated by the widespread appeal of Pedro Monlau's *Higiene del matrimonio o el libro de los casados* (1881) and Ángel Pulido's *Bosquejos médico-sociales para la mujer* (1875), medical manuals for marriage and maternity. Pulido's book includes a chapter that warns women of the dangers of reading fiction with sexual content, exemplified by the vogue of the 1880s for *naturalismo radical*. These novels by Eduardo López Bago, Alejandro Sawa and others enjoyed high levels of commercial success.[15] Émile Zola's school of physiology was also reported in the Spanish press as potentially dangerous to sensitive women.[16] In 1905 Antolín López Peláez, the Bishop of Jaca, expressed the advisability of women reading religious subject matter, but also emphasized the emergence of a significant new market for religious publications, one made up of women who had an extraordinary interest in reading.[17]

Blasco's turn-of-the-century fiction presents unequivocal moral portraits, exemplified by the wayward heroine of *Flor de Mayo* who is punished for adultery by the painful loss of her husband, lover and son at the end of the novel. Other novels appear to revel in their portrait of deviant feminine behaviour and role models who experience varying degrees of emotional loss in return for their transgressions. In *Cañas y barro*, the didactic element is at best contradictory: Neleta loses her son and lover, but succeeds in her goal of financial independence and social ambition. Of greater significance for the purposes of this analysis, however, is Blasco's spectacular route to an extensive and lucrative market. The key focus of his early novels on fantasies of the feminine provides circumstantial evidence that the author assumed both a female audience and demand for his fiction, an argument made all the more compelling by readership figures of the period and the increasing proportion of literate women, particularly in urban centres.

Blasco's newspaper *El Pueblo* contained regular contributions both on science and society, and was instrumental in the diffusion of local events including crime in Valencia, as well as contemporary debates about issues of social interest. As a daily newspaper intended for mass consumption, it is pertinent to note the number of advertisements included in each copy of *El Pueblo*, which promise cures for a number of common ailments including those associated with degeneration. On 20 October 1902, for example, under the title 'Los adelantos de la ciencia', an advertisement promises a cure for tuberculosis and its associated symptoms, including 'atonía (debilidad del estómago), digestiones laboriosas o difíciles, pirosis o acedías, inapetencia, gastralgias, [...], úlceras, hiperecloridia y toda clase de dispepsias'. Miraculous cures for syphilis through 'inyecciones vegetales' are also advertised, and the newspaper announces modern developments in medicine, including surgery for an arterial tumour performed for the first time in Valencia.[18] Every day articles were published on politics, science, literature and art, as well as local news. Sociological, cultural and political issues were therefore at the heart of the popular appeal of *El Pueblo*, in line with the newspaper's political and ideological aims, together with dissemination of information about mundane everyday life in Valencia. The newspaper serialized French naturalist novels in the *folletín*, including Zola's *La Débâcle* and *Vérité*. It is a mere truism to state that Blasco's work as a journalist was inseparably bound to his literary portrait of social ills, not least poverty, criminality and disease.

Furthermore *El Pueblo*, like other popular newspapers of the day, was peppered with advertisements for health and beauty products aimed at feminine consumption. This shrewd marketing is a good example of a consumer model identified by Charnon-Deutsch, who observes that by the end of the nineteenth century manufacturers 'quickly discovered that certain goods could be cheaply produced and sold at higher prices if they appealed to those who were in charge of the family's shopping'.[19] Women of the period, particularly the urban bourgeoisie, had access to numerous visual images that were invested with desirability: dance invitations, visiting cards, newspaper advertisements, fashion magazines such as *La Moda Elegante*, illustrated weeklies, and advertising posters. In the visual field, 'the production of "beautiful" images played a key role in shaping notions of proper and desirable feminine behaviour and could thus be considered a regulatory practice'.[20] Given that idealized visual representations of women were highly successful, it is logical to posit that a similar pattern held true for their literary counterparts. Fictional heroines and anti-heroines embodied equal potential both to foster desire for the wished-for self and also to alienate through the impossibility of achieving this desired alterity, whether idealized or transgressive. In other words, models of socially upright and deviant behaviour ('la mujer buena' and 'la mujer mala') were both invested with seductive appeal.

In the narrative realm of Blasco's early fiction, the portraits of wayward women and adulteresses were not a means of regulation or didacticism, but instead a desirable model for fantasies of Otherness. In *Cañas y barro*, Neleta's successful bid for economic, social and sexual independence held the potential for striking appeal to women readers. Whether or not the fatally alluring anti-heroine represents a persuasive source of moral degeneration in relation to scientific and social discourses of the period, her trajectory certainly enhanced the commercial viability of the novel through its draw to readers (including a high proportion of middle-class women) willing to meet the cost of the volume. Blasco was committed ideologically to the education of the masses, but in practice the lucrative income from both his novels and film adaptations stemmed from the attraction they held for middle-class audiences. In his analysis of the cinema adaptation of *Sangre y arena* (1916), David George shows that by casting the crowd as a threatening, proletarian rabble, the film in fact 'plays on middle-class fears of the masses in order to gain a greater degree of control over them as a potential film audience for the purposes of profit'.[21] There is, I conclude, a fundamentally productive tension in Blasco's early fiction between the representation of seductively degenerate women and the appeal to a broad reading demographic whose consumption of the novels assisted the promotion of the author to wealth and fame.

In Pardo Bazán's novel *La Tribuna* (1883), the working-class protagonist, Amparo, represents a threat to the social status through her leading role in the political mobilization of her fellow workers at the tobacco factory. She does so by reading Republican newspaper articles aloud to the group, a common practice among the working classes both due to cost and levels of literacy. Amparo's reading style is characterized in terms of feminine emotion and naivety: 'Su alma impresionable, combustible, móvil y superficial, se teñía fácilmente del color del periódico que andaba en sus manos, y lo reflejaba con viveza y fidelidad extraordinarias. [...] La fe virgen con que creía en la Prensa era inquebrantable'.[22] The evolving culture of consumption in late nineteenth-century Spain, then, spawned a widespread social fear on the part of the bourgeoisie because it represented a growing democratization of culture, as boundaries of class, gender and culture were eroded. The working-class masses who inhabited the city streets posed a threat to social order and bourgeois values. The prostitute and the criminal were seen as particularly dangerous figures within the public sphere, in a society defined by commodification and the rise of the masses.

In view of this threat, the regulation of 'deviant' behaviour was undertaken by hygienic medicine, scientific texts, visual imagery and also literature, as studies of late nineteenth-century Spain have shown.[23] Reading was thus posited as a form of consumption that posed a serious threat to bourgeois order during this period because it embodied female desire as a potent source of social decay and disease. At worst, female consumers of luxury goods would be tempted towards adultery and even prostitution to sustain the seductive appeal of self-adornment, a trajectory memorably delineated by Galdós's *La de Bringas* (1884).

In the 1910s and 1920s journals such as *La novela corta*, *El cuento semanal* and *Los contemporáneos* regularly published female writers as well as contributions by male authors including Unamuno and Valle-Inclán. Popular magazines such as *Ilustración Artística*, *Mundo Femenino* and *Blanco y Negro* held increasing appeal for women, despite dire warnings of the consequences of such frivolous reading habits. In his 1920 prologue to *Tres novelas ejemplares y un prólogo* Unamuno refers in derogatory terms to women as the predominant consumers of novels in Spain, and laments the prevailing influence of female readers on the shaping of literary creation (understood as a form of paternity). Unamuno thus positions women readers in the role of passive and undeserving consumers of male authorship, and he considers women's fiction as inferior for its frequent adherence to melodrama. Valle-Inclán expresses a similar frustration in an early scene that takes place in Zaratustra's bookshop in *Luces de bohemia* (1924) in which a girl comes to ask whether the next episode of *El hijo de la difunta* has been published. This is a disdainful nod to the type of serialized fiction consumed predominantly by middle-class female readers, represented here by Doña Loreta 'la del coronel'. The scene recalls the author's own early novel *La Cara de Dios*, a potboiler written for economic sustenance. Galdós of course published *por entregas* in the major literary magazines. The revised ending of *Doña Perfecta* in the book version is a telling example of the demands of serial publication.

Baroja was equally aware of his substantial female readership. Under the heading 'El amor y la literatura', in *El mundo es ansí* the author undertakes to explore female psychology, asserting that: 'Claro que en el fondo ni en el hombre existe algo más que lo humano, ni en la mujer algo más que lo femenino' (138). The male mind is associated with humanity; the female mind with femininity, a statement that betrays a wealth of problematic assumptions. Elsewhere, Baroja was ironic and pejorative about the absence of literary capacities of Spanish women in the context of their condescending lack of appreciation for burgeoning male writers. He asserted that Spanish women had no interest in reading anything of merit: 'a las mujeres españolas no les gusta leer. [...] Yo creo que la misma doña Emilia Pardo Bazán, que escribe muy bien, según dicen, no tiene sentido literario y filosófico alguno' (*OC*, v, 246–47).[24] Like the views cited above of fellow male intellectuals of the period, Baroja's statement points blatantly to the cultural exclusion of women in early twentieth-century Spain, as women were relegated to the position of inferior both from the perspective of cultural production and passive consumption.

Blasco's literary apprenticeship was undertaken through his forays in serialized fiction. Prior to the publication of *Cañas y barro*, the memorable ending of *Flor de Mayo* in which the cuckolded husband leads the men and boats of the fishing village of Cabañal to sea despite an impending storm had already appeared in the *folletín* of *El Pueblo* in 1895. Following the original serialization of *La barraca* in *El Pueblo*, only five hundred copies of this novel were sold, for one peseta each, with a total profit of just seventy-eight pesetas. Yet, by May 1899 critical acclaim led to serialization of *La barraca* in the popular Madrid daily *El Liberal*. As Nemesvari notes in his analysis of British sensation fiction, the 'literal meaning of sensationalism — an appeal to the senses, and to the sensual' explains uneasy contemporary responses to the form, 'particularly when that sensuality was explicitly connected to women'.[25] Sensationalist representations frequently focused on the erotic appeal of women's bodies, as succinctly demonstrated by Blasco's direct engagement with this literary mode and its close relationship to melodrama in *Cañas y barro*. Indeed, the term 'sensation novel' and its representational reliance on excess refers as much to its status within mass culture as it does to the content of this fluid genre. In addition to the inclusion of adultery and a sexual plot (*Flor de Mayo*, *Entre naranjos* and *Cañas y barro*), a notable common element of many of Blasco's early novels is the frequent loss of children.[26] In *La barraca* the death of the five-year-old child Pascualet represents the inexorable destiny of Batiste's family. Yet like the neonaticide of *Cañas y barro*, it is simultaneously at the heart of the novel's notoriety and marketability. Sensation fiction was thus, I contend, a key vehicle for the dissemination of popular versions of degeneration theory in the late nineteenth century, through the compelling draw of immorality and deviance, together with violent and sexualized women.

The democratic effects of print media (in relative terms) were key to Blasco's approach both to journalism and novel-writing, since this technology allowed the dissemination of culture from the aristocracy to both the bourgeoisie and working classes. Blasco aimed to reach a wide audience through his newspaper and serialized fiction, in line with Republican and Jacobean ideals. In 1905 he established *La novela ilustrada*, a collection of novels published in instalments, with the aim of reaching a large public by selling at an extraordinarily low price. Blasco was accused of instigating the rabble towards acts of political insurrection. Yet he viewed the politicization of the masses as a noble aim, and aimed to use both novels and film as instruments of democracy that sought to improve the level of education and cultural literacy of the proletarian masses. As Benedict Anderson has argued, the creation of a mass reading culture in the nineteenth century through the commercialization of print and through the education system established a set of common cultural values of a national community. The 'reading classes' were civilized members of society who promoted and shared these values.[27] Blasco Ibáñez accessed a large reading public through popular print media, but one whose revolutionary potential was limited by the appeal of traditional bourgeois values. Baroja maintained his commitment to producing a spectrum of intellectual, historical and philosophical fiction, but expressed vehement resentment towards Blasco's success.

By contrast to the elitism and cult of individualism of 'Generation of 1898' authors, Blasco is often labelled pejoratively as an 'escritor de masas'. His prose was condemned, even dismissed, by Baroja for being commonplace: 'Blasco Ibáñez, evidentemente, es un buen novelista; sabe componer, escribe claro; pero, para mí, es aburrido; es un conjunto de perfecciones vulgares y mostrencas, que a mí me ahoga. Tiene las opiniones de todo el mundo, los gustos de todo el mundo' (OC, VII, 734). It is widely acknowledged that the *noventayochistas* established an aesthetic formula that was based on the division between intellectuals and the masses, to whom 'lo vulgar' would appeal. Valle-Inclán was at the forefront of this derogatory approach to the general public, seeking instead a minority audience of intellectuals.

Women readers were subject to a similar double bind. They constituted a significant demographic in the consumption of novels, but were relegated by male literati of the period to the position of intellectual inferior, incapable both for reasons of biology and education of understanding and appreciating the works they consumed. Unamuno, Valle-Inclán and to some extent Baroja thereby rejected the very audience they attracted, and who provided a market for the literary and economic consumption of their works. Ortega y Gasset famously distinguished between *minoría y masa*. In *La rebelión de las masas* (1930), a collection of essays, the man of science represented for Ortega a precursor to the 'hombre-masa', and therefore a figure of perilous mediocrity: 'la ciencia experimental ha progresado en buena parte merced al trabajo de hombres fabulosamente mediocres, y aún menos que mediocres'.[28] In the prologues to his novels, Unamuno addressed his 'lector'; Blasco, by contrast, drew attention to his 'público', thereby conceptualizing his fiction in relation to spectacle.[29]

In the light of the derogatory comments made by Unamuno, Valle-Inclán and Baroja about their readership, my argument that Blasco wrote for a largely female audience may be placed in the context of theories of mass culture which was associated fundamentally with women. As Huyssen argues in his seminal work, 'the ominous expansion of mass culture throughout the social realm' was inscribed within modernism: 'political, psychological, and aesthetic discourse around the turn of the century consistently and obsessively genders mass culture and the masses as feminine, while high culture, whether traditional or modern, clearly remains the privileged realm of male activities'.[30] In other words, male authors produced genuine authentic literature, whilst women were identified as the 'avid consumer[s] of pulp'.[31] The elitist male realm stood in contrast to the subjective, emotional and passive referencing of women as readers of inferior literature. Mass audiences were feminized as emotional, irrational and intellectually weak. This paradigm is fundamental both in relation to gendered ideologies and classifications, but also to the elitism and individualism of the modernist artist. It underpins both the threat of female sexual desire and the rebellion of working-class men.

In this context, mass culture became synonymous with social corruption, through its blurring of existing class and gender relations. The availability of serialized fiction embodied this threat, through its association with the development of an organized working class, as Sieburth explains: 'Mass culture therefore meant, in the eyes of the dominant class, a threat to social control'.[32] Within bourgeois discourse, the working classes and the prostitute were invoked as threats to the higher order; nineteenth-century discourses on mass culture thereby metaphorically rendered the lower social body as a source of contamination.[33] It is a logical progression, therefore, that this type of symbolic displacement should have led to such widespread attempts to classify, order and contain promiscuity, madness and the corrupting legacy of mass production through the cultural and social myths of degenerationism.

In his memoirs, Baroja was derogatory both about Blasco's personality and his literary works. In 'Galería de tipos de la época', Baroja recalls meeting Blasco in Valencia in 1892 or 1893, and counters his reputation as a dashing Byronic figure through an unflattering physical portrait. He is described not as a dark and audacious figure, but instead as overweight with a high-pitched voice (OC, VII, 869). The resentment appears to have been mutual. Blasco was of the opinion that the title of the collection *Novelistas del siglo XX*, in which *El mayorazgo de Labraz* was due to appear, was 'una ridiculez, una petulancia' (869) and stated that Baroja's *La lucha por la vida* novels were 'estampas, pero no cuadros' (870). However, the primary source of resentment is resoundingly evident. By 1913 when they met in Paris, Blasco was not afraid to proclaim loudly his economic success.[34] In short, Baroja viewed Blasco as a financially successful writer, but not an authentic author, and dismissed his works as lacking literary interest.

The popularity of Blasco's novels during his lifetime fits awkwardly with his subsequent position within literary history. Critics have pointed to the 'conspiracy of silence' that surrounded the author during the Franco regime.[35] Even by the 1960s, approaching the centenary of his birth, positions were still polarized, in no small measure due to the writer's political affiliations and outspoken views which led to arrests, incarcerations and exile.[36] In 1932, under the Second Republic, a memorial tablet had been dedicated to him on the Avenida Blasco Ibáñez in Valencia, near the *plaza* which was named after him. In 1933 the body of Blasco was brought home to his native city and buried with military honours. By 1967, however, Juan Ignacio Ferreras stated that the author was 'un tabú'.[37] Without a street named after him, a plaque or a statue in Valencia, and the majority of his works banished from the library at the Universidad de Valencia, Blasco was effectively erased from the cultural and social history of the city for the duration of the dictatorship.

Blasco's popular version of degeneration theories were key to the numerous representations of immoral and adulterous women in his early works, evidence of a creative and profitable relationship between portraits of morally deviant women and popular consumption of his novels. In Baroja's works, the configuration of reproduction as a potential source of danger to the health of the nation, one capable of infecting the entire social body, presents an intriguing point of comparison. Blasco's creation of sexually assertive, financially independent women in novels such as *Entre naranjos* and *Cañas y barro* provides a persuasive indication of the author's awareness of the commercial agency of his readership. By contrast, Baroja's fictional portraits of women (Águeda de Aizgorri, María Aracil, Lulú) demonstrate their struggle in a traditional environment and the inevitable failure of emancipation. The urban prostitutes of Baroja's Madrid novels are trapped in poverty and squalor, but they do not accurately constitute embodiments of degeneration.

Bodies of Disorder has addressed the post-Darwinian context of degeneration theory, its assimilation and development in Spain. My analysis has focused on the powerful cross-fertilization of literature and popular versions of science (biology, anthropology, criminology) in early twentieth-century Spain. It provides a case study for the ways in which discourses of degeneration (moral, physical, national) played out in the novels of the period, across the categories of 'high' and 'low' art. My research on readership offers original evidence that both the canonical novels of the 'Generation of 1898' and the popular fiction of authors such as Blasco Ibáñez were written with a posited audience in mind, whether the lofty ideal of the intellectual male or the consumer power wielded increasingly by middle-class women.

The appeal of degeneration theory in Spain was strengthened and exacerbated by the powerful voices of regenerationism of Joaquín Costa and others, as the cultural potency of meta-narratives of degenerationism would reverberate through the early twentieth century and beyond. The understanding and representation of the degenerate female body and mind held significant implications for the nation's future in biological, spiritual and economic terms.[38] If the Spanish nation was in decline according to the national 'problem', then regeneration would depend on healthy reproduction through the medical, moral and social containment of childbearing women. In Baroja and Blasco Ibáñez, the influence of these ideas remains theoretical and incomplete: their novels both assimilate and resist positivist theories. In Spain, the later appropriation of regenerationist ideologies by Francoism provides a problematic context for our understanding of degenerationism in 'Generation of 1898' authors and their contemporaries. Indeed the question of assimilation and appropriation of degenerationism is nowhere more challenging than in their anticipation of fascist discourse. This is particularly pertinent to Francoist psychiatry in Spain. By the 1930s, Antonio Vallejo Nágera would put forward a policy of racial hygiene in a body of works including *Eugenesia de la Hispanidad y regeneración de la raza*. Vallejo Nágera's proposed cure for the racial degeneration of Spain would be found in the return to a strong religious faith, as well as imperial zeal.[39] In the final section of my book, I address the legacy and political implications of degeneration theories and discourses of eugenics within right-wing ideologies in the early decades of the twentieth century.

Degenerationism, Eugenics and their Legacy

Degenerationism was predicated on the perceived superiority of white, European domination alongside the implicit inferiority of non-European nations and by extension, those who embodied Otherness, including women and children. Yet it responded particularly to internal or national social divisions, and drew on a powerful language of social pathology. In Spain, as in other European countries, including Italy, France and England, the architects of medico-scientific discourse perceived contemporary problems such as crime, alcoholism, economic decline, prostitution and sexual deviance as evidence of socio-cultural crisis. Anarchism, too, as a political movement was deemed to be a source of disorder and chaos. In France, Taine supported the common medical view that social revolt could lead to widespread insanity, interpreting history in terms of the pathology of a sick nation. French *dégénérescence* gained momentum as a response to the social disorder of Revolution. Degenerationist theories focused on the individual — the criminal atavist, the cretin, the prostitute, the hysteric — in a bid to eradicate the sources of disease and disorder from society. Of course, specific national contexts must also be recognized. Italian criminal anthropology responded to a post-unification national context. However, Lombroso's school resoundingly grasped the public imagination across Europe, through the influential physiognomic analysis of the criminal who (with sufficient categorization) would eventually be recognizable by physical characteristics alone.

In nineteenth-century Spain, hygienists and psychiatrists were likewise engaged in the analysis and theorization of degeneration in relation to a number of diverse fields, including morality, criminality, alcoholism and poverty. These autochthonous discourses occurred alongside the theories of prominent European proponents of degenerationism; they were invigorated by social problems and receptive to prevalent currents of thought across national boundaries. By the 1880s, a fully formed thesis of degeneration had not yet been produced in Spain, although a number of studies were published that tackled the related issues of social and hygienic medicine. In 1884, the degenerationist elements of a developing industrial society underpinned Philiph Hauser's medico-social study of the nineteenth century, in which he identified the 'ley de la herencia y la transmisibilidad de los vicios orgánicos de los padres a los hijos'.[40] As Campos, Martínez and Huertas note, however, it would not be until the turn of the century that degenerationism would make a profound impact in social medicine in Spain.[41] In 1905, A. Muñoz Ruiz de Pasanis addressed the question of the degeneration of the Latin 'race' at the Academia Médico Quirúrgica in Madrid, and in 1906 delivered a paper on the role of alcoholism in racial degeneration.[42] These discourses were strongly allied with regenerationism and eugenics in early twentieth-century Spain. By 1911, J. Juderías would explain that Hygiene was not just about preventing disease and conserving health, but had the object of improving the race.[43]

Hygienic medicine in early twentieth-century Spain, therefore, posed the predicament of the Spanish nation in alarmist terms, a perceived danger that was only magnified by the military defeat of 1898. In the wake of the disaster, numerous texts were published that pointed to the decline and loss of Will of the Spanish people. In other words, national pathology was a potent metaphor in relation to Spain's perception of her place in the world, and the spirit of questioning of political, social and spiritual values at the turn of the century. In this context, *aboulia* became a key catchword, a term that conjured up the ailing nation and its all-embracing loss of Will, the potent symptom of Spain's ills, and a condition that underpins a number of prominent novels of 1902: Azorín's *La voluntad*, Unamuno's *Amor y pedagogía* and Baroja's *Camino de perfección*. The appeal of the term *aboulia* rested to a large extent on its elasticity, in the sense that it broadly encompassed the biological, the spiritual and the metaphysical, a condition that concisely denoted all aspects of Spain's national illness.

At the turn of the century, the biological degeneration of the Spanish nation was diagnosed in relation to a population that was becoming shorter, and one that was suffering the increasing incidence of mental and physical illness and birth defects. At its most extreme, degenerationists identified the anaemia, infertility and sterility of rural Spain as the heartland of an essential *hispanidad*.[44] The hereditary legacy of mental and physical traits was at the core of this belief in progressive degeneration; madness, alcoholism, tuberculosis and syphilis were all thought to be transmitted through successive generations. Addiction to morphine and tobacco were also believed to be inherited. Poverty, prostitution, criminality and moral deviance were regarded as both the cause and the symptoms of degeneration. As Jean Gayon notes, 'to varying degrees, turn-of-the-century biologists were all haunted by the idea that the "principle of heredity" might turn out to be a "force" that acted against the main principle of Darwinian evolution in such a way that heredity would either nullify the effects of selection or favour the return of ancestral characteristics'.[45]

Within these systems of early twentieth-century thought, the individual was part of a biological collective designated (variously) as the race, nation, heritage and homeland.[46] A pathological model of heredity therefore had far-reaching, even catastrophic consequences for the future. The widespread acceptance of a hereditary model for mental pathology, which would be exacerbated with each successive generation, forewarned of the ultimate exhaustion and extinction of the Spanish people. Even following the discovery of the germ that caused tuberculosis in 1882, hygienic medicine in Spain still posed the susceptibility of the ancestral race; the disease was a pathological expression of a degenerate and exhausted population. Like madness, tuberculosis represented the germination of a seed of destruction already present before birth, a dormant cell that formed *in utero*. Furthermore, those suffering from tuberculosis were actively discouraged from marrying, and thereby perpetuating a double predisposition for the disease in their offspring. This was implemented through the use of pre-marriage certificates which undertook to determine the state of health and predisposition to contract or transmit illness of the future spouse.

Across Europe, then, degeneration theories became a popular scientific response to social disorder and its manifestations, encompassing anarchism, socialism and popular revolt. In this context, Blasco's interest in the power of the masses is significant. In novels such as *La barraca* and *Entre naranjos*, the crowd is portrayed as a collective force of primitive emotion, the angry, proletarian mob that would gain momentum as demonstrated by the film adaptation of *Sangre y arena*. There is a contradiction, therefore, between Blasco's democratic aspiration to educate the masses and the specific appeal of the representation of the alcoholic and illiterate working classes for middle-class audiences, in the media of both fiction and film. Blasco, of course, was renowned for being a political agitator, and he experienced arrests, incarcerations and exile. In his novels, the collective is designated as an emotional and irrational force, prone to excessive reaction and weak in intellect, in line with late nineteenth-century metaphors of crowd behaviour. This is not a seductive image of the crowd, but instead a metaphor of degeneration that echoes Le Bon, and one that was prevalent in Blasco's novels, political speeches and newspaper articles.[47] Blasco's commitment to democratic and Republican ideals did not preclude the influential mediation of middle-class audiences in shaping his novels and film adaptations. Consciously or unconsciously, the trope of degenerationism defined key contemporary sources of bourgeois social anxiety: namely deviant femininity and the fear of the working classes.

The term 'eugenics' was coined in 1883 by Francis Galton, Darwin's half-cousin, and was defined as a science of improving stock and as 'practical Darwinism'.[48] The term, then, originated in Victorian Britain and offered a purportedly scientific approach to the perceived decline of the human race through illnesses such as syphilis and tuberculosis. According to Galton, the *stirp* ('descendant' or 'stock') was 'the sum-total of the germs, gemmules, or whatever they may be called, which are to be found, according to every theory of organic units, in the newly fertilised ovum'.[49] The structure of the *stirp* was symbolized by the curious analogy between heredity and a post office, in which the mail bags represented the fertilized egg, and the letters represented the 'germs and gemmules' that fill this space. According to Galton's science, heredity acquired a powerful bio-political dimension. His arguments against reproductive hybridity were fuelled by ill-concealed anxieties about social class.

Late nineteenth- and early twentieth-century eugenics were closely allied to the control of population, birth control and Malthusian economic theory. In Spain, of course, the deeply-rooted traditionalism of a Catholic society was paramount in the sustained identification of womanhood with motherhood, and the later development of feminist movements in comparison, for example, to Britain. Eugenics in early twentieth-century Spain was less hegemonic than its British counterpart, and more eclectic in its acceptance of a variety of ideas and theoretical frameworks.[50] In other words, Spanish eugenic discourses and social hygiene of the early twentieth century did not amount to monolithic political or scientific movement, despite their powerful legacy.

In 1904, the doctor Enrique Diego Madrazo wrote about the need for regeneration of the human race in *Cultivo de la Especie Humana — Herencia y Educación — Ideal de Vida*, in which the significance of heredity is placed above education. In Cataluña Dr Ignacio Valentí i Vivo, Professor of Legal Medicine and Toxicology at the University of Barcelona, participated in the First International Conference on Eugenics in 1912. Valentí published numerous articles and works on eugenics, including *Biología y Política* in 1889 and 'La Sanidad Nacional. Eugenesia y biometría' in 1910. In the latter, Valentí outlined a bio-political approach to social questions and racial decadence that was strongly influenced by British and German models of eugenics, including the work of Galton.[51] The paediatrician Andrés Martínez Vargas, another leading proponent of eugenics in early twentieth-century Spain, focused in particular on pre-marital certificates, as well as the care of the mother and child in relation to hygiene, sanitation and nutrition.[52] These ideas would be taken up in debates of the 1920s and 1930s by prominent figures such as Gregorio Marañón and the sex reformer Hildegart Rodríguez.

As Álvarez Peláez notes, eugenics established human characteristics, whether physical, mental or moral, as a product of heredity and absolute determinism. Education and environment were simply factors in the development of these hereditary characteristics, but they could not change the perceived problem of racial degeneration or decadence. Thus, in Spain as in England and other countries, the only way to overcome the progressive degeneration of the people, caused by the excessive reproduction of the inferior (working) classes and the under-reproduction of the better-equipped middle classes, was to take action. This constituted the control of reproduction by means of 'una "selección artificial" semejante a la que realizaban los criadores de animales para mejorar sus razas'.[53] In their early twentieth-century novels, Baroja and Blasco explore degenerationist paradigms but resist consistent adherence to their ideological premises. The specific post-Darwinian context of both degeneration theories and eugenics in the late nineteenth and early twentieth centuries must be acknowledged in weighing up their political and ideological legacy in relation to rightist ideologies of the 1920s, 1930s and beyond. In early twentieth-century Spain, the Primo de Rivera Dictatorship was the first authoritarian regime to appropriate regenerationist ideas, especially Costa's idea of the iron surgeon.[54]

Of course the concept of degeneration that came out of nineteenth-century discourses of criminality, urbanization and social pathologies later metamorphosed into a myth of 'negative eugenics' which dramatically obscured its post-Darwinian origins and which ultimately propelled the Holocaust in the 1940s. Degeneration originated as an idea applied to the sphere of biology, but it was soon transferred to other realms, including society and morality, where it continued to derive authority from its scientific roots. However, as Chamberlin discusses, its readiness to explain human existence was based fundamentally on metaphors of disease and derived metaphorical power from abstract metaphysics, not least the Book of Genesis.[55] *Degeneration: The Dark Side of Progress* traces and unravels these historical specificities in its analysis of the varying political agendas sustained by degenerative change, from twentieth-century Britain to its 'thoroughly malignant expression' in twentieth-century Germany, namely the Nazis' programme of applied eugenics.[56]

Degeneration had originated in the idea of difference, the deviation from an original type in scientific terms, and by extension from norms of behaviour. In both cases, degeneration represented a fall from grace in Biblical terms. However, the logical conclusion to the notion of backwards progress was that the degenerate could not be cured; the only possible courses of action were to classify and isolate, and ultimately to eliminate. Thus, 'the idea of degeneration became a monstrous intellectual legacy, something like the idea of progress. Degeneration as a word became so soiled by the realities that sprang from it, by the Holocaust and other inhumane actions, that it could no longer be used except as a term of opprobrium'.[57] The post-Darwinian context of degeneration and associated eugenic doctrines culminated eventually in the horrific legacy of applied eugenics and genocidal policies of 1940s Europe, with the ensuing metamorphosis of the term. As Greenslade notes, by 1963 the Professor of Eugenics at University College London could no longer tolerate the connotations of the title and renamed his post as the chair of 'human genetics'.[58] In this context, it is all too easy to divert attention from acknowledgement that the movement of eugenics in the late nineteenth and early twentieth centuries was extraordinarily broad.

Baroja's undeniably racist and infamous anti-Semitic statements have only encouraged his association with right-wing ideologies in Spain of the 1930s and 1940s. It is commonly accepted that the regenerationist agenda of the 'Generation of 1898' authors was later appropriated and distorted in Spain within Francoist ideologies of the 1930s and beyond. The relationship between Costa's ideas and authoritarianism is complex. None the less, as Balfour notes, some regenerationist discourses 'seeped into' right-wing ideology; in particular, the distrust of parliamentary politics, and the notion of an essential Spain, which was rooted in Castile and Catholicism.[59] The significance of Castilla as the soul of Spain for Unamuno, Azorín and others of their generation lent itself to reinterpretation within rightist discourse of the 1930s, as did the notion of *intrahistoria* and a mythical national identity. In particular, the concept of national character expressed by Ortega y Gasset provided a ready-made foundation for Francoist historiography, which drew on paradigms of racial determinism expressed by the 'Generation of 1898'.

Baroja briefly attempted a political career, running for municipal councillor in Madrid for the Republicans in 1909, and as a Republican candidate for Fraga (Huesca) in 1918. He was unsuccessful on both occasions, and in 1913 refused to run as a Conservative candidate for parliament. After the outbreak of the Civil War, in 1936, the author spent four years in self-imposed exile in Paris, returning to Vera de Bidasoa and Madrid in 1940. During the Civil War and Baroja's self-exile in France, Giménez Caballero made an ill-judged attempt to align the author with the ideology of the Franco regime, by publishing a selection of Baroja's writing entitled *Comunistas, judíos y demás ralea* (1938). The introduction was entitled 'Pío Baroja, precursor español del fascismo', an essay whose premise Baroja contested. He had no control over this collection, or its title, although it cannot be denied that the essays are infamously problematic.

This anthology included numerous quotations from Baroja's *César o nada* (1910), in which the protagonist asserts that Spaniards are individualistic and therefore require 'una disciplina férrea, de militares' (209). The myth of the natural tendency of Spaniards towards authoritarian government — conceived perhaps most famously by Ortega y Gasset's *España invertebrada* (1921) — was perpetuated, however, even by those who opposed the Franco dictatorship, notably the exiled historians Américo Castro and Claudio Sánchez Albornoz.[60] As Labanyi notes, 'by explaining Spanish history in terms of a mythical national character, the 1898 writers and their heirs necessarily end up advocating authoritarian solutions, for their appeal to racial determinism supposes that the people are incapable of improving themselves'.[61] Baroja was obviously influenced by racial paradigms, but failed to adhere ultimately to their logic, a fundamental contradiction that has implications for understanding the complexity of his political views.

In *El árbol de la ciencia* Iturrioz divides Spain into two types, the Iberian and the Semite: 'Al tipo ibérico asignaba el doctor las cualidades fuertes y guerreras de la raza; al tipo semita, las tendencias rapaces, de intriga y de comercio' (66). It should not be claimed that Iturrioz represents Baroja, since ironic distance negates the common argument that fictional characters are the mouthpieces of the author. However, the statement undeniably echoes the author's own anti-Semitic statements which associated Northern Europeans with science, Will and action; Semites with rhetoric and intrigue. The author objected vociferously to Freud's emphasis on erotic theory, and criticized psychoanalysis as 'palabrería judaica' (*OC*, VII, 1310).

Baroja consistently denounced both fascists and communists as 'enemigos de la libertad' (*OC*, V, 993), and was reluctant to be allied with any particular political party or ideology: 'Yo no iba a ser patrocinador ni defensor de ninguna teoría política' (*OC*, VIII, 741). The widespread view that Baroja's anarchist and Republican leanings were youthful political flirtations that he would subsequently discard, only to accept unquestioningly the values of Francoism in later years, demands further scrutiny. Certainly, as a younger man Baroja was aligned most strongly with Liberalism, as J. T. Reid's influential work of political thought in 1930s Spain attests.[62] Liberalism continued to offer a vital political philosophy for Baroja, in ideological if not practical terms. Jo Labanyi offers a potential solution to this dilemma, pointing to the 'political abstentionism' of the 1898 writers, who abandoned history in favour of the symbolic meaning of nature and the soul of Spain. There were unforeseen consequences for the realignment of their emphasis on national destiny by the architects of a dictatorship that would endure for nearly forty years.[63] In other words, Baroja moved from early political engagement towards a later stance of scepticism and disassociation. In *Ayer y hoy* of 1939 he wrote in favour of individualism and liberalism, but continued to express antipathy to democracy, socialism and communism, and hostility towards the Second Republic for its failure to deliver. Baroja's criticism of the Republic is evidence of his distrust of mass politics, his glaringly contradictory political trajectory and chameleonic political stance.

★ ★ ★ ★ ★

My book has aimed to contest the starkly divergent literary status and reputation of Baroja and Blasco through its challenge to established divisions between elite and mass culture, between canonical and popular fiction. Yet even in relation to language and form, the two authors share similarities. Baroja struggled with what he perceived as 'una técnica deficiente' (*OC*, VII, 892). Comparing the art of novel-writing with contemporary painters Darío de Regoyos and Ignacio Zuloaga, he expressed his desire for a direct form of language, free from convention and decoration: 'yo hubiera querido escribir en un idioma directo y sin frases hechas, y esto es imposible' (*OC*, VII, 892). Blasco Ibáñez wrote of his own search for an imperceptible form of language, one that would achieve the effects of visual communication: 'procuro siempre escribir sin oropeles retóricos, llanamente, con el propósito único de que el lector se olvide de que está leyendo, y al terminar la última página le parezca que sale de un sueño o que acaba de desvanarse ante sus ojos una visión cinematográfica'.[64] For different reasons, each author sought to achieve a form of language unhindered by rhetorical flourishes and excessive elaboration, in order to communicate with their audience on a subconscious or semi-conscious level. For both Baroja and Blasco Ibáñez, prose fiction stems from the writer's unconscious, beyond the rational, the linguistic and the formal.

Bodies of Disorder has sought to cast new light on the cultural assimilation and manifestation in early twentieth-century Spain of degeneration theories in their post-Darwinian and historical context through a case study of two prominent literary figures. Despite Baroja's open denigration of Blasco's commercialism, the questionable distinctions between elite and mass culture, between canonical and popular fiction, are powerfully challenged by the striking commonalities between each author's novelistic production. For Lawrence Levine, the hierarchy of cultural production misconstrues the categories of 'high' and 'low' art as permanent and immutable.[65] These distinctions ignore the hybridity and intrinsic commonalities between 'highbrow' literature and 'mass' culture.

My pairing of Baroja and Blasco is deliberately provocative in the challenge it issues to conventional literary histories of the period, and seeks to progress our conceptualization of the commonalities between intellectual, canonical fiction of the 'Generation of 1898' and their popular counterparts. By seeking to compare rather than to marginalize or segregate according to an established intellectual and cultural hierarchy, this study offers a new approach to the multiple crossings between popular science and literature, and between high and low art, in early twentieth-century Spain. Blasco's laconic — but persuasive — response to his exclusion from the 'Generation of 1898' was to cite the large readership that bought his books. *Bodies of Disorder* has analysed a comparable genealogy of gender and degeneration in these two authors, one canonical, one bestselling. By tracing shared cultural preoccupations of Blasco and Baroja in the context of degenerationism, the book repositions the Valencian author as markedly closer to the *noventayochistas* than hitherto acknowledged.

Notes to the Conclusion

1. Eduardo Betoret-París, 'El caso Blasco Ibáñez', *Hispania* (USA), 52 (1969), 97–102 (p. 99).
2. For an exception to this model, see Lou Charnon-Deutsch, 'What They Saw: Women's Exposure to and in Visual Culture in Nineteenth-Century Spain', in *A Companion to Spanish Women's Studies*, ed. by Xon de Ros and Geraldine Hazbun (Woodbridge: Tamesis, 2011), pp. 189–210. On models of female consumers in an Anglophone context, the reader is referred to Kate Flint, *The Woman Reader, 1837–1914* (Oxford: Clarendon, 1993); Elizabeth A. Flynn and Patrocinio P. Schweickart's classic edited volume *Gender and Reading: Essays on Readers, Texts and Contexts* (Baltimore: Johns Hopkins University Press, 1986); Catherine Golden, *Images of the*

Woman Reader in Victorian British and American Fiction (Gainesville: University Press of Florida, 2003); and Belinda Jack, *The Woman Reader* (New Haven: Yale University Press, 2012).

3. Luis Fernández Cifuentes, *Teoría y mercado de la novela en España: del 98 a la República* (Madrid: Gredos, 1982), p. 160.
4. These editions were the subject of a recent exhibition at the Casa-Museo Blasco Ibáñez in 2014, 'A la vuelta de un siglo: Editorial Prometeo (Valencia, 1914)', directed by Javier Lluch-Prats.
5. Juan Ignacio Ferreras, *La novela por entregas, 1840–1900* (Madrid: Taurus, 1972), p. 25 and Jean-François Botrel, 'La novela por entregas: unidad de creación y consumo', in *Creación y público en la literatura española* (Madrid: Castalia, 1974), pp. 111–55 (pp. 133–36). Both Ferreras and Botrel emphasize the large market attracted by the publication of the *entregas*, which frequently sold over 10,000 copies.
6. Eamonn Rodgers, 'Who Read Galdós? The Economics of the Book Trade in Nineteenth-Century Spain', in *New Galdós Studies: Essays in Memory of John Varey*, ed. by Nicholas G. Round (Woodbridge: Tamesis, 2003), pp. 11–25 (pp. 20–21).
7. Miguel de Unamuno, *Tres novelas ejemplares y un prólogo* [1920] (Madrid: Espasa-Calpe, 1931), p. 30.
8. Antonio Laguna Platero, *El Pueblo*, pp. 59–63. My thanks to the Hemeroteca de Valencia for providing access to historical accounts of *El Pueblo*.
9. M. C. Seonae, *Historia del periodismo español: el siglo XIX* (Madrid: Alianza Universidad, 1983), p. 204.
10. Rita Felski, *The Gender of Modernity* (Cambridge, MA: Harvard University Press, 1995), p. 62.
11. *La Ilustración Española y Americana*, 28.4 (30 January 1884), p. 64; cited by Tsuchiya, *Marginal Subjects*, p. 81.
12. Bram Dijkstra provides a range of European examples in *Idols of Perversity*.
13. See, for example, Pulido y Fernández's *Bosquejos médico-sociales*.
14. See María Carmen Simón Palmer, 'La mujer lectora', in *Historia de la edición y de la lectura en España, 1472–1914*, ed. by Víctor Infantes, François Lopez and Jean-François Botrel (Madrid: Fundación Germán Sánchez Ruipérez, 2003), pp. 745–53.
15. Stannard, *The Theme of Degeneration*, pp. 52–63.
16. Charles Bigot, 'Correspondencia de París', *Revista Contemporánea*, 30 April 1876, pp. 236–43 (p. 239).
17. Solange Hibbs-Lissorgues, 'El libro y la edificación', in *Historia de la edición y de la lectura en España, 1472–1914*, ed. by Víctor Infantes, François Lopez and Jean-François Botrel (Madrid: Fundación Germán Sánchez Ruipérez, 2003), pp. 650–61.
18. *El Pueblo*, 8 November 1902. My thanks to the Hemeroteca de Valencia for providing me with access to the newspaper archives. The Biblioteca Virtual has digitized copies online from 1903 onwards.
19. Charnon-Deutsch, 'What They Saw', p. 203.
20. Charnon-Deutsch, 'What They Saw', p. 205.
21. George, 'Cinematising the Crowd', pp. 91, 105.
22. Emilia Pardo Bazán, *La Tribuna* (Madrid: Cátedra, 1975), pp. 105–06.
23. Labanyi, *Gender and Modernization*, p. 55.
24. In *El tablado de Arlequín* (1904) he wrote in a similar vein that 'la mujer desarrolla poco su inteligencia; por eso siente poco el dolor moral' (*OC*, v, 42).
25. Richard Nemesvari, *Thomas Hardy, Sensationalism, and the Melodramatic Mode* (New York: Palgrave Macmillan, 2011), p. 11.
26. Round analyses the deaths of children in Galdós, as 'the impulse to regenerate succumbs to degeneration', in 'Galdós Rewrites Galdós: The Deaths of Children and the Dying Century', in *New Galdós Studies: Essays in Memory of John Varey*, ed. by Nicholas G. Round (Woodbridge: Tamesis, 2003), pp. 125–39 (p. 129).
27. Benedict Anderson, *Imagined Communities: Reflections on the Origin and Spread of Nationalisms* (London: Verso, 1983), p. 73.
28. José Ortega y Gasset, *La rebelión de las masas* (1930), in *Obras completas*, 6 vols (Madrid: Revista de Occidente, 1957), IV, 113–310 (p. 217).

29. Tomás, Introduction, *La maja desnuda*, p. 46.
30. Huyssen, *After the Great Divide*, p. 47.
31. Huyssen, *After the Great Divide*, p. 46.
32. Sieburth, *Inventing High and Low*, p. 6.
33. Sieburth, *Inventing High and Low*, p. 10.
34. 'En esta época Blasco quería demostrar que había llegado a la cumbre, que, con méritos o sin ellos, ganaba más que nadie' (871).
35. Cardwell, *Blasco Ibáñez: La barraca*, p. 16.
36. Cardwell, *Blasco Ibáñez: La barraca*, pp. 12–13 and Conte, 'Vicente Blasco Ibáñez'.
37. Cited in José Luis León Roca, 'Cómo escribió Blasco Ibáñez *La barraca*', *Les Langues Néo-Latines*, 180 (1967), 1–22 (p. 21).
38. Mark Mazower's, *Dark Continent: Europe's Twentieth Century* (London: Penguin, 1999) provides an influential analysis of the discourses that likened collective bodily health to the health of European nations during the interwar period. Chapter 3, 'Healthy Bodies, Sick Bodies', pp. 77–105.
39. On Vallejo Nágera's approach to eugenics and racial hygiene, the reader is referred to Sosa-Velasco, *Médicos escritores*, pp. 145–82 and Paul Preston, *The Spanish Civil War: Reaction, Revolution and Revenge* (London: Harper Perennial, 2006), p. 310.
40. 'El siglo XIX considerado bajo el punto de vista médico-social', p. 344.
41. Campos et al., *Los ilegales*, pp. 158–59.
42. *Primera y Segunda Conferencia sobre el tema ¿Está o no degenerada la raza latina?* (Madrid: Ginés Carrión Impresor, 1905), p. 7.
43. Campos et al., *Los ilegales*, pp. 160–61.
44. Campos et al., *Los ilegales*, p. 162.
45. Gayon, *Darwinism's Struggle for Survival*, p. 14.
46. Campos el al, *Los ilegales*, p. 164.
47. See George, 'Cinematising the Crowd', p. 103.
48. Karl Pearson, *The Life, Letters, and Labours of Francis Galton*, 4 vols (Cambridge: Cambridge University Press, 1914–30), II (1924), 86.
49. Francis Galton, 'A Theory of Heredity', *Journal of the Anthropological Institute*, 5 (1876), 329–48 (p. 330).
50. See Cleminson, *Anarchism, Science and Sex*, pp. 81–107 and Michael Richards, 'Spanish Psychiatry c.1900–1945: Constitutional Theory, Eugenics and the Nation', *Bulletin of Spanish Studies* 81.6 (2004), 823–48.
51. On eugenics in early-twentieth-century Spain, the reader is referred to Raquel Álvarez Peláez, 'Eugenesia, ideología y discurso del poder en España', in *Darwinismo social y eugenesia en el mundo latino*, ed. by Marisa Miranda and Gustavo Vallejo (Buenos Aires: Siglo XXI de Argentina Editores, 2005), pp. 87–143 (p. 99).
52. Álvarez Peláez, 'Eugenesia', p. 102.
53. Álvarez Peláez, 'La mujer española', pp. 181–82.
54. Before the Civil War the Catholic, nationalist right, particularly the CEDA, described parliamentary democracy as inherently 'degenerate'.
55. Chamberlin, *Degeneration*, p. 290.
56. Chamberlin, *Degeneration*, p. 290.
57. Chamberlin, *Degeneration*, pp. 293–94.
58. Greenslade, *Degeneration, Culture and the Novel*, p. 11.
59. Balfour, 'The Loss of Empire', p. 29.
60. Jo Labanyi, *Myth and History in the Contemporary Spanish Novel* (Cambridge: Cambridge University Press, 1989), p. 60.
61. Labanyi, *Myth and History*, p. 61.
62. J. T. Reid, *Modern Spain and Liberalism* (Stanford, CA: Stanford University Press, 1937).
63. Jo Labanyi, 'Nation, Narration, Naturalization: A Barthesian Critique of the 1898 Generation', in *New Hispanisms: Literature, Culture, Theory*, ed. by Mark I. Millington and Paul Julian Smith (Ottawa, ON: Dovehouse, 1994), pp. 127–49 (p. 147).

64. A. Laguna Platero, 'De propagandista de la política a propagador de la cultura: Vicente Blasco Ibáñez, un comunicador de éxito', *Debats*, 64–65 (1999), 121–35 (p. 126).
65. Lawrence Levine, *Highbrow/Lowbrow: The Emergence of Cultural Hierarchy in America* (Cambridge, MA: Harvard University Press, 1988).

BIBLIOGRAPHY

ALBERICH, JOSÉ, 'La biblioteca de Baroja', *Revista Hispánica Moderna*, 27.2 (1961), 101–12
ÁLVAREZ PELÁEZ, RAQUEL, 'La mujer española y el control de natalidad en los comienzos del siglo XX', *Asclepio*, 2 (1990), 175–200
—— 'Eugenesia, ideología y discurso del poder en España', in *Darwinismo social y eugenesia en el mundo latino*, ed. by Marisa Miranda and Gustavo Vallejo (Buenos Aires: Siglo XXI de Argentina Editores, 2005), pp. 87–143
ANDERSON, BENEDICT, *Imagined Communities: Reflections on the Origin and Spread of Nationalisms* (London: Verso, 1983)
ANDERSON, CHRISTOPHER L., *Primitives, Patriarchy, and the Picaresque in Blasco Ibáñez's 'Cañas y barro'* (Potomac: Scripta Humanistica, 1995)
ANON., 'Law and Insanity', *British Medical Journal* (1865), I, 275–77
AZORÍN, *La voluntad* (Madrid: Castalia, 1989)
—— 'Wagnerismo', *ABC*, 5 April 1952
—— 'Una cuestión', *ABC*, 2 September 1954
BACHOFEN, J. J., *Myth, Religion, and Mother Right: Selected Writings of J. J. Bachofen*, trans. by Ralph Manheim (Princeton, NJ: Princeton University Press, 1967)
BAHAMONDE MAGRO, ÁNGEL, and JESÚS MARTÍNEZ, *Historia de España: siglo XIX* (Madrid: Cátedra, 1994)
BALFOUR, SEBASTIAN, 'The Loss of Empire, Regenerationism, and the Forging of a Myth of National Identity', in *Spanish Cultural Studies: An Introduction*, ed. by Helen Graham and Jo Labanyi (Oxford: Oxford University Press, 1995), pp. 25–31
BAROJA, PÍO, 'Espíritu de subordinación', *El Globo*, 22 March 1903
—— *La ciudad de la niebla* (London: Nelson, 1932)
—— *Ayer y hoy* (Santiago: Ercilla, 1939)
—— *Obras completas*, 8 vols (Madrid: Biblioteca Nueva, 1946–51)
—— *La casa de Aizgorri*, in *Obras completas*, I (1946), 1–49
—— *Aventuras, inventos y mixtificaciones de Silvestre Paradox*, in *Obras completas*, II (1947), 7–150
—— *El árbol de la ciencia* (Madrid: Cátedra, 1989)
—— *Cuentos: Vidas sombrías* (Madrid: Caro Raggio, 1991)
—— *Camino de perfección (Pasión mística)* (Madrid: Caro Raggio, 1993)
—— *La busca*, prologue by Julio Caro Baroja (Madrid: Caro Raggio, 1997)
BEIZER, JANET, *Ventriloquized Bodies: Narratives of Hysteria in Nineteenth-Century France* (Ithaca, NY: Cornell University Press, 1994)
BENJAMIN, WALTER, *Charles Baudelaire: A Lyric Poet in the Era of High Capitalism*, trans. by Harry Zohn (London: Verso, 1989)
BERNALDO DE QUIRÓS, CONSTANCIO, and JOSÉ M. LLANAS AGUILANIEDO, *La mala vida en Madrid: estudio psico-sociológico* (Madrid: B. Rodríguez Serra, 1901)
—— *La mala vida en Madrid: estudio psico-sociológico con dibujos y fotografías fotograbados del natural* [1901], ed. by J. Broto Salanova (Huesca: Instituto de Estudios Altoaragoneses, 1998)

BETANCOR GÓMEZ, MARÍA JOSÉ, 'Eugenesia y pediatría: higiene infantil y "degeneración de la raza" en España a principios del siglo XX', in *Darwinismo social y eugenesia en el mundo latino*, ed. by Marisa Miranda and Gustavo Vallejo (Buenos Aires: Siglo XXI de Argentina Editores, 2005), pp. 641–63

BETORET-PARÍS, EDUARDO, 'El caso Blasco Ibáñez', *Hispania* (USA), 52 (1969), 97–102

BIEDER, MARYELLEN, 'Woman and the Twentieth-Century Spanish Literary Canon: The Lady Vanishes', *Anales de la literatura española contemporánea*, 17 (1992), 301–24

BIGOT, CHARLES, 'Correspondencia de París', *Revista Contemporánea*, 30 April 1876, pp. 236–43

BLANCO AGUINAGA, CARLOS, *Juventud del 98* (Madrid: Siglo XIX de España editores, 1970)

BLANCO, ALDA, 'Gender and National Identity: The Novel in Nineteenth-Century Literary History', in *Culture and Gender in Nineteenth-Century Spain*, ed. by Lou Charnon-Deutsch and Jo Labanyi (Oxford: Clarendon, 1995), pp. 120–36

BLASCO IBÁÑEZ, VICENTE, *Woman Triumphant (La maja desnuda)*, trans. by Hayward Keniston (New York: Dutton, 1920)

—— *Entre naranjos* (Buenos Aires: Austral, 1950)

—— *Obras completas*, 4th edn, 3 vols (Madrid: Aguilar, 1961)

—— *La maja desnuda*, ed. by Facundo Tomás (Madrid: Cátedra, 1998)

—— *Flor de Mayo* (Madrid: Cátedra, 1999)

—— *Cañas y barro* (Madrid: Alianza, 2003)

—— *La barraca* (Madrid: Alianza, 2004)

—— *La horda* (n.p., CreateSpace: 2013)

BOTREL, JEAN-FRANÇOIS, 'La novela por entregas: unidad de creación y consumo', in *Creación y público en la literatura española* (Madrid: Castalia, 1974), pp. 111–55

BREUER, JOSEPH, and SIGMUND FREUD, *Studies on Hysteria, 1893–1895*, trans. by James and Alix Strachey (Harmondsworth: Penguin, 1974)

BROWN, GERALD G., *Historia de la literatura española: el siglo XX* (Barcelona: Ariel, 1974)

CAMPOS MARÍN, RICARDO, JOSÉ MARTÍNEZ PÉREZ and RAFAEL HUERTAS GARCÍA-ALEJO, *Los ilegales de la naturaleza: medicina y degeneracionismo en la España de la restauración (1876–1923)* (Madrid: Consejo Superior de Investigaciones Científicas, 2000)

CAMPOS MARÍN, RICARDO, *Alcoholismo, medicina y sociedad en España (1876–1923)* (Madrid: CSIC, 1997)

—— 'La teoría de la degeneración y la profesionalización de la psiquiatría en España (1876–1920)', *Asclepio* 51.1 (1999), 185–203

CARDWELL, RICHARD A., *Blasco Ibáñez: La barraca* (London: Grant and Cutler, 1973)

—— 'Degeneration, Discourse and Differentiation: *Modernismo frente a noventa y ocho* Reconsidered', in *Critical Essays on the Literatures of Spain and Spanish America*, ed. by Luis T. González-del-Valle and Julio Baena (Boulder, CO: Society of Spanish and Spanish-American Studies, 1991), pp. 29–46

—— 'The Mad Doctors: Medicine and Literature in *fin de siglo* Spain', *Journal of the Institute of Romance Studies*, 4 (1996), 167–86

—— 'Deconstructing the binaries of *enfrentismo*: José-María Llanas Aguilaniedo's *Navegar pintoresco* and the finisecular novel', in *Spain's 1898 Crisis: Regenerationism, Modernism, Post-Colonialism*, ed. by Joseph Harrison and Alan Hoyle (Manchester: Manchester University Press, 2000), pp. 156–69

—— 'Blasco Ibáñez ¿escritor naturalista radical? Reconsideración de las novelas valencianas de Vicente Blasco Ibáñez', in *Vicente Blasco Ibáñez: 1898–1998. La vuelta al siglo de un novelista*, 2 vols (Valencia: Biblioteca Valenciana, 2000), I, 349–74

—— 'Oscar Wilde and Spain: Medicine, Morals, Religion and Aesthetics in the *Fin de Siglo*', in *Crossing Fields in Modern Spanish Culture*, ed. by Federico Bonaddio and Xon de Ros (Oxford: Legenda, 2003), pp. 35–53

CARLSON, ERIC T., 'Medicine and Degeneration: Theory and Praxis', in *Degeneration: The Dark Side of Progress*, ed. by J. Edward Chamberlin and Sander L. Gilman (New York: Columbia University Press, 1985), pp. 121–44

CAUDET, FRANCISCO, 'Reivindicación de Blasco Ibáñez frente a la crítica', in *Vicente Blasco Ibáñez, 1898–1998: la vuelta al siglo de un novelista*, ed. by Juan Oleza and Javier Lluch, 2 vols (Valencia: Generalitat Valenciana, Conselleria de Cultura i Educació, 2000), II, 680–99

CELAYA CARRILLO, BEATRIZ, *La mujer deseante: sexualidad femenina en la cultura y novela españolas (1900–1936)* (Newark: Juan de la Cuesta, 2006)

CERVERA BARAT, RAFAEL, *Alcoholismo y civilización* (Valencia: A. Cortés, 1896)

CHAMBERLIN, J. EDWARD, and SANDER L. GILMAN, eds, *Degeneration: The Dark Side of Progress* (New York: Columbia University Press, 1985)

CHARNON-DEUTSCH, LOU, and JO LABANYI, eds, *Culture and Gender in Nineteenth-Century Spain* (Oxford: Clarendon, 1995)

CHARNON-DEUTSCH, LOU, *Narratives of Desire: Nineteenth-Century Spanish Fiction by Women* (University Park: Pennsylvania State University Press, 1994)

—— *Fictions of the Feminine in the Nineteenth-Century Press* (University Park: Pennsylvania State University Press, 2000)

—— 'What They Saw: Women's Exposure to and in Visual Culture in Nineteenth-Century Spain', in *A Companion to Spanish Women's Studies*, ed. by Xon de Ros and Geraldine Hazbun (Woodbridge: Tamesis, 2011), pp. 189–210

CLEMINSON, RICHARD, *Anarchism, Science and Sex: Eugenics in Eastern Spain, 1900–1937* (Oxford: Peter Lang, 2000)

—— and Teresa Fuentes Peris, '"La mala vida": Source and Focus of Degeneration, Degeneracy and Decline', *Journal of Spanish Cultural Studies*, 10.4 (2009), 385–97

COMENGE Y FERRER, LUIS, *La medicina en el siglo XIX* (Barcelona: José Espasa, 1914)

CONTE, RAFAEL, 'Vicente Blasco Ibáñez: lecciones de un centenario', *Cuadernos hispanoamericanos*, 72 (1967), 507–20

COOKE, NICHOLAS FRANCIS, *Satan in Society* (Cincinnati: C. F. Vent, 1876 [1870])

DAVIS, LISA, 'Max Nordau, "Degeneración" y la decadencia de España', *Cuadernos hispanoamericanos*, 326–27 (1977), 307–23

DEAVER, WILLIAM O., 'Una deconstrucción feminista de *Camino de perfección*', *Crítica Hispánica*, 18.2 (1996), 267–73

DIJKSTRA, BRAM, *Idols of Perversity: Fantasies of Feminine Evil in Fin-de-siècle Culture* (New York and Oxford: Oxford University Press, 1986)

DOANE, MARY ANN, *Femmes Fatales: Feminism, Film Theory, Psychoanalysis* (London: Routledge, 1991)

ELLIS, HAVELOCK, *The Criminal* (London: Walter Scott & Co., 1890)

—— 'Précis of "Considerations on Infanticide" [Quelques Considérations sur l'Infanticide]. (Arch. d'Anthropol. Crim., January 18th, 1902) Audiffrent', *The Journal of Mental Science*, 48 (1902), 366

—— *From Rousseau to Proust* (London: Constable & Co., 1936)

ESCUDER, J. M., *Locos y anómalos* (Madrid: Sucesores de Rivadeneyra, 1895)

ESLAVA, RAFAEL G., *La prostitución en Madrid: apuntes para un estudio sociológico* (Madrid: Vicente Rico, 1900)

ESQUERDO, JOSÉ MARÍA, *Locos que no lo parecen: Garayo el Sacamantecas* (Madrid: Hospicio, 1881)

—— 'De la locura histérica', *Revista clínica de los hospitales*, 1 (1889), 1–9, 274–81, 337–40

ESQUIROL, JEAN ÉTIENNE DOMINIQUE, *Des Maladies mentales, considérées sous les rapports médical, hygiénique et médico-légal* (1838); trans. by E. K. Hunt, *Mental Maladies: A Treatise on Insanity* (Philadelphia: Lea and Blanchard, 1845)

FELSKI, RITA, *The Gender of Modernity* (Cambridge, MA: Harvard University Press, 1995)
FERNÁNDEZ, PURA, *Eduardo López Bago y el naturalismo radical: la novela y el mercado literario en el siglo XIX* (Amsterdam: Rodopi, 1995)
—— 'Orígenes y difusión del naturalismo: la especificidad de la práctica hispana', in *Revista de Literatura*, 58.115 (1996), 107–20
FERNÁNDEZ CIFUENTES, LUIS, *Teoría y mercado de la novela en España: del 98 a la República* (Madrid: Gredos, 1982)
FERNÁNDEZ VILLEGAS, F. ('Zeda'), 'Impresiones literarias', *La España Moderna*, 70 (1892), 202
FERRERAS, JUAN IGNACIO, *La novela por entregas, 1840–1900* (Madrid: Taurus, 1972)
FLINT, KATE, *The Woman Reader, 1837–1914* (Oxford: Clarendon, 1993)
FLINT, WESTON, and NOMA, *Pío Baroja: Camino de perfección (Pasión mística)*, Critical Guides to Spanish Texts, 37 (London: Grant and Cutler, 1983)
FLYNN, ELIZABETH A., and PATROCINIO P. SCHWEICKART, eds, *Gender and Reading: Essays on Readers, Texts and Contexts* (Baltimore: Johns Hopkins University Press, 1986)
FOREL, AUGUST, *The Sexual Question; A Scientific, Psychological, Hygienic and Sociological Study* [1906], trans. by C. F. Marshall (New York: Physicians and Surgeons Book Co., 1925)
FORSTER, E. M., *Aspects of the Novel* (Harmondsworth: Penguin, 1990)
FOUCAULT, MICHEL, *The History of Sexuality. Volume One. An Introduction*, trans. by Robert Hurley (Harmondsworth: Penguin, 1990)
—— *Discipline and Punish: The Birth of the Prison*, trans. by Alan Sheridan (Harmondsworth: Penguin, 1991)
FRASER, BENJAMIN, 'Baroja's Rejection of Traditional Medicine in *El árbol de la ciencia*', *Bulletin of Spanish Studies*, 85.1 (2008), 29–50
FREUD, SIGMUND, *The Standard Edition of the Complete Psychological Works of Sigmund Freud*, trans. under the general editorship of James Strachey, in collaboration with Anna Freud, assisted by Alix Strachey, Alan Tyson, and Angela Richards, 24 vols (London: Hogarth Press and the Institute of Psycho-Analysis, 1953–74)
FRIEDMAN, MELVIN J., 'The Symbolist Novel: Huysmans to Malraux', in *Modernism: A Guide to European Literature, 1890–1930*, ed. by Malcolm Bradbury and James McFarlane (London: Penguin, 1991), 453–66
FUENTES PERIS, TERESA, *Visions of Filth: Deviancy and Social Control in the Novels of Galdós* (Liverpool: Liverpool University Press, 2003)
—— 'Alcoholismo, anarquismo y degeneración en *La bodega* de Vicente Blasco Ibáñez', *Journal of Spanish Cultural Studies*, 10.4 (2009), 485–503
FUSTER, JOAN, *Recuerdo y juicio de Blasco Ibáñez en su centenario*, ed. by Manuel Bas Carbonell (Valencia: Societat Bibliogràfica Valenciana Jerònima Galés, 1998)
GALTON, FRANCIS, 'A Theory of Heredity', *Journal of the Anthropological Institute*, 5 (1876), 329–48
—— *Inquiries into the Human Faculty and its Development* (London: Macmillan, 1883)
GANIVET, ÁNGEL, *Obras completas*, ed. by Melchor Fernández Almagro, 2 vols (Madrid: Aguilar, 1961)
GASCÓ CONTELL, EMILIO, *Genio y figura de Blasco Ibáñez: agitador, aventurero y novelista* (Madrid: Afrodisio Aguado, 1957)
GAYON, JEAN, *Darwinism's Struggle for Survival: Heredity and the Hypothesis of Natural Selection*, trans. by Matthew Cobb (Cambridge: Cambridge University Press, 1998)
GENER, POMPEYO, *Literaturas malsanas* (Madrid: Fernando Fe, 1894)
GEORGE, DAVID, 'Cinematising the Crowd: V. Blasco Ibáñez's Silent *Sangre y arena* (1916)', *Studies in Hispanic Cinemas*, 4.2 (2007), 91–106
GILMAN, SANDER L., 'Sexology, Psychoanalysis, and Degeneration: From a Theory of Race to a Race to Theory', in *Degeneration: The Dark Side of Progress*, ed. by J. Edward

Chamberlin and Sander L. Gilman (New York: Columbia University Press, 1985), pp. 72–96

GINÉ Y PARTAGAS, JUAN, *Tratado teórico-práctico de freno-patología o estudio de las enfermedades mentales* (Madrid: Moya y Plaza, 1876)

GLICK, THOMAS F., MIGUEL ANGEL PUIG-SAMPER and ROUSAURA RUÍZ, eds, *The Reception of Darwinism in the Iberian World: Spain, Spanish America and Brazil* (Boston, MA: Kluwer Academic Publishers, 2001)

GOLDEN, CATHERINE, *Images of the Woman Reader in Victorian British and American Fiction* (Gainesville: University Press of Florida, 2003)

GÓMEZ DE BARQUERO, EDUARDO, *La España Moderna* 1/2/1903, Crónica literaria

GONZÁLEZ BLANCO, ANDRÉS, *Historia de la novela en España desde el romanticismo a nuestros días* (Madrid: Saenz de Jubera, 1909)

GRANJEL, LUIS, *Panorama de la generación del 98* (Madrid: Guadarrama, 1959)

GRANJEL, MERCEDES, *Pedro Felipe Monlau y la higiene española del siglo XIX* (Salamanca: Universidad de Salamanca, 1983)

GREENSLADE, WILLIAM, *Degeneration, Culture and the Novel, 1880–1940* (Cambridge: Cambridge University Press, 1994)

GREY, DANIEL, 'Women's Policy Networks and the Infanticide Act 1922', *Twentieth-Century British History*, 21.4 (2010), 441–63

GUIGOU Y COSTA, DIEGO, *Discurso leído en la sesión inaugural del año 1916 por el Académico numerario Dr D. Diego Guigou y Costa* (Santa Cruz de Tenerife: El Comercio, 1916)

HAIDT, REBECCA, '*Los besos de amor* and *La maja desnuda*: The Fascination of the Senses in the *Ilustración*', *Revista de Estudios Hispánicos*, 29 (1995), 477–503

HAMBROOK, GLYN, 'Baudelaire, Degeneration Theory and Literary Criticism in Fin de siècle Spain', *Modern Language Review*, 101.4 (2006), 1005–24

HARTMANN, KARL ROBERT EDUARD VON, *Philosophy of the Unconscious: Speculative Results According to the Inductive Method of Physical Science*, trans. by William Chatterton Coupland, 2nd edn, 3 vols (London: Trübner & Co., 1893)

HAUSER, PHILIPH, 'El siglo XIX considerado bajo el punto de vista médico-social', *Revista de España*, 101 (1884), 202–24, 333–58

—— *Madrid bajo el punto de vista médico-social*, 2 vols (Madrid: Establecimiento Tipográfico Sucesores de Rivadeneyra, 1902)

HEILMANN, ANN, 'Narrating the Hysteric: *Fin-de-Siècle* Medical Discourse and Sarah Grand's *The Heavenly Twins* (1893)', in *The New Woman in Fiction and Fact: Fin-de Siècle Feminisms*, ed. by Angelique Richardson and Chris Willis (Basingstoke: Palgrave, 2002), 123–35

HIBBS-LISSORGUES, SOLANGE, 'El libro y la edificación', in *Historia de la edición y de la lectura en España, 1472–1914*, ed. by Víctor Infantes, François Lopez and Jean-François Botrel (Madrid: Fundación Germán Sánchez Ruipérez, 2003), pp. 650–61

HOMANS, MARGARET, 'Representation, Reproduction, and Women's Place in Language', in *Literary Theory: An Anthology*, ed. by Julie Rivkin and Michael Ryan (Oxford: Blackwell, 1998), pp. 650–55

HUERTAS, RAFAEL, 'Niños degenerados: medicina mental y regeneracionismo en la España del cambio de siglo', *Dynamis*, 18 (1998), 157–79

—— 'Los niños de la "mala vida": la patología del "golfo" en la España de entresiglos', *Journal of Spanish Cultural Studies*, 10.4 (2009), 423–40

HUGHES, ROBERT, *Goya* (London: Harvill, 2003)

HUYSSEN, ANDREAS, *After the Great Divide: Modernism, Mass Culture, Postmodernism* (Bloomington: Indiana University Press, 1986)

INFANTES, VÍCTOR, FRANÇOIS LOPEZ, JEAN-FRANÇOIS BOTREL, eds, *Historia de la edición y de la lectura en España, 1472–1914* (Madrid: Fundación Germán Sánchez Ruipérez, 2003)

INMAN FOX, EDWARD, *Ideología y política en las letras de fin de siglo (1898)* (Madrid: Espasa-Calpe, 1988)
IRIGARAY, LUCE, *Speculum of the Other Woman*, trans. by Gillian G. Gill (Ithaca, NY: Cornell University Press, 1985)
JACK, BELINDA, *The Woman Reader* (New Haven: Yale University Press, 2012)
JAGOE, CATHERINE, 'Monstrous Inversions: Decadence and Degeneration in Galdós's *Ángel Guerra*', in *Culture and Gender in Nineteenth-Century Spain*, ed. by Lou Charnon-Deutsch and Jo Labanyi (Oxford: Oxford University Press, 1996), pp. 161–81
——, 'Sexo y género en la medicina del siglo XIX', in *La mujer en los discursos de género*, ed. by Catherine Jagoe, Alda Blasco and Cristina Enríquez de Salamanca (Barcelona: Icaria, 1998), pp. 305–48
JOHNSON, ROBERTA, 'Carmen de Burgos and Spanish Modernism', *South Central Review*, 18.1–2 (2001), 66–77
——, *Gender and Nation in the Spanish Modernist Novel* (Nashville, TN: Vanderbilt University Press, 2003)
JURKEVICH, GAYANA, '*Abulia*, 19th century Physiology and the Generation of 1898', *Hispanic Review*, 60 (1992), 181–94
——, *In Pursuit of the Natural Sign: Azorín and the Poetics of Ekphrasis* (London: Associated University Presses, 1999)
KIRKPATRICK, SUSAN, 'Fantasy, Seduction, and the Woman Reader: Rosalía de Castro's Novels', in *Culture and Gender in Nineteenth-Century Spain*, ed. by Lou Charnon-Deutsch and Jo Labanyi (Oxford: Clarendon, 1995), pp. 74–97
KRAMAR, KIRSTEN JOHNSON and WILLIAM D. WATSON, 'The Insanities of Reproduction: Medico-legal Knowledge and the Development of Infanticide Law', *Social Legal Studies*, 15.2 (2006), 237–55
LABANYI, JO, *Myth and History in the Contemporary Spanish Novel* (Cambridge: Cambridge University Press, 1989)
——'Nation, Narration, Naturalization: A Barthesian Critique of the 1898 Generation', in *New Hispanisms: Literature, Culture, Theory*, ed. by Mark I. Millington and Paul Julian Smith (Ottawa, ON: Dovehouse, 1994), pp. 127–49
—— *Gender and Modernization in the Spanish Realist Novel* (Oxford: Oxford University Press, 2000)
LAGUNA PLATERO, ANTONIO, *El Pueblo: historia de un diario republicano, 1894–1939* (Valencia: Institució Alfons el Magnànim, 1999)
——'De propagandista de la política a propagador de la cultura: Vicente Blasco Ibáñez, un comunicador de éxito', *Debats*, 64–65 (1999), 121–35
LE BON, GUSTAVE, *Psychologies des foules* (Paris: Allan, 1896)
LEÓN ROCA, JOSÉ LUIS, *Vicente Blasco Ibáñez* (Valencia: Prometeo, 1967)
——'Cómo escribió Blasco Ibáñez *La barraca*', *Les Langues Néo-Latines*, 180 (1967), 1–22
LEVINE, LAWRENCE, *Highbrow/Lowbrow: The Emergence of Cultural Hierarchy in America* (Cambridge, MA: Harvard University Press, 1988)
LEYS, RUTH, *Trauma: A Genealogy* (Chicago, IL: University of Chicago Press, 2000)
LITVAK, LILY, *Erotismo fin de siglo* (Barcelona: Bosch, 1979)
LOMBROSO, CESARE, *The Man of Genius* (London: Walter Scott, 1891)
——'Nordau's *Degeneration*: Its Value and Its Errors', *Century Illustrated Monthly Magazine*, October 1895, pp. 936–37
—— *Criminal Man according to the Classification of Cesare Lombroso* (New York and London: G. P. Putnam's Sons, 1911)
LOMBROSO, CESARE, and GUGLIELMO FERRERO, *Criminal Woman, the Prostitute, and the Normal Woman*, trans. and intro. by Nicole Hahn Rafter and Mary Gibson (Durham, NC: Duke University Press, 2004)

LONGHURST, CARLOS-ALEX, '*Camino de perfección* and the Modernist Aesthetic', *Bulletin of Hispanic Studies.* Special Homage Volume (1992), 191–203
—— '*Camino de perfección*: hacia la novela del inconsciente', *Insula*, 665 (May 2002), 20–23
—— 'Representations of the "Fourth Estate" in Galdós, Blasco and Baroja', in *New Galdós Studies: Essays in Memory of John Varey*, ed. by Nicholas G. Round (Woodbridge: Tamesis, 2003), pp. 73–97
—— 'Entre el naturalismo y el simbolismo: la primera novela de Baroja', *Ínsula*, 719 (2006), 19–21
—— 'La mala vida en Madrid según Blasco y Baroja: *La horda* y *La busca*', *Revista de Estudios sobre Blasco Ibáñez*, Ajuntament de Valencia, 1 (2012), 105–17
LÓPEZ NÚÑEZ, A., *La acción social de la mujer en la higiene y mejoramiento de la raza* (Madrid: M. Minuesa, 1915)
MALLADA, LUCAS, *Los males de la patria* (Madrid: Alianza, 1969)
MANCHEÑO, LAURA, 'Maternidad y familia en *Cañas y barro* y su adaptación televisiva: el caso de Rosa y Neleta', *Bulletin of Spanish Studies* 87.2 (2010), 177–94
MANGHAM, ANDREW, *Violent Women and Sensation Fiction: Crime, Medicine and Victorian Popular Culture* (Basingstoke: Palgrave Macmillan, 2007)
MARAÑÓN, GREGORIO, 'Biología y Feminismo', *Conferencia pronunciada en la Sociedad Económica de Amigos del País*, Sevilla, 21 February 1920 (n.p. [Madrid]: Sucesor de Enrique Teodoro, 1920), 47 pp.
MARCUS, SHARON, *Between Women* (Princeton, NJ: Princeton University Press, 2007)
MARISTANY, LUIS, *El gabinete del doctor Lombroso (Delincuencia y fin de siglo en España)* (Barcelona: Anagrama, 1973)
MAZOWER, MARK, *Dark Continent: Europe's Twentieth Century* (London: Penguin, 1999)
MCLAREN, ANGUS, *Twentieth-Century Sexuality: A History* (Oxford: Blackwell, 1999)
MEDINA, JEREMY T., *The Valencian Novels of Vicente Blasco Ibáñez* (Valencia: Albatros, 1984)
MÉRIMÉE, ERNEST, 'Blasco Ibáñez et le roman de mœurs provinciales' *Bulletin Hispanique*, 5.3 (1903), 272–300
MIRANDA, MARISA, and GUSTAVO VALLEJO, eds, *Darwinismo social y eugenesia en el mundo latino* (Buenos Aires: Siglo XXI, 2005)
MONLAU, PEDRO FELIPE, *Remedios del pauperismo: memoria para optar al premio ofrecido por la Sociedad Económica Matritense el 1 de mayo de 1845* (Madrid: Sociedad Económica, 1846)
—— *Estudios superiores de higiene pública y epidemiología (curso de 1868 a 1869: lección inaugural)* (Madrid: M. Rivadeneyra, 1868)
MORAL, CARMEN DEL, *La sociedad madrileña fin de siglo y Baroja* (Madrid: Turner, 1974)
MOREL, BÉNÉDICT, *Traité des dégénérescences physiques, intellectuelles et morales de l'espèce humaine* (Paris: n.pub., 1857)
MOSSE, GEORGE L., Introduction to Max Nordau, *Degeneration* (Lincoln and London: University of Nebraska Press, 1993), pp. xiii–xxxvi
MÜLLER-WILLE, STAFFAN, and HANS-JÖRG RHEINBERGER, *A Cultural History of Heredity* (Chicago, IL, and London: University of Chicago Press, 2012)
MULVEY, LAURA, 'Visual Pleasure and Narrative Cinema', in *Literary Theory: An Anthology*, ed. by Julie Rivkin and Michael Ryan (Oxford: Blackwell, 1998), pp. 585–95
MUÑOZ RUIZ DE PASANIS, A., *Primera y Segunda Conferencia sobre el tema ¿Está o no degenerada la raza latina?* (Madrid: Ginés Carrión, 1905)
MURGA, ALFREDO, '*Cañas y barro*: novela de V. Blasco Ibáñez'. *El Liberal*, 1 April 1903
MURPHY, KATHARINE, *Re-reading Pío Baroja and English Literature* (Oxford: Peter Lang, 2004)
NASH, MARY, 'Un/Contested Identities: Motherhood, Sex Reform and the Modernization of Gender Identity in Early Twentieth-Century Spain', in *Constructing Spanish Woman-*

hood: Female Identity in Modern Spain, ed. by V. L. Enders and P. B. Radcliff (Albany: State University of New York Press, 1999), pp. 25–49
NAVARRO FERNÁNDEZ, ANTONIO, *La prostitución en la villa de Madrid* (Madrid: Ricardo Rojas, 1909)
NEAD, LYNDA, *The Female Nude: Art, Obscenity and Sexuality* (London: Routledge, 1992)
NEMESVARI, RICHARD, *Thomas Hardy, Sensationalism, and the Melodramatic Mode* (New York: Palgrave Macmillan, 2011)
NIETZSCHE, FRIEDRICH, *The Case of Wagner*, in *The Birth of Tragedy and the Case of Wagner*, trans. by Walter Kaufmann (Harmondsworth: Penguin, 1976)
NORDAU, MAX, *Degeneration*, ed. by George L. Mosse (Lincoln and London: University of Nebraska Press, 1993)
NORRIS, NANCY ANN, 'Visión azoriniana del paisaje español', *Cuadernos de Aldeeu* 1.2–3 (1983), 373–83
NYE, ROBERT A., *The Origins of Crowd Psychology: Gustave Le Bon and the Crisis of Mass Democracy in the Third Republic* (London: Sage, 1975)
—— 'Sociology: The Irony of Progress', in *Degeneration: The Dark Side of Progress*, ed. by J. Edward Chamberlin and Sander L. Gilman (New York: Columbia University Press, 1985), pp. 49–71
OLEZA, JOAN, and JAVIER LLUCH, eds, *Vicente Blasco Ibáñez, 1898–1998: la vuelta al siglo de un novelista*, 2 vols (Valencia: Generalitat Valenciana, Conselleria de Cultura i Educació, 2000)
ORTEGA Y GASSET, JOSÉ, *La rebelión de las masas* (1930), in *Obras completas*, 6 vols (Madrid: Revista de Occidente, 1957), IV, 113–310
—— 'Pío Baroja: Anatomía de un alma dispersa', in *Meditaciones sobre la literatura y el arte (La manera española de ver las cosas)*, ed. by E. Inman Fox (Madrid: Castalia, 1988), pp. 117–94
OTIS, LAURA, *Organic Memory: History and the Body in the Late Nineteenth and Early Twentieth Centuries* (Lincoln and London: University of Nebraska Press, 1994)
PARDO BAZÁN, EMILIA, *Obras completas*, 3 vols (Madrid: Aguilar, 1973)
—— *La Tribuna* (Madrid: Cátedra, 1975)
PEARSON, KARL, *The Life, Letters, and Labours of Francis Galton*, 4 vols (Cambridge: Cambridge University Press, 1914–30)
PÉREZ ROJAS, JAVIER, 'Un período de esplendor: la pintura valenciana entre 1880 y 1918', in *Centro y periferia en la modernización de la pintura española (1880–1918)*, ed. by Carmen Pena (Barcelona: Ambit, 1993–94), pp. 162–98
PICK, DANIEL, *Faces of Degeneration: A European Disorder, c.1848–c.1918* (Cambridge: Cambridge University Press, 1989)
PRESTON, PAUL, *The Spanish Civil War: Reaction, Revolution and Revenge* (London: Harper Perennial, 2006)
PUÉRTOLAS VILLANUEVA, SOLEDAD, *El Madrid de la 'lucha por la vida'* (Madrid: Helios, 1971)
PULIDO Y FERNÁNDEZ, ÁNGEL, *Bosquejos médico-sociales para la mujer* (Madrid: Imprenta a cargo de Víctor Saiz, 1876)
—— *Sanidad pública en España y ministerio social de las clases médicas* (Madrid: Enrique Teodoro y Alonso, 1902)
QUINN, CATH, 'Images and Impulses: Representations of Puerperal Insanity and Infanticide in Late Victorian England', in *Infanticide: Historical Perspectives on Child Murder and Concealment, 1550–2000*, ed. by Mark Jackson (Aldershot: Ashgate, 2002)
RAFTER, NICOLE HAHN, and MARY GIBSON, Introduction, in Cesare Lombroso and Guglielmo Ferrero, *Criminal Woman, the Prostitute, and the Normal Woman* (Durham, NC: Duke University Press, 2004), pp. 3–33

RAMSDEN, HERBERT, *Baroja: La busca* (London: Grant and Cutler, 1982)
REDING, KATHERINE, 'Blasco Ibáñez and Zola', *Hispania* (USA), 6 (1923), 365–71
REID, J. T., *Modern Spain and Liberalism* (Stanford, CA: Stanford University Press, 1937)
REVUELTA EUGERCIOS, BÁRBARA A., *Los usos de la Inclusa de Madrid, mortalidad y retorno a principios del siglo XX (1890–1935)* (unpublished doctoral thesis, Universidad Complutense de Madrid, 2011)
RICHARDS, MICHAEL, 'Spanish Psychiatry c.1900–1945: Constitutional Theory, Eugenics and the Nation', *Bulletin of Spanish Studies*, 81.6 (2004), 823–48
RICHARDSON, ANGELIQUE, 'The Biological Sciences', in *A Companion to Modernist Literature and Culture*, ed. by David Bradshaw and Kevin J. H. Dettmar (Oxford: Blackwell, 2005), pp. 50–65
ROBIN, CLAIRE-NICOLLE, '*La horda* (1905) de Blasco Ibáñez: del "naturalismo" a la militancia', in *Vicente Blasco Ibáñez, 1898–1998: la vuelta al siglo de un novelista*, ed. by Joan Oleza and Javier Lluch, 2 vols (Valencia: Generalitat Valenciana, Conselleria de Cultura i Educació, 2000), I, 472–81
RODGERS, EAMONN, 'Who Read Galdós? The Economics of the Book Trade in Nineteenth-Century Spain', in *New Galdós Studies: Essays in Memory of John Varey*, ed. by Nicholas G. Round (Woodbridge: Tamesis, 2003), pp. 11–25
ROUND, NICHOLAS G., 'Galdós Rewrites Galdós: The Deaths of Children and the Dying Century', in *New Galdós Studies: Essays in Memory of John Varey*, ed. by Nicholas G. Round (Woodbridge: Tamesis, 2003), pp. 125–39
SACKETT, THEODORE A., 'Blasco Ibáñez y el IV centenario', *Hispania*, 75.4 (October 1992), 897–905
SCANLON, GERALDINE M., *La polémica feminista en la España contemporánea (1868–1974)* (Madrid: siglo veintiuno, 1976)
SCHOPENHAUER, ARTHUR, 'On Women', in *Essays and Aphorisms*, trans. by R. J. Hollingdale (London: Penguin, 1970), pp. 80–88
—— *The World as Will and Representation*, trans. by E. F. J. Payne, 2 vols (New York: Dover, 1969)
SELTZER, MARK, 'The Naturalism Machine', in *Sex, Politics, and Science in the Nineteenth-Century Novel*, ed. by Ruth Bernard Yeazell (Baltimore, MD: Johns Hopkins University Press, 1986)
SEONAE, M. C., *Historia del Periodismo Español: el siglo XIX* (Madrid: Alianza Universidad, 1983)
SHAW, DONALD L., 'More About *Abulia*', *Anales de la literatura española contemporánea*, 23.1–2 (1998), 451–64
SHAW, G. B., 'The Sanity of Art' (1907), repr. in *G. B. Shaw: Major Critical Essays*, ed. by Michael Holroyd (Harmondsworth: Penguin, 1986), pp. 309–60
SHOWALTER, ELAINE, *The Female Malady: Women, Madness and English Culture, 1830–1980* (New York: Penguin, 1987)
—— *Sexual Anarchy: Gender and Culture at the Fin de Siècle* (London: Virago, 2009)
SIEBURTH, STEPHANIE, *Inventing High and Low: Literature, Mass Culture, and Uneven Modernity in Spain* (Durham, NC: Duke University Press, 1994)
SIEGEL, SANDRA, 'Literature and Degeneration: The Representation of "Decadence"', in *Degeneration: The Dark Side of Progress*, ed. by J. Edward Chamberlin and Sander L. Gilman (New York: Columbia University Press, 1985), pp. 199–219
SIMÓN PALMER, MARÍA CARMEN, 'La mujer lectora', in *Historia de la edición y de la lectura en España, 1472–1914*, ed. by Víctor Infantes, François Lopez and Jean-François Botrel (Madrid: Fundación Germán Sánchez Ruipérez, 2003), pp. 745–53
SINCLAIR, ALISON, 'Unamuno y Baroja ante el debate arte / ciencia', *Rilce*, 15.1 (1999), 156–69

—— *Trafficking Knowledge in Early Twentieth-Century Spain: Centres of Exchange and Cultural Imaginaries* (Woodbridge: Tamesis, 2009)

—— 'Luxurious Borders: Containment and Excess in Nineteenth-Century Spain', in *A Companion to Spanish Women's Studies*, ed. by Xon de Ros and Geraldine Hazbun (Woodbridge: Tamesis, 2011), pp. 211–26

SOSA-VELASCO, ALFREDO J., *Médicos escritores en España, 1885–1955: Santiago Ramón y Cajal, Pío Baroja, Gregorio Marañón y Antonio Vallejo Nágera* (Woodbridge: Tamesis, 2010)

SOUFAS, C. CHRISTOPHER, *The Subject in Question: Early Contemporary Spanish Literature and Modernism* (Washington, DC: Catholic University of America Press, 2007)

STANNARD, MICHAEL W., *The Theme of Degeneration in the Work of Benito Pérez Galdós: A Study of Four Naturalist Novels* (Saarbrücken: Lambert Academic Publishing, 2012)

—— *Galdós and Medicine* (Oxford: Peter Lang, 2015)

STEPAN, NANCY, 'Biological Degeneration: Races and Proper Places', in *Degeneration: The Dark Side of Progress*, ed. by J. Edward Chamberlin and Sander L. Gilman (New York: Columbia University Press, 1985), pp. 97–120

STOTT, REBECCA, *Fabrication of the Late Victorian Femme Fatale: The Kiss of Death* (Basingstoke: Macmillan, 1992)

STRACHEY, JAMES, 'Sigmund Freud: A Sketch of his Life and Ideas', in Sigmund Freud, *On Sexuality: Three Essays on the Theory of Sexuality and Other Works* (London: Penguin, 1991), pp. 13–26

SULLOWAY, FRANK, *Freud, Biologist of the Mind: Beyond the Psychoanalytic Legend*, 1st paperback edn (Cambridge, MA: Harvard University Press, 1992)

TARDE, GABRIEL, *L'Opinion et la foule* (Paris: n.pub., 1901)

TILLYARD, S. K., *The Impact of Modernism, 1900–1920: Early Modernism and the Arts and Crafts Movement in Edwardian England* (London: Routledge, 1988)

TOLOSA LATOUR, MANUEL, *El Niño* (Madrid: La Gaceta Universal, 1880)

TOMÁS, FACUNDO, Introduction, *La maja desnuda* (Madrid: Cátedra, 1998), pp. 9–150

TOMLINSON, JANICE, *Goya in the Twilight of Enlightenment* (New Haven, CT: Yale University Press, 1992)

TRINIDAD FERNÁNDEZ, PEDRO, 'La reforma de las cárceles en el siglo XIX: las cárceles de Madrid', *Estudios de Historia Social*, 22–23 (1982), 69–188

TRUEBA MIRA, VIRGINIA, 'Lulú: el extraño personaje de *El árbol de la ciencia* de Pío Baroja', *Anales de la literatura española contemporánea* 28.1 (2003), 183–202

TSUCHIYA, AKIKO, *Marginal Subjects: Gender and Deviance in Fin-de-Siècle Spain* (Toronto: University of Toronto Press, 2011)

UNAMUNO, MIGUEL DE, 'Sobre la erudición y la crítica', *La España Moderna*, December 1905, pp. 5–26

—— *Tres novelas ejemplares y un prólogo* [1920] (Madrid: Espasa-Calpe, 1931)

VALIS, NOËL, 'On Monstrous Birth: Leopoldo Alas's *La Regenta*', in *Naturalism in the European Novel*, ed. by Brian Nelson (Oxford: Berg, 1992), pp. 191–209

VALLEJO NÁGERA, ANTONIO, *Eugenesia de la Hispanidad y regeneración de la raza* (Burgos: Editorial Española, 1937)

VÁZQUEZ, OSCAR E., 'Regenerating the "Man-Beast": Embodying Brutishness in *Fin de Siglo* Spanish Art', in *Picturing Evolution and Extinction: Regeneration and Degeneration in Modern Visual Culture*, ed. by Fae Brauer and Serena Kshavjee (Newcastle: Cambridge Scholars Publishing, 2015), pp. 107–25

—— *The End Again: Degeneration and Visual Culture in Modern Spain* (University Park: Pennsylvania State University Press, 2017)

VICKERS, PETER, 'Blasco Ibáñez y las novelas "sociales", 1903–1905', in *Vicente Blasco Ibáñez, 1898–1998: la vuelta al siglo de un novelista*, ed. by Joan Oleza and Javier Lluch, 2 vols (Valencia: Generalitat Valenciana, Conselleria de Cultura i Educació, 2000), I, 464–81

Viñeta-Bellaserra, José, *La sífilis como hecho social punible y como una de las causas de la degeneración de la raza humana* (Barcelona: La Academia, 1886)

Zola, Émile, *Nana*, trans. by George Holden (Penguin: Harmondsworth, 1979)

INDEX

aboulia (abulia) 7, 22, 35, 41, 50 n. 27, 51 n. 38, 102, 105, 113, 118, 120, 122, 131–32, 134, 137, 143, 145, 148, 151–52, 154 n. 39, 166–67
abúlico, el 93, 102, 114 n. 21, 124, 129, 133
acromatopsia 36
adultery 22, 83, 87, 118, 120–21, 123, 126–29, 132–34, 157, 159, 161–62
  adulteress, the 17, 118, 120–21, 125, 128, 131–33, 160
Alas, Leopoldo (Clarín) 5, 14, 31, 96 n. 29, 99, 152
  La regenta 96 n. 29, 99
Alberich, José 95 n. 7
Albufera, la 123, 126–27, 130–31, 133
alcoholism 1, 4, 8, 10–12, 21, 24 n. 5, 34, 39, 52–58, 62, 71, 72 n. 20 & 21 & 22, 76, 78, 81, 86, 88–89, 91–94, 99–101, 104, 108–09, 111, 113, 118, 120, 126–27, 130–31, 134, 135 n. 30, 140–41, 146, 151–52, 166, 167
alienists 14, 59
Álvarez Peláez, Raquel 96 n. 40, 101, 114 n. 17 & 18 & 20, 154 n. 28 & 29, 169, 174 n. 51 & 52 & 53
Amazon, the 3, 17, 53, 64–67, 100, 120–21, 125, 131
anarchism 9, 31, 80–81, 84, 98, 101, 105, 108, 110–11, 114 n. 19 & 23, 115 n. 48, 151, 166–67, 171, 174 n. 50
  anarchist journals in Spain 84, 114 n. 19
Anderson, Benedict 162, 173 n. 27
Anderson, Christopher L. 64, 72 n. 32 & 34, 134 n. 10, 135 n. 36
ángel del hogar 80, 91, 99, 125, 127
Anglophone fiction 19, 25 n. 23, 139, 156, 172–73 n. 2
d'Annunzio, Gabriele 69
atavism 11, 17, 21–22, 49, 53, 77–80, 82–84, 88–89, 91–92, 97–100, 102–03, 105, 110, 112, 124, 139, 151, 166
Azorín 7, 9, 29, 41, 51 n. 44, 66, 69, 72 n. 36 & 46, 73 n. 48, 134, 151, 167, 170
  Diario de un enfermo 9
  La sociología criminal 9
  La voluntad 7, 9, 29, 167

Bachofen, J. J.:
  Mother Law 66, 72 n. 38, 121
Bahamonde Magro, Ángel 98, 114 n. 5
Balfour, Sebastian 12, 25 n. 36, 170, 174 n. 59
Barcelona 19–20, 108, 168
Baroja, Julio Caro 81, 91, 95 n. 14, 112, 115 n. 46

Baroja, Pío:
  fiction:
    El árbol de la ciencia 22, 25 n. 24, 77, 87, 90, 103–05, 114, 114 n. 25, 134, 137–53, 153 n. 8 & 9 & 20, 154 n. 31, 171
    Aurora roja 110–11
    Aventuras, inventos y mixtificaciones de Silvestre Paradox 21, 38–39, 50 n. 34, 79, 151
    La busca 21–22, 24 n. 3, 55, 71, 76–78, 81–85, 88–95, 95 n. 1 & 14, 97–98, 100–03, 108, 110–14, 115 n. 46, 140, 150–51
    Camino de perfección 4, 9, 15–16, 19, 21, 24 n. 2, 25 n. 23, 28–42, 49, 50 n. 22 & 23 & 33 & 35, 51 n. 37, 52, 150, 167
    La casa de Aizgorri 4, 15–16, 21, 34, 38–40, 52–65, 70–71, 71 n. 13, 77, 138, 148–50
    César o nada 170
    La ciudad de la niebla 57, 149–50, 154 n. 34
    La dama errante 57, 149
    La lucha por la vida 76–77, 81, 90, 94, 105, 164
    Mala hierba 81, 87–88
    El mundo es ansí 149, 161
    'Patología del golfo' 24 n. 5, 110
    La raza 22, 77, 137, 149–50, 152
    Vidas sombrías 15, 52, 115 n. 43
  and ideas:
    anti-semitism 170–71
    as doctor of medicine 1, 10, 91–92, 137, 141, 154 n. 31
    political views 170–71
    racial theories 7, 138, 170
  non-fiction:
    Ayer y hoy 138, 153 n. 5, 171
    Desde la última vuelta del camino 88
    'Espíritu de subordinación' 110, 115 n. 42
    'Galería de tipos de la época' 164
    'Lejanías' 110
    'La raza y la cultura' 7, 138
Baroja, Ricardo 81, 87
Basque Country 7, 56–57, 77
Baudelaire, Charles 30, 45, 50 n. 7 & 10, 69, 96 n. 32
  Les Fleurs du mal 69
Beizer, Janet 34, 50 n. 24
Benjamin, Walter:
  Charles Baudelaire 87, 96 n. 32
Bernaldo de Quirós, Constancio 9, 77, 85–87, 95 n. 23 & 25, 96 n. 30 & 31

La mala vida en Madrid 9, 77, 87, 95 n. 23 & 25, 96 n. 30 & 31
Las nuevas teorías de la criminalidad 9
Bernard, Claude 10, 99, 106, 139
  Introduction à l'étude de la médecine expérimentale 10, 106
Betancor Gómez, María José 24 n. 11
Biblical symbols 8, 11, 96 n. 27, 120, 140, 146, 149, 151, 169
Bigot, Charles 173 n. 16
biological theories 1–9, 12–13, 15, 19, 22–23, 24 n. 14 & 15, 26 n. 49 & 63, 29, 32–33, 38–41, 46, 51 n. 38, 52–53, 55–59, 61–65, 71, 77–79, 81–84, 87, 89–90, 92–93, 95 n. 15, 96 n. 39, 97–98, 102–03, 106, 108, 110–11, 113, 124, 126–27, 129, 133, 137–43, 145–49, 151–52, 153 n. 7, 157–58, 163, 165, 167–69
birth control 96 n. 40, 101, 114 n. 17, 146, 168
Blanco, Alda 133, 136 n. 43
Blasco Ibáñez, Vicente:
  fiction:
    Arroz y tartana 123, 156
    La barraca 19, 63, 67–69, 72 n. 32 & 42 & 45, 113, 118, 123, 134 n. 1, 156–57, 162, 167, 174 n. 35 & 36 & 37
    La bodega 24 n. 5, 97
    Cañas y barro 3–4, 19, 22, 55, 63–64, 68, 72 n. 32, 94, 95 n. 2, 114, 118–34, 134 n. 9, 135 n. 15 & 18 & 32, 157, 159–60, 162, 164
    La catedral 97, 156
    Los cuatro jinetes del Apocalipsis 156
    Entre naranjos 3, 16, 21, 52–55, 63–71, 72 n. 33 & 36, 122, 133, 156, 162, 164, 167
    Flor de Mayo 43, 118, 122–23, 128, 132, 134 n. 2, 135 n. 15, 156–57, 159, 162
    La horda 21–22, 24 n. 3, 68, 71, 76–77, 87, 95, 97–98, 100–14, 114 n. 1 & 2 & 16 & 21, 115 n. 47
    La maja desnuda 21, 28–32, 42–49, 51 n. 42 & 43 & 47 & 50 & 58, 122, 174 n. 29
    Mare nostrum 156
    El papa del mar 156
    A los pies de Venus 156
    Sangre y arena 133, 136 n. 42, 160, 167
    Sónnica la cortesana 156
    social novels 97, 108, 115 n. 47, 119, 134 n. 1
    Valencian novels 6, 63–64, 68, 70, 72 n. 32, 115 n. 47, 118, 123, 130, 132–33, 134 n. 1, 135 n. 31 & 35
  and journalism 10, 119, 159, 162
    El Pueblo 11, 119, 123, 134, 134 n. 3, 156–57, 159, 162, 173 n. 8 & 18
  and publishing 119, 156, 173 n. 4
    La novela ilustrada 162
  and Republicanism 23, 95, 98, 108, 119, 123, 134 n. 3, 156–57, 162, 168

Botrel, Jean-François 156, 173 n. 5 & 14
bourgeoisie 100–01, 109, 160, 162
  bourgeois values 3–4, 12, 15, 29, 42, 44, 57, 61, 64, 66–67, 76–77, 80–81, 88, 90–91, 94, 99–101, 109–14, 118, 121, 126, 138, 143, 150, 153 n. 22, 157, 160–62, 164, 168
  see also middle classes
Breuer, Joseph:
  Studies on Hysteria 38, 51 n. 36, 64
Britain 2, 4, 8, 11, 16, 19, 114 n. 17, 124, 135 n. 16, 158, 162, 168–69, 173 n. 2
  see also Anglophone fiction; England
Brown, Gerald G. 51 n. 41
Buchez, Philippe 145, 151
  Introduction to Science 145
Burgos, Carmen de 16, 19, 26 n. 52, 44, 122
  La indecisa 122
  La que quiso ser maja 44, 122
  El veneno del arte 16

Campos Marín, Ricardo 12–13, 25 n. 20 & 31 & 33 & 38 & 41, 26 n. 42 & 43, 58, 72 n. 20 & 21, 80, 92, 95 n. 10 & 11, 96 n. 44, 125–26, 135 n. 26 & 27 & 29 & 30, 154 n. 30, 166, 174 n. 41 & 43 & 44 & 46
Cardwell, Richard 5, 24 n. 7, 25 n. 21, 26 n. 47, 41, 50 n. 6 & 12 & 29 & 30, 51 n. 40 & 51, 68, 72 n. 32 & 45, 134 n. 1, 174 n. 35 & 36
Carlson, Eric T. 71 n. 16, 72 n. 17 & 18 & 31
Casas, Ramon:
  Joven decadente. Después del baile 158
  Sífilis 17, 19–20, 122
Caudet, Francisco 108, 115 n. 34, 134 n. 3
Celaya Carrillo, Beatriz 19, 26 n. 62, 153 n. 22
Cervera Barat, Rafael 21, 58, 72 n. 21 & 22
Cestona, Guipúzcoa 10, 141
Chamberlin, J. Edward 24 n. 14, 25 n. 20, 26 n. 53, 71 n. 1 & 16, 95 n. 12, 169, 174 n. 55 & 56 & 57
Charcot, Jean Martin 34, 37, 54
Charnon-Deutsch, Lou 26 n. 54 & 58, 50 n. 31, 135 n. 16, 136 n. 43, 153 n. 11, 159, 172 n. 2, 173 n. 19 & 20
childbearing 22, 32, 139, 165
childbirth 45, 64, 98, 104, 123–24, 140, 143, 148–49
cholera 86, 98
cinema 67, 72 n. 40
  and Blasco Ibáñez 119, 136 n. 42, 160, 172, 173 n. 21, 174 n. 47
  see also film
city, the 3–4, 11, 33–35, 52, 71, 76–77, 81–82, 85, 87–88, 90–94, 97–101, 103, 108, 111–13, 124, 152, 156, 161, 164
  see also urban environment
Civil War, Spanish 170, 174 n. 39 & 54
Clarín, *see* Alas, Leopoldo
Clemenceau, Georges 110

Cleminson, Richard 5, 24 n. 5, 101, 104, 114 n. 19 &
   23, 115 n. 48, 174 n. 50
Comenge y Ferrer, Luis:
   La medicina en el siglo XIX 11, 25 n. 28
Comte, Auguste 110
Consejo Superior de Investigaciones Científicas (CSIC)
   8, 25 n. 20
Conte, Rafael 72 n. 32
Cooke, Nicholas Francis:
   Satan in Society 66, 72 n. 37, 134 n. 6
craniology 82, 98
criminality 1, 4, 6, 8–10, 12, 21–22, 49, 52, 55, 58,
   76–77, 79–85, 87, 91, 94, 97, 102, 105–07, 109, 113,
   115 n. 32, 118–20, 123–26, 129–30, 134, 135 n. 16
   & 30, 140–41, 146, 150, 158–59, 166–67, 169
   criminal, the 14, 77, 79, 80, 82–83, 86, 95 n. 17,
      104, 106, 161, 166
   criminal anthropology 10–11, 14–15, 17, 21, 77–79,
      82–83, 88, 92, 94, 98, 105, 107, 119, 166
   criminology 8, 77–78, 80, 87, 106, 124, 165
crowd, the 2, 21–22, 44, 67–68, 77, 95, 97–100, 105,
   108–12, 114 n. 4, 115 n. 36 & 39 & 40 & 41,
   136 n. 42, 160, 167–68, 173 n. 21, 174 n. 47
   see also Le Bon, Gustave; Tarde, Gabriel

Darío, Rubén 30, 128
Darwin, Charles 6, 15, 24 n. 19, 58, 104–05, 119, 139,
   144, 149, 168
   The Descent of Man 149
   Origin of Species 149
   Darwinism 4, 8, 24 n. 11 & 19, 72 n. 19, 79,
      81, 104–06, 113, 124–25, 165, 167–70, 172,
      174 n. 45 & 51
Davis, Lisa 25 n. 34
Deaver, William O. 51 n. 37
decadence:
   literary 26 n. 53 & 54, 30, 45, 69
   moral 19, 35, 126–27, 129
   national 1, 4–6, 12–14, 22–23, 37, 80, 82, 103, 110,
      168–69
determinism 6, 15, 21, 23, 27–28, 33, 37–42, 52–53,
   56–57, 59, 62–64, 68–71, 78. 82–83, 89, 93, 97,
   102, 105, 113, 120, 126, 128–31, 133, 135–36 n. 36,
   138, 148–50, 152, 154 n. 31, 169–71
   see also heredity
deviance 4–6, 10–11, 16–17, 21–23, 24 n. 8, 35, 39,
   53–54, 56, 65–66, 71, 78–79, 83–84, 86, 88, 93,
   100, 105–06, 114, 119–22, 124–27, 133–34, 144,
   159–62, 164, 166–68
Dijkstra, Bram 17, 26 n. 57, 122, 132, 134 n. 12,
   136 n. 39, 153 n. 12, 173 n. 12
disease 3–4, 8–11, 13–14, 17, 19, 30–31, 33, 35, 41,
   43–44, 46, 53, 58–59, 71, 76, 78, 81, 84, 86–91,
   94, 97–100, 102, 104, 106, 108, 112–13, 119, 124,
   134, 135 n. 30, 137, 141–42, 144, 150, 152, 159,
   161, 166–67, 169

Doane, Mary Ann 132, 136 n. 40
doctors:
   fictional 32, 45–46, 56–57, 59, 62, 64, 111, 137, 141,
      145–46, 148–50, 171
   medical 4, 9–10, 21, 24 n. 7, 34, 51 n. 40, 78, 83,
      89, 92, 95 n. 5, 106, 125, 142, 168
   see also medicine
Dujardin, Edouard 70

education 3, 19, 28, 34, 37–39, 55, 63, 85, 89, 100–01,
   106, 113, 119, 126, 133, 141, 151, 156, 160, 162–63,
   168–69
   of masses 101, 106, 119, 151, 160, 162
   of women 3, 19, 85, 89, 100, 141, 156, 163
Ellis, Havelock 30, 49, 51 n. 61, 78, 83, 95 n. 4 & 17,
   124, 135 n. 24
   The Criminal 83, 95 n. 17
   From Rousseau to Proust 51 n. 61
Empire, Spanish 25 n. 36, 80, 174 n. 59
England 7, 51 n. 59, 101, 122, 135 n. 22, 149, 166, 169
   see also Anglophone fiction; Britain
Escuder, J.M.:
   Locos y anómalos 12, 14, 25 n. 32, 55, 71 n. 10
Eslava, Rafael G.:
   La prostitución en Madrid 95 n. 21, 96 n. 29, 141,
      153 n. 17
España Moderna, La 9, 14, 25 n. 22, 50 n. 9, 125, 132,
   136 n. 38
Espina, Concha 19
Esquerdo, José María 11, 14, 25 n. 29, 145
   Locos que no lo parecen 11, 14, 25 n. 29
   'De la locura histérica' 145
Esquirol, Jean Étienne Dominique 14, 59, 124, 135 n. 20
   Des Maladies mentales 124, 135 n. 20
eugenics 13, 21, 90, 96 n. 40, 101, 104, 114 n. 19, 140,
   147, 165–66, 168–70, 174 n. 39 & 50 & 51
   and anarchism 101, 114 n. 19
   and Francis Galton 90, 104, 168–69
   and Francoist psychiatry 165, 174 n. 39
evolutionary theory 8, 16, 31, 94, 98, 125
extinction, of species 24 n. 12, 55, 58, 92, 100, 113, 167

Felski, Rita 158, 173 n. 10
feminism 17, 19, 51 n. 37, 59, 60, 80, 90, 96 n. 39, 122,
   136 n. 40, 139, 153 n. 11 & 14, 168
femme fatale 64, 66–67, 71, 121–22, 132, 134 n. 11,
   154 n. 24
   see also mujer fatal
Fernández, Pura 95 n. 6
Fernández Cifuentes, Luis 173 n. 3
Fernández Villegas, F. ('Zeda') 9, 25 n. 22
Ferreras, Juan Ignacio 156, 164, 173 n. 5
Ferrero, Guglielmo 26 n. 56, 83, 95 n. 4, 114 n. 10,
   134 n. 4 & 5
ficción de masas 1–2, 122
   see also popular fiction

film adaptation:
    and Blasco Ibáñez 10, 23, 133, 160, 167–68
    Torrent 133
    see also Hollywood; Blasco Ibáñez, fiction, *Sangre y arena*
fin de siècle 11, 17, 19, 24 n. 8, 26 n. 57 & 59, 28, 30–31, 50 n. 7, 53, 64, 66–67, 69, 80, 121–22, 128, 153 n. 14
    fin de siglo 1, 10, 12, 24 n. 7 & 12, 31, 44, 48, 55, 79–80, 92, 95 n. 1 & 5, 133, 135 n. 33, 153 n. 8
Flint, Kate 173 n. 2
Flint, Weston and Noma 4, 24 n. 2, 34, 50 n. 23
folletín 11, 119, 133–34, 156–57, 159, 162
Forel, August:
    The Sexual Question 139, 153 n. 13
Forster, E. M.:
    Aspects of the Novel 70, 73 n. 53
Foucault, Michel:
    Discipline and Punish 105–06, 115 n. 28
foundling hospital 123–24
    see also *inclusa*; la Inclusa (Madrid)
France 2, 6–12, 14, 21–22, 25 n. 31 & 38, 30, 34–35, 40, 42–43, 45, 50 n. 24, 52–53, 55–56, 58, 69, 72 n. 32, 78–79, 92, 94, 96 n. 45, 97–99, 124, 151, 166, 170
    see also naturalism; Zola, Émile
    see also translation, into French
Francoism 4, 164–65, 170–71
    Francoist psychiatry 165
Fraser, Benjamin 154 n. 31
Freud, Sigmund 15–16, 26 n. 49 & 50, 32–33, 37, 39–41, 49, 50 n. 19, 51 n. 36, 53–55, 57, 59–66, 71, 71 n. 3, 72 n. 27 & 30, 86, 171
    Beyond the Pleasure Principle 54
    'Heredity and the Aetiology of Neuroses' 16, 54
    The Interpretation of Dreams 15, 39–40, 65
    'Mourning and Melancholia' 40, 72 n. 27
    Studies on Hysteria 38, 51 n. 36, 64
    Three Essays on the Theory of Sexuality 15–16, 40, 50 n. 19, 65
    Totem and Taboo 16, 54
    and Oedipus complex 16, 54, 60
    and seduction theory 16, 54–55, 63–65
Friedman, Melvin J. 73 n. 52 & 54
Fuentes Peris, Teresa 5, 24 n. 5 & 8, 86, 90, 95 n. 27, 96 n. 41, 135 n. 34
Fuster, Joan 24 n. 10

Galdós, Benito Pérez 5, 17, 24 n. 3 & 8 & 17, 26 n. 46 & 54, 50 n. 32, 59, 72 n. 25, 85, 87, 98, 100, 103, 127–28, 130, 133, 135 n. 30, 152, 161, 173 n. 6 & 26
    Ángel Guerra 17, 26 n. 54, 130
    La de Bringas 87, 128, 161
    La desheredada 59, 87, 100, 135 n. 30
    Doña Perfecta 161

Tristana 133
Galton, Francis 90, 104–05, 114 n. 26, 146, 168–69, 174 n. 48 & 49
Ganivet, Ángel 7, 41, 51 n. 38 & 39, 152, 155
    Idearium español 7
Garbo, Greta 133
Garrido, Victoriano:
    La cárcel o el manicomio 14
Gascó Contell, Emilio 26 n. 51, 46, 51 n. 54 & 55, 73 n. 55
Gayon, Jean 58, 72 n. 19, 167, 174 n. 45
Gener, Pompeyo 14, 31, 50 n. 11
    Literaturas malsanas 31, 50 n. 11
'Generation of 1898' 1–2, 4–5, 9, 23, 29, 35, 42, 51 n. 38, 52, 119, 155, 163, 165, 170, 172
George, David 133, 136 n. 42, 160, 173 n. 21, 174 n. 47
Gilman, Sander L. 24 n. 14, 25 n. 20, 26 n. 53, 53–54, 71 n. 1 & 2 & 4 & 5 & 16, 95 n. 12 & 26, 134 n. 7 & 8
Giné y Partagás, Juan 14, 59, 72 n. 23 & 24
Gogh, Vincent van 49
Golden, Catherine 173 n. 2
Gómez de Barquero, Eduardo 132
Gómez Carrillo, Enrique 30, 45
de Goya y Lucientes, Francisco José 42–45, 51 n. 46 & 52 & 53
    La maja desnuda 42–45
Grand, Sarah:
    The Heavenly Twins 139, 153 n. 14
Granjel, Luis 154 n. 36
Granjel, Mercedes 153 n. 3
Greenslade, William 8, 24 n. 18, 25 n. 20, 50 n. 3, 83, 95 n. 16, 104, 114 n. 13 & 24, 170, 174 n. 58
Grey, Daniel 124, 135 n. 21
Guigou y Costa, Diego 6, 24 n. 11

Haidt, Rebecca 44, 51 n. 47
Hambrook, Glyn 50 n. 7 & 10
Hartmann, Eduard von:
    Philosophy of the Unconscious 15–16, 26 n. 48
Hauser, Philiph 86, 89, 95 n. 22, 96 n. 28 & 38, 99, 114 n. 6 & 22, 166, 174 n. 40
    Madrid bajo el punto de vista médico-social 95 n. 22, 96 n. 38, 114 n. 22
    'El siglo XIX considerado bajo el punto de vista médico-social' 96 n. 28, 114 n. 6, 174 n. 40
Hegel, Georg Wilhelm Friedrich:
    Lectures on the Philosophy of Religion 121
Heilmann, Ann 139, 153 n. 14
heredity 1, 4–5, 8, 10, 14–16, 21–23, 24 n. 13 & 16, 27, 33, 37, 53–54, 56, 58–59, 61–63, 70, 72 n. 19, 76, 81, 89, 92, 94, 97, 102, 108, 111, 118, 126–27, 129–30, 137–38, 143, 149–52, 167–69, 174 n. 49
    hereditary determinism 6, 12–13, 21–23, 28, 34–35, 37, 39–40, 42, 53, 55–59, 62–65, 69, 71, 78–79, 82–83, 88–90, 92–93, 98, 102, 105, 107, 113,

118, 120, 126, 128, 130–31, 138–39, 143, 148–52, 167, 169
Hibbs-Lissorgues, Solange 173 n. 17
highbrow fiction 2, 10, 172, 175 n. 65
Hollywood 2, 23, 133, 156
Holocaust, the 169–70
Huertas García-Alejo, Rafael 12, 24 n. 5, 25 n. 20 & 37, 126, 166
Hughes, Robert 45, 51 n. 46 & 53
Huysmans, Joris-Karl 44, 70, 73 n. 52
  À rebours 44
Huyssen, Andreas 67, 72 n. 41, 153 n. 1, 163, 174 n. 30 & 31
hygienic medicine 6, 15, 25 n. 31, 53, 81, 99, 104, 106, 130–31, 137, 145, 161, 166–67
  see also social medicine
hysteria 8, 10–11, 17, 21, 29–30, 32–38, 40, 42–43, 46, 48, 50 n. 24, 51 n. 36, 53–54, 58, 62, 64, 71 n. 3, 83, 92, 110, 137, 139–40, 143, 145, 147–48, 153 n. 14, 166

illegitimacy 37, 39, 57, 120, 123–26, 133–34
inclusa 123–25
  see also foundling hospital
Inclusa, la (Madrid) 123–24, 135 n. 17
indigence 4, 12, 21, 77–78, 84, 93, 97–99, 101–02, 105, 109, 111–12
  see also poverty
infant mortality 10, 22, 24 n. 11, 25 n. 24, 67, 90, 120–21, 123–25, 128–29, 132, 140–41, 145, 148, 151, 162, 173 n. 26
  see also infanticide; neonaticide
Infantes, Víctor 173 n. 14 & 17
infanticide 4, 22, 68, 85, 101, 114, 118–25, 130–31, 133–34, 135 n. 21 & 22 & 24 & 25
  see also neonaticide
infertility 128, 138, 167
  see also sterility, of nation
insanity 14, 22, 29–31, 44–45, 48–49, 54–55, 57–59, 61–62, 71, 84–85, 120, 123–24, 135 n. 16 & 20 & 22 & 23, 166
  see also madness; psychiatry
Institución Libre de Enseñanza 14
intrahistoria 170
Irigaray, Luce:
  Speculum of the Other Woman 72 n. 30
Italy 2, 10–11, 14, 43, 77–80, 92, 94, 166
  see also criminal anthropology; Lombroso, Cesare
'Itzea', Baroja's house 79

Jagoe, Catherine 26 n. 54, 50 n. 25
Jiménez, Juan Ramón 41
Johnson, Roberta 25 n. 23, 26 n. 52
journalism, journalists 10, 14, 49
  and Blasco Ibáñez 119, 159, 162
  see also newspapers; Pueblo, El

Jurkevich, Gayana 51 n. 38 & 44

Kirkpatrick, Susan 135 n. 16
Kleist, Heinrich von:
  Penthesilea 121
Krausists 14, 22, 106

Labanyi, Jo 22, 25 n. 35 & 36, 26 n. 44 & 54 & 64, 50 n. 31, 72 n. 39 & 43, 87, 95 n. 3, 96 n. 33 & 35 & 37, 106, 114 n. 9 & 15, 115 n. 29 & 30 & 31 & 37, 135 n. 16, 136 n. 43, 149, 154 n. 32, 170–71, 173 n. 23, 174 n. 60 & 61 & 63
Laguna Platero, Antonio 119, 134 n. 3, 157, 173 n. 8, 175 n. 64
Lavater, Johann Caspar:
  Essays on Physiognomy 79
law (discipline of) 3, 14, 90, 105–06, 135 n. 20 & 23 & 25, 151, 168
lawyers 4, 98
Le Bon, Gustave 22, 97–98, 108, 110, 114 n. 3 & 4, 168
  Psychologies des foules 22, 97, 114 n. 3 & 4
Legrain, Paul-Maurice 30, 50 n. 4, 58, 92, 94, 96 n. 43
Levine, Lawrence 172, 175 n. 65
Leys, Ruth 71 n. 6 & 7 & 8, 72 n. 35
literacy, rates of 89, 119, 156, 160, 162
Litvak, Lily 135 n. 33
Llanas Aguilaniedo, José M. 9, 25 n. 21, 31, 36, 77, 85–87, 95 n. 23 & 25, 96 n. 30 & 31
  Alma contemporánea 31, 36
  La mala vida en Madrid 9, 77, 85–87, 95 n. 23 & 25, 96 n. 30 & 31
  Navegar pintoresco 25 n. 21, 36
Llorca, Fernando 156
Lombroso, Cesare 1, 6, 10–11, 13–15, 17, 21–22, 26 n. 56, 30–31, 36, 49, 50 n. 5, 51 n. 60, 69–70, 77–80, 82–86, 89, 92, 95 n. 4 & 5 & 8 & 24, 97, 99–100, 106, 108, 114 n. 10, 119–21, 124–25, 134 n. 4 & 5, 140, 166
  Criminal Man (L'uomo delinquente) 11, 79–80, 95 n. 8
  Criminal Woman (La donna delinquente) 17, 21, 26 n. 56, 77–78, 83–86, 95 n. 4 & 19 & 24, 99–100, 114 n. 10, 119–21, 134 n. 4 & 5
  The Man of Genius (L'uomo di genio) 30, 51 n. 60
  and influence on Baroja 21, 79, 82
  and reception in Spain 14–15, 31, 77, 79–80, 125, 166
Longhurst, Carlos-Alex 4, 24 n. 3, 25 n. 23, 39, 50 n. 33 & 35, 56, 59–60, 71 n. 12, 72 n. 26, 76, 94, 95 n. 2, 96 n. 46, 136 n. 36
López Núñez, A. 153 n. 15

madness 12, 29–30, 34, 37, 48–49, 52, 55, 58–61, 70, 109, 124, 126, 130, 153 n. 10, 164, 167
  see also insanity; psychiatry
Madrid 9–10, 14, 21–22, 24 n. 3, 28, 34, 39, 43, 48, 55, 68, 71, 76–78, 80–82, 84–85, 87–90, 93–95,

95 n. 1 & 2 & 21 & 22 & 23 & 25, 96 n. 29 & 30 & 31 & 38, 97–98, 101, 103–04, 106, 108–09, 111–13, 114 n. 22 & 27, 115 n. 32 & 35, 123–24, 132, 135 n. 17, 137, 140–42, 144–45, 150, 152, 153 n. 17 & 19, 156, 162, 165–66, 170
Maeztu, Ramiro de 151
Mallada, Lucas 6, 13, 25 n. 40
   Los males de la patria 13, 25 n. 40
Malthus, Thomas Robert 101, 114 n. 17, 146
   Malthusian theory 84, 101, 168
Mancheño, Laura 134 n. 9 & 10
Manet, Édouard 45, 49
   Le Déjeuner sur l'herbe 45
   Olympia 45
Mangham, Andrew 135 n. 16
Marañón, Gregorio 24 n. 6, 90, 96 n. 39, 169
Marcus, Sharon 122, 133, 135 n. 13, 136 n. 41
Maristany, Luis 79
Martínez, Jesús 114 n. 5
Martínez Pérez, José 12, 25 n. 20, 126, 166
Martínez Ruiz, José, *see* Azorín
mass culture 72 n. 41, 100, 114 n. 14, 133, 162–64, 171–72
maternity 3, 6, 12, 19, 21–22, 33, 38–40, 52, 55, 57–63, 65, 86, 103, 114, 119, 121–22, 124, 126–29, 131–32, 134, 134 n. 9 & 10, 137, 139–40, 142–44, 147–50, 158
   see also motherhood
Maudsley, Henry 11, 66, 70
   The Pathology of Mind 66
   The Physiology of Mind 66
McLaren, Angus 26 n. 60
medicine 1–3, 6, 8–10, 14–15, 22, 24 n. 7, 25 n. 30 & 31 & 37, 26 n. 46, 32, 37, 50 n. 32, 53, 55, 66, 71 n. 16, 72 n. 17 & 18 & 25 & 31, 78, 81, 86, 89–90, 92, 99, 102, 104, 106, 112, 130–31, 135 n. 16, 137, 139–40, 145–49, 154 n. 31, 159, 161, 166–68
   see also doctors
Medina, Jeremy T. 63, 72 n. 32, 127, 130, 135 n. 31 & 35
melodrama 119, 135 n. 16, 156–57, 161–62, 173 n. 25
mental illness 12, 14, 59, 62, 66, 81, 135 n. 30
   mental health 10
middle classes 3, 29–30, 44, 52, 76, 80, 85, 91, 93, 98, 100, 109, 119, 138, 156, 158, 160–61, 165, 168–69
   see also bourgeoisie
Miranda, Marisa 24 n. 11, 174 n. 51
modernism 2, 9–10, 23, 25 n. 21 & 23, 26 n. 52 & 63, 29, 50 n. 35, 51 n. 59, 70, 72 n. 41, 73 n. 52, 137, 155, 163
   modernismo 24 n. 7, 30, 41, 68–69, 128
modernity 76, 97, 108, 113, 114 n. 14, 143, 173 n. 10
Monlau, Pedro Felipe 12, 25 n. 30, 35, 50 n. 26, 153 n. 3, 158
monomania (*monomanía*) 59
monstrosity 26 n. 54, 35, 89, 96 n. 29, 144, 169

Moral, Carmen del 95 n. 1, 141, 153 n. 16 & 18
Morel, Bénédict A. 1, 8, 10–14, 21, 31, 33, 53, 55, 57–59, 70, 71 n. 9, 78, 92, 94, 97, 113, 130, 138, 145–46, 150–52
   Traité des dégénérescences 8, 10, 55, 92
motherhood 4, 19, 38–41, 45–46, 51 n. 37, 53, 55, 57, 59–63, 65–66, 70, 72 n. 38, 76, 101–02, 104, 106, 119, 121, 123–24, 126–28, 139–40, 143–44, 149, 154 n. 33, 158, 168–69
Motherland 12–13
   see also maternity
mujer fatal 3, 17, 22, 65, 120–21, 127, 132–33
   see also femme fatale
mujer serpiente 3, 17, 37, 120–21, 128, 131
Müller-Wille, Staffan 24 n. 13 & 16
Mulvey, Laura 67, 72 n. 40
Muñoz Ruiz de Pasanis, A. 21, 166
Murga, Alfredo 127, 135 n. 32
Murphy, Katharine 25 n. 23, 153 n. 8

Nash, Mary 149, 154 n. 33
naturalism 4–6, 9–12, 14, 21–23, 24 n. 3 & 17, 29–30, 35, 42–43, 47, 53, 56, 62–63, 68–71, 71 n. 12, 72 n. 26 & 28 & 32, 73 n. 56, 75, 77–79, 81, 85, 94–95, 95 n. 2 & 6, 96 n. 29 & 45 & 46, 97–98, 106, 108, 113, 114 n. 21, 115 n. 47, 118–20, 123, 125, 128, 130–31, 134 n. 1, 136 n. 36, 140, 152–53, 158–59
Navarro Fernández, Antonio 153 n. 19
Nelken, Margarita 19
Nemesvari, Richard 162, 173 n. 25
neonaticide 22, 68, 118–20, 124–25, 134, 162
   see also infanticide
neurasthenia 8, 11, 21, 28–29, 32, 35–37, 42–43, 45–47, 57, 147, 150
neurosis 16, 21, 28–30, 32–35, 37–40, 42, 46, 49, 52–56, 59–62, 71, 137, 139, 143, 145, 148, 150–51
newspapers 11, 107, 109, 119, 156–57, 159–60, 162, 168, 173 n. 18
   see also journalism; *Pueblo, El*
New Woman 16, 19, 139, 153 n. 11 & 14, 158
Nietzsche, Friedrich 6–7, 28, 30, 57, 62, 105, 119, 137–38, 151, 153 n. 2
Nordau, Max 1, 4, 6, 10–11, 14–15, 17, 21, 25 n. 25 & 26 & 34, 28–37, 41–45, 47–49, 50 n. 1 & 2 & 4 & 5 & 13 & 14 & 17 & 21 & 28, 51 n. 49 & 56, 52, 69–70, 73 n. 49 & 50 & 51, 76, 79, 92, 96 n. 42, 119
   Degeneration 11, 17, 21, 25 n. 25 & 26 & 34, 28–37, 45, 47–49, 50 n. 1 & 2 & 4 & 5 & 13 & 14 & 17 & 21 & 28, 51 n. 49 & 56, 52, 69–70, 73 n. 49 & 50 & 51, 79, 92, 96 n. 42
   and influence on Baroja and Blasco 4, 6, 11, 15, 21, 28–29, 32–37, 41–44, 47–48, 79
   and reception in Spain 6, 14–15, 17, 25 n. 34, 28, 30–31, 119

Norris, Nancy Ann 51 n. 44, 72 n. 46
North America 149
   see also United States
Nye, Robert A. 95 n. 12, 114 n. 4, 115 n. 36 & 39 & 40 & 41

Oedipus complex 16, 39–40, 54–55, 59–61, 65
orphans, orphanage 85, 101, 105–06, 112
Ortega y Gasset, José 144, 154 n. 25, 155, 163, 170, 173 n. 28
   España invertebrada 170
   La rebelión de las masas 163, 173 n. 28
Otis, Laura 4, 24 n. 4, 73 n. 57, 138, 153 n. 6 & 7, 154 n. 37 & 38

Palmar, El 4, 118, 120, 125–27, 129–31
Pardo Bazán, Emilia 5, 15, 17, 31, 50 n. 8, 109, 115 n. 38, 133, 152, 160–61, 173 n. 22
   'Apuntes autobiográficos' 109
   Memorias de un solterón 17, 133
   La Tribuna 109, 160, 173 n. 22
patriarchy 66, 72 n. 32 & 34, 120–21, 127, 134 n. 10, 136 n. 36
Pearson, Karl 174 n. 48
Pérez Rojas, Javier 51 n. 44
pétroleuses 99
physicians, *see* doctors: fictional, medical
physiognomy 4, 33, 78–79, 82, 88, 97, 102, 108, 166
Picasso, Pablo 17–18, 81
   Les Demoiselles d'Avignon 17–18
Pick, Daniel 23 n. 1, 33, 50 n. 18 & 20, 55, 71 n. 9 & 11, 95 n. 9, 96 n. 43 & 47, 114 n. 8, 115 n. 44, 135 n. 28, 154 n. 27 & 35
popular fiction 1–2, 5, 9, 23, 32, 42, 52, 98, 165, 171–72
   see also *ficción de masas*
positivism 1, 4, 6, 14, 21, 23, 32, 41–42, 56, 77–80, 84, 93, 106, 142–43, 150–52, 165
poverty 1, 3–4, 8, 10, 12, 21, 56, 71, 76, 78, 81–82, 84–85, 87–94, 97–98, 100–03, 105–09, 111–13, 114 n. 21, 124, 126, 128, 130, 133, 141–45, 151, 159, 165–67
   see also indigence
primitivism 3, 11, 16–17, 52–54, 66–68, 72 n. 32 & 34, 77, 79–80, 82–84, 88, 97–103, 108, 110, 112–13, 121, 133, 134 n. 10, 136 n. 36, 139, 150, 167
Primo de Rivera, Miguel 169
prison 14, 100–01, 104–07, 111–12, 114 n. 27, 142
   Cárcel Modelo, la 106–07, 113
   see also Foucault, Michel
proletariat 3, 109–10, 112, 160, 162, 167
   see also working classes
Prometeo, Editorial 119, 156, 173 n. 4
prostitution 3, 8, 12, 17, 19, 21, 26 n. 56, 31, 48, 52, 55, 76–78, 80–81, 83–94, 95 n. 4 & 27, 98–99, 104–05, 109, 113, 121–22, 128, 137, 140–43, 150–52, 155, 158, 161, 164–67

psychiatry 6, 8–9, 11–15, 25 n. 31, 29, 40, 54–55, 58–59, 62, 66, 80–81, 98, 100, 139, 165–66, 174 n. 50
public health 8, 15, 85–86, 99
Pueblo, El 11, 119, 123, 134, 134 n. 3, 156–57, 159, 162, 173 n. 8 & 18
puerperal insanity 22, 124, 135 n. 22
Puértolas Villanueva, Soledad 95 n. 1, 107, 115 n. 32 & 35
Pulido y Fernández, Ángel 14, 26 n. 45, 87, 95 n. 27, 96 n. 34 & 36, 158, 173 n. 13
   Bosquejos médico-sociales para la mujer 87, 96 n. 34 & 36, 158, 173 n. 13
   Sanidad pública 14, 26 n. 45

Quinn, Cath 135 n. 22

race 4–8, 11, 13–16, 24 n. 14, 54–55, 63, 71 n. 1 & 9, 82, 86, 92, 100, 104–05, 110, 126, 137–40, 143, 145–46, 150–52, 166–68
Ramón y Cajal, Santiago 14, 24 n. 6
Ramsden, Herbert 95 n. 1
readership 2–3, 23, 29, 118, 122–25, 132–33, 135 n. 16, 155–65, 172, 172 n. 2
   women readers 3, 23, 118, 123, 133, 135 n. 16, 155–65, 172–73 n. 2
realism 5, 17, 25 n. 35, 30, 35, 42–43, 47, 78, 98, 118, 129, 133, 141
regenerationism 3–4, 6, 10, 12–13, 19, 21–23, 24 n. 12, 25 n. 21 & 34 & 36 & 37, 30, 35, 41–42, 49, 55, 80–81, 90, 93–94, 102, 104, 110, 113, 145, 151, 165–66, 168–70
Reid, J.T. 171, 174 n. 62
reproduction, human 3–8, 12, 15, 17, 19, 22, 46, 55, 72 n. 29, 87, 90, 98, 100–02, 104, 113–14, 118, 124–26, 133, 135 n. 25, 137–40, 143, 146–49, 158, 164–65, 169
Republicanism 23, 95, 98–99, 108–09, 114 n. 4, 119, 123, 134 n. 3, 156–57, 160, 162, 164, 168, 170–71
   and Baroja 170–71
   and Blasco Ibáñez 23, 95, 98, 108, 119, 123, 134 n. 3, 156–57, 162, 164, 168
Revolution 17, 22, 68, 98–100, 109–12, 150, 162, 166, 174 n. 39
Revuelta Eugercios, Bárbara A. 123, 135 n. 17
Rheinberger, Hans-Jörg 24 n. 13 & 16
Ribot, Théodule 139, 151–52
   Les Maladies de la volonté 152
Richards, Michael 174 n. 50
Richardson, Angelique 26 n. 63, 153 n. 14
Robin, Claire-Nicolle 114 n. 21
Rodgers, Eamonn 173 n. 6
Rodríguez, Hildegart 169
Round, Nicholas G. 24 n. 3, 173 n. 6 & 26
rural environment 4, 52, 56, 68, 71, 95 n. 2, 98, 151, 167

Sackett, Theodore A. 68
Salillas, Rafael 14
Salmerón, Nicolás 28
Salpêtrière (Paris hospital) 34
sanitation, public 15, 85, 87, 91, 93, 96 n. 27, 101, 103–04, 106, 112, 141–42, 152, 169
San Juan de Dios (Madrid hospital) 88, 137, 140–43, 152
San Sebastián 56, 146
savagery 11, 54, 66–68, 80, 83, 98–99, 121, 124
Scanlon, Geraldine M. 153 n. 11
Schopenhauer, Arthur 7, 10, 15–16, 25 n. 24, 40, 127, 138, 142–45, 148–49, 152, 153 n. 8 & 23
  'On Women' 143, 153 n. 23
  The World as Will and Representation 142
Seltzer, Mark 70, 73 n. 56
Sempere, Francisco 6, 119, 123, 156
sensationalism:
  and journalism 29, 107
  sensation fiction 3, 22, 67, 118–20, 123, 125, 130, 134, 135 n. 16, 157, 162, 173 n. 25
Seonae, M.C. 173 n. 9
serialized fiction 11, 22, 81, 119, 134 n. 2, 156–57, 159, 161–63
sexology 21, 53, 71 n. 1 & 2 & 4 & 5, 95 n. 26, 131, 134 n. 7 & 8
sexuality 12, 15–17, 19, 26 n. 60, 36–40, 49, 50 n. 19, 51 n. 57, 52–53, 56, 59, 61–62, 64–66, 68, 70, 78, 83–84, 86–88, 90, 119, 121–23, 125, 127, 131–33, 139, 143–44, 149
  and Sigmund Freud 15–16, 40, 50 n. 19, 53, 59, 65–66, 86
  and Cesare Lombroso 17, 78, 83–86, 119–21
  and Max Nordau 70
Shaw, Donald L. 35, 50 n. 27, 152, 154 n. 39
Shaw, George Bernard 49, 51 n. 61
Showalter, Elaine 19, 26 n. 59 & 61, 139, 153 n. 10
Sieburth, Stephanie 100, 114 n. 14, 164, 174 n. 32 & 33
Siegel, Sandra 26 n. 53
Simón Palmer, María Carmen 173 n. 14
Sinclair, Alison 25 n. 27, 136 n. 37
socialism 9, 81, 84, 98, 100, 105, 108, 110–11, 167, 171
social medicine 3, 9, 14, 22, 25 n. 31, 55, 86, 89–90, 92, 102, 112, 140, 146, 166
  see also hygienic medicine
Sorolla, Joaquín 43, 69
Sosa-Velasco, Alfredo J. 5, 24 n. 6, 56, 71 n. 14 & 15, 138, 153 n. 4, 174 n. 39
Soufas, C. Christopher 25 n. 23, 153 n. 8
Spencer, Herbert 6, 58, 81, 90, 104–06, 110, 119, 139, 144
Stannard, Michael W. 8, 24 n. 17, 25 n. 30, 26 n. 46, 50 n. 32, 72 n. 25, 100, 114 n. 11 & 12, 173 n. 15
Stepan, Nancy 7, 24 n. 14 & 15, 95 n. 15
sterility, of nation 1, 10, 23, 55, 92, 100, 113, 133, 151, 167
  see also infertility

Stott, Rebecca 134 n. 11, 154 n. 24
Strachey, James 26 n. 50, 32, 50 n. 19
suicide 8, 22, 34, 57, 83, 118, 120, 124, 129, 134, 148
Sulloway, Frank 26 n. 49
symbolism 21, 26 n. 50, 30, 36, 43, 45, 52, 60, 68–70, 73 n. 52 & 54
syphilis 3, 8, 10, 13, 17, 19, 37, 85–86, 88–89, 95–96 n. 27, 99–100, 119, 140–41, 146, 159, 167–68

Taine, Hippolyte 151, 166
Tarde, Gabriel 99, 108, 114 n. 7
  Les Lois de l'imitation 108
  L'Opinion et la foule 99, 114 n. 7
Tillyard, S.K. 51 n. 59
Tolosa Latour, Manuel 124, 135 n. 19
  El Niño 135 n. 19
Tomlinson, Janice 51 n. 52
translation of works:
  into English 48, 83, 156
  into French 28, 79, 113, 134 n. 1
  into Spanish 12, 28, 30, 79, 105
Trigo, Felipe 9–10, 156
Trinidad Fernández, Pedro 105, 114 n. 27
Trueba Mira, Virginia 142–43, 153 n. 20 & 21
Tsuchiya, Akiko 5, 17, 24 n. 8, 26 n. 55, 173 n. 11
tuberculosis 10, 25 n. 24, 89, 100, 119, 141, 144, 146, 159, 167–68
typhus 98

Unamuno, Miguel de 5, 7, 9, 29, 31, 41, 50 n. 9, 51 n. 38, 133–34, 152, 155–57, 161, 163, 167, 170, 173 n. 7
  Amor y pedagogía 9, 29, 167
  'Sobre la erudición y la crítica' 50 n. 9
  En torno al casticismo 7
  Tres novelas ejemplares y un prólogo 161, 173 n. 7
unconscious, the 15–16, 21, 26 n. 48, 29, 33, 37–41, 52–53, 59–60, 62–64, 67, 69–70, 172
United States 133, 146, 153 n. 11
  see also North America
urban environment 3–4, 8, 11, 21–22, 28, 33, 35, 41, 52, 55–56, 68, 71, 75–78, 82, 84–95, 95 n. 2, 97–106, 108–12, 141–43, 150–51, 155, 159–60, 165, 169
  see also city, the

Valencia 11, 14, 43, 51 n. 44, 52, 68, 123, 127–29, 135 n. 15, 157, 159, 164, 173 n. 8 & 18
  see also Blasco Ibáñez, Valencian novels
Valentí i Vivo, Ignacio 168
Valis, Noël 96 n. 29
Valle-Inclán, Ramón del 122, 128, 156, 161, 163
  Luces de Bohemia 161
  Sonata de estío 128
Vallejo, Gustavo 24 n. 11, 174 n. 51

Vallejo Nágera, Antonio 24 n. 6, 165, 174 n. 39
   Eugenesia de la Hispanidad y regeneración de la raza 165
vampire, the 67, 122, 128, 132
Vázquez, Oscar E. 7, 24 n. 12, 31, 50 n. 15
Vickers, Peter 115 n. 47
Viñeta-Bellaserra, J. 13, 25 n. 39
violence 17, 36, 55, 64, 66–68, 77–78, 82, 97, 99–101, 108, 110, 121, 123–25, 129, 131, 135 n. 16, 157, 162
   violent women 66–68, 77, 99–100, 121, 123–25, 131, 135 n. 16, 162
visual culture 7, 17, 19, 24 n. 12, 29, 31, 42, 50 n. 15, 72 n. 40, 121–22, 135 n. 13, 155, 158, 160–61, 172, 172 n. 2
voluntad 7, 35, 102, 112–13, 127, 129–31, 134
   see also Will

Wagner, Richard 30, 66, 69–70, 73 n. 48, 153 n. 2
   Tristan und Isolde 70
Wilde, Oscar 16, 24 n. 7, 30, 50 n. 6
   The Picture of Dorian Gray 16

Will, concept of 7, 13, 15, 22, 32, 35, 47, 56–57, 61–64, 66–67, 93, 103–04, 108, 112–13, 121, 127, 129, 142–50, 152, 166–67, 171
   see also voluntad
working classes 3–4, 22, 58, 67, 71, 76, 80, 87–88, 91, 94, 98–100, 103, 106, 108–09, 112, 123–24, 137, 160–64, 168–69
   see also proletariat

Zamacois, Eduardo 9, 134 n. 1
Zola, Émile 5–6, 9, 22, 30, 42, 45, 70–71, 72 n. 32, 73 n. 57, 76, 78, 94, 96 n. 45 & 46, 97, 106, 108, 111, 113, 115 n. 45, 118–19, 130, 134 n. 1, 138, 152, 158–59
   L'Assommoir 71, 73 n. 57
   La Bête humaine 76
   La Débâcle 119, 159
   Nana 111, 115 n. 45
   L'Œuvre 45
   Vérité 119, 159

www.ingramcontent.com/pod-product-compliance
Lightning Source LLC
LaVergne TN
LVHW061251060426
835507LV00017B/2012